MOTIF-INDEX

OF

MEDIEVAL SPANISH FOLK NARRATIVES

ΜΕDIEVAL & RENAISSANCE

TEXTS & STUDIES

VOLUME 162

MOTIF-INDEX

OF

MEDIEVAL SPANISH FOLK NARRATIVES

by

Harriet Goldberg

ϙEDIEVAL & RENAISSANCE TEXTS & STUDIES
Tempe, Arizona
1998

A generous grant from The Program for Cultural Cooperation between Spain's Ministry of Culture and United States Universities has assisted in meeting the publication costs of this volume.

Library of Congress Cataloging-in-Publication Data

Goldberg, Harriet.
  Motif-index of medieval Spanish folk narratives / by Harriet Goldberg.
      p. cm. — (Medieval & Renaissance texts and studies ; vol. 162)
  Includes bibliographical references and index.
  ISBN: 0-86698-203-5 (alk. paper)
  1. Folklore—Spain—Themes, motives.   2. Folklore—Spain—Classification.   3. Tales, Medieval—Themes, motives.   4. Tales, Medieval—Classification. I. Title. II. Series: Medieval & Renaissance texts and studies ; v. 162.
GR230.G57   1997
398.2'0946'0902—dc21   97–31019
                                                                                      CIP

⊚
This book is made to last.
It is set in Plantin,
smythe-sewn and printed on acid-free paper
to library specifications.

Printed in the United States of America

TABLE OF CONTENTS

SUMMARY OF MOTIFS

INTRODUCTION

The utility of an index of folk-motifs clearly lies in its ability to present in an orderly framework those transitory flashes of recognition that we experience upon hearing a familiar story or a familiar narrative component in a new context. A motif-index also shows us that all storytellers' bits and pieces are migratory and that they circulate in both time and space. Perhaps even more importantly, a motif index makes those of us interested in narratology increasingly aware of the possibilities for combining these narrative units. With this awareness we come close to penetrating the mystery of the nature of storytelling. In fact, we can say that the narrative impulse may derive energy from an unspoken awareness of the corpus of tales within a given culture. Robert S. Georges recognized that tale types are not just research tools: "The tale-type concept is one which is both rooted in, and is a manifestation of, intellectual or cognitive processes which are innate rather than learned" ("The Universality of the Tale-Type," 28). Surely this observation can be extended to include folk-motifs.

There are, of course, various ways to classify folktales. In the early days of organizing taxonomically the corpus of international folktales, Antti Aarne compiled his tale-type index (originally in 1910, revised 1928, translated into English by Stith Thompson 1960) topically: Animal Tales, Ordinary Folk-Tales, Jokes and Anecdotes, Formula Tales, and Unclassified Tales. A tale-type, according to David Azzolina, has three features: "A tale type is a story-line distinct from other story lines; . . . each tale type consists of a binding together or sequence of smaller units known as motifs; . . . a tale type is a kind of abstraction which is actually manifested in multiple versions or variants" (*Tale Type- and Motif-Indexes*, xii). In other words, a tale type simply says: "This is the story of a person / animal who . . ."

Aarne intended to collate complete recognizable folk narratives without isolating their components. He cautioned: "It might also naturally be conceivable to work out a classification of separate episodes and motifs, yet this would have necessitated such a cutting into pieces of all complete folktales that the scholar would be able to make a much more limited use of the classification" (cited by Thompson, *The Folktale*, 417).

Stith Thompson, however, was not deterred by this caveat and undertook the monumental task of designing an index of folk motifs because of the deficiencies in tale-type classification that he found. He explained: "A type is a traditional tale that has an independent existence" and may consist of one motif or more than one (*The Folktale*, 415). A motif, on the other hand, "is the smallest element in a tale having a power to persist in tradition." Some tale-types are made up of several motifs, but other tale-types are limited to one motif with a single outcome or result, without alternative possibilities. His definition falters when he gives the three classes into which motifs fall: actors ("gods, unusual animals, marvelous creatures like witches, ogres or fairies, conventionalized human characters"), items in the background of the action ("magic objects, unusual customs, strange beliefs"), and single incidents (*The Folktale*, 415–16). Clearly, actors or agents are easily identifiable and compatible, but, his "items" are a grouping of unlike quantities. It would require a creative stretch to see a relationship between magic objects and unusual customs. The third class, single incidents, obviously includes some motifs that coincide with tale types because they too can exist independently. Alan Dundes finds these disparities disquieting: "If motifs can be actors and incidents, then they are hardly units. They are not measures of a single quantity" ("From Etic to Emic Units" 63).[1]

Besides the classificatory difficulties in Aarne's index, Thompson found it further limited in that it does not include "such partly literary forms as the exemplum and the fabliau," nor does it treat non-European traditional tales (*Motif-Index*, 1.9 n. 3). To extend the system beyond Europe and beyond the simple folktale and jest, Thompson devised a potentially more inclusive scheme that catalogued single motifs, narrative raw material, "those details out of which full-fledged narratives are composed" (*Motif-Index* 1.10).[2] Thus, by identifying motifs — the transferable components of folktales — Thompson's index makes possible the discovery of cross-cultural narrative coincidences.[3]

The six-volume *Motif-Index* covered folktales, ballads, myths, fables, medieval romances, exempla, fabliaux, jest-books, and local legends, and it generated a series of applications of the technique to specific bodies of tales (1.12–18). Among these were John Keller's index of medieval Spanish exempla (*Motif-Index*, 1949) and a subsequent index with James H. Johnson of Aesopic fables ("Motif-Index Classification," 1954).[4]

The present volume fits into this genealogy of motif indexes by fulfilling two principal functions. First it expands and extends Keller's pioneering efforts. The utility of Keller's indexes has diminished since 1949, because new editions of the sources of *exempla*, fables, and folktales have been published since 1949. Apart from the obvious advantage that more recent texts are more readily accessible, these new editions are more reliable than their predecessors. Some texts had appeared only in nineteenth-century editions in *Biblioteca de Autores Españoles*. Second, the present volume surveys a wider range of texts than does Keller's, for example, more Aesopic fables, folktales from chronicles, Marian miracles, and other material excluded from the previous indexes. For instance, Alfonso X's *Cantigas* alone, although composed in *gallego-portugués* is a fruitful source of over four hundred peninsular Marian tales.

SOURCES

Because folktales are a frequent feature in works of fiction that are not mere collections, many of the entries in this index are a part of other

INTRODUCTION

longer literary works. An examination of a sample text shows that folktales function in two ways, either as plot devices that advance the action or as segments of ordinary dialogue. For example, we see in the *Libro del Cauallero Çifar* (80 entries) how the narrator begins his account of the early years of the hero Çifar with a series of folkloric episodes, all of which advance the action. First he sets limits to his hero's good fortune with a mysterious equine curse (D2089.3.2. *Magic spell causes knight's horses to die in ten days. Çifar* p. 5). Then the author frees Çifar to have knightly adventures unencumbered by wife and children with the following motifs from the life of Saint Eustace: He is separated from his young sons (R13.1.2. *Lion carries off child. Çifar* p. 26. B535.0.15. *Lion as nurse for child.* Child rescued when dogs pursue lion. *Çifar* p. 27). Then his wife is abducted by pirates and rescued by the Virgin Mary (V268.4.1. *Virgin Mary destroys devoted woman's abductors.* Gives her power to sail ship to safe port and to dispose of corpses of enemy. *Çifar* p. 29). The knight will make a second, advantageous but chaste marriage (T315.1. *Marital continence by mutual agreement.* Husband and wife to be celibate for two years to do penance for previous sin of husband [*Çifar* pp. 49–50]). Finally Çifar and his family will share a recognition and reconciliation scene (H11.1.5.3. *Sons recount separation from family.* Parents recognize them. *Çifar* pp. 55–56; R176.2. *Execution canceled.* King recognizes long lost wife. *Çifar* pp. 55–56).

Folktales, in addition to serving as convenient plot devices in extended narratives (sometimes through their cultural resonance), are also used as conversational devices. The author, instead of using a tale to advance the action, will cause a character in a larger narrative to interpolate an exemplary tale or at the very least allude to one in the course of trying to persuade another to undertake a course of action. See for instance the admonitory conversation between the empress of the *Islas Dotadas* and her consort, Roboán. She tells him the tale of Truth, Wind, and Water as a warning (Z121.2.1. *Truth, Wind and Water debate.* Wind and water easily found; truth must be guarded and never lost. Once lost never regained. *Çifar* p. 136). He must understand that once he departs, he will not be able to return. While the empress had used a tale to deliver a specific message, sometimes tales are part of an extended conversation, as in the father and son colloquy between Çifar, now king of Menton, and his sons. The wise king relates a series of folktales to teach them their princely responsibilities (pp. 75–108).

The *Libro de Buen Amor* is a rich source of tales used conversationally. The archpriest's pursuit of amatory adventure is facilitated by his engaging a go-between whose storytelling skill is rivaled by the adeptness of the witty women whom she seeks to persuade (40 entries). Typically, the lover's emissary tries to convince a haughty woman to succumb, and she in turn tells a cautionary tale about the unreliability of suitors.

Some tales have become so familiar that an allusion suffices to bring them to mind. In didactic works like *Castigos e documentos*, King Sancho frequently alludes to tales, knowing that they are a part of the general cultural legacy (e.g., J1153.1. *Susanna and the elders.* Prophet Daniel proves that elders had accused her falsely. *Castigos* 9.69). Therefore I have listed as entries brief narratives or even allusions to them wherever and however they appear in such didactic medieval texts as *Glosa castellana* (139 entries), *Poridat de las poridades* (3 entries), *Libro de las armas* (2 entries), and *Jardín de nobles donzellas* (22 entries).

Fables are represented by *Esopete ystoriado* (450 entries), but they also serve as plot devices in *La vida del Esopo*, the biographical narrative that precedes the fable collection. The *Libro de los gatos* has animal tales that illustrate Christian topics (85 entries). In *Calila e Dimna* (150 entries) and John of Capua's *Exemplario* (115 entries), tales are a plot device within the frame story that is in itself a folktale (K2131.2. *Envious jackal makes lion suspicious of his friend, the bull.* Lion kills bull. *Calila* p. 124; *Exemplario* 11r). In *Sendebar* (71 entries) and *Disciplina Clericalis* (73 entries) we find prevalent high-frequency folktales also set in a frame story.

For epic narratives, I rely on the *Primera crónica general* (34 entries) and the *Crónica abreviada* (39 entries), as well as the *Cantar de Mio Cid* (18 entries). For miracle tales, my principal Marian sources are Berceo's *Milagros* (41 entries) and Alfonso X's *Cantigas* (345 entries), along with *La vida de San Alejo* (30 entries) and *Los miraglos de Santiago* (40 entries). Of course, some texts have yielded only a few tales, and others abound in them. For a list of all the source texts and an indication of frequency, see "Source Texts, Abbreviations, and the Number of Entries."

METHODOLOGY

María Jesús Lacarra describes five kinds of brief narrative, and these groupings constitute a guide for the identification and inclusion of tales in this index.[5] (1) EXEMPLUM, a short account of events unique in time and place (anecdote); (2) FABULA, a tale that relates events in which the personages are animals (occasionally in contact with humans); (3) ALLEGORIA, a narrative susceptible of an allegorical interpretation; (4) DESCRIPTIO, an account of the custom, appearance, and characteristics of animals (from bestiaries) or plants; and (5) SIMILITUDO, a comparison of two activities (*"El libro de los gatos:* hacia una tipología," 26–34).

My specific methodology, however, relies on the system of classification developed by Stith Thompson. It is an existing, established system, and adhering to it both makes this index compatible with it (and thus easier for readers familiar with Thompson to use) and highlights the changes I have made. For example, I have added some new subdivisions to suit the medieval Spanish texts consulted: P462 Stonecutter, P463 Baker, P464 Shepherd, P465 Lawyer, P466 Doctors, W46 Compassion, W159 Arrogance. Within these subdivisions are some motifs not already added to the Thompson corpus by John Esten Keller (*Motif-Index* 1949).

I have made other, smaller changes in response to the weaknesses I perceive in Thompson's system. For example, María Jesús Lacarra is baffled that neither Thompson nor Keller had classified the tale of the two naked serving women in *Calila* (1984: pp. 194–95 n. 100). She connects it with its moral point "mote and beam parable" (Tubach 511).[6] However, she does not analyze the story to find the elements that combine to make this "a full-fledged narrative" that deals with the topic of judging the behavior of others. Briefly, the story tells of a man who had taken two captive women as wives. They are forced to serve him unclothed. One of them finds a scrap of cloth to cover her nakedness. Her companion accuses her of using that scrap of cloth to make herself sexually attractive to their husband. The jealous woman says to the husband: "Catad cómmo cubre esta su natura; et non lo faze sinon por que ayas sabor della et yoguieses con ella" ("See how she covers her private parts, so that you will want to lie with her"). I have assigned this to two narrative areas: (1) to the section dealing with sexual relationships, T472.1. *Women of vanquished city given to conquerors.* Two women must perform all duties naked. Out gathering wood, one covers genitals with scrap of cloth. Other one accuses her of lascivious thoughts. Accused told to look to own thoughts; (2) to unfair accusations, K2131.7. *Two female captives deprived of clothing.* One woman finds bit of cloth to cover herself. Second complains; captor reproaches her. She must look to her own shame, not that of another.

Although I add some circumstantial details to the entries in this index, they are not intended to be tale-types or plot summaries. Early classificatory schemes vacillated between listing motifs or tale types or a combination of both. If a tale-type is a plot summary that includes the basic events in a tale, it is a bundle of motifs, the smallest elements that persist in tradition. This bundle tells what the story is about.[7] Unfortunately, if one were to list only the smallest element in many tales, the index would be excessively reductive. For example: B11.2.1. *Dragon as compound animal* is not sufficiently descriptive. Thompson adds: "(serpent or crocodile, with scales of a fish for covering, and feet and wings and sometimes the head of an eagle, falcon, or hawk, and the forelimbs and sometimes the head of a lion)."

As I have noted above, a major flaw in Thompson's scheme is the mixed nature of his categories (e.g., R. CAPTIVES AND FUGITIVES are actors; Q. REWARDS AND PUNISHMENTS are outcomes; K. DECEPTIONS are strategies), but another difficulty is that many tales contain more than one motif. For example, in the present volume is J643.1. *Frogs demand a live king.* King Log. Jupiter has given them a log, but they find him too quiet. He then gives them a stork who eats them all. The wrongheaded demand for a king is one motif; the granting them an inanimate ruler is another. In this second motif a god mocks the group. Their further dissatisfaction with the inanimate king is still another motif, and finally the punishment meted out to them in the form of a stork king who will eat them is still another motif.

Furthermore, the assignment of many tales to one category or another is arbitrary and subjective, and many tales fit logically in more than one category. Consider the thematic content of tales of adultery that can fit into several categories (K. DECEPTIONS, T. SEX, P. SOCIETY). Besides viewing these tales thematically, can we classify them according to the intent of the storyteller? If such is the case, then these salty tales could be jokes intended to provoke laughter (X. HUMOR), stern warnings against sexual irregularity (T. SEX), admonishments to avoid deceptive women (K. DECEPTION). Thus some of these stories must appear several times for appropriate classification.

Beyond the obvious organizational flaws of Thompson's system, the language of many existing entries is clearly in need of revision. Torberg Lundell commented: "The *Motif-Index* in general (1) overlooks gender identity in its labeling of motifs, thus lumping male and female actions or characters under the same, male-identified heading or (2) disregards female activity or (3) focuses on male activity at the cost of female" ("Gender-Related Bias," 150). She also notes that "passive constructions abound. While they appear to project generalizations and objective statements, their effect is vitiated by their silence regarding the active person" ("Gender-Related Bias," 152). On a superficial level, I have transformed all the "girls" into young women if they are of a certain age. Furthermore, I have shifted the point of view in some motifs. Keller's entry "W167.2. *Woman's stubbornness causes loss of chance to go on pilgrimage.* She nags her husband until in rage he breaks the leg of their donkey" now reads: "W167.2. *Stubbornness causes loss of chance to go on pilgrimage.* Husband and wife quarrel. Infuriated husband breaks wife's leg (donkey's leg)." The compiler's bias is also evident in G303.9.4.4. *"Devil persuades bishop to sin with nun."* My wording shares the responsibility more or less equally: *"Devil persuades bishop and nun to sin."*

A final difficulty inherent in Thompson's method is his fastidiousness concerning obscene material in the fabliaux: "Fabliaux with obscenity as the only point have been excluded, though good jests with risqué elements are retained" (*Motif-Index*, 1.17). One can only wonder what the boundary is between a good jest and an obscene one,[8] but there is no doubt that Thompson is over-delicate in his treatment of sexual topics. This timidity is particularly apparent in the division he assigns to sexual activity or rather the activities he omits.[9] The juxtaposition of topics verges on the bizarre. He explained: "In 'T' are treated together the motifs dealing with sex. . . . Here particularly come wooing, marriage, married life, and the birth of children, as well as sundry types of sexual relations" (*The Folktale*, 425). If it were possible to change some categories, I would place T100–T199. MARRIAGE, T200–T299. MARRIED LIFE, and T600–T699. THE CARE OF CHILDREN in the section devoted to societal organization P. SOCIETY where we find such subdivisions as P200–P299, the family that includes P210 Husband and wife, P230 Parents and children, and P250 Brothers and sisters.

Compilers of motif-indexes who depend on Thompson and opt to add new entries either mark an entry in Thompson's *Motif-Index* with an asterisk and the name of the person who had originated it or mark new entries with an asterisk without explanation.[10] Haim Schwarzbaum, in his study of a collection of animal fables (*The Mishlé Shu'alim [Fox Fables]*), for example, does the former. I have chosen to mark new entries with an asterisk without crediting the source, and on occasion, have added new subdivisions, such as "X590. Jokes on masters and servants." Although it might have been less awkward to open a new subdivision about the devil, I have followed Thompson's lead and use "G303 Devil," a maneuver that requires longer numbers than are common in the rest of the index.

I use the following conventions: The italicized word at the beginning of each entry in the list of "Texts Examined for Motifs" is the abbreviation for that entry. There are separate lists of abbreviations and of the number of entries in "Source Texts, Abbreviations and the Number of Entries." I have added a listing that explains the citations that do not refer to simple page numbers, "Notations Explained." Entries are cross-indexed with Frederic Tubach's *Index Exemplorum: A Handbook of Medieval Religious Tales.* The concordance "Correspondences between Motif Numbers and Tubach Topical Numbers" lists more than 1,100 correspondences.

NOTES

1. One wonders if Nikita Elisséef's formulation does not offer a more logical base. For him a motif is "un élément qui constitue un épisode complet." He finds in each motif a second element, the fundamental idea expressed by the motif, e.g., "keeping a child safe from destiny." He calls this second element the theme, and includes a third "l'accessoire épique" that is an object that drives the action, e.g., a magic ring (*Thèmes et Motifs des "Mille et Une Nuits,"* 85). In his index he categorizes each tale by these three components, narrative point, moral point, and motivating agent. See also "Classification of Tales" in *Esopete ystoriado (Toulouse 1488),* ed. Victoria Burrus and Harriet Goldberg, xvii–xxi.

2. Ralph S. Boggs compiled the *Index of Spanish Folktales* that added subdivisions to those of Aarne and also included an invaluable alphabetical index. Stanley Robe extended Aarne's work with an index of tale types from Mexico, Central America, and the Hispanic United States. Various folklorists provided specialized motif-indexes to augment Thompson's monumental work. Rotunda collected the motifs peculiar to the Italian novella following Thompson's scheme. See Azzolina's bibliography which serves as a useful guide despite the flaws noted by Hans Jörg Uther in his review of Azzolina's work. Edward Neugaard has prepared an index of medieval Catalan folktales with an informative preface and a bibliography worth consulting. Reginetta Haboucha has amassed a huge volume of tale types and motifs of Sephardic folktales.

3. Proppian causality is susceptible to re-interpretation into a new sequentially-arranged narrative scheme. In Propp's scheme, narrative elements are identified insofar as they move the action forward. The narrative shape of the Russian fairy tale, first viewed as a rigidly designed series of causative events, is thus expanded and encompasses other folk narratives. The bare

bones of the causative sequence becomes a conflation of motifs around "certain structural units" (Meletinsky, "Structural-Typological Study," 21). To try to force exempla lacking in "certain structural units" into the rigid causative Proppian scheme is fruitless.

4. Just what the word *exemplum* means has led to some convoluted speculation. Haim Schwarzbaum proposed two alternatives: a tale "employed as a rhetorical device for various purposes of a conspicuously didactic nature," or a story "representing a rather practical code of behavior, shrewdness and wisdom ... characteristic of the common folk and the practical experience of life" (1979: p. v).

5. Because of the shifting chronology in the *romancero*, ballad narratives, many of which begin in the Middle Ages and continue in the twentieth century, are not included.

6. Matthew 7:24, "Judge not that ye be not judged. For with what judgement ye judge, ye shall be judged; and with what measure ye mete, it shall be measured to you again. And why beholdest thou the mote that is in thy brother's eye, but considerest not the beam that is in thine own eye?"

7. Although Stith Thompson insists on a distinction between types and motifs, many of his entries are tale types. See for example: U31. *Wolf unjustly accuses lamb and eats him.* When all the lamb's defenses are good the wolf asserts the right of the strong over the weak. (The wolf had accused the lamb of stirring up water despite the fact that the lamb was downstream from the wolf). See also the motif-index in *Esopete ystoriado (Toulouse 1488)*, ed. Victoria Burrus and Harriet Goldberg, 223–41 and an analysis based on "narrative hinges" (essential pivotal function) and "tale roles" (actors) (243–54). Alan Dundes has proposed a refinement of the concept of the motif. He suggests a distinction between "etic" and "emic" narrative elements. A motifeme is a minimal distinctive narrative unit ("From Etic to Emic Units," 61–72).

8. The multifaceted approach to folktales is evident in the case of tales that deal with sexual matters (Goldberg, "Sexual Humor in Misogynist Medieval Exempla," in *Women in Hispanic Literature*).

9. For example, Elisséef, less timid, devotes a section to "Pédérastie" and "Pédérastie feinte" (*Thèmes et Motifs des "Mille et Une Nuits,"* 148).

10. Haim Schwarzbaum identifies motif numbers created by Holbek, Bodker, Thompson-Balys, Noy, Bodker-Nielssen and Keller-Johnson, marking them with an asterisk (*The Mishlé Shu'alim [Fox Fables]*, 584–600).

Texts Examined for Motifs

Cantigas   Alfonso X, el Sabio. *Cantigas de Santa María*. Ed. Walter Mettman. 3 vols. Madrid: Castalia, 1986.

PCG   ——. *Primera crónica general de España*. (*Estoria de España*.) 2 vols. Ed. Ramón Menéndez Pidal. Madrid: Gredos, 1955.

Amadís   *Amadís de Gaula*. Ed. Angel Rosenblat. Adiciones Alicia Redondo Goicoechea. Odres Nuevos. Madrid: Castalia, 1987.

is this the only or the best edition of Amadís de Gaula?

Barlaam   *Barlaam e Josafat*. Ed. John E. Keller and Robert W. Linker. Clásicos Hispánicos, Serie II, Ediciones Críticas XXI. Madrid: CSIC, 1979.

Milagros   Berceo, Gonzalo de. *Obras completas*. II *Milagros de Nuestra Señora*. Ed. Brian Dutton. London: Tamesis, 1971.

Calila   *Calila e Dimna*. Ed. J. M. Cacho Blecua y María Jesús Lacarra. Madrid: Castalia, 1984.

CMC   *Cantar de Mio Cid*. Ed. Alberto Montaner. Biblioteca Clásica 1. Barcelona: Editorial Crítica, 1993.

Exemplario   Capua, Juan de. *Exemplario contra los engaños y peligros del mundo (1493)*. I-1994, *Biblioteca Nacional, Madrid*. Ed. Francisco Gago Jover. Madison: Hispanic Seminary of Medieval Studies, 1989.

Castigos   *Castigos e documentos para bien vivir ordenados por el rey Don Sancho IV*. Ed. Agapito Rey. Indiana University Publications Humanities Series No. 24. Bloomington: Indiana University Press, 1952.

Castigos
MS A BNM
6559   *Castigos e documentos del rey don Sancho*. (MS A BN 6559 with interpolated material from the Spanish gloss of Egidio Romano *Regimiento de príncipes*.) Ed. Pascual de Gayangos. BAE 51. Madrid: Rivadeneyra, 1860.

Castigos
MS A BNM
6559
ADYMTE 0   *Castigos e documentos para bien vivir ordenados por el rey Don Sancho IV*. Ed. Charles B. Faulhaber. ADMYTE Vol. 0. Madrid: Micronet, 1993.

Danza   Danza de la muerte. *Para una antología de la literatura castellana medieval: La Danza de la Muerte.* Ed. Margharita Morreale. Annali del Corso di Lingue e Letterature Straniere 6. Bari: Publicazioni dell' Università de Bari, 1964.

Esopete   *Esopete ystoriado (Toulouse 1488).* Eds. Victoria Burrus and Harriet Goldberg. Madison: Hispanic Seminary of Medieval Studies, 1990.

Espéculo   *El espéculo de los legos: texto inédito del siglo XV.* Ed. José Mª Mohedano Hernández. Madrid: CSIC, 1951.

Compendio   Fray Martín de Córdoba. *Compendio de la fortuna.* Ed. Fernando Rubio Alvarez. Madrid: Biblioteca "La Ciudad de Dios," 1958 (also in BAE 171). Reissued in *Prosistas castellanas del siglo XV.* Ed. P. Fernando Rubio Álvarez O.S.A. Biblioteca de Autores Españoles 171. Madrid: Atlas, 1964.

Jardín   ———. *Jardín de nobles donzellas.* Ed. Harriet Goldberg. UNCSRLL 137. Chapel Hill: University of North Carolina Press, 1974.

Glosa   García de Castrojeriz, Fray Juan. *Glosa castellana al Regimiento de príncipes de Egidio Romano.* Ed. Juan Beneyto Pérez. Biblioteca Española de Escritores Políticos. 3 vols. Madrid: Instituto de Estudios Políticos, 1947.

Teodor   *La historia de la Donzella Teodor: ein spanisches Volksbuch arabischen Ursprungs.* Ed. Walter Mettman. Wiesbaden: Akademie der Wissenschaften und der Literatur, Abhandlungen der Geistes- und Sozialwissenschaftlichen Klasse, Jahrgang 1962, No. 3. Mainz: Akademie der Wissenschaften und der Literatur; Wiesbaden: Franz Steiner, 1962.

Lucanor   Juan Manuel. *Libro del Conde Lucanor.* In *Obras completas.* 2 vols. Ed. José Manuel Blecua. Biblioteca Románica Hispánica IV. Textos, 15. Madrid: Gredos, 1981.

Abreviada   ———. *Crónica abreviada.* In *Obras completas.* 2 vols. Ed. José Manuel Blecua. Biblioteca Románica Hispánica IV. Textos, 15. Madrid: Gredos, 1981.

Armas	———. *Libro de las armas*. In *Obras completas*. 2 vols. Ed. José Manuel Blecua. Biblioteca Románica Hispánica IV. Textos, 15. Madrid: Gredos, 1981.
Estados	———. *Libro de los estados*. In *Obras completas*. 2 vols. Ed. José Manuel Blecua. Biblioteca Románica Hispánica IV. Textos, 15. Madrid: Gredos, 1981.
Ultramar	*La gran conquista de Ultramar*. Ed. Louis Cooper. 4 vols. Bogotá: Instituto de Caro y Cuervo, 1979.
Mocedades	*Las Mocedades de Rodrigo* in Deyermond, Alan D. *Epic Poetry and the Clergy*. London: Tamesis, 1968: pp. 221–76.
Alexandre	*Libro de Alexandre*. Ed. Jesús Cañas Murillo. Madrid: Editora Nacional, 1978.
Apolonio	*Libro de Apolonio*. Ed. Carmen Monedero. Madrid: Castalia, 1987.
Çifar	*Libro del Cauallero Çifar*. Ed. Marilyn A. Olsen. Madison: Hispanic Seminary of Medieval Studies, 1984.
Gatos	*Libro de los gatos*. Ed. Bernard Darbord. Annexes des Cahiers de Linguistique Hispanique Médiévale 3. Paris: Klincksieck, 1984.
Talavera	Martínez de Toledo, Alfonso. *Arcipreste de Talavera o Corbacho*. Ed. Michael Gerli. Madrid: Cátedra, 1979.
Santiago	*Los Miraglos de Santiago*. (*Biblioteca Nacional de Madrid MS 10252.*) Ed. Jane E. Connolly. Acta Salmanticensia. Textos Recuperados V. Salamanca: Universidad de Salamanca, 1990.
San Alejo	*La "Vida de San Alejo": Versiones castellanas*. Ed. Carlos Alberto Vega. Acta Salmanticensia. Textos Recuperados II. Salamanca: Universidad de Salamanca, 1991.
Grisel	Matulka, Barbara. *The Novels of Juan de Flores and Their European Diffusion: A Study in Comparative Literature*. New York: New York University Comparative Literature Series, 1931.
Crestomatía	Menéndez Pidal, Ramón. *Crestomatía del español medieval*. 2 vols. Seminario Menéndez Pidal. Madrid: Universidad de Madrid, Facultad de Filosofía y Letras, 1966.

Disciplina Petrus Alfonsi. *The "Disciplina Clericalis" of Petrus Alfonsi*. Latin to German and edition by Eberhard Hermes (translated into English by P. R. Quarrie). Berkeley and Los Angeles: University of California Press, 1977.

Disciplina ——. *Disciplina Clericalis*. Trans. Esperanza Ducay. Introduction and notes by María Jesús Lacarra. Zaragoza: Guara, 1980.

Poridat Pseudo-Aristóteles. *Poridat de las poridades*. Ed. Lloyd Kasten. Madrid: pvt. pub., 1947.

LBA Ruiz, Juan. *Libro de buen amor*. Ed. G. B. Monypenny. Madrid: Castalia, 1991.

a.b.c. Sánchez de Vercial, Clemente. *Libro de los enxenplos por a.b.c.* Ed. John Esten Keller and Louis Jennings Zahn. Madrid: CSIC, 1961.

Sendebar *Sendebar*. Ed. María Jesús Lacarra. Madrid: Cátedra, 1989.

Epitus Severin, Dorothy Sherman. "'E ynfante Epitus': The Earliest Complete Castilian Version of the 'Dialogue of Epictetus and the Emperor Hadrian'," *Bulletin of Hispanic Studies* 62 (1985): 25–30.

Voragine Voragine, Jacobus de. *The Golden Legend. Readings on the Saints*. Trans. William Granger Ryan. 2 vols. Princeton: Princeton University Press, 1993.

Source Texts, Abbreviations, and the Number of Entries

a.b.c. = *Libro de los enxenplos por a.b.c.*, 1046 entries
Abreviada = *Crónica abreviada*, 39 entries
Alexandre = *Libro de Alexandre*, 24 entries
Amadís = *Amadís de Gaula*, 1 entry
Apolonio = *Libro de Apolonio*, 16 entries
Armas = *Libro de las armas*, 2 entries
Barlaam = *Barlaam e Josafat*, 54 entries
Calila = *Calila e Dimna*, 150 entries
Cantigas = *Cantigas de Santa María*, 345 entries
Castigos = (ed. Agapito Rey) *Castigos e documentos*, 88 entries[*]
Castigos = (BAE 51 + ADMYTE 0) = *Castigos e documentos*, 170 entries
CMC = *Cantar de Mio Cid*, 18 entries
Çifar = *Libro del Cauallero Çifar*, 80 entries
Compendio = *Compendio de la fortuna*, 3 entries
Crestomatía = *Crestomatía del español medieval*, 1 entry
Danza = *Danza de la muerte*, 1 entry
Disciplina = *Disciplina Clericalis*, 73 entries
Epitus = *Epitus*, 1 entry
Esopete = *Esopete ystoriado*, 450 entries
Espéculo = *El espéculo de los legos*, 600 entries
Estados = *Libro de los estados*, 8 entries
Exemplario = *Exemplario contra los engaños y peligros del mundo*, 117 entries
Gatos = *Libro de los gatos*, 85 entries
Glosa = *Glosa castellana*, 139 entries
Grisel = *Grisel y Mirabella*, 1 entry
Ilustres mujeres = *De las ilustres mujeres en romance*, 63 entries
Jardín = *Jardín de nobles donzellas*, 22 entries
LBA = *Libro de buen amor*, 40 entries
Lucanor = *Libro del Conde Lucanor*, 128 entries
Milagros = *Milagros de Nuestra Señora*, 41 entries
PCG = *Primera crónica general (Estoria de España)*, 34 entries
Poridat = *Poridat de las poridades*, 3 entries
San Alejo = *La Vida de San Alejo*, 30 entries
Santiago = *Los miraglos de Santiago*, 40 entries
Sendebar = *Sendebar*, 71 entries
Talavera = *Arcipreste de Talavera*, 140 entries
Teodor = *La historia de la Donzella Teodor*, 21 entries
Tubach = *Index Exemplorum*, 1,106 entries[**]
Ultramar = *La gran conquista de Ultramar*, 46 entries
Voragine = *The Golden Legend*, 1 entry

[*] If an item appears in the 1293 version (ed. Agapito Rey), its appearance in the glossed version of MS A BNM 6559 is not noted (BAE and ADMYTE).
[**] Entries marked cf. differ circumstantially but share the same folk motif.

Notations Explained

a.b.c. = number of individual *exemplum* (Paris MS; *exempla* not in Paris MS are noted)

Abreviada = book + chapter

Alexandre = numbers of four-line *coplas* (c., cc.)

Amadís = book + chapter

Apolonio = numbers of four-line *coplas* (c., cc.)

Cantigas = numbers of individual *cantigas*

Castigos = chapter + page in 1952 edited by Agapito Rey

Castigos MS A BNM 6659 = chapter + page in 1860 edited by Pascual Gayangos BAE

Castigos MS A BNM 6659 ADMYTE 0 = chapter + page (recto, verso) in CD ROM ed. Faulhaber 1993

CMC = verse numbers (v., vv)

Disciplina = numbers of individual *exemplum*

Espéculo = numbers of individual *exempla* + pages

Exemplario = folio number (verso or recto)

Gatos = tale number + page

Ilustres mujeres = (name) chapter + folio number (verso, recto)

LBA = numbers of four-line *coplas* (c., cc.)

Lucanor = *exemplum* number

Milagros = miracle number

PCG = volume + chapter + page

Santiago = chapter + page number

Sendebar = frame narrative = page number; *exempla* = day + tale number

Talavera = part + chapter + page number

Ultramar = volume number + book + chapter + page number

*All other notations refer to page numbers in the edition listed in the "Texts Examined for Motifs."

Critical Works Consulted

Aarne, Antti. *The Types of the Folktale: A Classification and Bibliography. Antti Aarne's Verzeichnis der Märchentypen (Folktale Fellows Communications No. 3)*. Trans. and enlarged Stith Thompson. Folktale Fellows Communications No. 184. Helsinki: Academia Scientiarum Fennica, 1964.

Azzolina, David S. *Tale Type- and Motif-Indexes: An Annotated Bibliography*. New York and London: Garland, 1987. (Review by Hans Jörg Uther, *JAF* 102 [1989]: 479–84.)

Boggs, Ralph Steele. *Index of Spanish Folktales*. Folklore Fellows Communications 90. Helsinki: Academia Scientiarum Fennica, 1930.

Dundes, Alan, ed. "From Etic to Emic Units in the Structural Study of Folktales," in *Analytic Essays in Folklore*. The Hague: Mouton, 1975, 61–72.

Elisséef, Nikita. *Thèmes et Motifs des "Mille et Une Nuits:" Essai de Classification*. Beirut: Institut Français de Damas, 1949.

Georges, Robert A. "The Universality of the Tale-Type as Concept and Construct." *Western Folklore* 42 (1983): 21–28.

Goldberg, Harriet. "Sexual Humor in Misogynist Medieval Exempla," in *Women in Hispanic Literature: Icons and Fallen Idols*. Ed. Beth Miller. Berkeley, Los Angeles, and London: University of California Press, 1983, 67–83.

Haboucha, Reginetta. *Types and Motifs of the Judeo-Spanish Folktales*. New York and London: Garland, 1992.

Keller, John Esten. *Motif-Index of Medieval Spanish Exempla*. Knoxville: University of Tennessee Press, 1949.

Keller, John E., and James H. Johnson. "Motif-Index Classification of Fables and Tales of *Ysopete Ystoriado*." *Southern Folklore Quarterly* 18 (1954): 85–117.

Lacarra, María Jesús. "*El libro de los gatos:* hacia una tipología del 'enxiemplo'," in *Formas breves del relato (Coloquio Casa de Velásquez-Departamento de Literatura Española de la Universidad de Zaragoza.) Madrid, Febrero de 1985*. Ed. Yves-René Fonquerne y Aurora Egido. Zaragoza: Secretariado de Publicaciones de la Universidad de Zaragoza, 1986, 19–34.

Legman, Gershon. "Toward a Motif-Index of Erotic Humor." *JAF* 75 (1962): 227–48.

Lundell, Torberg. "Gender-Related Biases in the Type and Motif Indexes of Aarne and Thompson," in *Fairy Tales and Society: Illusion, Allusion, and Paradigm.* Ed. Ruth B. Bottigheimer. Philadelphia: University of Pennsylvania Press, 1986, 149–63.

Meletinsky, Eleazar. "Structural-Typological Study of Folktales," in *Soviet Structural Folkloristics: Texts by Meletinski, Neklidov, Novik, and Segal with Tests of the Approach by Jilek and Jilek-Aall, Reid, and Layton.* Ed. P. Maranda. The Hague: Mouton, 1974, 19–59.

Neugaard, Edward J. *Motif-Index of Medieval Catalan Folktales.* Medieval & Renaissance Texts & Studies 96. Binghamton, NY: MRTS, 1993.

Noy, Dov. "Motif-index of Talmudic-Midrashic Literature." Ph.D. Diss. (Indiana University, 1954).

———. *Ha-Mashal be Sifrut ha-Aggada:Tipusim u-Motivim* (Tale-Types and Motifs of Animal Tales: Aarne-Thompson 1-299). Jerusalem: Hebrew University, 1960.

Robe, Stanley L. *Index of Mexican Folktales, including Narrative Texts from Mexico, Central America, and the Hispanic United States.* Berkeley, Los Angeles, and London: University of California Press, 1973.

Rotunda, D. P. *Motif-Index of the Italian Novella in Prose.* Bloomington: Indiana University Press, 1942.

Schwarzbaum, Haim. "International Folklore Motifs in Petrus Alphonsi's *Disciplina Clericalis.*" *Sefarad* 21 (1961): 267–99; 22 (1962): 17–59, 321–44; 23 (1963): 54–73.

———. *The Mishlé Shu'alim (Fox Fables) of Rabbi Berechiah Ha-Nakdan: A Study in Comparative Folklore and Fable Lore.* Kiron: Institute for Jewish and Arab Folklore Research, 1979.

Thompson, Stith. *The Folktale.* New York: Holt Rinehart and Winston, 1946. Reprint: Berkeley: University of California Press, 1977.

———. *Motif-Index of Folk-Literature: A Classification of Narrative Elements in Folktales, Ballads, Myths, Fables, Mediaeval Romances, Exempla, Fabliaux, Jest-Books, and Local Legends.* 6 vols. Bloomington and Indianapolis: Indiana University Press, 1955.

Tubach, Frederic C. *Index Exemplorum: A Handbook of Medieval Religious Tales.* Folktale Fellows Communications No. 204. Helsinki: Academia Scientiarum Fennica, 1969.

A. MYTHOLOGICAL MOTIFS

A0–A99. CREATOR
A100–A499. GODS

A100–A499. The gods in general.

A106.2.2. *Satan's fall from heaven.* Failed in attempt to equal God. *Castigos* 9.70.

*A106.2.3. *Satan tempts Eve with apple.* Knowledge will make her God's equal in wisdom. *Talavera* 2.9.184.

A139. Nature and appearance of the gods: miscellaneous.

*A139.6.1. *God's voice tells faithful to seek out holy man.* They must ask him to pray for them. *San Alejo* p. 77.

A160. Mutual relations of the gods.

A163. Contests among the gods.

*A163.2. *Neptune and Minerva dispute* name to be given to city of Athens. Women of city win by one vote. Neptune, angered, brought floods to city. *Jardín* pp. 243–44; Tubach 3462.

A500–A599. DEMIGODS AND CULTURE HEROES

A510. Origin of the culture hero (demigod).

*A511.1.5.1. *Culture hero mysteriously or magically engendered* by royal personage in disguise. *Alexandre* cc. 1063–64; Tubach 124.

A600–A899. COSMOGONY AND COSMOLOGY
A900–A999. TOPOGRAPHICAL FEATURES OF THE EARTH

A930. Origin of stream.

A941. Origin of springs.

*A941.7.4. *Spring breaks forth* at young Jesus's command to palm tree to bend and bring forth water. *Castigos* MS A BNM 6559 31.146 (ADMYTE 0 30v).

A1000–A1099. WORLD CALAMITIES AND RENEWALS

A1018. Flood as punishment.

*A1018.4. *Neptune (angered by feminine votes for Minerva)* causes flood to come to Athens. To appease him, citizens promise to deprive women of right to vote. *Jardín* pp. 243–44; Tubach 3462.

*A1018.5. *World without kings punished* for lack of order and discipline by flood. *Castigos* 9.75–76.

A1021. *Deluge: escape in boat (ark).* *Castigos* MS A BNM 6559 90.226 (ADMYTE 0 33r); *Estados* 1.27; Tubach 3478.

A1100–A1199. ESTABLISHMENT OF NATURAL ORDER

A1160. Determination of months.

*A1161. Julius Caesar adds intercalary year; February gains day. *Glosa* 1.2.6.94–95; *Castigos* MS A BNM 6559 (ADMYTE 0 104*v*).

*A1162. *Roman emperors chose twelve months* parallel with twelve zodiacal signs, with vestigial names of ten-month scheme. *Abreviada* 1.124.

A1200–A1699. CREATION AND ORDERING OF HUMAN LIFE
A1200. Creation of man.

*A1212.1. *Man created in God's image.* Woman created so that they might procreate. *Estados* 1.38.

A1275.1. *Creation of first woman from man's rib.* Created thus so that all humankind might have common origin. *Jardín* p. 145.

A1300–A1399. Ordering of human life.
A1310. Ordering of human's bodily attributes.

*A1313.3.4.2. *Women have two breasts* so that they can nurse a son and a daughter. *Estados* 1.27.

A1330. Beginnings of trouble for man.

A1331. *Paradise lost.* Original happy state is lost because of one sin. *Estados* 1.38.

A1331.1. *Paradise lost* because of forbidden fruit. *Estados* 1.38.

A1333. *Confusion of languages.* Divine retribution for building tower of Babel. *Glosa* 3.1.6.35.

A1370. Origin of mental and moral characteristics.
A1383. Origin of shame for nakedness.

A1383.1. *Shame for nakedness appears to first woman (and man).* Adam hears God's voice; is frightened and ashamed. Covers self and Eve. *Castigos* 9.74–75.

A1391. *Why other members must serve belly.* Result of a debate between members of the body. *Esopete* p. 66; *Glosa* 2.3.16.311; Tubach 570.

A1400–A1499. Acquisition of culture.
A1440. Acquisition of crafts.

A1441.2. *Origin of practice of yoking oxen,* yoking young with old so that young might learn to pull plow. *Esopete* pp. 64–65.

A1500–A1599. Origin of customs.

A1541.4.1. *Origin of Sabbath* dedicated to Mary from a feast dedicated to Venus. *a.b.c.* 262.

*A1599.4.1. *Why humans always look at own excreta.* Think they may have passed brains. *Esopete* pp. 14–15.

A2200–A2599. ANIMAL CHARACTERISTICS
A2200. Cause of animal characteristics.

A2232.1. *Camel asks for horns:* punishment is short ears. *Esopete* p. 121; Tubach 838.

A2232.2. *Bees pray for lethal sting:* punishment is that first sting is suicidal. *Esopete* p. 112.

A2232.7. *Peacock has ugly feet to prevent too great arrogance.* When tail is raised, is aware of great beauty; when tail is lowered, is ashamed of ugly feet. *Espéculo* 380[1].281; Tubach 3631.

*A2282.1. *Swallows nest near humans* after other birds do not heed warning about hemp-seeds for hunter's nets. *Esopete* p. 39; cf. Tubach 4686.

A2300–A2399. Causes of animal characteristics: body.

A2310. Origin of animal characteristics: body covering.

*A2311.10. *Goat claims holiness* because its hair is used to make hair shirts. Its beard is never cut to make it beautiful to behold. *Gatos* 27.

*A2311.11. *Why bats have fur and no feathers.* *Esopete* p. 62; Tubach 501.

A2320. Origin of animal characteristics: head.

A2325.4. *Why camel has short ears.* *Esopete* p. 121; Tubach 838.

A2326. Origin and nature of animals' horns.

*A2326.3.3.1. *Antelopes' horns are entangled* in tree branches. They cry out and hunters find and kill them. *Gatos* 12; *Esopete* p. 63; Tubach 4589.

A2346. Origin and nature of animal's sting.

A2346.1. *Why bees die after sting.* Punishment for request for lethal sting. *Esopete* p. 112.

*A2346.3. *King of bees has no stinger* to make him compassionate. *Glosa* 1.2.15.143; *Castigos* MS A BNM 6559 (ADMYTE 0 38r, 115v); Tubach 547.

A2356. Origin and nature of animal's back.

A2356.2.7. *Ass boasts that cross marking on back* (shoulders) is reward for being beast who bore Christ on Palm Sunday. *Gatos* 27.

A2400–A2499. Causes of animal characteristics: appearance and habits.

A2430. Animal characteristics: dwelling and food.

*A2431.3.9. *Why eagles do not nest in dungbeetle season.* Beetles destroy their eggs. *Esopete* p. 109.

A2440. Animal characteristics: carriage.

A2441.4.2. *Cause of crab's walk.* Learned from mother. *Esopete* pp. 119–20; Tubach 1311.

*A2441.5. *Why vultures drop bones from great heights.* They drop bones they cannot break. *Gatos* 5.

A2460. Animal characteristics: attack and defense.

*A2466.3. *Fox plays dead*, extends its tongue to trap prey. Eats them when they come near. *Gatos* 53; Tubach 2176.

A2490. Other habits of animals.

A2491.1. *Why bat flies by night.* *Esopete* p. 62.

A2491.1.1. *Why bat sleeps by day.* *Esopete* p. 62.

*A2491.6. *Why nightingales sing at night.* *Esopete* p. 63.

*A2492.3. *Why horses first permitted themselves to be saddled* and bridled. *Esopete* pp. 77–78; Tubach 2619.

A2493. Friendship between animals.

*A2493.36. *Friendship between mouse and dove.* Mouse gnaws net and frees captured ringdoves. *Calila* p. 202; *Exemplario* 42v.

A2494. Enmity between animals.

A2494.7.1. *Enmity between monkey and lion. Esopete* p. 67.

*A2494.7.4. *Enmity between carnivores and herbivores.* Lion and bull represent their group. Pact between them fails at instigation of other animals. Lion kills bull. *Calila* p. 168; *Exemplario* 13r; *Lucanor* Ex. 22.

A2494.12.2. *Enmity between mongoose and snake. Calila* p. 173.

*A2494.12.11. *Enmity of lion and leopard.* Lion hates leopard because it is product of union between a lion and a *pardo*: leopard hates lion because it is fearless. *a.b.c.* 210; cf. Tubach 3014.

A2494.13. Enmities of birds.

*A2494.13.13. *Enmity of birds*: falcon and nightingale. *Esopete* pp. 62–63.

*A2494.13.13.1. *Enmity between falcon and kite.* Falcon asks why kite permits falcon to dominate him. Explanation: kite lacks falcon's heart. *Espéculo* 51.35.

*A2494.13.14. *Enmity between owls and crows.* Bitter war, crow is spy to help crows defeat enemy. *Calila* pp. 224–52; *Exemplario* 53v–56v; *Lucanor* Ex. 19; Tubach 1358.

A2497. Monogamy among animals.

*A2497.2. *Monogamy among animals.* Male storks and male lions will kill mate if she is unfaithful. *Espéculo* 24.17–18; *Glosa* 2.1.8.40.

A2500–A2599. Animal characteristics: miscellaneous.

A2520. Disposition of animals.

*A2522.8. *Some flies bite and cause pain.* Some create filth, and others make noise. *Gatos* 10.

A2540. Other animal characteristics.

*A2543. *Why snails travel very little.* They carry their own house. *Gatos* 51.

A2545. Animal given certain privileges.

*A2545.3.1. *Dogs eat kill first.* When they are sated, crows can eat what is left. *Gatos* 17.

*A2562. *Why leopard is aggressive.* Is fruit of adultery between lion and *pardo. Espéculo* 28.19.

A2800–A2899. MISCELLANEOUS EXPLANATIONS

A2851. *The four characteristics of wine.* Noah plants vineyard; fertilizes with blood of lions for anger, lambs for foolishness, pigs for lustfulness, and apes for wit. *a.b.c.* 421; Tubach 5093.

B. ANIMALS

B0–B99. MYTHICAL ANIMALS

B10. Mythical beasts and hybrids.

B11. Dragon.

B11.2.1. *Dragon as compound animal* (serpent or crocodile, with scales of a fish for covering, and feet and wings and sometimes the head of an eagle, falcon, or hawk, and the forelimbs and sometimes the head of a lion). *Ultramar* II.2.241.341–42.

B11.2.13.1. *Blood of dragon venomous.* Causes leprosy in his slayer who is cured miraculously by Virgin Mary. *Cantigas* 189.

B11.6. Deeds of dragons.

B11.6.5. *Dragon guards hermit's food.* Frightens off robbers. *a.b.c.* 3.

*B11.10.4. *Dragon holds sinner down with tail* and with its head sucks soul from sinner's mouth. *a.b.c.* 438.

B11.11. Fight with dragon.

B11.11.9. *Fight with dragon.* Hero frees countryside of marauder; avenges brother's death. *Ultramar* II.2.243–48.346–59.

B16. Devastating animals.

*B16.1.4.3. *Devastating swine.* Industrious ants make anthill. Pigs come and trample it. *Espéculo* 62.43–44.

B20. Beast-human.

B24. *Satyr. Combination of man and goat. Esopete* pp. 126–27.

B30. Mythical birds.

B32.1. *Phoenix* renews youth. *Alexandre* cc. 2475–76.

*B32.2. *Eagle when flies close to sun* is consumed by fire and renews itself. *Espéculo* 78.50–51.

*B39.2. *Magical bird song* bewitches hearer. Owl's harsh song portends death. *Disciplina* 8.58–59; cf. Tubach 3556.

B80. Fish-human.

B80.2. *Monster half-man, half-fish* attacks laundress in river. Other laundresses come to her aid and kill monster. *Esopete* p. 166.

B100–B199. MAGIC ANIMALS

B120. Wise animals.

B123.1. *Wise serpent.* Injured by man, refuses reconciliation. *Esopete* p. 36; Tubach 4251.

B147. Animals furnish omens.

B147.2.1. Bird of good omen.

B147.2.1.1. *Two crows good omen. Esopete* p. 16.

B147.2.2. Bird of bad omen.

B147.2.2.1. *Crows as bird of ill omen. Esopete* p. 16; *Castigos* MS A BNM 6559 57; Tubach 1366.

*B147.2.2.1.1. *Crows seen on left bad omen, seen on right good omen. CMC* vv. 10–11.

B147.3. Other animals furnish omens.

B147.3.1.2. *Bees leave honey on lips of infant.* (Plato) to show future eloquence. *a.b.c.* 180.

*B147.3.1.3. *Ants leave grains of wheat on lips of infant* as sign of future wealth. *a.b.c.* 180; Tubach 293.

*B147.3.1.4. *Egg magically caused to bring forth chick with mature comb* (sign of future greatness of unborn child). *a.b.c.* 180.

B151. Beast determines road to be taken.

B151.1.1.2.1. *Ass carries usurer's body to the gallows* instead of to the church. *Espéculo* 567.461–63; Tubach 375.

B160. Wisdom-giving animals.

B161. *Wisdom from serpent.* Helps man to prosper. *Esopete* p. 52; Tubach 4251.

B170. Magic birds, fish, reptiles.

*B172.5.1. *Magic hawk.* Catches all prey at which it is loosed. *Çifar* p. 137.

B176.1.1. *Serpent as deceiver in paradise. Estados* 1.38.

B180. Magic quadrupeds.

*B182.1.3.2. *Magic mastiff.* Is able to bring down any fleeing stag. *Çifar* p. 135.

B184. Magic quadrupeds: ungulata.

*B184.1.1.4. *Magic horse that neither eats nor drinks* is faster than wind. *Çifar* p. 137.

B200–B299. ANIMALS WITH HUMAN TRAITS

B217. Animal languages learned.

*B217.9. *Aesop learns animal language.* Magical reward for kindness to angel. *Esopete* p. 3.

B230. Parliament of animals.

*B236.1.1. *Election of king of birds.* Owl (raven) elected. Crow argues against it; persuades birds to revoke election. *Calila* p. 230; *Exemplario* 52r.

B240. King of animals.

B240.4. *Lion as king of beasts. Esopete* pp. 35, 67, 78, 98–100.

B241.2.2. *King of monkeys. Esopete* p. 77.

B242.1.1. *Eagle king of birds. Esopete* pp. 17–18.

B242.1.8. *Owl proposed as king of birds. Calila* p. 230; *Exemplario* 52r; Tubach 3554.

B242.2.2. *King of doves. Esopete* pp. 49–50.

B250–B259. Religious animals.

B251.1.1. *Animals worship infant Jesus. Castigos* MS A BNM 6559 31.145 (ADMYTE 0 92v).

*B256.13. *Serpent guards monastery garden* from thief. *a.b.c.* 178; *Glosa* 3.2.23.214.

B259.4. *Bees in hive build church of wax* to contain consecrated host and figure of Virgin Mary and Child. *Cantigas* 208; cf. Tubach 2662.

*B259.4.2. *In praise of Virgin Mary swarm of bees makes wax* to restore candles in church. *Cantigas* 211.

B260–B269. Animal warfare.

B260.1. *Two groups of animals make peace treaty* (wolves, sheep). *Esopete* pp. 2, 19, 65; Tubach 5357.

B261.1. *Bat in war of birds and quadrupeds.* Because of ambiguous form, joins first one side and then the other. Discredited. *Esopete* p. 62; Tubach 501.

MOTIF INDEX OF

B263.3. *War between crows and owls (ravens)*. Crows victors because of espionage. *Calila* pp. 225–52; *Exemplario* 50r–62r; *Lucanor* Ex. 19; Tubach 1358.

B267. Animal allies.

B267.1. *Alliance of dog and wolf*. *Esopete* pp. 93–94.

B267.2. *Alliance of sheep and dogs*. *Esopete* pp. 2, 19, 65; Tubach 5357.

B270. Animals in legal relations.

*B270.3. *Lawsuit between wolf and fox*. *LBA* cc. 321–71; *Esopete* p. 54.

*B270.4. *Lawsuit between dog and sheep*. Wolf, vulture, and kite testify falsely for dog. Sheep loses. *Esopete* p. 34.

*B270.5. *Lawsuit between stag and sheep*. Wolf's presence at trial intimidates sheep. Repayment to be made in absence of wolf. *Esopete* p. 52.

B274. Animal as judge.

*B274.1. *Ape as judge in lawsuit*, greyhound lawyer for wolf, sheepdog lawyer for fox. *LBA* cc. 321–71; *Esopete* p. 54.

*B274.2. *Fox is judge in dispute between man and snake*. a.b.c. 312.

*B274.3. *Fox is judge in dispute between farmer and wolf*. a.b.c. 363.

B275.1.3.2. *Wolves and wild pigs condemned to death in lion's court* for killing and eating sheep. *Gatos* 20; Tubach 5330.

B290. Other animals with human traits.

B291. Animal as messenger.

B291.1.11. *Swallow as messenger*. Tells knight that Virgin Mary and her son Jesus Christ will help him save his wife from her enemies. *Ultramar* I.1.104.216.

B299. Other animals with human traits: miscellaneous.

*B299.1.2. *Panther takes revenge on men who injured him*. Spares those who treated him kindly. *Esopete* p. 76.

*B299.11. *Animals obey nature's law*. Carnivores do not eat their own species. *Estados* 1.24.

*B299.12. *Animals obey nature's law*. Herbivores only eat what they need. *Estados* 1.24.

*B299.13. *Animals are chaste by nature*. Only mate when they will procreate. *Estados* 1.24.

B300–B599. FRIENDLY ANIMALS

B300–B349. Helpful animals: general.

B301.1.1. *Faithful dog* follows master's dead body when cast into river. There he keeps body afloat. a.b.c. 59; Tubach 1700.

*B301.1.1.1. *Faithful dog* takes food to imprisoned master. a.b.c. 59.

B301.8. *Faithful lion* follows man who saved him from serpent. a.b.c. 185; Tubach 3057.

B320. Reward of helpful animal.

*B321. *Crow advises eagle* to drop shelled prey on rocks to open it. They share food. *Esopete* p. 37.

B325.1. *Animals bribed with food*. Thief tries to bribe watchdog with meat. *Esopete* p. 50; *LBA* cc. 166–80.

B330. Death of helpful animal.

B331. Helpful animal killed by misunderstanding.

*B331.1.2. *Falcon left hunter's hand* (without release). Strangled self in flight. *Espéculo* 55.38.

B331.2. *Llewellyn and his dog.* Dog has saved child from serpent. Father sees bloody mouth and kills the dog. *Sendebar* Day 5 Tale 12; *Calila* p. 265; *Exemplario* 67v; Tubach 1695.

B335.2. *Life of helpful animal demanded as cure* for feigned sickness. Flesh of monkey said to be cure. *Esopete* p. 67.

B336. *Helpful animal threatened by ungrateful person.* Lion raised by man is beaten and driven away. Later refuses reconciliation; wounds healed, insults did not. *Castigos* MS A BNM 6559 27.142 (ADMYTE 0 86r–86v).

B350–B399. Grateful animals.

B360. Animals grateful for rescue from peril of death.

B361. *Lion and eagle grateful for rescue from pit.* Lion brings kill to rescuer; eagle leads him to treasure. *a.b.c.* 207.

*B361.1. *Jackal and cubs rescued from pit.* Grateful to man who freed them. *a.b.c.* 185.

B362. *Animals grateful for rescue from drowning.* Ant and dove. *Esopete* p. 111.

B363.1.1. *Lion is freed from net* by mouse in return for previous kindness. *Esopete* p. 38; Tubach 3052.

B370. Animal grateful to captor for release.

B371.1. *Lion spared mouse: mouse grateful.* Later releases lion from net. *LBA* cc. 1425–34; *Esopete* p. 38; Tubach 3052.

B374.1. *Lion eternally grateful to man* for having freed it from serpent. *a.b.c.* 185; Tubach 3057.

B380. Animals grateful for relief from pain.

B381. *Thorn removed from lion's paw* (Androcles and the Lion). In gratitude, the lion later rewards the man. *Esopete* p. 61; *Espéculo* 47.31–32; cf. *Esopete* p. 111; *a.b.c.* 186; Tubach 215, 2771.

*B381.3, *Hyena, grateful to monk for having cured blindness of cubs,* brings him food and skins. *a.b.c.* 50; Tubach 2714.

B390. Animals grateful for other kind acts.

*B391.1.4. *Snake grateful for food and shelter.* Snake's offspring kills human's child. Mother snake kills offender and departs from human's house. *a.b.c.* 205; cf. Tubach 4251.

B400–B499. Kinds of helpful animals.

B400. Helpful domestic beasts.

*B401.2. *Horse grabs arm of thief* and will not let go until thief is caught. *a.b.c.* 242; Tubach 2608.

B411.2. *Helpful ox.* Hides fugitive deer. *Esopete* p. 67; Tubach 4596.

B430. Helpful wild beasts.

B437.2 *Helpful mouse* gnaws net, frees lion. *Esopete* p. 38; Tubach 3052.

*B437.2.1. *Helpful mouse gnaws net of captured ringdoves* to free them. *Calila* p. 202; *Exemplario* 41r.

B449. Helpful wild beasts: miscellaneous.

MOTIF INDEX OF

*B449.4. *Helpful hyena.* Brings food to hermit. *a.b.c.* 50; cf. Tubach 2711, 2714.

*B449.5. *Bear guards holy man's sheep.* *a.b.c.* 329; Tubach 519.

B457.1. *Helpful dove.* Saves ant. *Esopete* p. 111.

B469. Helpful birds: miscellaneous.

*B469.11. *Eagle brings large fish to feed starving saint* and his company. Grateful saint takes half and returns half to eagle. *Espéculo* 3.5.

*B469.12. *Helpful swan.* Enchanted swan leads knight in magical boat to places where his knightly protection is needed. *Ultramar* I.1.68.119–20.

B480. Helpful insects.

B481.1. *Helpful ant.* Returns previous favor of dove. *Esopete* p. 111.

B490. Other helpful animals.

B491.1. *Helpful serpent.* *Esopete* pp. 52, 89–90.

B500–B599. Services of helpful animals.

B510. Healing by animals.

B513. *Remedy learned from overhearing animal meeting.* Hero learns how to cure his own blindness, restore princess's speech, and cure king's blindness. *Gatos* 28.

B522. Animal saves man from death sentence.

B522.1. *Serpent shows condemned man how to save prince's life.* Bites prince and then shows man the proper remedy. By thus ingratiating self, man is freed from false accusation. *Calila* p. 318.

B525. *Lion spares man he is about to devour.* Androcles. *Esopete* p. 61; *Castigos* 27.141; Tubach 215.

*B525.1.1. *Lion spares Christian martyr.* Repects her virginity. *Jardín* p. 253; cf. Tubach 3072.

*B525.2. *Lions spare Daniel's life.* God had rewarded him for saving Susanna from false accusations. *Castigos* 9.70.

B535. Animal nurse.

*B535.0.15. *Lion as nurse for child.* Child rescued when dogs pursue lion. *Çifar* p. 27; cf. Tubach 5350 (wolf).

*B535.0.16. *Doe as nurse for seven abandoned princelings* left in desert. *Ultramar* I.1.56.93; cf. Tubach 5350 (wolf).

B540. Animal rescuer or retriever.

B545.1. *Deer freed from net by friendly animals*: crow, mouse, and tortoise. To save slow moving tortoise from hunter, deer feigns death. Crow perches on deer. Deer arises, escapes. Archer pursues and mouse gnaws ropes to free tortoise. *Calila* p. 221; *Exemplario* 49r.

B545.2. *Rat (mouse) gnaws net.* *Esopete* p. 38; *Calila* p. 202.

B552. Man carried by bird.

B552.1. *Alexander* carried through air by two griffins with meat held in front of them. *Alexandre* cc. 2496–2504; Tubach 125.

B558.1. *Boat drawn by swan.* Swan Knight arrives in kingdom and departs in boat drawn by his swan-brother. *Ultramar* I.1.71.126, I.1.135.275–76.

B560. Animals advise people.

B562.1.3. *Birds show man treasure.* Doves saved from death by monk show him where to dig for treasure. *Calila* p. 334.

B563.5. *Wild leopards guide Jesus and Holy Family* through wilderness. *Castigos* MS A BNM 6559 31.145 (ADMYTE 0 91*v*).

B575. Animals as constant attendant of human.

*B575.2.1. *Man raises baby goat.* Tries to keep it as a companion animal. She runs off to join other wild goats grazing in fields. His servants bring her back to house and kill other wild goats. *Barlaam* pp. 156–57.

B580. Animal helps man to wealth and greatness.

*B581.1. *Serpent brings wealth* to farmer. *Esopete* pp. 89–90; Tubach 4251.

B700–B799. FANCIFUL TRAITS OF ANIMALS

*B701. *Animals help each other.* Sheep shelter others from sun; deer will carry each other across rivers; cranes guide other cranes in flight. *Espéculo* 87.5.

B730. Fanciful color, smell, etc. of animals.

B732. *Panther's sweet smell* attracts other animals and protects it from other beasts. *Espéculo* 50.35; cf. Tubach 3583.

B741.2. *Neighing of stallions in Assyria* impregnates mares. *Esopete* p. 22.

*B749. *Eel opens clam/oyster/conch shell.* Uses pebble to wedge it open to eat flesh. *Espéculo* 63.44–45.

*B752.1.1. *Enchanted swan sings to signal Swan Knight* he must depart kingdom in boat. *Ultramar* I.1.134.274–75.

*B765.4.2. *Cow thought to have given birth to snake.* She flees; snake pursues; traps her legs and drinks her milk. Teats and legs are blackened. *Esopete* p. 166.

B770. Other fanciful traits of animals.

B773. Animals with human emotions.

*B773.1.1. *Cranes love each other,* have a king whose laws they obey, and migrate as a group. *a.b.c.* 60.

*B773.4. *She-wolf ashamed because she stole holy man's bread.* He prayed for her and forgave her. *a.b.c.* 29; Tubach 5344.

*B773.5. *Crows care for aged parents. a.b.c.* 41; Tubach 642.

C. TABU

C0–C99. TABU CONNECTED WITH SUPERNATURAL BEINGS

C10. Tabu: profanely calling up spirit (devil).

C12. Devil invoked: appears unexpectedly.

*C12.4.2. *Man inadvertently breaks tabu* by calling out to devil (servant) to help with shoes. Devil appears. *a.b.c.* 113; Tubach 1605.

*C12.4.3. *Cleric stubs toe on stone and inadvertently praises devil's power.* He is punished with paralysis and blindness. *Cantigas* 407.

C20. Tabu: calling on ogre or destructive animal.

C25. *"Bear's-food."* To urge on his horses, a man threatens them with the bear, calling them "bear's-food." The bear hears and comes for them. *Esopete* pp. 144–45.

*C25.2. *Child threatened with wolf (ogre).* Esopete* p. 119.

*C25.2.1. *"Wolf food."* To urge his ox on, man angrily says he will feed him to wolf. Wolf comes to claim promised food. *Disciplina* 23; *a.b.c.* 363; cf. J2066.5.

C30. Tabu: offending supernatural relative.

C32.2.1. *Tabu: asking name of supernatural husband.* Swan Knight tells new wife that she must not ask him his name. *Ultramar* I.1.68.120.

C32.2.2. *Tabu: asking where supernatural husband comes from.* Swan Knight tells new wife that she must not ask him what country he came from. *Ultramar* I.1.68.120.

C50. Tabu: offending the gods.

*C51.4.1.1. *Bee offends Jupiter* when she asks him for power to kill men. *Esopete* p. 112; see A2346.1.

C54. Rivaling the gods.

*C54.1. *Multiparous woman declares self superior to goddesses of fertility.* Her fecundity was superior to theirs. *Ilustres mujeres* 14.21r–22r (Niobe).

*C54.2. *Woman skilled at weaving and spinning* challenged Pallas Athena to a contest. Defeated, she hanged herself. *Ilustres mujeres* 17. 2424v–25r (Arachne).

C55.3. *Beekeeper puts consecrated Host into beehive to make colony thrive.* Bees build an altar and put Host on it. He repents sacrilege and shows the miracle to public. *Espéculo* 254.172.

*C55.3.1. *Beekeeper puts consecrated Host into beehive.* Virgin Mary and Child appear in hive. *Cantigas* 128, 208; Tubach 2662.

C93. Tabu: trespassing sacred precinct.

*C93.3.1. *Tabu: privy in churchyard.* Saint appears to hermit. Tells him privy's odor is offensive near church. He must move it. *Espéculo* 212.146.

C94. Tabu: rudeness to sacred person or thing.

C94.1.1. *The cursed dancers.* Dancers rude to priest on Christmas Eve. Curses them to keep dancing until released. *Espéculo* 132.90–91; Tubach 1419.

*C94.1.4. *Gambler curses Virgin Mary.* Terrible smell issues from his heart. *a.b.c.* 55; cf. Tubach 2240.

C94.4.1. *Tabu: calling profanely on God's eyes.* Gambler's eyes fall out. *a.b.c.* 236; Tubach 1949.

C100–C199. SEX TABU

*C110.2. *Tabu: sexual intercourse* on night previous to coming to church.

Devils torment guilty woman. Saint's prayers cure her. *Espéculo* 96.64–65.

*C114.1.1. *Tabu: incest.* Widow commits incest with son. Forgiven by Virgin Mary. *a.b.c.* 274.

*C114.3. *Tabu: incest.* Servant holds candle while nobleman commits incest with a relative. *a.b.c.* 166.

*C114.4. *Tabu: incest.* Mother tries to commit incest with son. He refuses and she accuses him of attempted rape. *a.b.c.* 172; Tubach 2734.

*C116.1. *Tabu: sexual intercourse in public place.* Saint invited by a prostitute offers to have sex with her before a crowd. She will not out of shame; he asks then how much more shame should she have before God. *Espéculo* 350.250.

C119. Miscellaneous tabus concerning sexual intercourse.

*C119.1.2.1. *Tabu: sexual intercourse on day of consecration of church.* Violators taken by devil. Saint's prayer frees them. *Espéculo* 277.185.

*C119.1.2.2. *Tabu: sexual intercourse on feast day.* Defiant couple found dead embracing in bed next day. *Espéculo* 279.186.

C200–C299. EATING AND DRINKING TABUS

C221. Tabu: eating meat.

*C221.0.1. *Ascetic (fasting jackal)* vows not to eat meat. *Calila* p. 309.

*C221.0.2. *Tabu: eating meat on Sabbath.* Warriors who violate tabu captured and killed. Those who ate only bread victorious. *Cantigas* 277.

C230. Tabu: eating at certain time.

*C235.1. *Tabu: eating meat during Lent.* Saint has only bacon to give guest during Lent. Both partake as sign of saint's hospitality. *Espéculo* 297.207–8; cf. Tubach 3243.

C270. Tabu: drinking certain things.

*C271.1. *Tabu: drinking milk of any other than one's own mother.* Angel appears to pregnant woman warning that baby is not to have wet-nurse. *Ultramar* I.1.84.168–69; Tubach 3283.

C400–C499. SPEAKING TABUS

C400. Speaking tabu.

*C400.01. *Old man traveling in company with monks* maintains silence as a sign of wisdom. *a.b.c.* 335.

*C400.02. *Philosopher in desert* gains serenity without speaking. *a.b.c.* 403.

C401.2. *Tabu: speaking during seven days of danger.* Horoscope indicates when to be silent. *Sendebar* p. 73.

C410. Tabu: asking questions.

*C411.1. *Tabu: asking for reason of an unusual action.* King forbids that anyone ask him why he never laughs. *Çifar* p. 130.

*C411.2. *Tabu: speaking.* Consort of fairy queen must not address her subjects nor ask questions of them. *Çifar* p. 67.

C411.4. *Tabu: asking questions.* Wife violates tabu (asks forbidden questions) and Swan Knight must leave her. *Ultramar* I.1.127–35.264–76.

C430. Name tabu.

C436. *Tabu: disclosing one's identity.* Saint must not reveal identity to his father. *San Alejo* p. 74.

C600–C699. UNIQUE PROHIBITION

C601. Unique prohibition announced by mysterious voice.

C601.1. *Heavenly voice tells pope he may not enter church.* To save money, he ceased payment for eternal oil lamp placed there by Constantine. *Espéculo* 214.147.

C603. Other unique prohibitions.

*C603. *Entry to palace forbidden.* King opens locked palace and enters despite prohibition. Opens locked chest despite prohibition. King who breaks tabu will lose his kingdom to invaders portrayed on cloth in chest. *PCG* 1.553.307; *Abreviada* 2.100.

*C604. *Kissing hands of empress forbidden.* *Çifar* pp. 134–37.

C610. The one forbidden place.

*C610.01. *Wife ordered to guard household* in husband's absence. She is forbidden to enter oven. Digging around oven she is crushed when wall falls. *a.b.c.* 307; Tubach 5277.

C611.1. Forbidden door.

*C611.1.2. *Church doors will not let woman sinner* pass through. All others enter freely. Prays to Virgin Mary and is permitted entry. *Cantigas* 98.

C620. Tabu: partaking of the one forbidden object.

C621. *Forbidden tree.* Fruit of all trees may be eaten, except one. *Estados* 1.38.

C700–C899. MISCELLANEOUS TABUS

C770.1. *Overweening pride forbidden.* Man proud that he and his clan have never known want or unhappiness is swallowed by earth with all his belongings. *a.b.c.* 287; Tubach 3938.

C771.1. *Tabu: building too high a tower* (Tower of Babel). *Glosa* 3.1.6.35.

C777. Excessive worry.

*C777.1. *Merchant not to fret* over goods on ship at sea. Cannot sleep, eat, nor drink. Thinks every wind will cause ship to sink. *Castigos* 7.64.

C900–C999. PUNISHMENT FOR BREAKING TABU

C901.4. Punishment for breaking tabu: assigner suffers own penalty.

*C901.4.2. *Consul violates sanctuary.* Kills enemies captured in church. Later takes sanctuary himself and emperor executes him. *Espéculo* 211.146.

C950. Person carried to otherworld for breaking tabu.

*C951. *Knight breaks tabu.* Asks emperor why he never laughs. Set adrift in boat without oars that takes him to otherworld. *Çifar* p. 130.

C961. Transformation to object for breaking tabu.

C961.1. *Transformation to pillar of salt* for breaking tabu. *Castigos* 50.212.

D. MAGIC

D0–D699. TRANSFORMATION

D10. Transformation to person of different sex.

*D12.0.1. *Transformation: man to woman.* Man drinks water from magical spring. Transformation reversed by tricking a demon. *Sendebar* Day 4, Tale 8.

D117. Transformation: person to rodent.

*D117.1.1. *Transformation: person to rat.* Hermit prays that God transform rat-maiden back into rat so that she may marry rat. *Calila* p. 244; *Exemplario* 58v; Tubach 3428.

D130. Transformation: human to domestic beast.

D136. *Transformation: man to swine. Ilustres mujeres* 36.43r–43v (Circe).

*D141.1.1. *Transformation: young woman to puppy.* Woman threatened with transformation if she will not acquiesce to a sexual request. *Sendebar* Day 4, Tale 10; *a.b.c.* 234 (not in Paris MS); *Disciplina* 13; Tubach 661.

D150. Transformation: man to bird.

D161.1. *Transformation: man to swan* when magic golden chain is removed from neck. *Ultramar* I.1.58.99; cf. Tubach 1884.

D315. Transformation: rodent to human.

D315.1. *Rat-maiden.* Hermit prays to God that a rat be changed into a girl. Raises her as daughter. *Calila* p. 244; *Exemplario* 58v; Tubach 3428.

D350. Transformation: bird to person.

*D361.2. *Swans changed back into youths* by replacement of golden chains around neck. *Ultramar* I.1.68.118; cf. Tubach 1884.

D450–D499. Transformation: object to object.

*D451.10. *Transformation: wood becomes stone.* Rustic who chopped wood on saint's day is reproached by neighbor. Defends self: "This wood would turn to stone, if it were wrong to chop it today." It changes to stone. *Espéculo* 275.185; Tubach 5371.

*D454.3.1.2. *White chasuble, stained red with wine,* miraculously returned to white by Virgin Mary. *Cantigas* 73.

D470. Transformation: material of object changed.

*D470.1. *Water in river transformed to copper* by magician, Virgil. *LBA* c. 266.

*D470.2. *Saint changes maggots in sores of nun* into precious stones. *a.b.c.* 342; Tubach 2266.

D530. Transformation: putting on skin or clothing.

D536. Transformation: removing chains from neck.

D536.1. *Transformation to swans by taking golden chains off neck.* Evil countess orders servants to remove chains from grandsons' necks before killing them. Swans escape. *Ultramar* I.1.58.98–99; Tubach 1884.

D630. Transformation and disenchantment at will.

*D630.1.1.1. *Power of self-transformation wrested from demon* by trickery. *Sendebar* Day 4, Tale 8.

D700–D799. DISENCHANTMENT

D788. Disenchantment by sign of cross.

*D788.1. *Saint makes spring water safe* from serpent with sign of cross. *Espéculo* 136.95–96; Tubach 1347.

D800–D1699. MAGIC OBJECTS

D800–899. Ownership of magic objects.

D810. Magic object as gift.

*D811.3. *Thread supplied magically* to sew new altar cloths for church. *Cantigas* 273.

D812.8. *Magic object received from lady in dream.* Candle crushed in dream. Nun awakes with piece of candle in hand. *Castigos* MS A BNM 6559 4.95; cf. Tubach 847.

*D812.16. *Gloves and ring given to saint in dream.* Sends for them from distant place as evidence of appearance in dream. *Espéculo* 300.208–9.

D871. Magic object traded away.

D876. *Magic treasure animal killed.* Goose that laid the golden egg. *Esopete* p. 127.

D900–D1299. Kinds of magic objects.

D906. Magic wind.

*D906.1. *Forbidden church burial,* pope orders that his remains be placed in front of closed church doors. Magic wind blows them open as sign of his worthiness. *a.b.c.* 33; Tubach 2370.

*D906.2. *Extraordinary wind* blows arrows shot against Christians back against enemy. *PCG* 2.568.323; *Castigos* MS A BNM 6559 10.108 (ADMYTE 0 36r); *Abreviada* 2.115; Tubach 349, 4773.

D910. Magic body of water.

D915. Magic river.

*D915.7. *Magic river carries worldly debris.* *Espéculo* 37.26.

D927. Magic spring.

*D915.8. *Magic river* rises to drown liars. *Esopete* pp. 100–1.

D927.1. *Gods create magic spring* in desert. *Alexandre* cc. 1170–75; *Castigos* MS A BNM 6559 31.146 (ADMYTE 0 92r).

*D927.6. *Magic spring* transforms man into woman. *Sendebar* Day 4, Tale 8.

D960. Magic gardens and plants.

D978. *Magic herbs* sought by wise man on quest to India in hope of finding way of resuscitating the dead. *Exemplario* 5r–5v; *Calila* pp. 99–102.

D990. Magic bodily members: human.

*D992.4. *Magic skull* as source of secret political information. *Espéculo* 147.100.

D997. Magic internal organs: human.

*D997.1.2. *Heart of woman devoted to Virgin Mary* bears image of Virgin. Observed in autopsy. *Cantigas* 188; cf. Tubach 1338, 2497, 2498.

D1030. Magic food.

*D1031.1.2. *Monks complain about shortage of bread.* Abbot tells them to have faith and patience. Next day, sacks of flour for bread are left at their door. *Espéculo* 398.295–96; Tubach 766, 2566.

*D1032.1.1. *King's faith in Virgin Mary brings him food for guests.* Four shiploads of fish arrive magically. *Cantigas* 386.

D1039. Magic food: miscellaneous.

*D1039.3. *Monk complains about food.* Virgin Mary tells him to touch it to her Son's wounds; it will sweeten. *Espéculo* 5.5–6.

*D1039.4. *Monk leaves monastery because of food.* Jesus Christ touches bread to his wounds; it sweetens. *Espéculo* 6.6.

D1040. Magic drink.

D1040.1. *Drink supplied by magic.* Virgin Mary replenishes wine at celebration of her feast day. *Cantigas* 351.

D1050. Magic clothes.

*D1052.2. *Magic chasuble* given to S. Ildefonso by Virgin Mary not to be worn by any other. It strangles his unworthy successor. *Milagros* 1; *Cantigas* 2; *Espéculo* 375.275–76.

D1053.1. *Pupil returns from dead* to warn master of futility of his studies. Wears magic cloak lined with perilous fire. Droplet from cloak burns master's hand. *a.b.c.* 417; Tubach 1103.

D1065. Magic footwear.

*D1065.2.1. *Magic slippers given to woman by suitor.* Woman unable to remove them upon husband's return until Virgin Mary helps her. *Cantigas* 64.

D1070. Magic ornaments.

*D1071.2. *Magic stones engraved with image of Virgin Mary and Child.* Have power to enlighten literally and figuratively. *Cantigas* 29.

D1130. Magic buildings and parts.

D1131. *Magic castle.* Knight led to magic castle at bottom of enchanted lake. *Çifar* p. 67.

D1162. Magic light.

D1162.2. *Magic candles* dance on altar when placed there by unrepentant sinner. *Espéculo* 492.389.

*D1162.3. *Virgin Mary gives minstrel who sings her praise a magic candle.* Churchman tries to put candle in candlestick, but it returns to the singer's *vihuela* (guitar). *Cantigas* 8.

*D1162.3.1. *Magically curative candle will stay lit only for minstrels.* Will not burn for bishop. *Cantigas* 259.

*D1162.4. *Candles kept alight magically by Virgin Mary* were placed in church by man devoted to her. *Cantigas* 116.

D1170. Magic utensils and implements.

*D1171.6.5. *Magic drinking vessel.* Man suffering with a swollen mouth and face, unable to drink, cured by glass brought by pilgrims from shrine. *Santiago* 12.74–75.

*D1171.7.2. *Magic pitcher will not hold water.* Given task to fill it, sinner prays to Virgin Mary for help. Fills it with own tears. *Cantigas* 155.

*D1206.1.1. *Sickle magically stuck to man's hand* because he cut grain on a feast day. Removed magically when he offered sickle to St. Peter. *a.b.c.* 164; *Cantigas* 289.

D1210. Magical musical instruments.

D1222. *Magical horn* (ivory, gold, and precious jewels), negligently left in palace to burn in terrible conflagration, saved from fire by magical swan. *Ultramar* I.1.137.278–79.

D1273.1. Magic numbers.

D1273.1.2.1. *Five as a magic number.* Five joys of the Virgin, five senses, five fingers. *Milagros* 4.

*D1273.1.2.2. *Five as a magic number.* Five wounds of Jesus Christ. *Castigos* 9.72.

D1298. Magic firewood.

D1298.1. *Magic firewood bleeds when cut and curses man who had sent him.* Monk's servant sent to cut it on Sabbath. Returned to monastery to find monk had disappeared. *Espéculo* 280.186–87.

D1300–D1599. Function of magic objects.

D1300. Magic object gives supernatural wisdom.

*D1300.4.1. *Stone said to give magic wisdom:* wisdom to fools; restore hearing to deaf, speech to mutes, sanity to madmen; cure sick; chase demons. Revealed to be Jesus Christ. *Barlaam* p. 48.

D1310. Magic object gives supernatural information.

*D1310.4.4. *Magic sign to show that soul is freed of torment.* Black hair combings secreted by dead lover turn white when she is freed. *Espéculo* 353.251–52; Tubach 2397.

D1317.1. *Buttocks as magic watcher.* Woman tells slave she can supervise him even while she sleeps. *Esopete* p. 16.

D1344. Magic object gives invulnerability.

D1344.11. *Magic sword to give invulnerability* given to infant Alexander. *Alexandre* c. 94.

D1380. Magic object protects.

D1381.5. *Knight protected in battle by magic shirt.* Virgin Mary's shirt makes him invulnerable. *Cantigas* 148.

*D1381.5.1. *Virgin Mary's skirt repels besiegers of city.* Leader is struck blind. After siege is lifted, skirt disappears and eyesight restored. *Espéculo* 373.274.

D1381.11.1 *Magic circle protects from wild animals.* *Ultramar* II.2.254–57.370–78.

D1381.20. *Sacred relics of Virgin Mary* protect ships from pirate's attack. *Cantigas* 35.

D1385. Magic object protects from evil spirits.

D1385.19.1. *Saint's hose protect* woman from incubus. *a.b.c.* 116; Tubach 1118.

D1400. Magic object overcomes person.

D1400.1.16. *Magic pennant* enables bearer to succeed in any undertaking. *Çifar* p. 138.

D1402.7. *Sword that causes death* to foe when drawn given to young Alexander. *Alexandre* c. 94.

D1443. Magic object expels animals.

*D1443.2. *Saint excommunicates flies* that are plaguing a monastery. They all die. *Espéculo* 269.181.

D1500. Magic object controls disease.

*D1500.0.2. *Book devoted to Virgin Mary* has curative powers when placed on royal body. *Cantigas* 209.

D1500.1.7.2. *Magic healing spittle.* Jesus cures blind man with saliva. *Castigos* 1.39–40.

*D1500.1.7.3.5. *Blood flows from side of crucifix* that has been stomped upon and tormented. Used as cure. *a.b.c.* 91; Tubach 1373.

D1505. Magic object cures blindness.

D1505.5.4. *Magic spring cures blindness.* Location overheard by man blinded by monkey-king. *Gatos* 28.

D1507. Magic object restores speech.

D1507.5. *Magic cake* chewed first by a fox restores speech of princess. *Gatos* 28.

D1515. Magic antidote for poison.

*D1515.2.2. *Words of mass* can protect humans from snake venom. *Castigos* 4.54.

D1520. Magic object affords miraculous transportation.

*D1524.9.1. *Magic wind transports hero.* Saint's boat is carried at great speed to destination. *San Alejo* p. 74.

D1525. *Magic submarine (boat).* Alexander explores sea floor. *Alexandre* cc. 2305–17; *Castigos* MS A BNM 6559 153.33 (ADMYTE 0 104v); Tubach 123.

D1550. Magic object opens and closes.

D1551. *Waters magically divide and close* (Red Sea). *Castigos* MS A BNM 6559 15.122.

D1557.1. *Pilgrims denied entrance to tomb of Santiago* pray to him. Saint causes doors to shatter and they enter. *Santiago* 18.94–96.

D1560. Magic object performs other services for owner.

D1561.2.2. *Magic treasure.* Magic treasure (coins hidden in mouse hole) gives mouse power to leap into basket of food suspended up high by hermit. Deprived of treasure, loses power. *Calila* p. 210; *Exemplario* 45v.

*D1561.2.5. *Magic power in six golden chains* changes when melted down. Metalworker able to make requested vessel from one chain; reserves five. *Ultramar* I.1.58.100.

D1600–D1699. Characteristics of magic objects.

D1620. Magic automata.

*D1622.4. *Image of Virgin Mary placed in bed by nuns* changes color and tosses and turns as if she were in labor. *Cantigas* 361.

D1624.2. *Crucifix bleeds* after being stabbed. *a.b.c.* 90; Tubach 1373.

D1639.2. *Image of Virgin saves painter* who had painted ugly picture of devil. Devil had pulled scaffold away. *Cantigas* 74; *a.b.c.* 263; Tubach 3573.

*D1639.2.1. *Image of Virgin* cures queen at point of death. *Cantigas* 256.

D1650. Other characteristics of magic objects.

D1652.1.1. *Charitable person's supply* of bread is inexhaustible. *a.b.c.* 146, 147; *Espéculo* 169.114; *Cantigas* 203; Tubach 766.

D1654. Immovable object.

D1654.9.1. *Corpse cannot be moved.* Corpse of priest's concubine magically too heavy to carry. Only other concubines can carry her. *Espéculo* 111.72–73; Tubach 1265.

D1654.11. *Letter in hand of dead saint (pilgrim) can only be removed by pope* (abandoned wife, patriarch, bishop, king). *San Alejo* pp. 78–79; *Armas* p. 128.

*D1654.11.2. *Letter in hand of dead convert to Christianity* can only be removed by bishop who converted him. *a.b.c.* 283.

D1700–D2199. MAGIC POWERS AND MANIFESTATIONS

D1710–D1799. Possession and means of employment of magic powers.

D1712. Soothsayer (diviner, oracle).

D1712.3 *Interpreter of dreams.* Bishop interprets king's dream. *a.b.c.* 61; Tubach 1785.

*D1712.4. *Queen casts lots and reads stars* to foretell future. Three brothers born in France will come to conquer holy land. *Ultramar* I.1.166.323.

*D1712.4.1.1. *Interpreter of dreams.* False interpretation given by king's enemy. Must kill family and advisers, bathe in their blood, and destroy his defenses to avoid losing his realm. *Calila* p. 280; *Exemplario* 70v.

D1713. Magic powers of hermit (saint).

*D1713.1. *Magic powers of saint.* Beam for construction of church in honor of saint found to be too short. Saint magically extends it. *Espéculo* 206.143–44; cf. Tubach 512.

*D1713.2. *Saint's prayers* enable man to return from dead to do penance. *a.b.c.* 129; Tubach 4151.

*D1713.3. *Saint holds scorpions* and cuts them in half without peril. *a.b.c.* 237; Tubach 4151; cf. Tubach 4279.

*D1713.4. *Magic powers of saint* enable him to win dice game with gambler. *a.b.c.* 252; Tubach 2239, 4151.

*D1713.5. *Magic powers of saint* show him face of death. *a.b.c.* 296; Tubach 4151.

*D1713.6. *Magic powers of saint* give him second sight. *a.b.c.* 378; Tubach 4151.

*D1713.7. *Saint magically causes emperor's throne to burn.* Emperor forced to rise and show him signs of reverence. *Espéculo* 464.368.

*D1713.8. *Flood waters stop miraculously* at door of saint's church. *a.b.c.* 31; Tubach 2091.

*D1713.9. *Infant Jesus commands date palm to bend down* to give shade in desert. *Castigos* MS A BNM 6559 31.145 (ADMYTE 0 92v).

*D1713.10. *Infant Jesus chases dragons away* to protect family. *Castigos* MS A BNM 6559 31.145 (ADMYTE 0 92v).

D1714. Magic powers of person without sin.

*D1714.2. *Saint saves man who had pledged fealty to Satan.* *a.b.c.* 23; *Milagros* 2, 14; *Talavera* 1.13.90.

D1719. Possession of magic powers: miscellaneous.

D1719.6. *Magic power of holy cross.* Man taught power of cross. Moses' magic rod was of the wood of the cross. *Espéculo* 142.98; cf. Tubach 5373.

*D1719.6.1. *Magic power of cross.* Enchanted skull unable to speak in presence of sign of cross. *Espéculo* 147.100.

*D1719.6.2. *Magic power of holy cross.* David's weapon against Goliath prefigured cross. *Espéculo* 148.100–1.

*D1719.6.3. *Magic power of cross.* Victim saves self from murder by making sign of cross with his arms. *a.b.c.* 94.

D1726. Magic power derived from deity.

*D1726.0.2. *Old man prays that God grant him power to stay awake* during spiritual sermons and to fall asleep during evil speech. *Espéculo* 175.119.

D1745. Magic power rendered ineffective.

*D1745.1.1. *Magician's power rendered ineffective* when king recites John 1:1. "In the beginning was the word." *Espéculo* 530.417.

*D1745.3. *Witch comes to cure young saint's headache.* He sends her away. *Espéculo* 529.417.

D1760. Means of producing magic power.

D1766.1.2. *Prayers of woman* cause Virgin Mary to show her the infant Jesus. *a.b.c.* 280; Tubach 1021, 1022.

D1766.1.3. *Garment produced by prayer.* Man's prayer to Virgin Mary weaves garment for her. *a.b.c.* 276; *Cantigas* 274; Tubach 3913.

D1766.1.4. *Pain stopped by prayer.* Priest must give up fornication; in exchange, pains are cured by saint's prayers. *Espéculo* 110.72.

D1766.1.7. *Cleric prays to Santiago* for release from captivity. He appears, unchains prisoners magically, and leads them to freedom. *Santiago* 1.45–48, 11.73–74; 14.77–79; cf. Tubach 926 (Virgin Mary).

*D1766.1.7.1. *Prisoner's wife prays for his release.* Released, he tells her that in prison, he felt himself freed from his restraints. *a.b.c.* 318; *Espéculo* 247.169; Tubach 3893.

*D1766.1.7.2 *Prisoner chained cruelly* miraculously released from chains at tierce when mass was said for him. *Espéculo* 249.170.

D1766.1.8. *Food produced by prayer.* Cleric unable to feed workmen who are repairing church dedicated to saint prays to saint for help. Finds an oven full of bread. *Espéculo* 207.144.

*D1766.1.8.1. *Bishop trapped in hill of sand.* His wife mourned and left offerings of food, wine, and candles in church for a year, failing one day. He was sustained magically for a year (failing one day) until he was rescued. *Espéculo* 154.106–7.

*D1766.1.8.2. *Sailor drowning at sea saved* by mass at moment when it was said for him. Magically supplied with bread. *Espéculo* 251.170–71; Tubach 4148.

*D1766.1.9. *Prayers of community* led by saint defeat devil. *a.b.c.* 23.

*D1766.1.10. *Hermit prays for companionship.* Bear comes to serve him. *a.b.c.* 329; Tubach 519.

*D1766.1.11. *Prayers of holy man* cause four evildoers to sicken and die. *a.b.c.* 329; Tubach 519.

*D1766.1.12. *Prayers bring rain.* Farmers shown how to pray devoutly. *a.b.c.* 331; cf. Tubach 3885.

*D1766.1.13. *Prayer.* Man enters church dark, heavy with sin accompanied by devil. He prays, and leaves light, bright, and accompanied by an angel. *a.b.c.* 332.

*D1766.1.14. *Captive's prayers move mountain. a.b.c.* 170; Tubach 3424.

*D1766.1.15. *Prince throws weapons down and prays for victory.* Wins battle. *a.b.c.* 32; Tubach 3875.

D1766.6. Magic result from sign of the cross.

*D1766.6.4.1. *Sign of cross.* Saint makes sign of cross over poisoned wine and is able to drink it without danger. *Espéculo* 141.98.

*D1766.6.4.2. *Sign of cross.* Saint makes sign of cross and wine glass containing poison breaks and spills contents. *Espéculo* 138.96.

*D1766.6.4.3. *Sign of cross.* Evil spirit conjured away by sign of cross. Sign of cross cures bishop's ruddy face. *a.b.c.* 157.

D1766.7. Magic results from uttering powerful name.

*D1766.7.1.2. *Philosophers come to dispute with bishop* to show him he should return to their ancient faith. He orders them to be silent in Christ's name, and they lose power of speech. *a.b.c.* 431; Tubach 4560.

D1766.7.3. *Magic results produced in name of saint.* Pilgrim falls into sea, calls out to Santiago. Friend throws shield to him. Travels safely to port under Santiago's protection. *Santiago* 10.72–73.

D1800–D2199. Manifestations of magic power.

D1810. Magic knowledge.

D1810.0.2. *Magic knowledge.* Devil disguised as magician conjures up magical skull to tell envoy of enemy's plans. *Espéculo* 147.100.

D1810.0.3.1. *Saint perceives cheat.* He knows that a boy has hidden a basket of fruit sent him by a friend. He warns boy that a snake has hidden in basket. *a.b.c.* 393; Tubach 4259.

D1810.0.3.2. *Saint perceives cheat.* Pilgrims hide their clothes in woods and then ask saint to clothe them. He tells them to return and get their own clothes in woods. *a.b.c.* 378; Tubach 3805.

D1811. Magic wisdom.

*D1811.3. *Poet calls on Virgin Mary* for perfect line in poem to her. *Cantigas* 202.

D1812. Magic power of prophecy.

*D1812.3.3.0.4. *Captive interprets royal dream.* Grateful king frees him. *a.b.c.* 61.

D1812.3.3.8. *Pregnant woman's dream reveals future of unborn child. a.b.c.* 180; *Ultramar* I.1.84.169, I.1.144.290–91; *Alexandre* cc. 348–49.

*D1812.3.3.8.1. *Father's dream* that sun's rays emanated from pregnant wife's womb. Prophecy of future greatness of unborn child. *a.b.c.* 180.

*D1812.3.3.12. *Death of bishop revealed* in deacon's dream. *a.b.c.* 65.

D1812.5. Future learned through omens.

D1812.5.0.1 *Omens from sneezing* (flatulence). Omen makes wolf leave food behind in hope of better. *LBA* cc. 766–79; *Esopete* p. 91–93.

D1812.5.0.2. *Kill bird that lands on head.* Omen of personal gain or loss to realm. Good ruler chooses not to kill. *Castigos* MS A BNM 6559 57.184.

D1812.5.1.4. *Eclipse as evil omen.* Tubach 1475.3; *Alexandre* c. 1227.

*D1812.5.2.12. *Omen.* Bird left serpent's egg in king's lap. Sign that unborn son would rule the world. *a.b.c.* 180.

*D1812.5.2.13. *Omen.* Hen's egg heated produced a crested chick. Omen that unborn royal child would be a son who would rule empire. *a.b.c.* 180.

D1813. Magic knowledge of events in distant place.

*D1813.1.3.1. *Dream warns king of uprising and danger to Christian church.* King and queen have same dream of Virgin Mary and child in danger of fire. *Cantigas* 345.

*D1813.5. *Jesus comes to bishop in dream to lead him to interment of Saint Martha.* Sends for saint's gloves and ring as evidence of his presence. *Espéculo* 300.208–9.

D1814. Magic advice.

D1814.2. *Advice from dream.* St. James appears, tells king he will defeat enemy. *PCG* 2.629.360.

*D1814.2.1. *Advice from dream.* Angel appears in dream to three knights. They must go to holy land and capture it. *Ultramar* I.1.188.362–63.

*D1814.2.2. *Advice from dream.* Cleric dreams of birds of prey; must hunt usurers. *Espéculo* 565.461.

D1815. Magic knowledge of strange tongues.

D1815.2. *Magic knowledge of language of animals.* Aesop rewarded for kindness to traveler. *Esopete* p. 3.

D1816.2. Lost object discovered by magic.

*D1816.2.1.1. *Lost object discovered by magic.* Stolen ring lost in river, recovered in fish's belly. *Cantigas* 369; Tubach 4102.

*D1816.2.2. *Lost animal (falcon) discovered miraculously.* Virgin Mary helps noble hunter to find lost falcon. *Cantigas 366.*

*D1816.2.3. *Lost sheep brought safely home by Virgin Mary. Cantigas 398.*

*D1816.2.4. *Stolen necklace returned to owner by Virgin Mary.* Necklace, borrowed by poor woman for wedding, stolen. *Cantigas 212.*

*D1816.2.5. *Lost ring recovered.* Royal ring found by traveler and returned to owner who had prayed to Virgin Mary. *Cantigas 376.*

D1817. Magic detection of crime.

*D1817.0.1.7. *God disguised as pilgrim says he has eyes in back of neck.* Saw theft of pig by barber. *Espéculo 553.445;* Tubach 1018.

D1817.0.2. *Magic sight of blind bishop* sees that an archdeacon is about to poison him. Drinks poison but sends message that evil archdeacon will not succeed him because he will die magically. *a.b.c.* 239; Tubach 697.

D1820. Magic sight and hearing.

D1820.1.1. *Magic sight of blind holy man* lets him see that king is king. *a.b.c.* 239.

D1821.7. *Knight entering a monastery decided to remain mute* to avoid error. Muteness enables him to see demons carry off soul of dying knight, and angels carrying off soul of another knight. *a.b.c.* 409.

D1825. Kinds of magic sight.

D1825.3.2. *Magic power of sight.* Sees angel in form of bright star over heads of good people or dark star over the heads of evil people. *a.b.c.* 203; *Espéculo 481.378.*

D1825.3.3.1. *Magic power to see souls after death.* Souls of the just fly through air and souls of the damned fall. *Espéculo 336.237–39.*

D1830. Magic strength.

D1831. *Magic strength resides in hair.* Samson, shorn by Delilah, is left powerless. *Castigos MS A BNM 6559 22.138 (ADMYTE 0 80r).*

*D1831.4. *Magic strength in lion skin.* Woman convinces Hercules to take off magic garb and to discard magic club. *Ilustres mujeres 21.27v–28v* (Iole).

*D1835.7. *Magic strength of short-statured knight-warrior* derived from faith and moral rectitude (died a virgin). *Castigos 1.38–39;* Tubach 4656.

D1840. Magic invulnerability.

D1840.1.2. *Magic invulnerability of saint.* Able to sunder poisonous snakes with his bare hands. *a.b.c.* 237; Tubach 4279.

D1840.1.2.1. *Saint invulnerable to poison.* Drinks poison; is saved by divine protection. *Estados 1.62;* Tubach 4151.

D1840.1.4. *Man protected from damnation by good works.* Gave store of good works to save sinner. Devils will take saintly man now bereft of good works. Generous act judged sufficient for salvation. *a.b.c.* 138.

D1841. Invulnerability from certain things.

*D1841.1.2. *King's robes unmarked by mud.* Kneels to honor host, rises unsoiled. *Castigos MS A BNM 6559 16.127 (ADMYTE 0 66r);* Tubach 1110.

*D1841.1.3. *Invulnerability from sword blows.* Image of Virgin Mary resists blows of enemies. *Cantigas* 215.

*D1841.1.4. *Words of mass give invulnerability* from venom of poisonous snakes. *Castigos* 4.54.

D1841.3. *Burning magically evaded;* monk survives when cell set afire; survives being thrown into fiery furnace. *a.b.c.* 389; Tubach 2038.

D1841.3.2. *Invulnerability from fire.* Image of Virgin Mary resists burning by enemies. *Cantigas* 215.

D1841.3.3. *Sacred book or manuscript does not burn in fire.* Book of St. James's miracles does not burn. *Santiago* p. 45.

D1841.4.4. *Rain or snow avoids certain places according to desire of saint or monk.* Saint makes sign of cross and creates an area free of rain in a storm. *Espéculo* 140.97.

*D1841.4.6. *Invulnerability from drowning.* Image of Virgin Mary resists drowning by enemies. *Cantigas* 215.

*D1841.4.7. *Woman pilgrim falls into sea,* calls upon Virgin for help. Is saved. *Cantigas* 383.

D1845.2. *Clothes confer invulnerability.* Hero as infant given magic gifts. *Alexandre* cc. 100–6.

D1846.4.2. *Virgin Mary sends maidens to anoint dying man.* Magic anointing restores him to life. *Cantigas* 204.

D1880. Magic rejuvenation.

*D1882.1.1. *Magic rejuvenation.* Monk, after suffering wasting disease, prays to Virgin Mary and is rejuvenated. Appears to be twenty. *Cantigas* 141.

D1890. Magic aging.

*D1890.0.1. *Magic aging.* Monk falls to knees at mention of Virgin Mary. Sickens and ages rapidly. *Cantigas* 141.

D1920. Other permanent magic characteristics.

D1925.3. *Barrenness removed by prayer.* After years of prayer childless couple have child. *San Alejo* p. 68; *Sendebar* p. 67; *Cantigas* 43.

D2000. Magic forgetfulness.

D2011.1. *Years seem moments while man listens to song of bird.* Monk in search of heaven follows bird of paradise. Returns to monastery 200 years later. *a.b.c.* 181; *Espéculo* 290.201; *Cantigas* 103; Tubach 3378.

D2020. Magic loss of speech.

*D2021.2. *Gambler punished for blasphemy.* Tongue grew a palm's length and he lost power of speech. *a.b.c.* 52; Tubach 677; cf. Tubach 4906.

D2025. Magic recovery of speech.

*D2025.6. *Magic recovery of speech* as reward for hospitality to traveler. *Esopete* pp. 3–4.

*D2025.7. *Son, born mute, recovers speech* when his father is in danger. Cries out warning. *a.b.c.* 173.

D2031. Magic illusion.

D2031.5. *Man magically made to believe self to be* bishop, archbishop, cardinal, and pope. When he refuses to reward the magician, the latter shows him the reality. *Lucanor* Ex. 11.

D2050–D2099. Destructive magic powers.

D2070. Bewitching.

*D2071.0.4. *Women with double pupils* kill those who anger them with a glance. *Glosa* 2.3.20.340.

*D2071.0.5. *Men kill enemies* with eyes like a basilisk. *Glosa* 2.3.20.340.

D2072.0.1. *Sword made magically helpless.* Executioner's arm paralyzed; unable to behead holy man. *a.b.c.* 295.

D2072.0.3. *Ship held back miraculously.* Man devoted to Virgin Mary is captive of Moorish pirates. Ships cannot leave port until he is released. *Cantigas* 95.

*D2072.7. *Thief prevented magically from leaving church.* Virgin Mary keeps him there until he confesses and returns stolen money to fellow pilgrim. *Cantigas* 302.

D2080. Magic used against property.

D2086.1. *Sword magically dulled* in attempted execution of innocent woman. *a.b.c.* 14; Tubach 4697.

*D2086.2.1. *Executioner's sword unable to behead prisoner* under protection of Santiago. *Santiago* 20.99–101.

*D2089.3.2. *Magic spell causes knight's horses to die* in ten days. *Çifar* p. 5.

D2090. Other destructive magic powers.

D2091.11. *Black cloud magically blown* upon army of hero's enemy. They are blinded and begin striking each other. *Ultramar* I.1.105.218.

*D2091.17. *Enemy's arrows deflected from target magically* so that they turn against the archer. *PCG* 2.568.322–24.

D2093. *Walls (Jericho) overthrown by magic.* *Castigos* MS A BNM 6559 69.198.

D2100–D2199. Other manifestations of magic power.

D2105. Provisions magically furnished.

*D2105.2.1. *Magically furnished food supply.* Virgin Mary rewards man for his generosity to her when she visited him in disguise. *Cantigas* 335.

D2106. Magic multiplication of objects.

D2106.1.5. *Multiplication of loaves and fishes.* Jesus made five loaves and two fish to feed 5,000 people. *Castigos* MS A BNM 6559 54.181.

D2120. Magic transportation.

D2125.1. *Magic power to walk on water.* Saint sends disciple to save a youth from drowning. Obedience gave him magical power to walk on water. *Espéculo* 416.314.

D2140. Magic control of elements.

D2140.1. *Control of weather by holy man's prayers.* Friars had prayed for rain in vain; holy man's prayers more powerful; they bring rain. *a.b.c.* 266.

D2140.1.1. *Storm magically stilled,* Jesus appears to Simon and other fishermen and saves them from storm at sea. *Castigos* MS A BNM 6559 8.100; *Castigos* MS A BNM 6559 84.217 (ADMYTE 0 22r); cf. Tubach 4649.

D2141.0.9. *Virgin Mary causes storm at sea* to impede escape of Moorish pirates who have plundered Christian settlement. They return and turn over spoils to king. *Cantigas* 379.

D2142. Winds controlled by magic.

D2142.0.2. *Winds free warship trapped in narrow river.* Caused by prayers to Virgin Mary. *Cantigas* 271.

D2142.1. *Wind produced by magic.* Woman has power to cause winds to produce tempests. *Ilustres mujeres* 16.23v (Medea).

D2143. Precipitation controlled by magic.

D2143.1.3. *Holy man magically produces rain* by praying. *a.b.c.* 331; Tubach 3885.

*D2143.1.3.1. *Preaching friar promises rain to flock* if they will repent sins and pray to Virgin Mary. *Cantigas* 143.

D2143.2.1. *Church spared in flood because of prayers.* Flood waters reached doors of church. *a.b.c.* 31; Tubach 2091.

*D2143.4.2. *Image of Virgin Mary placed in vineyard protects it from hailstorm* that devastates other vineyards in vicinity. *Cantigas* 161.

D2148.3. *Virgin Mary will halt volcanic eruption* if good man writes a poem in her praise. *Cantigas* 307.

D2149.4. Magic control of gravitation.

*D2149.4.3. *Stonemason, falling from great height,* calls upon Virgin Mary. He hangs by fingertips until she comes. *Cantigas* 242, 249.

*D2149.4.4. *Virgin Mary saves workmen* when sand hill collapses and smothers them. *Cantigas* 252.

*D2149.4.5. *Virgin Mary saves assembled worshipers.* Keeps great wooden beam from falling. *Cantigas* 266.

D2150. Miscellaneous magic manifestations.

D2151.1.3. *Sea calmed by prayer to Santiago.* Saint saves ship in storm. *Santiago* 9.69–72.

*D2151.9. *Magic control of waters.* Bishop's prayers dry up flood and mend destroyed walls of city. *a.b.c.* 332.

D2152. Magic control of mountains.

D2152.1. *Magic leveling of mountain.* Christians remember Matthew 17:20. To obey sultan's orders to level a mountain, they use prayer. *a.b.c.* 170; *Espéculo* 281.188–89; Tubach 3424.

*D2152.1.1. *God causes mountain to fall* on enemy of Christian army. *PCG* 2.568.323.

*D2152.1.2. *Mountains caused to fall.* Alexander prayed that mountains seal off captives who had offended their own god. *Espéculo* 283.189–90.

*D2152.6. *Virgin Mary's image's roar causes earth tremors* to protect monk from prosecution for minting money illegally. *Cantigas* 164.

D2156. Magic control over animals.

D2156.5. *Horned vipers easily controlled by saint.* *a.b.c.* 237; Tubach 4279.

*D2156.12. *Saint shuns eating meat.* Requests fish at father's table. A great fish was caught for him where none had ever been seen. *Espéculo* 2.4–5.

*D2156.13. *Hero fearlessly leads lion by collar back into cage.* CMC vv. 2282–2304.

D2158. Magic control of fires.

D2158.1. *Magic kindling of fire.* Enchanter's spell causes fire to be kindled only in contact with a particular woman's private parts. *LBA* c. 263.

D2158.2. *Magic extinguishing of fire.* Virgin Mary's image uses veil to extinguish church fire. *Cantigas* 332.

D2161. Magic healing power.

*D2161.2.4. *Magic candle that protects against erysipelas* given to devotees by Virgin Mary. *Cantigas* 259.

*D2161.2.5. *Cure by holy man effected in absence of patient.* a.b.c. 63; *Castigos* MS A BNM 6559 87.221.

D2161.3. Magic cure of physical defect.

D2161.3.1. *Blindness magically cured.* Spring cures all in kingdom who are blind. *Gatos* 28.

D2161.3.1.1. *Eyes torn out magically replaced.* Monkey-king orders eyes of truth-teller ripped out. Blinded person overhears animals speak of secret spring that restores his eyes and cures blindness. *Gatos* 28.

D2161.3.2. *Magic restoration of severed hand.* a.b.c. 273, 391; *Cantigas* 206, 265; Tubach 2419.

D2161.3.6. *Loss of speech magically cured* by bread (prechewed by fox). *Gatos* 28.

D2161.3.6.1. *Magic restoration of cut-out tongue.* Gambler who loses at dice blasphemes and cuts out own tongue. Virgin Mary pardons him and restores it. *Cantigas* 174.

D2161.4. Methods of magic cure.

D2161.4.9. *Baptism as magic cure.* *Espéculo* 73.49 (gout); *Espéculo* 74.50 (paralysis); *Espéculo* 75.50 (elephantiasis); *Espéculo* 76.50 (fever).

*D2161.4.9.1. *Blindness magically cured by prayer.* Jesus cures blind man. *Castigos* MS A BNM 6559 82.221–22.

*D2161.4.9.2. *Blindness magically cured.* Saint orders blind man to see in Jesus's name. *Espéculo* 282.189.

*D2161.4.9.3. *Blindness magically cured.* Jesus uses saliva to restore blind man's sight. *Castigos* 1.39.

D2161.5. Magic cure by certain persons.

D2161.5.1. *Holy man prescribes cure for paralysis.* Emperor's son paralyzed by joy; cured by anger at preferential treatment of enemy. a.b.c. 204.

*D2161.5.1.1. *Angel appears to man who had sinned by heeding devil's admonition that he accumulate savings.* Angel cures his gangrenous foot when he repents. a.b.c. 355.

*D2161.5.2.3 *Cure by milk of Virgin Mary.* Saint's sight restored. *Cantigas* 138.

D2161.5.2.4.1. *Emperor severs hand of purported traitor.* Severed hand restored by Virgin Mary. a.b.c. 273; Tubach 2419.

*D2161.5.2.4.2. *Severed limb restored by Virgin Mary.* Man suffering pain of erysipelas severed own foot. She restored foot and cures other sufferers' pain. *Cantigas* 134.

*D2161.5.2.4.3. *Severed limbs restored by Virgin Mary.* Woman pilgrim's son captured by thieves who cut off his hands and take out his eyes. Pilgrim prays to Virgin and she restores his hands and eyes. *Cantigas* 146.

*D2161.5.2.4.4. *Severed tongue replaced by Virgin Mary.* Man punished by heretics able once again to sing her praises. *Cantigas* 156.

*D2161.5.2.4.5. *Severed hand restored by Virgin Mary.* Pope severs hand kissed by woman. Restored miraculously by Virgin Mary. *a.b.c.* 391; *Cantigas* 206; Tubach 2419.

*D2161.5.2.4.8. *Severed limbs restored by Virgin Mary.* Young man kicked mother. Begged mother's pardon but could not enter church until he severed offending foot. Virgin restored it. *Cantigas* 127.

D2161.5.2.5. *Woman poisoned by spider venom cured* by Virgin Mary. *Espéculo* 363.266; *Castigos* MS A BNM 6559 82.216.

*D2161.5.2.5.1. *Chaplain swallows spider from communion chalice.* Virgin Mary cures him; spider leaves body through arm. *Cantigas* 222.

D2161.5.2.6. *Terrible headaches that prevent monk (nun) from praying cured by Virgin Mary.* *a.b.c.* 279; Tubach 2488.

*D2161.5.2.7. *Virgin Mary removes arrow piercing face (eye) of devotee.* *Cantigas* 126, 129.

*D2161.5.2.8. *Blindness cured by Virgin Mary* in exchange for vow to go to church and to abstain from meat. *Espéculo* 562.456.

*D2161.5.5.1. *Angel cures man's foot* after hearing him confess that he had sinned by accumulating wealth. *a.b.c.* 355.

D2163. Magic defense in battle.

*D2163.3.1. *Statue of Virgin Mary intercepts arrow* to protect those behind her in defense of precious monstrance. *Cantigas* 51.

*D2163.3.1.1. *Virgin Mary protects knight from enemies.* She surrounds him magically with garland of roses. *Cantigas* 121.

*D2163.3.1.2. *Devils cause playful battle at festival to turn serious.* Virgin Mary intervenes so that combatants are not hurt. *Cantigas* 198.

*D2163.5.3. *Military leader, facing defeat, threw down arms and prayed.* Troops rallied and prevailed against enemy. *a.b.c.* 32; Tubach 3875.

*D2163.5.4. *Bishop's prayers visit enemy troops with flies and stinging insects.* Horses and camels flee and siege of city is lifted. *a.b.c.* 332; Tubach 2754.

D2167. Corpse saved from corruption.

*D2167.0.1. *Corpse magically saved from corruption.* Holy man always said Ave Maria. Body buried beneath tree whose leaves bore legend "Ave Maria." *a.b.c.* 43.

*D2167.0.2. *Corpse magically saved from corruption* because of previous devotion to Virgin Mary. When grave was opened aromatic flowers issued from uncorrupted corpse's mouth. *Milagros* 3.

*D2167.0.3. *Corpses magically saved from corruption.* Saint and wife lived chastely for thirty-six years. Disinterred, bodies uncorrupted. *Espéculo* 93.63–64.

*D2167.0.4. *Corpses magically saved from corruption.* Emit sweet fragrance. *Barlaam* pp. 349–50.

D2174. Magic dancing.

D2174. *Magic dancing. Enchanted persons dance till released.* Priest curses young dancers for levity and lustfulness on Christmas Eve. They cannot detach selves and must dance until a year passes. *Espéculo* 132.90–91; Tubach 1419.

D2176. Exorcising by magic.

D2176.3.4. *Holy monk drives demon* out of his attacker. *a.b.c.* 291.

*D2176.3.4.1. *Young shepherd's seizures caused by demonic possession.* Devils drown him. Child's uncle makes pilgrimage and Virgin Mary casts out devils and revives youth. *Cantigas* 197.

*D2176.3.5.1. *Virgin Mary drives demon* out of possessed woman who prayed to her. *Cantigas* 298.

*D2176.3.6. *Mother prays that Virgin Mary drive demon out of possessed child.* She is then able to speak. *Cantigas* 343.

D2176.5. *Burning cut hair* to prevent witchcraft. *a.b.c.* 424.

*D2176.7. *Sinner enters church dressed in black* accompanied by devil; prays and leaves light and clear and accompanied by angel. *a.b.c.* 330.

E. THE DEAD

E0–E199. RESUSCITATION

E63. Resuscitation by prayer.

*E63.3. *Husband says to jealous wife that he loves another woman, the Virgin Mary.* Wife stabs self, and Virgin responds to his prayers by resuscitating wife. *Cantigas* 84.

*E63.4. *Virgin Mary revives man thought to be dead.* Already placed in coffin. *Cantigas* 223.

*E63.5. *Virgin Mary revives pilgrim struck by lightning.* He sits up and reproaches companion who had doubted. *Cantigas* 311.

E100. Resuscitation by medicines.

E101. *Resuscitation by ointment.* Woman thought to be dead revived by salve and heat. *Apolonio* c. 308.

E105. *Resuscitation by herbs.* Sage sent in quest to India to find herbs with power of resuscitation. *Exemplario* 5r–5v; *Calila* pp. 99–102.

E120. Other means of resuscitation.

E121.3. *Resuscitation by Virgin Mary.* After three miscarriages, woman has still-born child. Child brought back to life. *Cantigas* 118, 224.

*E121.3.1. *Little girl who had drowned resuscitated by Virgin Mary* during funeral rites. *Cantigas* 133.

*E121.3.1.2. *Resuscitation by Virgin Mary (Santiago).* Man devoted to Santiago, tricked into castrating self dies on pilgrimage. Corpse taken for burial revives. *Santiago* 17.86–94.

*E121.3.1.3. *Princess sickens and dies; resuscitated by Virgin Mary.* Cantigas 122.

*E121.3.2. *Son of Moorish woman resuscitated by Virgin Mary.* Mother
converts to Christianity. *Cantigas* 167.

*E121.3.2.1. *Newly betrothed son dies in fall.* Resuscitated by Virgin
Mary because of mother's prayers. Youth and betrothed enter religious orders. *Cantigas* 241.

*E121.3.2.2. *Woman neglects promise to make pilgrimage; son dies.* Prays
to Virgin Mary who resuscitates child dead for four days. *Cantigas*
347.

*E121.3.2.3. *Virgin resuscitates child* whose parents brought him to her
shrine. *Cantigas* 381.

*E121.3.3. *Woman's last surviving son dead three days resuscitated* by
Virgin Mary. *Cantigas* 168.

*E121.3.4. *Virgin Mary resuscitates boy* killed and buried by Jew because
the boy sang "Gaude Maria." *Cantigas* 6.

*E121.3.5. *Virgin Mary restores life to drowned child.* Transports him to
destination of parents' pilgrimage. *Cantigas* 171.

*E121.3.5.1. *Man fleeing Moorish raiders commends dead son to Virgin
Mary.* Returns to house after attack, finds house untouched and son
alive and well. *Cantigas* 323.

*E121.3.6. *Virgin Mary resuscitates robber whose soul demons have carried
off.* Mother prayed to Virgin who restored his life. *Cantigas* 182.

*E121.3.7. *Woman killed by robbers resuscitated by Virgin Mary* so that
she can confess. *Cantigas* 237.

*E121.3.8. *Virgin Mary resuscitates girl* bleeding from the eyes and
thought to be at point of death for three days. *Cantigas* 378.

E121.4. *Resuscitation by St. James.* Prayers to Santiago enabled childless
couple to have child. He dies when on pilgrimage. Santiago resuscitates him. *Santiago* 3.50–52; Tubach 971.

E121.5. *Resuscitation by holy man (priest).* Disconsolate widow had not
permitted interment. *a.b.c.* 286; Tubach 4082.

E121.5.2. *Resuscitation by holy man.* Grieving mother pleads with saint
to revive her son. He does. *a.b.c.* 301.

E150. Circumstances of resuscitation.

*E169. *Man makes wax figure of valued falcon that has died.* Takes it to
church and prays to Virgin Mary. She resuscitates bird. *Cantigas* 352.

*E169.1. *Royal scribe makes wax figure of dying horse.* Takes it to church
and prays to Virgin Mary. Horse survives. *Cantigas* 375.

*E169.2. *During royal hunt, king's pet weasel is trampled by horse.* King
calls on Virgin Mary to save its life. Animal revives. *Cantigas* 354.

E171. *Virgin Mary resuscitates half-flayed mule* in response to little boy's
prayers and promise of candle. *Cantigas* 178, 228.

E200–E599. GHOSTS AND OTHER REVENANTS
E200–E299. Malevolent return from the dead.
E234. Ghost punishes injury received in life.

MOTIF INDEX OF

E234.0.2. *Ghost punishes person who mocks it.* St. Gregory strikes dead evil successor. *a.b.c.* 100; cf. Tubach 3817.

E235. Return from dead to punish indignities to corpse, or ghost.

E235.4.3.1. *Corpse of usurer* rises up, destroys church furnishings, beats monks, kills one, because his soul was suffering torments despite promises that soul would be prayed out of hell. *a.b.c.* 149; Tubach 5031.

E235.7. *Return from dead to capture thief of sheep.* Corpse emanates power to hold thief captive and to make stolen sheep adhere to him. Thief has to pass the tomb of a holy man with his stolen sheep magically stuck to him so that he was caught. *a.b.c.* 99; Tubach 1498 b.

*E235.9. *Disinterred corpse spits gold at grave robbers.* They flee. *a.b.c.* 123.

E243. *Ghosts in cemetery attack bishop* who had suspended priest who had said requiem mass for dead each day. *a.b.c.* 297; Tubach 2424.

E300–E399. Friendly return from the dead.

*E301. *Prior returns from dead to tell pious sacristan of his torment and of how the Virgin Mary had led him to heaven.* Sacristan related all to the chapter. *Milagros* 12; *Espéculo* 333.234, 376.276.

E301.1. *Monk appears to friend* to tell him he has been saved because of his life as a religious. *Espéculo* 503.395, 510.402–3.

*E301.2. *Cleric who had refused to accept bishopric returns from dead* to tell scholar he was better off than those church officials among the damned. *Espéculo* 471.371.

*E301.3. *Monk returns from dead tormented* because he had given a pair of shoes to a nephew without permission. Asks friend to get shoes and to return them to free him from torment. *Espéculo* 480.377–78; Tubach 4347.

*E301.4. *Monk returns from dead to ask for prayers to shorten his stay in purgatory.* Abbot and monks cut short chapter meeting to pray for him. *Espéculo* 488.385.

*E301.5. *Dead monk tortured and ugly appears to friend* to warn him that pride in disputation and scholarship will be punished. *Espéculo* 540.434.

*E301.6. *Friendly return of dead monk.* Grateful for thirty days of continuous masses said for him. *Espéculo* 150.104–5.

*E301.7. *Dead cleric returns to tell friend he is damned.* Asked why confession and sacrament did not save him replied that they had no effect, because he acted out of fear of God, not out of love. *Espéculo* 552.444–45; Tubach 1188 a) 1.

*E301.8. *Pilgrim returns from dead to warn companions* to take leave of their feudal lord who is going to die badly. Lord falls from horse and surrenders soul to demons. *Santiago* 16.81–85.

*E301.9. *Soul of dead man returns.* Warns that he had wasted his time on earth. *Espéculo* 406.303.

*E301.10. *Dead woman returns to warn another of peril of self-adornment.* Condemned to comb hair painfully with iron comb. *Jardín* p. 285; *Glosa* 2.1.21.106.

*E302. *Aristotle appears to scholar* who asks him for genus and species of logic. Dead philosopher answers that in hell there is no scholarship, only torment and intemperate winds. *Espéculo* 335.235.

*E303. *Scholar returns from dead* to tell friend that he read devil's message written on his hand; devil grateful for fools who come to hell because of bad churchmen. *Espéculo* 470.371.

E310. Dead lover's friendly return.

*E312. *Young woman returns to ask lover to say mass for her.* Their carnal desire was sin. He says mass and enters religious order. *Espéculo* 353.251–52.

E320. Dead relative's friendly return.

E323. *Dead mother returns,* grateful to son for having completed her penance. *Espéculo* 166.111–12.

E323.4. *Mother returns from the dead* to tell son of torments of hell and joys of heaven. *Espéculo* 56.38–39.

*E323.9. *Dead mother returns.* Suffers, covered with fiery serpents. Cleric son's prayers cannot help because she had adorned herself excessively in life. *Espéculo* 432.326–27.

E325. *Dead sister's ghost returns resplendent.* Saint's acts of penance had freed her from torment. *Espéculo* 163.110.

E326. *Dead brother permitted to return to life* to repent his sins and save his soul. While on earth he asks pope to say mass for his dead brother to free him from purgatory. *Milagros* 10.

*E326.1. *Dead brother's friendly return.* Tells brother he has gone directly to heaven because of his pilgrimage to Holy Land. *Espéculo* 144.99.

E360. Other reasons for friendly return from the dead.

*E361.4. *Young woman, delivered from purgatory, returns* to thank deacon (to thank her employer) who had prayed that she benefit from all his pilgrimages, charity, and good works. *Espéculo* 317.222, 318.222–23.

E365. Return from death to ask forgiveness.

*E365.0.1. *Woman thought to have died without stain on character* returns to tell confessor she had offended her mother during her lifetime. Devils now torment her. *Espéculo* 440.334; *a.b.c.* 336.

E365.1. *Woman thought to have died without stain on character* returns to tell confessor that she had listened to and enjoyed secular music. Asks forgiveness. *Espéculo* 5.92–93; Tubach 1188 a) 4.

E366. Return from death to aid living.

E366.1. *Return of dead monk to tell how Virgin Mary had saved him from devils.* Monk's body twisted and became discolored when devils were tormenting him. *Cantigas* 123.

*E367.6. *Soul of nun returns to preach repentance.* Out of shame she had not repented her sins when alive. *a.b.c.* 75; Tubach 1188 a) 4.

E368. *Pupil returns from dead to warn master of futility of his studies.* Wears magic cloak bearing sophistries lined with perilous fire. Droplet from cloak burns master's hand *a.b.c.* 417; *Espéculo* 278.185–86; Tubach 1103.

*E369. *Dead apostate's hand swells with blood and points to heaven.* He cries out that another had defeated him. *Espéculo* 54.37–38.

E400–E599. Ghosts and revenants: miscellaneous.

E410. The unquiet grave.

*E410.3. *Murdered child's grave* hidden in stable, uncovered by rooting pig. *Talavera* 1.24.117.

E411. *Saint asks if head is of a Christian or of a pagan.* Severed head's soul in hell. Cannot rest. *a.b.c.* 435; *Espéculo* 330.231–32; Tubach 3111.

E411.0.2.1. *Man stole houses and orchard dedicated to St. Lawrence and St. Ines.* St. Lawrence bruised his arm on Judgement Day. Virgin pleads for him. Permitted to return to body (bruise is visible) for thirty days to do penance and then to die. *a.b.c.* 129; *Espéculo* 215.147–48.

*E411.0.2.1.1. *Man stole from churches.* Given chance to return to body to do penance. *Espéculo* 216.148.

E411.0.2.2. *Unconfessed person cannot rest in grave.* Priest who delayed to hear confession wept. God grants return for penance. *a.b.c.* 386; *Espéculo* 122.82; Tubach 1188 b) 2.

*E411.0.2.3. *Grave of excommunicated person opened,* found to be filled with foul boiling water. Bishop absolves dead man and body turns to dust. *Espéculo* 272.183; Tubach 1924.

E411.0.5.1. *Rich man's body dragged from grave by demons* and thrown into grave in unblessed ground. *a.b.c.* 398; *Espéculo* 513.405–6; Tubach 1254.

E411.0.6. *Earth rejects body.* Unrepentant sinner told earth will not be his tomb; he will be eaten by birds and beasts. Prophecy fulfilled. *Espéculo* 99.66–67; Tubach 1270.

*E411.0.6.1. *Earth rejects buried severed arm* of young woman magically cursed to dance for a year. *Espéculo* 132.90–91.

*E411.0.9. *Sinner buried in church.* Voice from grave says, "I am burning." Grave opened to find only shroud. *a.b.c.* 400; *Espéculo* 514.406; Tubach 1137.

*E411.0.9.1. *Priest who had sex with goddaughter dies* after seven days. Fire rises from grave consuming it totally. *a.b.c.* 404; Tubach 2037.

E411.4. *Usurer cannot rest in grave.* Insists that monks remove body from church. *Espéculo* 564.460–61.

*E411.4.1. *Usurer tormented in grave* rises up and attacks monks who had promised to pray for him. *a.b.c.* 149; Tubach 5031.

*E411.11. *Dead knight cannot rest.* Had desecrated cemetery attacking a man. Asks friend to make amends to hermit he had injured. *Espéculo* 213.146–47; Tubach 2944 d).

*E411.12. *Dead canon cannot rest because committed sin of vainglory.* Asks for prayers of other canon. *Espéculo* 295.204; Tubach 1464 e).

E412. Person under religious ban cannot rest in grave.

E412.1. *Excommunicated person cannot rest in grave.* Nuns threatened with excommunication leave their grave in church when deacon says that all excommunicated ones must leave. *Espéculo* 267.180–81; Tubach 1925.

*E412.1.1. *Excommunicated suffer even in grave.* Their bones are restless. *Espéculo* 271.182–83.

E412.2. *Unbaptized person can stay in paradise only if he is baptized.* *Espéculo* 77.50; cf. Tubach 475.

*E412.6. *Dead man had not completed penance of three years.* Friend says it for him, and he returns partially each year until he is whole at end. *Espéculo* 165.111; Tubach 3660.

*E412.7. *Dead nun cannot rest until penance completed.* Abbess and other nuns do it and she is released from torment. *Espéculo* 167.112; cf. Tubach 3213.

*E412.8. *Dead scholar in hell.* Guilty of greed, vainglory and lust. *Espéculo* 296.204–5.

E415. *Dead mother cannot rest* until son completes her penance. *Espéculo* 166.111–12; Tubach 3667.

E415.2. *Dead man returns to rebuke relatives* because they had not sold his horse and given money to poor. *a.b.c.* 298; *Espéculo* 261.176; Tubach 3349.

*E415.2.1. *Dead scholar cannot rest* until friend who has kept his belongings sells them and gives money to poor. *Espéculo* 162.109–10; Tubach 3349.

*E415.2.2. *Dead monk cannot rest* until brothers give his belongings to poor. *Espéculo* 164.110–11; Tubach 3349.

*E415.3.1. *Dead cleric returns to rebuke bishop* who had not used money left him to pay for masses. *Espéculo* 266.178; Tubach 3349.

E415.4. *Dead cannot rest until money debts are paid.* Returns weighed down with chains. Debts paid, chains will be lifted. *Espéculo* 264.177–78; cf. Tubach 1499.

*E415.5. *Dead cannot rest until stolen goods are returned.* *Espéculo* 265.178.

E420. Revenants.

E421.1.1. *Ghost visible to one person alone.* Monk, seated with others, alone sees soul of his brother who died at distant place. *a.b.c.* 25.

E425.2.3. *Revenants as recently dead abbot and monks.* Beat cellarer who had not distributed alms to poor to honor their deaths. *Espéculo* 163.112–13.

E430. Defense against ghosts and the dead.

*E434.8.2. *Sign of cross.* Jew in Apollo's temple banishes evil spirits with sign of cross. Saves bishop from sin. Is converted. *a.b.c.* 92; *Espéculo* 137.96.

E440. Walking ghost "laid."

E446.2.1. *Ghost laid by burning lock of hair.* Devil appears disguised as woman's dead son tells her to find holy relic (Virgin Mary's golden hair) and to climb a very tall tree for special branches. Her confessor tells her to burn hair. Ghost disappears. *a.b.c.* 424; Tubach 2276.

E480. Abode of the dead.

*E481.1.3. *Daughter visits mother in hell* where she sees mother in torment. Chooses not to follow mother's evil ways. *Espéculo* 88.61; Tubach 1450.

*E481.1.4. *Daughter visits father in heaven* where he disports self happily with the saints. Chooses to live good life like her father's. *Espéculo* 88.61; Tubach 1450.

E490. Meetings of the dead.

*E499.5. *Dead in cemetery rise up* to attack bishop who has removed priest who said daily prayers for them. Bishop restores priest. *a.b.c.* 297; *Espéculo* 153.106, 155.107; Tubach 2424, 3214.

*E499.6. *Dead in cemetery rise up* gratefully to receive holy water and prayers offered every Monday by bishop. *Espéculo* 156.107.

*E499.7. *Dead in cemetery* give responses to prayer for dead. *Espéculo* 157.108, 158.109.

E530. Ghosts of objects.

E533.2. *Self-tolling bells.* When saint's soul leaves body, all bells in city toll. *San Alejo* p. 77.

E540. Miscellaneous actions of revenants.

*E586.0.1. *Dead person's soul returns at moment of death.* *a.b.c.* 26.

E586.1. *Dead return on burial day.* Souls seen ascending by travelers at sea. *a.b.c.* 26.

E600–E699. REINCARNATION

E630. Reincarnation in object.

E631.0.2. *Flowering tree from grave* with "ave" on leaves. Grows from tomb as reward. Disinterred, body preserved, roots of tree came from cadaver's mouth. *a.b.c.* 43; Tubach 430.

E631.0.2.1. *Illiterate knight could only learn to read "Ave Maria."* Flowering plant grew on his grave; on each leaf "Ave Maria" was written in gold letters. Root of plant grew from cadaver's mouth. *a.b.c.* 328; *Espéculo* 378.277; Tubach 427.

E700–E799. THE SOUL

E720. Soul leaves or enters body.

*E721.0.1. *Man's soul leaves his body.* Views four fires representing principal sins of world. Returns to body that is marked by a burn from these fires on shoulder and cheek. *a.b.c.* 308; Tubach 818.

*E721.0.2. *Widow's soul is carried to grave of sinner buried in sacred ground* as warning against sin. Body is corrupted and malodorous. *Espéculo* 515.406.

E721.1. *Soul leaves body in sleep.* Dream is experience of extracorporeal sojourn. *a.b.c.* 142.

*E721.1.2.6. *Soul of monk leaves body to be judged in heaven.* Returns, tells brothers of judgement and then dies. *Espéculo* 466.369.

E721.6. *On return to body* soul crosses on scythe blade (sword blade) as bridge. *a.b.c.* 142.

*E721.11. *Monk vows silence.* Muteness enables him to see souls departing from dying people. *a.b.c.* 316.

E722.1. Form of soul as it leaves body at death.

E722.1.1. *Soul as black or white spirit hovers over coffin.* a.b.c. 203; *Espéculo* 481.378.

*E722.2.1.2. *Soul is invisible* as it leaves the body of a friar. a.b.c. 24.

*E722.2.13. *Soul heard to speak as it departs.* Reproaches person and promises torment in hell. *Espéculo* 104.69.

*E722.2.14. *Soul of poor man taken by Jesus Christ.* He is promised comfort in heaven. *Espéculo* 447.343.

*E722.3.4. *Monk sees soul of brother* at moment of brother's death in a distant city. a.b.c. 25; Tubach 4551.

*E722.3.5. *Men at sea saw soul on way to heaven.* Later learned it was soul of a pious man who had died at that moment. a.b.c. 26; Tubach 4551.

E723.6. *Appearance of his wraith as announcement of person's death.* Cleric appears to servant on trip for master. *Espéculo* 61.42–43.

E727. Relation of body to soul.

E727.1. *Debate of body and soul.* Crestomatía 2.465–69.

E728. Evil spirit possesses person.

E728.1. *Bishop expels evil spirit from his calumniator.* a.b.c. 157.

*E728.1.2. *Devil cast out of calumniator by prayers of calumniated person.* a.b.c. 117.

E730. Soul in animal form.

E732.1. *Soul in form of dove* leaves mouth of saintly monk as he dies. Ascends to heaven. a.b.c. 27; Tubach 1760, 4551.

E740. Other forms of the soul.

E741.1.1.2. *Star as sign of birth of hero*; supernatural birth of culture hero. *Alexandre* c. 8.

E750. Perils of the soul.

E751. *Souls at Judgement Day.* The just rewarded by youthful form and will be in air with God; unjust will be tormented below. *Castigos* MS A BNM 6559 89.225.

*E752.1.1.2. *Devil disguised as magician acquires man's soul* in exchange for marriage with beloved. a.b.c. 23; *Talavera* 1.13.90; Tubach 3566.

E752.2. *Soul carried off by demon (Devil).* *Castigos* MS A BNM 6559 89.226; Tubach 4548.

*E752.2.1. *Rich man, greedy and avaricious, about to die, asks for one night's delay.* Devils take soul in morning. a.b.c. 119; Tubach 1050.

E754. Saved souls.

E754.1.3.1. *Monk who had denied God is given penance to pass three weeks in cave* awaiting restoration of soul. Asked three times what he had seen. Third time saw soul return. a.b.c. 106.

E754.1.9. *Soul captive in block of ice* used to relieve bishop's gout. Bishop says thirty masses to free captive soul. a.b.c. 28; *Espéculo* 151.105; Tubach 2717, 4151.

E754.1.10. *Devil denied soul of monk.* Shown switches used to beat him to cleanse his soul. *Espéculo* 453.352.

E754.2. *Knight follows Jesus' steps in Jerusalem.* Prays on Mt. Olivet that his soul follow to heaven. Prayer answered. a.b.c. 434.

E755. Destination of soul.

E755.2.1.1. *Soul of sinner wrenched from bodies with pitchforks by devil.* Soul carried off to hell; angels come with music to transport souls of good people. *a.b.c.* 293; *Espéculo* 444.341–42; Tubach 4553.

*E755.2.7.1. *Priest's soul seen in hell's torment. Espéculo* 109.72; Tubach 2514.

*E755.2.7.2. *Soul of dying man is spied in hell* by diabolically possessed woman capable of prophecy. He is there because his piety was insincere. *Lucanor* Ex. 40.

E756. Contest over souls.

E756.1. *Angels and devils ready to fight for good abbot's soul. a.b.c.* 30; Tubach 237.

E756.4.1. *Soul of gambler won by saint in dice game.* Dice miraculously split to make higher score for saint. *a.b.c.* 252; Tubach 2239.

*E756.4.2. *Saint regains pact youth signed with devil.* Soul restored. *a.b.c.* 23; *Talavera* 1.13.90; Tubach 3572.

E760. Life index.

*E765.4.3.2. *Abbot and pupil will die at same moment.* Death predicted by image of Infant Jesus. *Cantigas* 353; Tubach 1475 b) 1.

E783. Vital head.

*E783.9. *Severed head rejoins body.* Virgin Mary protects man whose head had been severed by thieves. *Cantigas* 96.

F. MARVELS

F0–F199. OTHERWORLD JOURNEYS

F10. Journey to upper world.

F11.1. *Abbot in coma for three days.* In heaven being judged, dies happy. *a.b.c.* 303 (not in Paris MS).

F11.3. *Simple man journeys to heaven* and learns names of those who will die from pestilence; proof: returns able to speak foreign tongues. *a.b.c.* 383.

F81. Descent to lower world of dead.

*F88. *Monk travels to hell to see those in torment.* Sees a monk whose sin was daily drunkenness who hopes for deliverance because he had lit a lamp before St. Nicholas's altar every day. *Espéculo* 196.137.

F110–F199. Miscellaneous otherworlds.

F129.4. *Journey to otherworld island.* Hero in oarless boat lands on shore of otherworld where doors open magically to him. *Çifar* p. 133.

F160. Nature of otherworld.

F174.2. *Hero welcomed to otherworld by beautiful women* who bring him a palfrey to ride to the court of their empress. *Çifar* p. 133.

F185. Otherworld queen.

F185. *Otherworld queen gifted with second sight* but cannot foretell future. *Çifar* p. 133.

F200–F699. MARVELOUS CREATURES
F302. Fairy mistress.

F302.3.2. *Fairy (demon) offers gifts to man to be her lover.* She offers a magic hound, a hawk, and a horse. *Çifar* pp. 134–36.

F305. Offspring of fairy and mortal.

*F305.4. *Child of fairy and mortal born seven days after conception.* Reaches maturity in seven days. *Çifar* p. 68.

F310. Fairies and human children.

F312.1. *Supernatural beings bestow gifts at birth of hero.* Sword and shield made by Vulcan; belt and sheath made by Philosophy; two good fairies give magical shirt that is protection from drunkenness and lust; other fairies give magic tunic that is protection from disloyalty, cold and heat; cloak that is protection from fear and sloth. *Alexandre* cc. 89–103.

F370. Visits to fairyland.

F377.1. *Supernatural lapse of time in paradise.* Knight, in French court, awakes after three years believes it was only three days. *a.b.c.* 181; *Espéculo* 291.201–2.

*F377.1.1. *Supernatural lapse of time in paradise.* Cleric granted wish to follow bird to paradise, spends three hundred years. Returns to monastery. *Cantigas* 103; *a.b.c.* 181; *Espéculo* 290.201; Tubach 3378.

F400–F499. Spirits and demons.
F420. Water spirits.

F420.5.1.7.4. *Water spirit returns* silver axe to woodchopper in place of the one he has lost. *Esopete* p. 112.

F460. Mountain spirits.

F460.1.2. *Mountain woman has breasts so long* she folds them at her waist (throws them over her shoulder). *LBA* c. 1019.

F470. Night spirits.

*F471.2.0.2. *Holy man gives woman a token* to free her from incubus. *a.b.c.* 116.

F480. House spirits.

F480.2. *Serpent as house spirit* whose presence guarantees prosperity. *Esopete* p. 52; Tubach 4251.

F500–F599. Remarkable persons.
F510. Monstrous persons.

F511.0.2.1. *Two-headed person.* Baby born with two heads each one facing the other; two bodies joined at chest (conjoined twins). *Esopete* p. 166.

F560. Unusual manner of life.
F565. Women warriors or hunters.

F565.1. *Amazons.* Women warriors create own kingdom (Marsepia & Lampedon). *Abreviada* 1.467; *Ilustres mujeres* 11.17r–18r; *Jardín* 249; cf. Tubach 92.

F565.1.2. *All male children* killed by Amazons or given to fathers (Marsepia & Lampedon). *Abreviada* 1.467; *Ilustres mujeres* 11.17r–18r.

F570. Other extraordinary human beings.

F582. *Poison damsels.* Woman nourished on poison is fatal to sexual partners. Damsel sent to Indian king bit him; he died. *Poridat* 41; *Glosa* 1.2.34.237; Tubach 3830.

F591.1. *Prince (emperor) who never laughs* punishes any who ask him why. *Çifar* p. 130; cf. Tubach 4994.

*F591.3. *Holy man who never laughs* does so when devil is discomfited in church. *a.b.c.* 382.

F600–F699. Persons with extraordinary powers.

F610. Remarkably strong man.

F628. *Strong man as mighty slayer* (Samson). *Castigos* MS A BNM 6559 22.138 (ADMYTE 0 80r).

F640. Extraordinary powers of perception.

*F642.4.1. *Remarkable application of logic* enables philosopher to say that a worm is hidden in stone. Perceived its unusual warmth. *a.b.c.* 313; Tubach 5391.

F645. Marvelously wise man.

F645.3. *Remarkable application of logic* enables philosopher to say that horse had been nurtured by an ass. Does not run like horse but like an ass. *a.b.c.* 313.

F700–F899 EXTRAORDINARY PLACES AND THINGS

F715. Extraordinary river.

*F715.7.1. *River will punish liars* who pass over it. *Esopete* pp. 100–1.

F720. Submarine and subterranean world.

F721.5. *Underwater castle.* Knight is carried away by mysterious woman. *Çifar* p. 67.

F770. Extraordinary buildings.

F771.2.4.1. *Indulgent king pleases wife by surrounding palace* with lagoons filled with rosewater and spices, and sugar and spice wetlands. *Lucanor* Ex. 30.

F772.1. *Tower of Babel: remarkably tall tower designed to reach sky. Glosa* 3.1.6.35.

F772.2.6. *Flying tower* that touches neither the earth nor the sky. Plan: boys urge birds to fly by means of meat held out in front of them. Trick: someone must deliver meat to boys. *Esopete* p. 22.

F810. Extraordinary trees, plants, fruits, etc.

*F811.2.2.1 *Tree whose leaves bear "ave"* grows on grave of holy man. Disinterred, body is preserved, and roots are growing from mouth. *a.b.c.* 43; Tubach 430.

F815.1. *Vegetables (plants)* mature in miraculously short time. Are planted, mature, and give fruit each day anew. *Çifar* p. 68.

F841. Extraordinary boat.

*F841.2.8. *Boat without oars.* Comes to shore long enough for man to get in. *Çifar* p. 130.

*F841.2.9. *Boat without oars.* Fleeing princess finds a boat supplied with food and embarks. Disembarks in a barren place to which all were forbidden entry. *Ultramar* I.1.47.82.

F900–F1099. EXTRAORDINARY OCCURRENCES

F910. Extraordinary swallowings.

F912. *Victim kills swallower from within.* Hydrus (fabulous water serpent) enters sleeping crocodile's mouth, bites its heart, and kills it. *Gatos* 13; see Tubach 1326.

F930. Extraordinary occurrences concerning seas or waters.

F930.1. *Book of saint's miracles* immersed in water emerges unharmed. *Santiago* p. 45.

F933. Extraordinary occurrences with springs.

F933.1.2. *Magic spring* flows from roots of date palm at command of Infant Jesus. *Castigos* MS A BNM 6559 31.145–46 (ADMYTE 0 92v).

*F933.1.4. *Spring bursts forth in front of altar* eight days before death of king. *PCG* 2.964.645.

F940. Extraordinary underground disappearance.

*F941.2.2.1. *Monastery swallowed by earth for year.* At end of year Virgin Mary causes it to reappear; all occupants are safe. *Cantigas* 226.

F950. Marvelous cures.

F950.2. *Physician prescribes anger* to cure patient's paralysis. Titus, enraged at servant's indulgent treatment of despised enemy and servant's neglectful treatment of him, is cured. *a.b.c.* 204.

*F950.4.1. *Demonically induced illness to be cured by marriage with cleric.* Virgin Mary reproaches the bride and groom who both opt for religious lives. *Cantigas* 125.

F950.7. *Marvelous cure.* Jesus cures centurion's wife from a distance without seeing her. *Castigos* MS A BNM 6559 86.221.

*F950.7.1. *Cure by holy man effected in absence of patient.* *a.b.c.* 63; *Castigos* MS A BNM 6559 87.221.

*F950.8.1. *Lovesick man cured by marriage* with object of his affection. *Çifar* pp. 9–11; *Disciplina* 2.

F952. Blindness miraculously cured.

*F952.0.3. *Saint whose sight was restored miraculously* prays that God restore his blindness. Will see angels without interference of worldly sight. *Espéculo* 319.224.

F954. Muteness miraculously cured.

F954.5. *Mute person speaks.* Mute son cries out to warn father of danger. *a.b.c.* 173; *Glosa* 2.2.4.133.

F959. Marvelous cures: miscellaneous.

*F959.6.3. *Virgin Mary cures youth's madness induced by drinking poison* intended to harm his benefactor. *Cantigas* 334.

F960. Extraordinary natural phenomena: elements and weather.

*F960.1.2. *Extraordinary natural phenomena at birth of hero.* Sun darkened, sea turbulent, earth trembling, hailstorms, anomalous births. *Alexandre* cc. 8–11.

F963.2. *Extraordinary wind* blows arrows shot against Christians back against enemy. *PCG* 2.568.323; *Castigos* MS A BNM 6559 10.108; *Abreviada* 2.115; Tubach 349, 4773.

*F968.1.1. *Lightning bolt kills false accuser* of saintly person. *a.b.c.* 15, 172; Tubach 3046.

*F968.1.2. *Lightning bolt cleaves* blasphemer in two. *a.b.c.* 324; Tubach 680.

F1010. Other extraordinary events.

F1021.5. *Scoffing woman challenges Virgin Mary* who transports her through air to shrine leaving her prostrate before altar. *Cantigas* 153.

F1041.8.2. *Madness from grief.* Mother is cured of madness by Virgin Mary after death of young son. *Cantigas* 331.

F1051. Prodigious weeping.

F1051.1. *Barrel filled miraculously with penitent's tears.* Sinner unable to repent given task to fill barrel. Not able to fill it, returns and sheds a tear. *Espéculo* 117.77–78.

*F1051.1.1. *Tears of remorse wash away stain* of sin marked on man's palm. Man swore allegiance to devil by placing thumb on palm of other hand. Left indelible mark. *Espéculo* 119.78.

F1066. *Arrow shot at heaven angrily returns bloody.* Gambler, angry over losses, blasphemously shoots at God and Virgin Mary. *a.b.c.* 36, 236; *Cantigas* 154; Tubach 324.

F1066.1. *Blasphemer plunges knife in ground* to show how he would treat Virgin Mary's womb. Knife comes out bloody. *a.b.c.* 54; *Tubach* 2937.

F1068.2. *Wound received in dream.* Still there when person wakes. God punished one who provoked another to perjure self. *Glosa* 3.2.23.213.

F1097. *Virgin Mary keeps Moorish and Christian armies* from seeing one another. Next day they make peace and retire to own territories. *Cantigas* 344.

G. OGRES

G10–G399. KINDS OF OGRES

G10–G99. Cannibals and cannibalism.

G50. Occasional cannibalism.

G60. Human flesh eaten unwittingly.

G61. *Relative's flesh eaten unwittingly.* Flesh of courtier's children served to him by cruel king. *Castigos* MS A BNM 6559 13.118 (ADMYTE 0 52v).

G70. Occasional cannibalism: deliberate.

*G72.2.1. *During siege of Jerusalem,* starving mother eats own child. *Castigos* 5.55; *PCG* 1.135; Tubach 1851.

G72.2.2. *Siege of Antioch.* Starving army rabble eats corpses of enemy dead. *Ultramar* II.2.150.222.

G300–G399. Other ogres.

G303. Devil (The Devil, Satan).

G303.3. Forms in which devil appears.

G303.3.0.1. *Devil in hideous form.* Man who saw devil would rather burn in an oven than see him again. *Espéculo* 189.130.

*G303.3.0.2. *Devils appear in hideous form,* hairy bodies, huge teeth, terrible eyes, sulfurous flames from nostrils. *Espéculo* 190.130–31.

G303.3.1. Devil in human form.

*G303.3.1.3. *Devil as a distinguished-looking knight* consoles an impoverished man. *Castigos* MS A BNM 6559 83.216.

G303.3.1.3.1. *Devil as a raffish traveler (ribaldo)* makes offer for man's soul. *Castigos* MS A BNM 6559 89.225.

G303.3.1.12.2. *Devil as beautiful woman* tries to seduce bishop (hermit). *a.b.c.* 388; *Espéculo* 179.121–23; *Castigos* 37.177–78; Tubach 214.

G303.3.1.12.2.1. *Devil as beautiful young woman* seduces man. She offers him a hunting dog that can catch any beast, a hawk that can capture any prey, and a horse that is faster than the wind. He must ask his wife the empress for the dog, for the hawk, for the horse. *Çifar* pp. 134–36.

G303.3.1.12.3. *Devil as young woman* whom celibate had known in his youth torments him. *a.b.c.* 411; Tubach 1535.

*G303.1.12.3.1. *Devil comes to hermit's cave in form of distressed woman.* He feeds, shelters and clothes her. When he reaches for her she disappears and devil materializes. *Castigos* 37.177–78.

G303.3.1.12.4. *Devil as old woman* tries to seduce monk from cloister. *a.b.c.* 115; Tubach 1553.

G303.3.1.15. *Devil appears as Jew* to entice cleric to deny his belief. *Castigos* MS A BNM 6559 82.215; *a.b.c.* 261; *Milagros* 24; *Cantigas* 3.

G303.3.1.16. *Devil appears as recently deceased son* to tempt mother to risk her life. *a.b.c.* 424.

G303.1.17. *Devils appear in form of neighboring people* who had come to dine. *a.b.c.* 112; Tubach 1648.

*G303.3.1.26. *Devil as magician.* Learned magic arts as prisoner of Moors. *Espéculo* 147.100.

*G303.3.1.27. *Devil as magician.* Promised wealth and worldly honor to youth. *Espéculo* 149.101–2.

*G303.3.1.28. *Devil as pilgrim.* Advocates life of secular social responsibility in world over spiritual asceticism. *San Alejo* pp. 104–6.

*G303.3.1.29. *Devil as black man* accompanied by herd of boars menaces monk. Virgin Mary chases them away. *Cantigas* 83; cf. Tubach 2461.

*G303.3.1.30. *Devil as priest* who can predict the future. Accuses woman of incest. Is vanquished by her protector, the Virgin Mary.

a.b.c. 274.

★G303.3.1.31. Devil as Moorish customer in brothel. Exchanges blows with monk-reformer. *a.b.c.* 229.

G303.3.2. The devil in superhuman form.

G303.3.2.1. *Devil appears as Christ.* Saint recognizes the imposture. *Castigos* 1.37; MS A BNM 65591.1.88 (ADMYTE 0 3r); Tubach 1536.

G303.3.2.2. *Devil appears as angel.* Tells abbot to revise order's rules. *a.b.c.* 4; Tubach 19.

★G303.3.2.6. Devil appears as angel. Tells monk to fast for eight or nine days. *a.b.c.* 4; *Espéculo* 7.6–7; Tubach 1529.

G303.3.3. Devil in animal form.

G303.3.3.1.4. *Devil in form of bull.* Appears to drunken cleric. *Milagros* 20; Tubach 1812.

G303.3.3.2.7. *Devil in form of monkey.* Tells archbishop that money in his chest belongs to devil. *Espéculo* 59.42.

★G303.3.3.2.11. Devil in form of spider bites over-adorned woman. Abbot brings Host to banish it. *Espéculo* 429.325.

G303.3.5. Devil changes shape.

★G303.3.5.4. Devil sequentially in form of bull, hairy savage man, and then lion menaces monk. Monk flees to church and Virgin Mary saves him. *Cantigas* 47; Tubach 1812.

★G303.3.5.5. Devil appears sequentially as lion, bear, serpent, griffin, basilisk to frighten man. *Barlaam* p. 328.

G303.4. The devil's physical characteristics.

G303.4.8.1. *Devil has putrid odor* because of sins. Exists only to trap souls of sinners. *Espéculo* 451.349.

G303.6. Circumstances of devil's appearance.

★G303.6.1.8. Demon laughs when sees another clutch at a woman's skirt. She lifts skirt and demon falls in mud. *a.b.c.* 407; *Espéculo* 426.324–25; Tubach 1660.

G303.6.2.8. *Devil appears to dying man* who rebukes him. *Espéculo* 181.123.24.

★G303.6.2.8.1. Devil appears to dying man who pleads for more time. Dies trying to evade devils. *Espéculo* 188.130.

G303.9. Deeds of the devil.

★G303.9.4.3.1. Devil gets ring from faithful wife by trickery. Tells husband it was reward for having sex with her. *San Alejo* p. 106.

G303.9.4.4. *Devil persuades bishop and nun to sin. a.b.c.* 92; Tubach 1436.

★G303.9.4.8.1. Devil demands that bishop deny Christ and Mary and to renounce Christianity in exchange for ecclesiastical post. *a.b.c.* 261.

★G303.9.4.8.2. Devil makes man his vassal; must deny Jesus and the Virgin Mary to gain worldly success. *Cantigas* 281.

★G303.9.4.8.11. Devil tempts youth to deny Christ. Youth flees making sign of cross. *Espéculo* 149.101–2.

★G303.9.4.11. Devil in form of victualer. Tempts monks. Only one takes food from him. *a.b.c.* 111; Tubach 210.

*G303.9.4.12. *Devil poses as pagan god.* Monk must deny Christianity to win woman. Loses soul. *a.b.c.* 106.

G303.10. Allies and possessions of the devil.

G303.10.5. *Where the devil can't reach, he sends an old woman.* False old woman convinces husband to kill wife. *a.b.c.* 370 (not in Paris MS); *Lucanor* Ex. 42; *Esopete* pp. 149–50; Tubach 5361.

*G303.10.20. *Snake is messenger of devil.* Sent to tempt Eve. *Estados* 1.39.

G303.15. Places haunted by the devil.

G303.15.3. *Devils haunts a house.* Cleric's servant protected; made sign of cross on all sides of house. *Espéculo* 61.42–43; *a.b.c.* 240.

G303.16. How the devil's power may be escaped or avoided.

G303.16.1. *Wife pledged to devil.* Virgin Mary substitutes self for a woman whose husband had pledged her to the devil. *a.b.c.* 268; *Espéculo* 374.274–75; Tubach 5283.

*G303.16.1.1. *Demons cause monk and knight's wife to run off with monastery's funds and husband's fortune.* Arrested, Virgin Mary saves them and orders demons to take their shape and place in prison. *Espéculo* 372.272–74; Tubach 3370.

*G303.16.1.2. *Cleric can escape devil's power if he takes* portion of his hoarded treasure and gives it to poor. Fails, demons guard treasure. *Espéculo* 61.42–43; cf. Tubach 4948.

*G303.16.1.3. *Disorderly monks threatened by devils* call out to Virgin Mary. Devils spare them. *Espéculo* 526.412–13.

*G303.16.1.4. *Devil defeated by saint's ability to answer riddle.* *a.b.c.* 388; Tubach 214.

G303.16.2. Devil's power avoided by prayer.

*G303.16.2.1.2. *Devil's power avoided by prayer.* Monk who was tempted by devil-victualer's spices, prays and saves self. *a.b.c.* 111; *Espéculo* 420.319; Tubach 210.

G303.16.2.3.4. *Nun eating unblessed lettuce eats demon. Is possessed.* *a.b.c.* 93; *Espéculo* 139.96–97; Tubach 3503.

*G303.16.2.3.6. *Devil's power avoided by prayer.* Simple friar's prayers will protect him from demons even though the words confound him. *Espéculo* 419.318–19; Tubach 1594.

*G303.16.2.3.7. *Monk's prayers deter demonic messenger.* Devil cannot pass spot where monk prays for fifteen days. *Espéculo* 422.320; Tubach 3276.

*G303.16.2.3.8. *Bishop's prayer banishes devil* who had posed as good man's servant. *Cantigas* 67.

G303.16.3. Devil's power avoided by the cross.

*G303.16.3.4.1. *Sign of cross.* Jew vanquishes devil by making sign of the cross. Saves saint from sin. *a.b.c.* 92; *Espéculo* 137.96.

G303.16.5. Administering sacrament destroys devil's power.

*G303.16.5.3. *Devil vanquished when priest passes by carrying the Host.* *a.b.c.* 432; Tubach 1602.

*G303.16.5.4. *Devil in form of incubus exorcised.* *a.b.c.* 116.

*G303.16.5.5. *Devil vanquished when paralyzed man calls upon Jesus in his heart.* Remembers his passion. *Espéculo* 442.336–37.

*G303.16.8.1. *Demons leave at mention of Jesus's name. Espéculo* 409.306.

*G303.16.8.2. *Demons seek place where Jesus's name is unknown.* Dwell in pagan idols. *Espéculo* 410.306.

*G303.16.8.3. *Demons leave man's body at command of Virgin Mary. Cantigas* 109; Tubach 3449.

*G303.16.8.4. *Monks who had left monastery* protect selves from devils by calling upon Virgin Mary. Return to monastery grateful for deliverance. *Cantigas* 254.

G303.16.9. *Devil impotent because of confession* of wife's lover who is absolved. Devil tells husband that wife committed adultery, but he cannot remember with whom. *a.b.c.* 354; Tubach 1508.

G303.16.11. Various holy persons save one from devil.

G303.16.11.5. *Saint disputes devil.* Devil is superior because he never eats nor sleeps. Saint sleeps, eats, but has humility; devil has none. *Espéculo* 308.218.

G303.16.15. *Holy man frees demonically possessed man.* Devil slaps holy man on cheek, and holy man turns other cheek. Devil defeated by his humility. *Espéculo* 309.218–19, 433.330.

*G303.16.15.1. *Devil is denied soul* when monk does penance for three weeks in cave. Soul returns. *a.b.c.* 106.

*G303.16.15.2. *Holy man chases devil away* with noise made from shaking tear-stained object worn around neck. *Espéculo* 349.248.

G303.16.19. Miscellaneous ways in which devil may be escaped or his power destroyed.

*G303.16.19.21. *Devil asks saint for apple,* but is unable to utter word *"caridad"* in request. Receives apple; it burns his hand, and he flees. *Espéculo* 85.57.

G303.24. The devil in church.

G303.24.1.3. *In church, devil writes names of people who misbehave.* Holy man laughs when he sees that he has run out of room to list them. *a.b.c.* 382; *Espéculo* 180.123; Tubach 1630.

*G303.24.1.4.1. *Devil unable to record names of all who misbehave in church;* frustrated, pounds on wall; disappears. *a.b.c.* 382. Tubach 1630.

G303.24.1.7. *Devil writes down names of those who sleep in church. a.b.c.* 382.

*G303.24.1.10. *Holy man permitted to pray for three days in church.* Man possessed by devil attacks him. Holy man throws devil out of church and out of man's body. *a.b.c.* 291.

G303.25. Miscellaneous devil motifs.

*G303.25.3.1. *Devils prefer to be in monastery where sinners resist them strongly* (where they are needed) rather than in the world where sinners are weak. *a.b.c.* 412; *Espéculo* 182.124; Tubach 3329.

*G303.25.3.2. *Single devil suffices for dwelling of usurers.* Many devils necessary in monastery where monks are harder to catch. *Espéculo* 566.461.

*G303.25.3.3. *Devil in monastery* prevails in choir (lateness, early departure), dormitory (oversleep, think evil thoughts), refectory (overeat, excessive fasting). Cannot enter chapter. *Espéculo* 184.125–26.

*G303.25.3.4. *Devils in monastery* stop up ears of those who sleep during prayers, open the mouths of those who yawn, and sit astride those who do not resist them. *Espéculo* 421.319–20.

*G303.25.20. *Before dying, fortune teller (witch) tells children to take precautions to protect grave from devils.* Devils break through and capture her soul and carry her off screaming, seated on black horse with great iron hooks on its back. *Espéculo* 527.415–16.

G400–G499. FALLING INTO OGRE'S POWER
G400. Person falls into ogre's (devil's) power.

G405. *Man on hunt* falls into she-devil's power. *Sendebar* Day 3, Tale 6.

H. TESTS

H0–H199. IDENTITY TESTS: RECOGNITION
H10. Recognition by common knowledge.

H11.1. *Recognition by telling life story.* Dead saint's account of life causes parents to recognize him. *San Alejo* p. 79.

*H11.1.5.1. *Recognition by hearing lament.* Captive in brothel cries out about her lost parents. Father recognizes her. *Apolonio* cc. 530–40.

*H11.1.5.2. *Hero recounts events of life.* Long-lost wife recognizes him. *Apolonio* cc. 585–89.

*H.11.1.5.3. *Sons recount separation from family.* Parents recognize them. *Çifar* pp. 55–56.

H50. Recognition by bodily marks or physical attributes.

H51.2. *Recognition by joined toes.* Imposture uncovered. Abandoned princess recognized. *Ultramar* I.2.43.570.

H71. Marks of royalty.

*H71.10.8. *Wild horse bows* before prince. *Alexandre* c. 117; Tubach 96.

H84. Tokens of exploits.

*H84.5. *Ring taken as proof* of woman's infidelity. *San Alejo* p. 112.

H94. Identification by ring.

H94.0.1. *Recognition of wife's ring in friend's possession* informs husband of her unfaithfulness. *Espéculo* 125.83.

H94.5. *Identification through broken ring.* Son uses half-ring given to mother to identify self to father and stepmother. *PCG* 743.441–42, 751.446–48; *Abreviada* 2.295.

H105. Parts of bodies as tokens of slaying.

*H105.8. *Severed head of enemy* proof of slaying. Knight presents severed head to emperor. *Ultramar* I.1.80.158.

H119. Identification by cloth or clothing: miscellaneous.

*H119.3. *Bishop does not recognize impoverished mother* when she wears borrowed finery. She returns wearing humble garments, and he recognizes her. *Espéculo* 441.334–35; Tubach 3420.

H150. Circumstances of recognition.

H151.4. *Recognition by cup in sack*: alleged stolen goods. Cup is placed in the sack of Joseph's brethren (Aesop, pilgrim); they are (he is) accused of theft. This gives cause for recognition. *Esopete* p. 23; *a.b.c.* 38; cf. Tubach 3796.

*H151.11.1. *Recognition*. Son identifies self to his parents after he has defended mother in judicial combat to save her from execution for adultery. *Ultramar* I.1.64.112–13.

H171. Animal (object) indicates election of ruler.

*H171.0.1. *One who shoots arrow that kills four birds at once* will be king. *Ultramar* I.1.166.326.

*H175.6. *Horse is recognized as having been raised by ass because of gait.* Sultan is recognized as son of a baker because his reward to philosopher is loaves of bread. *a.b.c.* 313; Tubach 2611.

H200–H299. TESTS OF TRUTH

H210. Test of guilt or innocence.

H215. *Magic manifestation at execution* proves innocence. Executioner unable to kill innocent woman. *a.b.c.* 14; Tubach 4697.

H218. Trial by combat.

H218.0.1. *Vindication by champion.* Woman accused of adultery saved by knight who fights accuser. *Lucanor* Ex. 44; *Ultramar* I.1.68.120.

H218.0.1.1. *Vindication by champion.* Noble women robbed of lands. Need champion in judicial combat. *Ultramar* I.1.70–80.123–57, I.1.80.157–60.

H218.0.2. *Long-lost son is champion* in judicial combat of mother accused of adultery. Saves her. *Ultramar* I.1.64.111–12.

H220. Ordeals. Guilt or innocence thus established.

H221.2. *Ordeal by red-hot iron.* Saint made to walk on heated iron bars to prove her chastity. *Espéculo* 94.64; Tubach 3109.

*H221.2.3. *Ordeal by red-hot iron.* Adulterous woman confessed and could handle hot iron bar without pain. Sinned again, was burned by cold iron bar as she put it in fire. *Espéculo* 493.389; Tubach 59.

H221.3. *Ordeal by burning oil.* St. John not burned by boiling oil. *Espéculo* 95.64.

*H221.6. *Falsely accused wife proved innocent* when she survives burning at stake. Had prayed to Virgin Mary. Perjured lover burns to death. *Cantigas* 185.

H240. Other tests of truth.

*H242.2. *Scourge marks on body* prove that God had appeared in dream. *a.b.c.* 65.

H251. Test of truth by magic object.

H251.3.4. *Stick with money in it breaks* and betrays thief, who swears his innocence. *a.b.c.* 234; *Espéculo* 459.358; Tubach 3352.

H252. Act of truth.

*H252.7. *Act of truth: hemorrhage stopped.* Is test of truth that priest's concubine is a demonic beast. *Espéculo* 115.74–75.

H253. Oaths before gods as test of truth.

*H253.1. *Bishop accused of simony must swear innocence* in name of Father, Son, and Holy Spirit. Proved guilty; cannot utter "Holy Spirit." *Espéculo* 465.368–69.

H300–H499. MARRIAGE TESTS

H301. *Excessive demands to prevent marriage.* Here St. Catherine demands perfection in prospective husbands. At last she receives Jesus. *Castigos* MS A BNM 6559 81.214; Tubach 899.

H400–H459. Chastity tests.

H412. Chastity test by ordeal.

*H412.7.3. *Chastity ordeal: jumping.* Wife leaps from high place to prove chastity. Protected by Virgin Mary, she is unharmed. *Cantigas* 341.

H430. Chastity index.

H439.1.1. *Painting on wife's stomach as chastity index.* Husband paints lamb on stomach before leaving on trip. Stays away years; returns to find ram portrayed (painted by lover in his absence). Wife retorts: lamb had matured with the years. *LBA* cc. 474–85.

H460. Wife tests.

H473. Test of wife's obedience.

H473.2. *Test of wife's obedience: the one command.* Upon wife's insistence that he test her by giving her one command, husband tells her not to go into the oven. She does and oven collapses on her. *a.b.c.* 307; cf. Tubach 5278.

*H473.3.1. *Test of wife's obedience.* Husband, knowing his wife is inclined to be contrary, leaves her two unguents; warns her not to apply poisonous one but to use other one. She disobeys and dies. *Lucanor* Ex. 27; cf. Tubach 5278.

*H474.1. *Husband proves wife's total obedience.* She agrees with all his absurd statements: direction of a river's flow, identifying cows as mares. *Lucanor* Ex. 27.

H479. Wife tests: miscellaneous.

*H479.3. *Husband puts wife's chastity to test.* Has men offer her gifts. She finally succumbs to promise of jewels. *Ilustres mujeres* 26.33v–43v (Prochris); cf. Tubach 5194.

H480. Father tests.

H486.2. *Test of paternity:* shooting at father's corpse. Youngest of supposed sons refuses to shoot and is judged the only genuine son of dead emperor. *a.b.c.* 174; Tubach 1272.

H490. Other marriage tests.

H491. Test of mother's and father's love for children.

*H491.2. *Fathers carry children on head to save them from flood,* even

MOTIF INDEX OF

dying. Mothers stepped over and on children trying to escape to safety. *Castigos* 5.55.

H500–H899. TESTS OF CLEVERNESS
H510. Tests in guessing.
*H511.1.3. *Wrong choice.* Two royal wives must choose between a gift of a crown or of splendid clothes. Favorite chooses crown and is berated. *Calila* p. 280; *Exemplario* 70r.
H530–H599. Riddles.
H540. Propounding riddles.
H540.3. *King propounds riddle.* Suitor for princess's hand will lose head if he cannot answer. *Apolonio* c. 15; cf. Tubach 4098.

H543.1. *Devil held off from person by answering his riddles.* St. Andrew, the bishop, and the devil. Devil, in form of beautiful woman, visits bishop. St. Andrew appears as pilgrim, answers devil's questions, and defeats devil. *a.b.c.* 388; Tubach 214.

*H548.2. *King poses riddle to rival monarch.* Solver to get tribute or pay tribute for failure. *Esopete* p. 20

*H548.2.1 *Calendar riddle.* *Esopete* pp. 22–23.

*H548.2.2. *River-and-fish riddle.* *Apolonio* cc. 505–6.

*H548.2.3. *Reed-grass-and-paper riddle.* *Apolonio* cc. 507–8.

*H548.2.4. *Boats-and-water riddle.* *Apolonio* cc. 509–10.

*H548.2.5. *Bathhouse-and-bather riddle.* *Apolonio* cc. 511–12.

*H548.2.6. *Anchor riddle.* *Apolonio* cc. 513–14.

*H548.2.7. *Mirror riddle.* *Apolonio* cc. 520–21.

*H548.2.8. *Four-wheels-of-cart riddle.* *Apolonio* cc. 522–23.

*H548.3. *Clever slave bests rivals* in slave market with riddling responses. *Esopete* pp. 6–7.

*H548.4. *Riddles as test of wit.* Prince poses riddles to youth at court. Youth confounds prince. *Epitus* pp. 26–29.

*H548.5. *Riddles as test of wit.* Slave woman (Teodor) answers riddles propounded by king and sages. Confounds them all. *Teodor* pp. 105–34.

*H548.6. *Customer and entertainer in brothel exchange riddles.* *Apolonio* cc. 505–23.

H561. Solvers of riddles.
H561.5. *King and clever minister.* King propounds riddles and questions to his clever minister. *Esopete* pp. 22–23.

*H561.5.1. *Clever minister gives enigmatic answer in riddle form* to king's request that he describe court. *Esopete* p. 23.

*H561.11. *Servant saves master from mob.* Master's advice solves riddle who will first see sun at daybreak. First light of day appears in western sky. Mob pardons master and makes him king. *a.b.c.* 401.

H565. *Riddle propounded from chance experience.* Arrival of unknown person in strange land. *Apolonio* cc. 518–19.

*H566. *Clever slave woman answers series of riddles* based on knowledge of biblical, theological, and classical truths. *Teodor* 125–29.

H570. Means of solving riddles.

H572. *Reductio ad absurdum* of riddle: stallions of Babylon. Why is my mare restless when stallions of Babylon neigh? Hero beats cat for having strangled a cock last night in Babylon (impossible distance away). *Esopete* p. 22.

H580. Enigmatic statements.

H588.7. *Father's counsel*: find treasure within a foot of the ground. (Sons dig everywhere and thus loosen soil of vineyard which becomes fruitful.) *Esopete* pp. 113–14.

*H594.4. *Enigmatic responses* to queries concerning place of origin and birth. *Esopete* p. 6; *Epitus* 26–29.

H600. Symbolic interpretations.

H604. *Symbolic meaning of spiced and bitter tongue* served at dinner. *a.b.c.* 248; *Esopete* pp. 12–13; Tubach 4898, 4916.

H605. *Angel teaches through parable* that work is prayer. Shown man who twists rope and prays. *a.b.c.* 7, 333; Tubach 275.

*H605.1. *Physician gives king symbolic prescription* for salvation. *Çifar* p. 75.

H606. *Symbolic interpretation of sin.* Priest drags heavy sack of sand behind him to show how men are hindered by sin. *a.b.c.* 1; Tubach 4413.

*H606.1. *Symbolic interpretation of sin.* Pilgrim carries heavy iron staff penitentially. Freed of burden at end of pilgrimage. *Cantigas* 253.

H607. Discussion by symbols.

H607.1. *Disputation between Greeks and Romans.* Greek shows one finger, open palm; Roman shows three fingers and clenched fist. Greek thinks gestures mean monotheism, Trinity, divine power; Roman sees them as menacing physical gestures. *LBA* cc. 46–63; Tubach 2275.

H617. Symbolic interpretation of dreams.

*H617.1. *Duke dreams of being in a magic forest*, attacked by four lions, three fierce bears, and two flying dragons followed by ferocious dogs. Wife interprets it as a warning that his enemies were coming to attack him. *Ultramar* I.1.112.231–32.

*H617.2. *Countess (pregnant) dreamt of a griffin and two eagles* who cleared temple in Jerusalem of rats, bats, and owls that had nested on altars. Placed on a throne by them, a griffin pecks out her heart and entrails and encircles the city with them. Interpreted: her lineage will be honored in holy land. *Ultramar* I.1.144.290–91.

H630. Riddles of the superlative.

H631.5. *What is strongest? Truth.* Royal handmaidens debate relative power of kings, of wine, of women, and of truth. King judges debate and chooses truth. *Castigos* 33.157–58.

*H631.5.1. *What is strongest?* Debate among wind, water, and truth. Truth wins. *Çifar* p. 136.

H642.2. *What is highest?* The empyrean heavens. *a.b.c.* 338; Tubach 214.

*H648.3. *What is best thing God has done?* The diversity and nobility of human visages. *a.b.c.* 338; *Espéculo* 179.121–23; Tubach 214.

H659. Riddles of the superlative: miscellaneous.

*H659.7.3. *What is greatest good?* Charity. *a.b.c.* 96.

*H659.7.3.1. *Woman poses riddle to king who desires her.* She will be his if he answers correctly. What is the best character trait? Conscience (shame). *Lucanor* Ex. 50; Tubach 954.

H659.7.4. *What is the greatest villainy?* Stealing. *a.b.c.* 96.

H659.19. *What is easiest to lose and impossible to recover?* Truth. *Çifar* p. 136.

*H659.27. *What is strongest?* Rat-maiden wants most powerful mate of all. Sun covered by clouds; clouds controlled by winds; mountain blocks winds; mountain gnawed by rodents, therefore she must marry a rat. *Calila* p. 244; *Exemplario* 58v; Tubach 3428.

*H659.28. *What ages man most rapidly?* Sleeping with many women. *Teodor* 116.

*H659.29. *What is heaviest thing in world?* Obligation. *Teodor* 123.

*H659.30. *What is sharpest thing in world?* Tongue of men and of women. *Teodor* 123.

*H659.31. *What is faster than arrow in flight?* Thoughts. *Teodor* 123.

*H659.32. *What is faster and more burning than fire?* Human heart: *Teodor* 123. Angry man's heart: *Teodor* 129.

*H659.33. *What is sweeter than honey?* Parental love: *Teodor* 123. Profit: *Teodor* 129.

*H659.34. *What is bitterer than bile?* Bad children. *Teodor* 123.

*H659.35. *What is the most incurable of illnesses?* Foolish, shameless daughter: *Teodor* 123. Madness: *Teodor* 129.

*H659.36. *What is harder than steel?* Truth. *Teodor* 124.

*H659.37. *What is best and worst thing in world?* Words. *Teodor* 129.

H680. Riddles of distance.

H682. Riddles of heavenly distance.

H682.1.10. *How far from earth to heaven?* The devil knows for he has fallen this distance. *a.b.c.* 338; *Espéculo* 179.121–23; Tubach 214.

*H682.1.11. *Where is earth higher than the heavens?* In the Empyrean, where Jesus was raised from earth. *a.b.c.* 388; *Espéculo* 179.121–23.

H690. Riddles of measure.

H696.1.1. *How much water is in the sea?* Stop all the rivers, and I will measure it. *Esopete* p. 15; *Sendebar* Day 8; cf. Tubach 4028.

H900–H1199. TESTS OF PROWESS: TASKS

H900–H999. Assignment and performance of tasks.

H910. Assignment of tasks in response to suggestion.

H919.4. *Impossible task assigned by aggrieved person.* One-eyed man demands eye from man accused of having deprived him of his. Must remove remaining eye to see if it matches one removed by adversary. *Sendebar* Day 8, Tale 22.

H920. Assigners of tasks.

*H927.3. *Angel comes to hermit* to tell him to send young man to defend his mother in judicial combat to prevent her execution for adultery. *Ultramar* I.1.63.108.

*H927.4. *Angel appears to youth assigning him task* of being defender of widows, orphans and those who have been disinherited. *Ultramar* I.1.63.109.

*H931.3. *Seemingly impossible task assigned to get rid of clever slave*: find a man without cares. *Esopete* p. 13.

H933. Princess sets hero tasks.

*H933.0.1. *Princess assigns three tasks* to prospective suitors. She marries the first to accomplish them. *Abreviada* 1.10.

H950. Task evaded by subterfuge.

*H951.1. *Countertasks.* Hold back rivers and streams. Hero will drink sea if conditions are met. *Esopete* p. 15.

H970. Help in performing tasks.

*H984.1.1. *Task performed with help of Virgin Mary.* Sinner unable to fill magic pitcher with water for two years, prays to Virgin Mary. His tears finally fill pitcher. *Cantigas* 155.

H1000–H1199. Nature of tasks.

*H1049.5. *Task: Find a man without cares. Esopete* p. 13.

H1110. Tedious tasks.

H1111. *Task: carrying hundreds of sheep across stream. a.b.c.* 156; *Disciplina* 12; *Esopete* p. 144; Tubach 4310.

H1129.10.1. *Impossible task: assembling huge quantity of fleas*: many-colored, separated according to sexual identity. *Sendebar* Day 8, Tale 22.

H1130 Superhuman tasks.

H1142.3. *Task: drinking the seas dry*; countertask: stop all the rivers. *Sendebar* Day 8, Tale 22; *Esopete* p. 15.

H1200–H1399. TESTS OF PROWESS: QUESTS

H1210. Quest assigned.

*H1210.2.1. *Quest assigned by king.* King sends sage to India in search of magic herbs that will resuscitate the dead. *Exemplario* 5r–5v; *Calila* pp. 99–102.

H1370. Miscellaneous quests.

H1376. Spiritual quests.

H1376.1. *Young prince protected from knowledge of death* goes out into city and comes upon old man who tells him of its inevitability. *Barlaam* pp. 42–43; *Estados* 1.7.

H1376.2.1. *Spiritual quest.* Holy man prays that he be shown face of Death; it is a horrific beast with a human voice. *a.b.c.* 296; Tubach 5082 b.

H1400–H1599. OTHER TESTS

H1400 Fear test.

H1406.1. *Fear test.* Threat of burning to death innocent person in order to frighten another. *Esopete* pp. 13–14.

H1510. Tests of power to survive.

*H1511.5. *Widow proves innocence of dead husband* by holding red-hot metal. *a.b.c.* 365; Tubach 1284; cf. Tubach 2759.

H1531.2. *Vain attempt to kill man on stairway set with razors. LBA* c. 267.

H1550–H1569. Tests of character.

*H1551. *Physiognomist found to have unfavorable traits.* Explains that his science is true and that he has had to work to overcome the characteristics his face shows. *Çifar* p. 78.

H1553. Test of patience.

H1553.2. *Kings and emperors suffer criticism* and reproof without displaying anger. *Castigos* MS A BNM 6559 31.147.

H1553.3. *Test of patience:* those who enter city gates must endure insults of old men there who mock them. *a.b.c.* 214; Tubach 3622.

H1553.4. *Monk shows patience by enduring blow* with stool thrown by abbot. *a.b.c.* 238; Tubach 3619.

H1553.5. *Test of patience.* Monk fails in test of patience. Tries to live apart to test it. Loses temper at a cup which overturns and breaks it; fails again. *a.b.c.* 221; Tubach 252.

*H1553.7. *Test of patience.* Would-be philosopher endures insults from great philosopher. Told he had proved himself by keeping quiet retorted: "I would have known I was a philosopher if you had been silent." *a.b.c.* 408; Tubach 3748.

H1554. Test of curiosity.

H1554.1. *Test of curiosity: mouse hidden between two plates.* Monk boasts of strong character; told by companion not to lift the upper plate. Tempted, he lifts it, and mouse escapes. *a.b.c.* 376; Tubach 3427.

H1556. Tests of fidelity.

*H1556.0.3. *Fidelity of vassals.* Show devotion by drinking exudations from count's leprous lesions. *Lucanor* Ex. 44.

*H1556.0.4. *Fidelity of son.* King gives son, suspected of disloyalty, his sword. Must not resort to poison or hired assassin. Son repents and swears loyalty. *Glosa* 2.2.2.128–29; Tubach 4485.

H1558. Test of friendship.

H1558.1. *Test of friendship: the half-friend.* Son brags to father of many friends. Father tells son to kill a calf (hog) and tell his friends he has killed a man and ask help in concealing body. All drive him away, and only his father's half-friend remains true to him in his feigned trouble. *a.b.c.* 18; *Disciplina* 1; *Çifar* pp. 7–8; *Esopete* pp. 137–39; *Castigos* 35.165–68; *Lucanor* Ex. 48; *Espéculo* 49.34–35 (ADMYTE 0 111*v*–113*r*); Tubach 2216, 2407.

H1558.1.1. *Test of friendship.* Of three friends, the least loved proves true in emergency. *a.b.c.* 16; *Barlaam* pp. 115–18; *Espéculo* 35.24–25.

H1558.2. *Test of friendship: whole friend.* In despair, man gives himself up as murderer rather than endure further misery. His friend tries to take on himself the guilt and be substituted. Real murderer touched by his generosity, confesses. *Çifar* pp. 9–11; *Disciplina* 2; Tubach 2208.

*H1558.2.1. *Test of friendship: whole friend.* Man gives up his betrothed to friend whose sickness can only be cured by love. *Çifar* pp. 9–11; Tubach 2215.

*H1558.11. *Test of friendship*: to take slap publicly from friend. *Castigos* MS A BNM 6603 36.158 (ADMYTE 0 92v–93r).

H1561. Tests of valor.

*H1561.2.4. *Test of valor* among three knights. First two attacked enemy as they came near. The most valiant waited until enemy attacked him before fighting back. *Lucanor* Ex. 15.

H1565. Tests of gratitude.

H1565.1. *Test of gratitude.* Magician makes pupil believe he has gained high office. Though he had promised teacher great rewards, pupil does not keep promise. Magically removed from high office. *Lucanor* Ex. 11; Tubach 3137.

*H1565.2. *Test of gratitude.* Prince sends courtiers a series of presents: good, better, best, and even better than best. First courtier rejects them all. Second sends his thanks. Ungrateful one jailed; grateful one rewarded further. *a.b.c.* 206.

H1569. Tests of character: miscellaneous.

*H1569.2. *Test of ability to reign.* King's youngest son shows willingness to serve and to learn. *Lucanor* Ex. 24.

*H1569.3. *Test of worry-free nature.* Philosopher tries to shake stolidity of peasant. To frighten him, threatens to immolate wife. Peasant, unshaken, asks for delay so that own wife can be added to fire. *Esopete* pp. 13–14.

*H1569.4. *Test of ability to keep secret.* Husband tells wife secret; he has given birth to a crow. She cannot keep secret. *Glosa* 2.1.24.119–20; cf. Tubach 5269.

H1570–H1599. Miscellaneous tests.

H1573. Religious tests.

H1573.2.2. *Angel in disguise tests saint's generosity.* Begs for platter of food sent him by his mother. Saint gives silver platter to him. *a.b.c.* 137; *Espéculo* 236.159–60; Tubach 5076.

*H1573.2.4. *King tests courtiers' wisdom.* Chests adorned with gold and precious stones contain putrefying remains; chests containing royal treasures covered with pitch. *Barlaam* pp. 56–58; *Espéculo* 449.343–44; Tubach 967.

H1578. Test of sex: to discover person masking as other sex.

*H1578.1.4.3. *Test of sex.* Boy masking as girl: given choice of playthings, chooses arms, not fripperies. *Alexandre* cc. 411–15.

H1584. Tests of space.

*H1584.3. *Land measured according to amount encompassed by hide of ox.* Dido orders hide to be cut in thin strips; thus gains large territory (Dido). *Ilustres mujeres* 40.47r–49v; *PCG* 1.53.34–35; *Abreviada* 1.16.

H1596. Beauty contest.

H1596.1. *Golden apple as prize in beauty contest.* Judgement of Paris. *Glosa* 3.3.17.379–80.

*H1596.4. *Ape-mother brags to Jupiter* that her child will win the beauty contest. All laugh. *Esopete* pp. 122–23; cf. Tubach 4873.

H1599. Contest among demons.

*H1599.1. *Test of evil.* Devils vie: first caused a war; second caused storms at sea, killed many; third caused marital strife and many deaths; fourth lived in desert and caused a monk to succumb to fleshly desires; fifth triumphed because caused saint to touch a woman with palm of hand. *a.b.c.* 92.88–90; *Espéculo* 183.124–25; Tubach 1663.

J. THE WISE AND THE FOOLISH

J0–J199. ACQUISITION, POSSESSION OF WISDOM (KNOWLEDGE)

J10. Wisdom (knowledge) acquired from experience.

J15. *Serpent having injured human refuses reconciliation.* He knows that neither can forget his injuries. *Esopete* pp. 52, 89–90; *a.b.c.* 74; Tubach 4251.

*J15.1. *King's son and bird's son brought up together.* Bird kills young boy and king has bird's son killed. Bird refuses reconciliation because knows that neither can forget injuries. *Calila* p. 273.

*J15.1.1. *Snake having tried to poison man by secreting poison in cooking pot,* refuses reconciliation because knows that man will never forget. *Exemplario* 43r; Tubach 4251.

*J15.1.2. *Snake's offspring bites and kills human benefactor's son.* She kills offender and leaves, never to return. *a.b.c.* 205; Tubach 4251.

*J15.2. *Lion raised by man is beaten and driven away.* Later refuses reconciliation; wounds healed, insults did not. *Castigos* MS A BNM 6559 27.142 (ADMYTE 0 86r–86v).

J16. *Dove disregards experience* and loses brood building nest in same place where she lost former brood. *Calila* p. 352.

*J16.1. *Lazy trout ignores danger.* Does not save self from fishermen as had two companions. *Calila* p. 149; *Exemplario* 18r.

J17. *Tiger learns through experience to fear man. Esopete* p. 123.

*J17.2. *Young lion learns through experience to fear man.* In spite of the warning of his father, he searches for man and is trapped and beaten. *Esopete* pp. 98–100.

J21. Counsels proved wise by experience.

J21.1. *"Consider the end."* Barber sees inscription over door: "Whatever you do, do wisely, and think of the consequences." He is hired to cut king's throat, drops razor, and confesses. *a.b.c.* 69.

J21.2. *"Do not act when angry."* Counsel proved wise by experience. Man returns home after long absence and sees man lying with his wife. Restrains self and learns that it is son born soon after his departure. *Lucanor* Ex. 36.

*J21.2.1.1. *"Do not act when angry."* Master will not punish servants when angry. Asks steward to do it. *a.b.c.* 219; *Castigos* MS A BNM 6559 31.148; *Glosa* 1.2.14.135–36; Tubach 3991.

J21.5. *"Do not leave the highway."* Counsel proved wise by experience. Short cut proves longer in time. *a.b.c.* 414; *Disciplina* 18; Tubach 4111.

J21.12. *"Rue not a thing that is past."* Man lets bird go and then, having listened to bird's false declaration that she had a precious gem in her body, tries to climb a tree after her and falls. *Esopete* pp. 142–43; *a.b.c.* 124; *Disciplina* 22; *Çifar* p. 76; *Barlaam* pp. 92–94; cf. Tubach 5324.

*J21.12.1. *"Never give up what you have in your hand."* Man releases captive bird in the hope of greater reward. Bird escapes. *a.b.c.* 124; *Disciplina* 22; *Çifar* p. 76; *Esopete* pp. 142–43; *Barlaam* pp. 92–94.

J21.12.3. *"Do not try to acquire what cannot be acquired."* Man tries vainly to recapture bird he has released. *a.b.c.* 124; *Disciplina* 22; *Çifar* p. 76; *Esopete* pp. 142–43; *Barlaam* pp. 92–94. See also *a.b.c.* 300 (not in Paris MS, *Perdita res irrecuperabilis non est dolenda*). Tale not given.

J21.13. *"Do not believe what is beyond belief."* Man believes when bird tells him she has a precious gem in her body. *a.b.c.* 124; *Disciplina* 22; *Çifar* p. 76; *Esopete* pp. 142–43; *Barlaam* pp. 92–94.

*J21.13.1. *Previously injured serpent warns farmer repeatedly not to believe advice* from one whom one has injured. *Esopete* pp. 89–90.

J21.14. *"Never try to reach the unattainable."* Man cannot reach the heights to which a bird can fly. Cannot catch escaped bird. *Çifar* p. 76; *Esopete* pp. 142–43.

J21.32. *"Do not marry more than one woman."* Man who wanted three wives marries one and is greatly weakened. Loses power to turn mill-stone. *LBA* cc. 181–216; Tubach 3182.

*J21.53. *Elderly monk told: "Stay in your cell.* Do not go to city where you will fornicate." He goes; fathers a child; returns lamenting birth of child of disobedience. *a.b.c.* 176; Tubach 3323.

*J21.54. *Dove told not to throw fledglings to fox* but to tell fox she must climb tree if she wants to eat them. Saves fledglings. *Calila* p. 353; *Exemplario* 91v.

*J22.1 *Precept of the lion to his sons*: beware of man. *Esopete* pp. 98–99.

J26. *Romans learn from vanquished enemy* that enemies can be won more by kindness than by cruelty. *a.b.c.* 289 (not in Paris MS); Tubach 4127.

*J26.1. *Christian does not heed Jew's declaration that* in his faith he has the right to take the belongings of anyone who is not a Jew. Horse and belongings stolen. *a.b.c.* 202; Tubach 2796.

*J28. *Friar, living alone, away from community in hope of controlling anger*, finds himself overcome by anger by simple act of filling a jug with water in his solitude. Returns to monastery. *a.b.c.* 221; Tubach 252.

*J29. *Foolish monk disdains disobedience in others.* Companion traps mouse between two plates and warns him not to lift top one. Fool unable to obey releases mouse. *a.b.c.* 376; Tubach 3427.

J30. Wisdom (knowledge) acquired by inference.

*J30.01. *Philosopher reads gloomy epitaph* and decides to give up worldly life and to become a hermit. *Disciplina* 32.

*J30.02. *Philosophers recognize disparity between golden sepulcher* and the reality of death. *Disciplina* 33; *Espéculo* 382.282.

*J31.3. *Holy man's simple statement of faith* vanquishes disputation of scholar (heretic). *a.b.c.* 250; Tubach 2548.

J32. *Arrow as man's message* shows lion (tiger) how terrible man himself must be. *Esopete* p. 123.

J50. Wisdom (knowledge) acquired by observation.

*J51.1. *Fox learns from fate of other animal.* Fox learns wisdom of giving lion's share after seeing punishment meted out to wolf. *LBA* cc. 82–88; *Gatos* 15; Tubach 3069.

J52.2. *King descends to bottom of sea in glass barrel* to learn wisdom from observing fishes. *Castigos* MS A BNM 6559 153.33 (ADMYTE 0 104v); *Glosa* 1.2.6.94; Tubach 123.

*J55.1. *Bad judge flayed and skin put on the judgement chair.* His son, the new judge, taught by fate of father to be good judge. *a.b.c.* 223; Tubach 2855, 2859.

*J56.1.1. *Ruler learns lesson from virtuous bishop* with ruddy and pimply face. Bishop casts out devils from sword bearer. Lesson: do not judge a person by appearance. *a.b.c.* 157.

*J57. *Ruler learns to be merciful* from example of bees who die after they sting. *a.b.c.* 381.

J80. Wisdom (knowledge) taught by parable.

*J80.0.1. *Wisdom taught by parable*: the good shepherd. *Barlaam* p. 103.

*J80.0.2. *Wisdom taught by parable*: the seed sown on good and sterile ground. *Barlaam* p. 51; *Castigos* MS A BNM 6559 50.176.

*J80.0.3. *Wisdom taught by parable*: turbulence of powder dissolved in water subsides in time. *a.b.c.* 82; *Espéculo* 496.392.

*J80.0.3.1. *Wisdom taught by parable*: storm-tossed ship should be saved and not crashed on rocks. Sinner should be welcomed back into monastery. *a.b.c.* 351.

*J80.0.4. *Wisdom taught by parable*: guests who do not attend wedding are idolaters who refuse God's invitation. *Barlaam* p. 86.

*J80.0.5. *Wisdom taught by parable*: seven wise and seven foolish virgins. Wise virgins come with oil for lamps. *Barlaam* p. 87.

*J80.0.6. *Wisdom taught by parable*: the prodigal son. *Barlaam* pp. 102–3.

*J80.0.7. *Wisdom taught by parable*: the good shepherd. *Barlaam* pp. 103–4.

*J80.0.8. *Wisdom taught by parable*: the unjust steward. *Barlaam* pp. 127–28.

*J80.0.9. *Wisdom taught by parable*: man tells tale of farmer who yoked a calf and an ox to tame unruly calf. *Esopete* pp. 64–65.

J80.3. Wisdom (knowledge) taught by symbolic act.

*J80.3.1. *Wisdom taught by a symbolic act*: monk frightened by evil thoughts. Abbot tells him to bare his chest and try to receive the wind. Just as he cannot do this, he cannot prevent thoughts from coming to him. *a.b.c.* 290.

*J80.3.2. *Wisdom taught by a symbolic act*: basket of sand is abbot's sins. *a.b.c.* 1; Tubach 4413.

*J80.3.3. *Wisdom taught by a symbolic act*: chests adorned with gold and precious stones contain putrefying remains; chests containing royal treasures covered with pitch. *Barlaam* pp. 56–58; Tubach 967.

*J80.3.4. *Wisdom taught by symbolic act*: angel in vision twists rope. Prayer is work. *a.b.c.* 7; Tubach 275.

*J80.3.5. *Wisdom taught by symbolic act*: confessor shows sinner heavy sack of wheat; sinner tries to lift it; holy man pulls against him. Sinner's unwillingness to change is like pull toward earth. *Gatos* 38; *Espéculo* 404.302.

*J80.3.6. *Wisdom taught by symbolic act*: saint sends pupil unclothed to market. He is to bring back meat balanced on his head. Packs of dogs and flocks of birds attack him. They are like the devils who attack ascetics who withdraw from world. *Espéculo* 475.376.

*J80.4. *King likens trumpets of death to the call all sinners face when they know they will die.* *a.b.c.* 192, 292; Tubach 4994.

*J80.4.1. *Holy man teaches lesson to nephew who had suffered injury.* Holy man publicly embraces offender and makes peace with him. *Espéculo* 437.331.

*J80.5. *King tells fable of mule who refused to acknowledge his low-born father.* Poet rewarded because he acknowledges his base parentage. *a.b.c.* 199; *Disciplina* 4; Tubach 3829.

*J81.4. *Parable comparing filling a hole with sea water using a small spoon* with the task of putting the truth about the Trinity in a book. *a.b.c.* 413; *Espéculo* 539.433–34.

*J81.5. *Parable comparing siege of a city with task of resisting temptation.* Monks must deprive selves of food and water as do besiegers to cities. *Espéculo* 541.437.

*J81.6. *Holy man explains God's image in tranquil, meek hearts.* Image's movement is like coin dropped into glass of water. *Espéculo* 340.240–41.

*J81.7. *Holy man teaches carnally tempted young monk.* Just as mother weans infant by applying bitter medicine to nipples, he must think of bitter punishment for carnal sins after death. *Espéculo* 380.281.

*J83.1. *Philosopher teaches princeling by showing him ravens quarreling over devastated kingdoms.* Youth recognizes that he has been devastating his own realm. *Lucanor* Ex. 21.

MOTIF INDEX OF

*J83.2. *Wise man tells Alexander that even lions, when they die, are perches for birds of prey.* a.b.c. 86; Tubach 148.

*J88.1. *Wise man warns that thief's marriage will swell number of thieves* just as marriage of sun would create new suns to dry up world. *Esopete* p. 35; Tubach 4677.

*J88.2. *Wisdom taught by parable.* Worse to be bitten by an angry rabid dog than by a dog who uses teeth to carry pups. a.b.c. 232.

*J89. *Dishes of poorly seasoned tongues* and of well-seasoned ones compared to unkind and kind speech. a.b.c. 248; *Esopete* p. 13; Tubach 4898, 4916.

*J94.1. *Saint learns how to achieve peace of mind* by seeing man who worked and then prayed. Work and prayer are answer. a.b.c. 333; Tubach 275.

*J99.3. *Friar told that those who do not sow and reap* will starve even before those who sow and reap badly. *Espéculo* 405.302–3.

*J99.4. *Even if hen is given barn full of grain,* she will not stop scratching the ground: likewise woman will not desist from adultery (told by Venus to Jupiter in defense of adultery). *Esopete* p. 167.

J100. Wisdom (knowledge) taught by necessity.

J101. *Crow drops pebbles into water jug* to raise level. *Esopete* p. 126.

J120. Wisdom (knowledge) from children.

J121. *Wisdom from child.* Ungrateful man refused warm cloth to his father. His own son begged warm cloth to save for the day when he too will refuse it to his father. a.b.c. 337; Tubach 2001.

J122.1. *Wisdom from child.* Seducer refrains when child tells him he is foolish. A man is foolish to leave his family and to go whoring. *Sendebar* Day 8, Tale 20.

*J122.1.1. *Joint depositor tricks old woman.* She mistakenly pays him in court: child advises old woman to demand presence of all three joint depositors before she repays money entrusted to her. *Sendebar* Day 8, Tale 21; Tubach 3353.

J130. Wisdom (knowledge) acquired from animals.

*J132.1. *Crow advises eagle to drop snail* to break its shell. *Esopete* p. 37.

*J133.7. *Animal gives wise example to man.* Cock serves (sexually) fifteen hens; man can serve only one woman. *Esopete* p. 167.

J140. Wisdom (knowledge) through education.

*J142.3. *Illiterate knight wants to learn to read.* Can only learn two words: *"Ave Maria."* a.b.c. 44.

J144. *Well-trained kid obeys mother goat:* does not open to wolf. *Esopete* p. 51; cf. Tubach 2312.

J147. *Child sheltered to keep him in ignorance of sadness, death, aging, and infirmity.* Useless. *Barlaam* p. 22.

*J148. *Emperor insists that offspring be prepared.* Sons to learn manly arts: running, jumping, throwing lances, swimming; daughters, spinning and weaving. a.b.c. 325; *Glosa* 2.1.13.67; Tubach 5383.

J150. Other means of acquiring wisdom (knowledge).

J151. Wisdom from old person.

*J151.1.1. *Aged master hidden by servant during revolt.* Master's advice solves riddle who will first see sun at daybreak. First light of day appears in western sky. Mob pardons master and makes him king. *a.b.c.* 401.

*J151.5. *Aged nursemaid taught her charge temperance.* Not permitted wine. *a.b.c.* 51.

*J151.6. *Aged man counsels travelers.* "Take main road, not short cut." *a.b.c.* 414; *Disciplina* 18; Tubach 4111.

J152. Wisdom (knowledge) from sage (teacher).

J152.1. *Wisdom of simple living.* Cynical philosopher (Socrates/Diogenes) lives in half of a large earthenware vessel: open part toward the sun, closed part toward the wind and the rain. *a.b.c.* 427; *Disciplina* 28; cf. Tubach 1673.

*J152.7. *Wisdom from philosopher.* Urinates while walking to protect head from noon-day sun, to keep feet from burning, and to escape urine's odor. *Esopete* pp. 7–8.

*J152.8. *Philosopher advises courtier.* Advises him to deceive king. Willing to follow him in exile. *a.b.c.* 75; *Barlaam* pp. 26–31; *Lucanor* Ex. 1.

*J152.9. *Wisdom from philosopher.* Tells knights that giving is greatest virtue and robbing the greatest vice. Reproaches them for taking and robbing every day. *a.b.c.* 96.

*J152.10. *Wise man cannot tell king what God is.* The more he tries, the more he fails. King gives sage three days to tell him. Cannot do it. *a.b.c.* 107; Tubach 2903.

*J152.11. *Philosopher confines pupil and self in room* for six months until pupil knows all. *Sendebar* p. 72.

*J152.12. *Philosopher counsels illegitimate princeling* to wear garments to remind himself of both his noble and base lineage. *a.b.c.* 189.

*J152.13. *Philosopher writes Alexander's epitaph* about Death's powers. *a.b.c.* 294.

*J152.14. *Philosopher is king's superior.* Is guided by reason and king by will. *a.b.c.* 259.

*J152.15. *Holy man counsels emperor against vengeance* against citizens who had dishonored statue of late empress. Saved from killing many. *a.b.c.* 342 (not in Paris MS); see also *a.b.c.* 437.

*J152.16. *Philosopher reinterprets royal dream.* Prophecies of new interpretation come true. *Calila* p. 280.

*J152.17. *Philosopher answers riddle for king:* most important human virtue is conscience. *Lucanor* Ex. 50; Tubach 954.

*J152.18. *Philosopher advises father* to marry daughter to poor man who is good. *a.b.c.* 422; *Lucanor* Ex. 25; cf. Tubach 1444.

J152.19. *Man warned not to eat philosopher's cabbages.* Told: "If you want to eat them, you will be a truth teller, not a flatterer." *Castigos* MS A BNM 6559 (ADMYTE 0 107r).

J153. Wisdom (knowledge) from holy man.

*J153.3. *Hermit explains why God granted water for garden* but did not allow inappropriate crop to flourish. To pray for rain is to presume

MOTIF INDEX OF

greater wisdom than God's. *a.b.c.* 104; Tubach 3885.

★J153.4. *Dying saint tells disciples to love one another* as they carry him to church. *Espéculo* 82.56.

★J153.5. *Holy man explains anger.* It should not reside in heart but only in face. *Espéculo* 339.240.

★J153.6. *Holy man advises pupil* to be like a stone when struck. *Espéculo* 434.330, 435.330.

★J153.7. *Saint on deathbed gives monks rules.* Do not offend others, but apologize if you do; believe in the good sense of others; do not seek revenge if offended. *Espéculo* 505.397–98.

★J153.8. *Wisdom acquired from saint.* Santiago appears to devoted man who insists that the saint is a fisherman. Tells him he is God's warrior knight. *Santiago* 19.97–99.

J154. Wise words of father.

J154. *Wise words of dying father.* Search for treasure by digging soil of vineyard. *Esopete* pp. 113–14.

★J154.0.1. *Wisdom from father* in form of *sententiae*. *Esopete* p. 21; *Çifar* p. 75.

★J154.0.2. *Wisdom from father.* Youth learns the nature of friendship. *Esopete* pp. 137–39; *Castigos* 35.165–68; *Lucanor* Ex. 48; *Espéculo* 49.34–35; *Çifar* pp. 7–8.

J154.1. *Dying saint leaves wise message to monks.* Message is cryptic (*Ubi? Ibi?*) but is finally made clear. *a.b.c.* 182.

★J154.2. *Wise words from father.* Weed small area of field each day until whole field is free of thorns. *Espéculo* 403.301–2.

J155. Wisdom (knowledge) from women.

J155.4. *Wife as adviser.* King's dream misinterpreted, reluctant to follow advice, is advised by wife to delay and to seek advice of philosopher. *Calila* p. 280.

★J155.4.1. *Wisdom from wife.* King unable to conquer enemy is advised by queen that he try to conquer by using contrary measures as do physicians: good for evil, kindness for cruelty. *a.b.c.* 302; *Castigos* MS A BNM 6559 (ADMYTE 0 115r); *Çifar* pp. 124–25; *Glosa* 1.2.27.204.

★J155.9. *Wisdom from astute old woman.* Counsels banker against fraudulent depositors. *Esopete* pp. 139–40; *a.b.c.* 163; *Disciplina* 15; Tubach 3355, 4969.

J156. Wisdom (knowledge) from fools and madmen.

★J156.5. *Wisdom from madman.* Why does hunter spend so much on useless activity? *Esopete* p. 152.

★J156.5.1. *Wisdom from simple person.* Holy man mortified self to rid self of lustful temptations to no avail. Simple pilgrim told him to eat and to regain strength and to serve God. *a.b.c.* 80, 326, 347; Tubach 3906.

★J156.5.2. *Wisdom from foolish neighbor.* Cut cat's ears and burn off her fur to keep her from wandering. *Espéculo* 356.254–55.

J157. Wisdom from dream.

*J157.4. *King is judged in dream.* a.b.c. 61.

J163. Wisdom purchased.

J163.4. *Good counsels bought.* Counsels sold at different prices: "In land where you do not know the cuisine, fill up on first dish you are served" costs a small sum; more valuable counsel is "Do not act when angry." *Lucanor* Ex. 36; cf. Tubach 5324.

J164. Wisdom from God.

*J164. *Wisdom acquired from God's voice.* Saint counseled to use humility to avoid worldly snares. a.b.c. 194, 231.

*J164.1. *Wisdom from Mother of God.* Virgin Mary explains nature of Host to doubting cleric. *Cantigas* 149.

*J164.2. *Virgin Mary appears to monk.* Tells him he must love her, honor her, and praise her. *Cantigas* 296.

J166. Wisdom (knowledge) from visual signs.

J167. *Wisdom from continual reminder* of foolishness in past. Unjust judge skinned, his skin stretched over a stool kept in presence of subsequent judges. a.b.c. 223; Tubach 2859; cf. Tubach 2855.

J168. *Inscription of walls for condensed education.* Sendebar p. 72.

*J168.1. *Roman temple* designed to teach by arrangement of figures and wall inscriptions. a.b.c. 212.

J172. Account of punishments in hell brings about repentance.

J172.1. *Angels take dying saint to heaven,* but voice says he first must see vileness of devils so that he can confess even small sins he may have forgotten. *Espéculo* 191.131.

J180. Possession of wisdom.

J181.1. *Years not counted.* Philosopher counts age from time he began to serve God. Is only forty or forty-five instead of chronological seventy years. *Barlaam* pp. 148–50; Tubach 484.

J190. Acquisition and possession of wisdom: miscellaneous.

*J191.3. *Wisdom acquired from future experience.* Holy man fears three things: departure of soul from body, appearance before Jesus for judgement, sentence to be passed on him. *Espéculo* 195.135.

J200–J1099. WISE AND UNWISE CONDUCT

J200–J499. Choices.

J210. Choices between evils.

*J210.2. *Choice between time in purgatory or illness.* God rewards saint with choice. He chooses illness. *Espéculo* 485.384–85, 491.386–87; cf. Tubach 4263.

*J210.3. *Peasant given choice by nobleman.* Pay forty marks, take forty blows, or eat forty onions. Tries to eat onions; fails, endures the blows; fails and must pay marks anyway. *Espéculo* 489.385.

J211. Choice: free poverty or enslaved wealth.

J211.2. *Town mouse and country mouse.* Latter prefers poverty with safety. *LBA* cc. 1369–85; *Esopete* pp. 36–37; *Gatos* 11; Tubach 3281.

*J211.3. *Dog chooses safety of master's care* to promised reward offered by thief. *LBA* cc. 166–80.

J212. Choice: simplicity with safety or grandeur with danger.

J212.1. *Ass envies horse in fine trappings.* Sees him after severely wounded after joust, suffering and put to work in the fields. *LBA* cc. 237–45; *Esopete* p. 62; cf. Tubach 2615.

J215. Present evil preferred to change for worse.

J215.1. *Don't drive away the flies.* Wounded animal (man) refuses to have flies driven away since they are now sated and their places will be taken by fierce and hungry flies. *a.b.c.* 225; *Espéculo* 70.47; Tubach 2087.

J215.1.3. *Do not pluck off well-fed leeches.* Wolf crosses lake to escape pursuit. Tries to rid self of leeches but must cross lake again. Is advised to keep the sated leeches rather than to leave place for new hungry ones. *Çifar* p. 106.

J215.1.4. *Old man chooses occasional loud chirp of swallows* rather than never-ending but soft chirp of sandpipers. *Lucanor* Ex. 39.

J215.2.1. *Old woman prays for safety of cruel tyrant.* Fears that a worse one will succeed him. *a.b.c.* 380; *Castigos* MS A BNM 6559 33.153 (ADMYTE 0 106v).

J215.4. *Monk goes to wilderness to escape worldly work and to lead contemplative life.* In wilderness was tormented by wasps and flies and suffered great hunger. Returns because he must work to live. *a.b.c.* 428; *Espéculo* 341.242–43.

*J215.4.1. *Newly arrived friar criticizes abbot for working in garden.* Given cell, awaits in vain a call for meal. Must work and pray to eat. *Espéculo* 342.243–44; Tubach 5386.

*J215.5. *Holy man's cell far from water.* Moves it nearer. Angel walks behind him and says: "I am counting your steps to reward you according to your effort." Returns cell to far off location. *Espéculo* 343.244.

*J215.6. *Knight urges others into battle.* The wounds they will receive will make them forget the ones they already have. *Lucanor* Ex. 37; cf. Tubach 508.

J216. Choice of deaths.

J216.2 *Lamb prefers to be sacrificed in temple* rather than to be eaten by wolf. *Esopete* pp. 128–29.

J216.5. *Warrior count prefers to die in battle* instead of in retirement. Thus will his name be famous for his deeds. *Lucanor* Ex. 16.

J217. Unsatisfactory life preferred to death.

J217.2 *Discontented ass longs for death* but changes mind when he sees skins of dead asses at fair (longing misplaced because his skin made into drums). *Esopete* pp. 66–67; cf. Tubach 394, 1747.

*J217.3. *Envious ass, desiring easy life of pig who does not work and is fed,* changes mind when he sees pig is slaughtered for meat. *Gatos* 35; Tubach 3771.

J218. Enemies make peace rather than slay each other.

*J218.2. *Mortal enemies called upon to rule jointly* make peace. *Glosa* 3.1.2.17.

J221. Choice: small injustice permitted rather than to cause trouble.

J221.3. *Man would rather pay 500 florins he did not owe* than to have it said he did not pay debts. *a.b.c.* 159; Tubach 1498.

J225. Choice: apparent injustice over greater wrong.

J225.0.1. *Angel and hermit.* Angel takes hermit with him and does many seemingly unjust things. Later shows why each was just. *a.b.c.* 230; Tubach 2558.

J225.0.1.1. *Angel explains why sinful rich man is buried with honors,* and pious monk is devoured ignobly by lion. Evil will suffer in afterlife, good will not. *a.b.c.* 105; *Espéculo* 511.404; Tubach 3107.

*J225.0.4. *Angel explains apparent injustice to hermit.* Squire lost knight's money sack; charcoal burner found it. Knight cut squire's foot off. Angel explained: Knight lost money because he had stolen it; charcoal burner found money that had belonged to his father. Squire lost foot for having kicked his mother. *Espéculo* 15.11; Tubach 2558.

J225.4. *Angel kills man.* Done because man is plotting a murder. *a.b.c.* 230.

J229.8. *Contentment with evil master (tyrant) for fear of worse successor.* *a.b.c.* 380; *Castigos* MS A BNM 6559 33.153 (ADMYTE 0 106v).

J230–J299. Real and apparent values.

*J234. *Hermit learns that knight's bravery* in battle against infidel army is as valuable as is his life of devotion. *Lucanor* Ex. 3; Tubach 2561.

*J235. *Monk asks abbot what to do with property.* Abbot tells him he has three choices: give it to Church so that he will be given preference; give it to his family so that they treat him well; give it to the poor so that he will do the right thing. *a.b.c.* 290.

*J235.1. *Philosopher absorbed in study* will not be interrupted even to save self from marauders. Is killed. *Castigos* MS A BNM 6559 15.122, 15.58 (ADMYTE 0 15v); *Glosa* 1.2.7.98.

*J235.2. *Philosopher so absorbed in study* forgets to lift food to mouth at mealtimes. *Castigos* MS A BNM 6559 15.122; *Glosa* 1.2.7.97.

J240–J259. Choice between useful and ornamental.

J242.2. *Pine and thorn bush dispute as to their usefulness.* Beauty of form does not give worth; pine grows slowly but it will withstand storms. *Esopete* p. 124.

J242.5. *Peacock and crane in beauty contest.* Better to be able to soar like crane than to strut like peacock. *Esopete* p. 123.

J242.6. *Contest in beauty between swallows and crows (ants and flies).* Worth lies not in beauty. *Esopete* p. 53.

J245. Useful and ugly preferred to expensive and beautiful.

*J245.2.1. *Humble man becomes king.* Chooses humble food over royal fare. *a.b.c.* 81; Tubach 3843.

*J245.3. *King prefers ruling smaller territory of satisfied subjects* than larger one with rebellious ones. Gives up territory. *a.b.c.* 289.

J247. Goodness preferred to wealth.

J247.1. *Man advised to find good husband for his daughter, not a rich one.*

a.b.c. 422; *Lucanor* Ex. 25; *Castigos* MS A BNM 6559 (ADMYTE 0 59*r*); Tubach 1444.

*J247.2. *Pope's wealth and hermit's poverty are equal.* *a.b.c.* 122.

J260–J279. Choice between worth and appearance.

*J260.0.1. *Holy man, small of stature, found on ladder lighting lamps.* His greatness of spirit contradicts appearance. *Espéculo* 313.220.

J262.1. *Noisy things often empty.* Fox finds drum in tree. Makes loud noise in wind, but when fox opens it, drum is empty. *Calila* p. 135.

J280. Quality preferred to quantity.

*J282. *Man troubled by bird song* must choose between ridding house of swallows with superior song and sparrows. Swallows come and go, but sparrows stay all year long. *Lucanor* Ex. 39.

J300–J329. Present values chosen.

J320. Present values preferred to future.

J321.2. *Little fish in net kept* rather than wait for uncertainty of greater catch. *Esopete* pp. 124–25.

J321.4. *Present joys preferred to future ones.* Dying man shows soul all the good things it can enjoy if he remains alive. Pleasures of future less certain. *Lucanor* Ex. 4.

*J321.5. *Three trout.* First sees danger (fishermen) and escapes; second, having delayed, finds escape blocked and plays dead. Third is lazy and is caught. *Calila* p. 149; *Exemplario* 18*r*.

J330–J369. Gains and losses.

J340. Choices: little gain, big loss.

J341.1. *Fox prefers to bear weight of tail* rather than give part of it to ape. *Esopete* p. 66; Tubach 297.

J342. High wages bring expensive living.

J342.2. *Visitor refuses royal offer of wealth* and comfort because king's expenses are equal to income. Knows that in emergency wealth will not be there. *a.b.c.* 155; *Disciplina* 26; Tubach 2917.

J344. What one has is neglected in search for other things.

J344.1. *The monkey and the lost lentil.* Lets fall all others he has in his hand in order to search for one dropped lentil. *Calila* p. 292; *Exemplario* 73*v*.

*J344.3. *Wolf neglects present food* in hope of finding better. *LBA* cc. 766–79; *Esopete* pp. 91–93.

J347. Wealth and glory sacrificed for freedom and virtue.

J347.1. *Man refuses vast wealth* because it would cause him to become covetous. *Castigos* MS A BNM 6559 11.140.

J347.2. *King lays aside crown since it brings too many cares.* *Glosa* 1.1.8.43.

J347.2.1. *Crown accidentally bestowed on knight* refused. Crown falls on head; he will not accept power. *Glosa* 1.1.8.43–44; *Castigos* MS A BNM 6559 (ADMYTE 0 42*v*).

J347.3. *Duke's son chooses exile* and honor over licentious life in father's court. *Castigos* 1.41–42; Tubach 362.

J347.4. *Rich merchant worries constantly* about investments; poor man is free from worry. *Castigos* 7.64.

J347.5. *Man rejects three beds*: marriage (marital bed inhabited by dangerous beasts); royal power (royal bed inhabited by dangerous beasts); wealth (rich person's bed inhabited by dangerous beasts). Chooses a stair that leads to spiritual happiness. *Gatos* 23.

*J347.6. *Young man uses inherited wealth to feed starving populace.* Rebuked, he replies that he had not put it where it could be stolen or destroyed, but rather in a safe place that would benefit kingdom. *a.b.c.* 395; *Disciplina* 29; Tubach 4963.

J350. Small inconvenience, great gain.

*J351.2. *Fox, in danger of being caught, plays dead.* Allows tail to be cut off, teeth to be pulled, ears to be cut off, but will not permit heart to be removed. *LBA* cc. 1412–21; *Lucanor* Ex. 29; Tubach 2176.

J352.2. *Snake suffers indignity of serving frog king as his mount (vehicle).* Eats only those frogs given to him by king. *Calila* p. 248; *Exemplario* 61r.

*J353. *Saint asked why he is so thin and wasted.* Fear of God dries bones just as fire dries wood. *Espéculo* 549.443.

J356. *Less inconvenience found in fighting while tired* than losing all for a little rest. *Lucanor* Ex. 37.

J357. *Priest gives donkey to poor* because worry for its safety distracts him from prayer. *a.b.c.* 327; Tubach 381.

J369. Small inconvenience, large gain: miscellaneous.

*J369.0.1. *King chooses small inconvenience* of personal troubles to great troubles for realm. *Castigos* 57.184.

J369.2. *Ape throws away nut* because of its bitter rind. *Esopete* p. 153; *Gatos* 50; *Espéculo* 57.39; Tubach 3510.

*J369.3. *Hungry man grudgingly invited to eat accepts invitation.* Knows that eating is more important than pride. *Lucanor* Ex. 17.

J370. Choices: important and unimportant work.

J371.1. *Bull refuses to fight goat.* Bull being pursued by lion tries to go into cave. Goat refuses to let him in. Bull must go on, for with lion pursuing, he has no time to fight goat. *Esopete* p. 122.

J372. *"This is Alaquen's addition."* King's invention of flute with extra hole compared with the construction of great mosque. *Lucanor* Ex. 41.

*J373. *Holy man leaves cell each day to go to shore for stones to build cells for others.* Pupil challenges him because of his advanced age and fragility. *Espéculo* 344.244–45.

J390. Choices: kind strangers, unkind relatives.

J391.1. *Lamb chooses her foster mother*, the she-goat. Owes more to her than to her own mother who has deserted her. *Esopete* pp. 50–51.

J400–J459. Choice of associates.

J401. Scarcity of real friends.

*J410.0.2. *Half-friend.* Son tells father he has many friends. Father replies that he only has one half-friend. Tells son to tell his many friends he has killed a man and needs their help. They refuse. He sends him to his half-friend who offers to help him. *Disciplina* 1; *a.b.c.* 18; *Çifar* pp. 7–8; *Esopete* pp. 137–39; *Lucanor* Ex. 48; Tubach 2216.

J410. Association of equals and unequals.

J411.1. *The lion (boar) and the ass.* Ass laughs at lion. Lion does not care to dirty his teeth to bite him. *Esopete* p. 36; Tubach 3060.

J411.3.1. *Noble poets refuse to associate with poet of lowly lineage.* Rebuked by king. *a.b.c.* 183; *Disciplina* 3; Tubach 3829.

J411.4. *Peasant ashamed of being thrown off by ass.* Shameful to be thrown by such a creature. *Esopete* pp. 24–25.

J411.5. *Wolf tries to make friends with lion.* Killed. *Esopete* pp. 85–86.

*J411.5.1. *Pig tries to make friends with sheep.* Is carried off. *Esopete* pp. 85–86.

J413. Unprofitable association of unequals.

*J413.2. *Alexander the Great* was raised with a rascal and learned to behave like him. *Espéculo* 531.420.

J420. Association of strong and weak.

J425. Weak fear company of strong.

J425.1. *Earthen and brazen pots in river.* Brazen pot thinks they should stay together for company. Earthen pot, however, fears approach of brazen pot. *Esopete* p. 122.

J426.1. *Association of rat with cat ceases as soon as mutual danger has passed.* Mouse helps wild cat escape from snares in such a way that escape is possible. *Esopete* p. 38; *Calila* p. 267; *Exemplario* 67v.

J440. Association of young and old.

J441.1. *Old ox yoked with young ox.* Thus kept in order. *Esopete* pp. 64–65.

J445.1. *Foolish youth* in love with ugly old woman. Does not see her flaws. *Gatos* 8; *Esopete* p. 64; Tubach 2454.

J450. Association of the good and the evil.

J451. Contagiousness of bad company.

*J451.1.1. *Weasel caught with mice and killed* in spite of pleas. *Esopete* p. 54; Tubach 5228.

J451.2. *Stork killed along with cranes.* Ill-advised association ends fatally. *Esopete* p. 111.

*J451.2.1. *Cricket caught among locusts.* *Esopete* pp. 19–20.

*J451.3.1. *Contagiousness of bad company.* Two scholars in an inn; arrested along with other customers. *a.b.c.* 349 (not in Paris MS); *Disciplina* 7; Tubach 2431.

J452. *Bad associates bring death to bishop.* Lawyer lost his soul for him; doctor lost his life. *a.b.c.* 160; Tubach 2999.

*J453. *Appearance of associating with women in brothel damages reputation of good man.* Pious man innocently in alley of whores criticized. *Lucanor* Ex. 46.

J460. Unnecessary choices.

J461. Senseless debate of the mutually useful.

J461.1. *The belly and the members.* Debate as to their usefulness. All mutually useful. *Esopete* p. 66; Tubach 570.

J466. Senseless debate about usefulness.

J466.2. *Senseless debate.* Which is the greater: St. John the Baptist or St. John the Evangelist. Saints appear in dreams of debaters urging them to make peace. *a.b.c.* 57; Tubach 2829.

*J466.3. *Senseless debate.* Which is the most important: hearing mass or hearing sermons. Kings of France and England dispute. *Espéculo* 33.22.

J480. Other choices.

J482.1. *Widow refuses second marriage.* If husband is good, she will fear to lose him; if bad, she will repent. *a.b.c.* 368; Tubach 3180.

J482.2.2. *Father chooses poor wise man* over rich fool for daughter's husband. *Castigos* MS A BNM 6559 15.122 (ADMYTE 0 58v); Tubach 1444.

J482.3. *Young man advised to choose wife* whose mother and grandmother were chaste. *a.b.c.* 386 (not in Paris MS); Tubach 955.

J485. *Three sins of the hermit.* Given choice of covetousness, lust, or drunkenness. Chooses drunkenness, and cannot avoid committing the others. *a.b.c.* 127; *LBA* cc. 529–43; *Espéculo* 199.139; Tubach 1816; *Apolonio* cc. 54–55; cf. Tubach 2569, 4130.

*J485.1. *Three choices of holy man.* Read religious books; give them to others to read; sell them to give proceeds to poor. Saint says fourth choice is not to own anything. *Espéculo* 476.376.

J495. *Monk chooses contemplative* solitary life to avoid sin. *a.b.c.* 82.

J500–J599. Prudence and discretion.

J512. Animal should not try to change nature.

J512.6. *Crow tries to imitate partridge's (dove's) walk.* Only spoils its own. *Calila* p. 304; *Exemplario* 78r.

*J512.16. *Daw tried to imitate eagle.* Attempts to carry off lamb. Fails. *Esopete* p. 109.

J514. One should not be too greedy.

J514.1. *Kite tries to carry off so many partridges* that he drops them all (that an archer shoots him easily). *Gatos* 39; *Espéculo* 17.12; Tubach 3608.

J514.2. *Wolf tries to eat bowstring.* Finds archer, boar, and stag dead. Decides to save meat and eat only the bowstring. Bow hits him in head and kills him. *Calila* p. 212; *Exemplario* 46v.

J514.4. *Greedy pig looks up into tree* waiting for fruit thrown to him by ape. This causes his death. *Sendebar* Day 5, Tale 11.

J552. Intemperate pugnacity.

J552.3. *Serpent (weasel)* tries to bite a file. *Esopete* p. 65.

J557. Intemperance in undertaking labor.

J557.1.1. *True penance even for a day is effective.* Man counseled that forty days, even three days might be excessive. *a.b.c.* 290, 296 (not in Paris MS).

*J557.2. *Two travelers carry unequal burdens.* One adds to his burden and dies. The other lightens his load and survives. *a.b.c.* 260 (not in Paris MS).

J565. Intemperance in fasting.

*J565.2. *Young woman devoted to Virgin Mary* takes no food for a month and dies. *Cantigas* 188.

J570. Wisdom of deliberation.

J571.4.2. *Master, when angry,* will not punish steward who has ruined him for fear that punishment would be excessive. *a.b.c.* 219, 220, 150 (not in Paris MS) text not given, only title ("Iracundus non debet modo aliquando liberare"); Tubach 3991.

*J571.5.1. *Avoid hasty judgement.* Wife counsels king to delay killing all members of his court because of a dream. He may regret his action. *Calila* p. 280.

*J571.6.1. *Judge not lest you be judged.* Abbot admonished by angel not to judge sins of monks. *a.b.c.* 226.

*J571.6.2. *Judge not.* Sinner may have confessed and repented; accusation may not be true. *a.b.c.* 227, 228.

J572.1. *Bravest know how to wait.* Three men are pursued in battle. First throws self on enemies; second waits a little; third does not fight until the enemy begins. Third one is bravest. *Lucanor* Ex. 15.

J580. Wisdom of caution.

J581.2. *Lovers quarrel about means of escaping* without being caught by husband. Escape route not as described. They are caught by returning husband. *Calila* pp. 111–12.

J581.3. *Monk's enemies quarrel* and thus save him. Thief wants to steal his cow; devil wants to capture his soul. They quarrel over precedence and he awakens. *Calila* p. 239; *Exemplario* 56v; Tubach 4787.

J600–J799. Forethought.
J610. Forethought in conflict with others.
J613. Wise fear of the weak for the strong.

J613.1. *Frogs fear increase of sun's power* (through marriage) will dry up their puddles. *Esopete* p. 35; Tubach 4677.

J620. Forethought in prevention of other's plans.
J621. Destruction of enemy's weapons.

J621.1. *The swallow and the hemp-seeds.* Birds to eat seeds. Heedless birds are caught in nets made from hemp grown from seeds. Swallow departs and makes nest in safety of human dwellings. *Esopete* p. 39; *Lucanor* Ex. 6; *LBA* cc. 745–54; Tubach 4686.

*J621.1.2. *Trees not to supply wood for woodman's axe handle.* *Esopete* p. 65; Tubach 444.

J624. Uniting against a common enemy.

J624.1. *Mountain goats butting each other* shed blood. Fox laps up spilled blood and is killed by goats. *Calila* p. 138; *Exemplario* 14r.

J624.3. *Enemy brothers unite* to fight a common enemy when outsider begins to insult one of them. *a.b.c.* 311; Tubach 714.

*J624.4. *Horses, who had previously been enemies,* unite when their owners turn them over to lion, a common enemy. *Lucanor* Ex. 9.

J634. King takes measures against assassination.

J634.1. *King, to avoid possible assassination,* singes beard rather than have barber shave him. *Castigos* MS A BNM 6559 25.141 (ADMYTE 0 84*v*); *Glosa* 1.1.6.32.

*J634.1.1. *King, to avoid possible assassination,* has queen's quarters searched before entering. *Castigos* MS A BNM 6559 25.141 (ADMYTE 0 84*v*); *Glosa* 1.1.6.32–33.

J640. Avoidance of other's power.

J642.2. *Traitor convinces king (Rodrigo) to turn swords into plowshares.* Enemy prevails. *Glosa* 2.2.19.29.

J643. Care against future tyranny.

J643.1. *Frogs demand a live king.* King Log. Jupiter has given them a log, but they find him too quiet. He then gives them a stork who eats them all. *Esopete* p. 49; *LBA* cc. 199–206; Tubach 2221; cf. Tubach 292 (ants).

*J643.2.1. *Hawk eats doves* who have elected him king. *Esopete* pp. 49–50; cf. Tubach 1755, 3554.

J644.1. *Fox sees all tracks going into lion's den but none coming out.* Does not enter and saves self. *Esopete* p. 78; Tubach 2169.

J651. Inattention to danger.

*J651.1.1. *Hawk, engaged in eating nightingale's chicks,* is caught by hunter. *Esopete* pp. 62–63.

J651.2. *Man, inattentive to the danger of drowning,* persists in crossing river overburdened by load of precious stones. Drowns. *Lucanor* Ex. 38.

*J651.3. *Inattention to danger.* Man is perched on branches over stream. Dreaded serpent awaits his fall. Two mice are gnawing his branches. Ignoring peril, he sees a beehive above and eats honey. Branches are eaten through, and he falls into mouth of awaiting serpent. *Calila* p. 120; *Exemplario* 10*v*–11*r*.

*J651.4. *Man, pursued by unicorn,* climbs tree and eats apples, enjoys view. There are poisonous snakes, toads, and other perils at foot. Roots of tree are gnawed, and he falls into serpents' pit. *Gatos* 48; *Barlaam* pp. 113–15; *Espéculo* 379.280; Tubach 5022.

J655. Approaching danger too familiarly.

*J655.3. *Fox laps up blood shed by battling goats.* *Calila* p. 138; *Exemplario* 14*r*.

J656. Avoiding things which are harmful by nature.

J656.1. *Thornbush blamed by fox* for wounding him. He should have known better than to lay hold of something whose nature is to lay hold of others. *Esopete* p. 110.

*J656.2. *Emperor, fearful of lightning,* takes pains to protect palace against it. Goes out hunting on clear day, but storm overtakes him; he is killed by lightning. *Çifar* p. 27.

J657. Care in selecting the creature to carry one.

J657.2. *Tortoise requests flight to see fields and mountains.* Eagle drops him and eats him. *Gatos* 1; *Esopete* p. 119; Tubach 625, 1832.

J657.3. *Crane persuades fish to let him move him from one lake into another,* eats fish. *Calila* p. 143; *Exemplario* 16*r*–16*v*.

J670. Forethought in defenses against others.

J671. Practical and impractical defenses.

J671.1. *Belling the cat.* Mice decide that a bell should be put on cat, but none are willing to tie it on. *Gatos* 55; Tubach 566.

*J673.2. *Prophet unperturbed when surrounded by enemy.* Tells servant that more soldiers are on his side than against him. In morning, forces massed to protect prophet are seen. *a.b.c.* 58.

J680. Forethought in alliances.

J681. Alliances which make both parties vulnerable.

J681.1. *Rat and frog tie paws together to cross stream.* Both carried off by kite. *a.b.c.* 58; *Esopete* pp. 24, 34; *LBA* cc. 407–16; *Gatos* 18; Tubach 3425.

J700–J749. Forethought in provision for life.

J701.2. *King improves kingdom* by making it smaller, stronger, and richer before leaving it to his sons. *a.b.c.* 289; Tubach 2909.

J702. Necessity of work.

J702.2. *King (queen) teaches children to work at all tasks* to prepare them for future needs. *a.b.c.* 325; Tubach 5383.

J710. Forethought in provision for food.

J711. In time of plenty provide for want.

J711.1. *Ant and the lazy grasshopper.* Lazy bird (grasshopper) is put to shame by thrift of industrious bird (ant). In winter he is in distress. *Esopete* p. 79.

*J711.1.1. *Ant and the greedy fly.* Fly bites whom he will and eats best food from tables but only in the summer; in winter he dies while ant is secure from the cold beneath the earth. *Esopete* p. 53; Tubach 2097.

J711.3. *King for a year provides for future.* Knowing that the custom is that he is to be deposed and exiled naked and without food to an island in a year, he has provisions sent to island beforehand. *Lucanor* Ex. 49; *a.b.c.* 366; *Barlaam* pp. 121–23; *Espéculo* 243.163; Tubach 2907.

J711.5. *Industrious ant works always at its harvest to keep it dry.* Brings stored grain out into sun to keep it safe. *Lucanor* Ex. 23; Tubach 265.

J750–J799. Forethought: miscellaneous.

J758. Beware of an interested adviser.

*J758.4. *Beware of interested adviser.* Crow advises eagle to drop snail to break shell. Crow eats meat of snail. *Esopete* p. 37

J800–J849. Adaptability.

J810. Policy in dealing with great.

J811. Wisdom of concession to power.

J811.1. *The lion's share.* Wolf divides booty unevenly giving entrails to ailing lion. Lion kills wolf. Fox then divides: gives lion meat and takes bones. *LBA* cc. 82–88; *Gatos* 15; *Espéculo* 534.422; Tubach 3069.

J811.1.1. *Lion divides the booty.* Best part goes to himself as king of beasts; second, as strongest; third, as most valiant; fourth: "touch it if you dare." *Esopete* p. 35.

*J811.2.1. *Lion, having broken vow of abstinence* from meat, asks courtiers if his breath smells bad. Those who say yes, he kills. Monkey praises its fragrance and survives. *Esopete* p. 67; cf. Tubach 2205.

J811.4. *Ruler angered by evil spoken about him* is placated by gentle explanation that they were spoken when drunk. *a.b.c.* 419.

*J811.5. *Ruler told he forgets nothing, except injuries.* Must learn to pardon injuries. *Castigos* MS A BNM 6559 31.148 (ADMYTE 0 96r); *Glosa* 1.2.14.134.

J815. Unpleasant truths must be withheld from the great.

J815.1. *Liar rewarded by ape-king.* King of apes asks visitors how they like his children (courtiers). Truthful visitor tells that they are very ugly and is punished. Liar praises their beauty and receives reward. *Esopete* p. 77; *Gatos* 28; Tubach 304.

J816. Tact in reproving the great.

J816.4. *Woman tactfully restrains amorous king.* Sendebar Day 1, Tale 1; *Lucanor* Ex. 50; Tubach 954.

*J816.5. *King's mother (lion's mother)* urges him not to kill falsely accused counselor (fasting jackal). *Calila* p. 311.

*J816.6. *Conqueror's mother convinces him to be merciful to enemy.* *Glosa* 2.2.4.139.

J817. *A soft answer turns away wrath.* Captives of Romans tells them that merciful treatment will result in peace. *a.b.c.* 289 (not in Paris MS); Tubach 4127.

*J817.4. *Pagan priest beats monk* who had addressed him rudely but admires his teacher who treats him respectfully. *a.b.c.* 218; Tubach 1237.

*J817.5. *Courtier gives king chance to exculpate self* by relating tale of farmer frightened by lion's paw prints. King understands and excuses himself from blame answering that lion may have been on land but had not hurt anyone. *Sendebar* Day 1, Tale 1.

J830. Adaptability to overpowering force.

J832. *Reeds bend before wind (flood).* Save themselves while oak is uprooted. *Esopete* p. 80.

*J836. *Courtier pretends he will join king in retreat* to leave the court and live in the wilderness. *a.b.c.* 75, 215 (not in Paris MS); *Barlaam* pp. 25–29; *Lucanor* Ex. 1.

J850–J899. Consolation in misfortune.

J860. Consolation by a trifle.

J861.1. *Consoled by a drop of honey.* Man in pit, precariously supported by branches being gnawed by rodents, surrounded by perils, comforts self eating honey from hive. *Calila* p. 120; *Exemplario* 10v–11r.

J869.1. *Doves (partridges) in net* console themselves because they think trapper's tears are from pity for them. *Esopete* pp. 76–77; *Lucanor* Ex. 13; Tubach 1773, 3606.

J870. Consolation by pretending that one does not want the thing one cannot have.

J871. *The fox and the sour grapes.* Pretends that the grapes he cannot reach are sour. *Esopete* p. 75.

J880. Consolation by thought of others worse placed.

J881.1. *More timid than the hare.* Hares take heart when they see that frogs are more timid than they. *Esopete* p. 51.

J883.1. *Poor man sadly reduced to eating grain* usually fed to cattle is consoled by seeing other man following him eating his discarded husks. *Lucanor* Ex. 10.

J893. Consolation: spiritual recompense for temporal misfortune.

J893.1. *Consolation.* Saint tells blind man that even flies have eyes but that only man has eyes of the soul. *a.b.c.* 63.

*J893.1.2. *Blind woman consoled.* Sight is occasion of sin. *a.b.c.* 63; Tubach 1950.

*J893.2. *Sick man denied cure.* Told that sickness is necessary to cleanse soul. *Espéculo* 320.224.

*J893.3. *Sick man denied cure.* Rust is to iron as sickness is to humankind. Heat burns it away. *Espéculo* 321.224.

*J893.4. *Saint prays that arrow wound not be healed.* Pain will strengthen him spiritually. *Espéculo* 323.225.

*J893.5. *Dying man asks friends not to pray for cure but for a good end.* Better to suffer here than in afterlife. *Espéculo* 324.225.

*J893.6. *Man who fell ill every year* laments when one year he does not. Fears that God has forgotten him. *Espéculo* 325.225–26.

*J893.7. *Man whose three companions fall ill* takes care of them. Laments his own good health because God had forgotten him. *Espéculo* 326.226.

J893.8. *Man feels closer to God when ill than when well.* Cleric will pray that he not be cured. *Espéculo* 327.226.

J900–J999. Humility.

J910. Humility of the great.

*J911.2. *Friar fasted for seventy weeks to gain understanding.* Failed and went to ask for help of other friar. Angel praised his acknowledgment of ignorance. *Espéculo* 314.220.

J912. Wise man humble in death.

J912.1. *Dying king (sultan) orders that shroud be displayed* to public. It is all he will take with him. *a.b.c.* 121; *Espéculo* 386.283; Tubach 4355.

J912.2. *King accepts offer of monument* for his death as reminder of his mortality and as lesson to others. *a.b.c.* 294.

J912.3. *Rich man (king) humbled by realization he cannot take wealth with him.* He laments the lack of servant after death but learns that he can lean on God. *Espéculo* 388.284.

*J912.3.1. *Rich man (usurer) ordered that one-third of wealth be buried with him.* Devils seen tossing gold in cadaver's throat. *a.b.c.* 123; Tubach 5039.

*J912.3.2. *King declares his love for Jesus* upon receiving Host at moment of death. *Espéculo* 31.21.

*J912.4.1. *Great king says: "Many call me king of great armies. I say I am king of dust."* *Espéculo* 305.214–17.

*J913.1. *Humble man becomes king.* Falls ill because of change of diet. Wise man advises he return to simple foods. *a.b.c.* 81; Tubach 3843.

*J913.2. *King unable to protect self from fly.* Even kings are unable to prevail against all. *Espéculo* 312.219–20.

J914.1. *King David dances with common youths before the Ark of the Covenant* to humble himself and please God. *Castigos* MS A BNM 6559 16.127 (ADMYTE 0 66v).

*J914.2. *King shows humility.* Offers drink to holy man before self. Holy man humbly serves his chaplain before himself. *Espéculo* 225.152.

*J914.3. *Holy father removes clothes and bathes self and clothes in river.* Shows humility in face of grand receptions planned for him. *Espéculo* 311.219.

*J914.4. *St. John Patriarch* used clay drinking vessels to avoid arrogance. *Espéculo* 383.282.

*J914.5. *On day man is elected emperor, stonemason brings three kinds of marble.* Must choose stone for tomb. *Espéculo* 384.282.

J914.6. *King (Xerxes) weeps,* knows he will be dead in 100 years. *Castigos* MS A BNM 6559 (ADMYTE 0 88v).

J915. *King of humble lineage cannot be flattered.* Will not permit it. *a.b.c.* 10; Tubach 2906.

J916. *Abbot warned of official visit* dresses as a beggar. Avoids vainglory. *a.b.c.* 5; Tubach 13.

*J916.1. *Precentor refuses to accept praise for wise words.* *a.b.c.* 9.

J921. *Noble and ugly holy man embraces man who calls him ugly* saying he loves those who see him as he really is. *a.b.c.* 320; Tubach 5016.

*J922. *Humble abbot covers his face* to hide such a worldly thing from people. *a.b.c.* 63.

*J922.1. *Noble man gives up costly garments when enters religious order.* Better to save soul in vile garments than to be damned in fine silk. *Espéculo* 427.325.

J950. Presumption of the lowly.

J951.1. *Ass in lion's skin unmasked* when he raises his voice (when ears are seen projecting from skin). *Esopete* p. 120; *Gatos* 22; Tubach 386.

J951.2. *Crow (jay) in peacock's (pigeon's) feathers unmasked.* *Esopete* p. 53; *LBA* cc. 285–90; Tubach 1360.

J951.4. *Weasel paints self (dusts self with flour)* to deceive mice. *Esopete* p. 75.

*J951.6. *Ram in mastiff's skin unmasked* when thorns tear skin. *Esopete* p. 98.

J952. Lowly animal tries to move among its superiors.

*J952.6. *Frog attempts to be a great physician.* Shamed by fox. *Esopete* p. 120; Tubach 1692.

*J952.7. *Two smaller rams ridicule large ram in flight from danger* which they do not see. *Esopete* p. 78.

J953. Self-deception of the lowly.

J953.1. *Dog proud of his clog.* Thinks it is a decoration. *Esopete* pp. 120–21.

*J953.10.1.1. *Flea descends from camel's back* and tells him he can rest. Camel replies that flea's weight made no difference. *Esopete* p. 79.

*J953.19. *Mule scornful of fly that threatens to bite him.* He will hasten but only in fear of master's whip. *Esopete* p. 53.

*J953.20. *Ass thinks all animals fear him because hares flee when he brays.* Lion humbles him. *Esopete* p. 78; cf. Tubach 386.

J954. Foolish boast of ancestry by lowly.

J954.1. *Mule boasts of grandfather who was war-horse.* Refuses to acknowledge father who was an ass. *a.b.c.* 199; *Disciplina* 4; Tubach 3432, 3829.

J955. Lowly tries in vain to be greater than it is.

J955.1. *Frog in vain tries to be as big as an ox.* Bursts. *Esopete* p. 54; Tubach 2219.

J956. *Ambitious branch chosen as king of trees.* Vine and fig tree have refused. *Esopete* p. 1; Tubach 751.

J1000–J1099. Other aspects of wisdom.

J1010. Value of industry.

*J1012. *King spends nights in study.* Invents self-filling lamp to study through the night without interruption. *Glosa* 1.2.7.96–97; *Castigos* MS A BNM 6559 15.121 (ADMYTE 0 58r).

J1020. Strength in unity.

J1022. *Fight of lions and bulls.* Lion (here wolf) succeeds only when bulls are separated. *Esopete* pp. 123–24.

J1024. *Ringdoves (quails) caught in net.* Rise up in a body and escape. They fly to mouse friend of leader who gnaws the net and frees them. *Calila* p. 202; *Exemplario* 41r–42r.

J1025.1. *Cranes, when united defeat all enemies.* When they fight among themselves they are destroyed. *a.b.c.* 60; Tubach 1315.

J1025.2. *Cats unite in battle against wolf.* Each one attacking distinct parts of his body. They destroy wolf. *Calila* p. 343; *Exemplario* 88r.

*J1025.3. *Horses who had previously been enemies unite* when their owners turn them over to lion. *Lucanor* Ex. 9.

*J1025.4. *Deer unite and hunters cannot attack them.* *Espéculo* 102.68; Tubach 1503.

J1030. Self-dependence.

J1032. *Stag found by master when overlooked by servants.* Hides under hay and escapes until master himself comes. *Esopete* p. 67; Tubach 4596.

J1033. *Gardener who plants vegetable tends it best* (why wild plants grow better than tended ones). *Esopete* pp. 9–10.

J1040. Decisiveness of conduct.

J1041.2. *Miller, his son, and the ass.* Miller blamed when he follows his son on foot; when he takes son's place on the ass; when he takes his son behind him; and when he puts son in front of him. *Esopete* pp. 153–54; *Lucanor* Ex. 2; Tubach 382.

J1050. Attention to warnings.

*J1054.1. *Chick disregards mother hen's warning* to stay under her wing. Kite carries him off. *Gatos* 36.

J1060. Miscellaneous aspects of wisdom.

J1061.1. *The cock and the sapphire (pearl).* Prefers a single corn to a peck of pearls. *LBA* cc. 1387–91; *Esopete* p. 33; Tubach 3635.

J1062.1. *Frog as beauty doctor* unable to cure his own ugliness. *Esopete* p. 120; Tubach 1692.

J1063.1. *Mother crab blames children for not walking straight. Esopete* pp. 119–20; Tubach 1311.

J1064. Futility of trying to teach the stupid.

J1064.1. *Bird killed by apes* who will not believe her warning that firefly is not a fire. *Calila* p. 170; *Exemplario* 25r.

*J1064.2. *Swallow unable to convince other birds to eat hempseeds* to prevent humans from using hemp for nets. *LBA* cc. 745–54; *Lucanor* Ex. 6; Tubach 4686.

*J1064.3. *Partridges will not believe warning* that hunter with tears in his eyes intends to capture them. *Lucanor* Ex. 13; *Esopete* pp. 76–77.

J1072. Person to be judged by own qualities, not by clothes.

*J1072.3. *King leaves bathhouse wearing rags.* Not recognized; is mistreated. *Lucanor* Ex. 51.

*J1072.4. *Madman in rich household given master's clothes.* Others cannot distinguish between them. *Espéculo* 40.27.

J1074. Value of silence.

*J1074.1.2. *Value of silence.* Would-be philosopher endures insults from great philosopher. Told he had proved himself by keeping quiet retorted: "I would have known I was a philosopher if you had been silent." *a.b.c.* 408; Tubach 3748.

*J1074.1.3. *Value of silence.* Abbot holds stone in mouth for three years to learn how to be silent. *a.b.c.* 409; *Espéculo* 525.412; Tubach 4627.

*J1074.1.4. *Value of silence.* Bishop answered plea for edification with meaningful silence. *Espéculo* 523.411–12.

*J1074.1.5. *Value of silence.* Monk relies on scriptural verse that warns against misspeaking. *Espéculo* 524.412.

*J1074.3. *Vow of silence* gives man power to see demons and angels carry off departing souls. *a.b.c.* 409.

J1085. Money does not always bring happiness.

J1085.3. *King sees poor man who is far happier than himself. a.b.c.* 350.

J1100–J1699. CLEVERNESS

J1100–J1249. Clever persons and acts.

J1110. Clever persons.

J1114.0.1. *Clever slave.* Maimundus makes clever retorts to master. *Disciplina* 27.89–90; *a.b.c.* 195; Tubach 4288.

*J1114.0.2. *Clever servant* asked how much he could eat. Asks if questioner means his food or the food of another. If another, he would eat as much as possible. *a.b.c.* 195.

J1140. Cleverness in detection of truth.

J1141.14. *Thief of church funds threatened with excommunication.* Returns money and is absolved. *Espéculo* 170.114–15.

J1144. Eaters of stolen food detected.

J1144.1. *Eaters of stolen food* detected by the giving of an emetic. *Esopete* pp. 2–3.

J1150. Cleverness connected with giving of evidence.

J1152. *Witness cannot speak language of accusation: discredited.* Rejected lover taught two parrots in a particular language to accuse mistress of household of infidelity. When tested, the birds know nothing more of the language. *Calila* p. 198; *Exemplario* 38v–39r; cf. Tubach 632, 3147.

J1153.1. *Susanna and the elders.* Prophet Daniel proves that elders had accused her falsely. *Castigos* 9.69; *Glosa* 2.2.6.248; Tubach 4584.

J1154.1. *Parrot (magpie) unable to tell* husband details of wife's infidelity. Wife simulates a rainstorm while cage is covered so that parrot gives husband a false report. *Sendebar* Day 1, Tale 2; *Exemplario* 25v–26v; cf. Tubach 632, 3147.

J1160. Clever pleading.

J1161.1. *The two (three) joint depositors.* Two men entrust money to women; she may pay it only in the presence of both. One comes to her to tell her his partner is dead. She hands over money. Other, still alive, demands his money. Before judge, first one must produce his "dead" partner. Cannot do it. *a.b.c.* 78; *Sendebar* Day 8, Tale 21; Tubach 3353.

J1161.4. *Money in the stick.* Before swearing, the borrower hands a stick containing the borrowed money to the lender. He then swears it has been repaid. *a.b.c.* 234; *Espéculo* 459.358; Tubach 3352.

J1161.9. *Drunk philosopher wagers that he can drink the ocean dry.* Agrees to do so if the others will hold back streams emptying into the ocean. Agreed only to drink the ocean. *Esopete* p. 15.

J1162.4. *Clever pleading.* Youth in court for calling king a fool, proves truth of statement because king allowed himself to be duped by alchemist. *Çifar* pp. 128–29; *Lucanor* Ex. 20; cf. Tubach 89.

*J1162.5. *Lawsuit over property.* Plaintiff sleeps during proceedings; unwilling to see brother's unhappiness. Recovers his property. *Espéculo* 101.67–68.

J1164. *Clever pleading.* Knight haled before king for beating blasphemer. Tells king just as he would fight to protect king's name, so he should fight to protect the name of the King of Kings. *a.b.c.* 53.

J1169. Clever pleading: miscellaneous.

J1169.4. *The ass beheaded.* Alexander vows to sacrifice first thing he meets. It is a man riding an ass. Man pleads that ass preceded him. King amused, man spared. *a.b.c.* 118; Tubach 3289.

J1170. Clever judicial decisions.

J1171.1. *Solomon's judgement: the divided child.* Two women claim child. Judge offers to cut it in two. Real mother refuses. *Castigos* 9.69; Tubach 4466.

J1172.1. *Not the same purse as was lost.* Finder of purse with 100 gold coins and a golden serpent (800 guldens) returns it and asks for reward. To avoid giving reward, owner says there had been two serpents (900 guldens). In court, wise intermediary helps finder. Judge rules that finder may keep purse because it was not the one lost. *a.b.c.* 367; *Disciplina* 17; *Esopete* pp. 141–42; Tubach 874, cf. 4090.

J1172.3. *Ungrateful animal returned to captivity.* A man rescues a serpent (bear) who in return seeks to kill his rescuer. (Snake liberated by shepherd bites him when freed.) Fox as judge advises the man to put the serpent back into captivity. *Esopete* pp. 86–87; *a.b.c.* 312; *Disciplina* 5; Tubach 4254, 4262.

*J1172.3.3. *Clever judge.* Suspects that miscreant is hidden in hollow tree. Orders that fire be set to smoke him out. *Calila* p. 171; *Exemplario* 26v–27r; Tubach 4954.

J1174.1. *Youth to be killed for kissing duke's daughter* (pleads his love for her). Duke says: "If we kill those who love us, what shall we do with those who hate us?" Same prince forgives member of court who spat at him. *a.b.c.* 67.

J1176.2. *Measuring the dregs.* Some full and some half-full oil casks left with man by landlord, who accuses him of theft. Fraud detected by measuring the dregs. Half-full casks's dregs were measurably less than full casks's. *a.b.c.* 390; *Disciplina* 16; *Esopete* pp. 140–41; *Glosa* 3.2.21.197–98; Tubach 3524.

J1179. Clever judicial judgements: miscellaneous.

*J1179.1.1. *Lawsuit: neither plaintiff awarded judgement.* Both fox and wolf suspect and legally unable to bring complaint. *Esopete* p. 54.

*J1179.5.1. *Flea pleads innocence.* When he bites man he is only following rules of nature. *Esopete* p. 113; Tubach 2081.

J1179.13. *Cardinal's clever decision.* The monks who arise earliest may sound bells for matins. There had been a great argument between clerics associated with the church and monks associated with a religious order. *Lucanor* Ex. 31.

J1180. Clever means of avoiding legal punishment.

*J1181.4. *Man sentenced to be hanged* is permitted to choose tree for his hanging. Cannot find suitable tree. *a.b.c.* 130; Tubach 4790.

*J1181.5. *Sentenced to have eyes taken out,* asked if he could select the instrument (*el clavo*). Favor granted, but then he could not find a nail that suited him. *a.b.c.* 151; Tubach 1947.

*J1189.4. *Judge, forced to sentence own son* to the loss of both eyes as punishment for adultery, offers one of his own so that law is satisfied. *a.b.c.* 224; *Glosa* 1.2.11.113–14; Tubach 1944.

*J1189.5. *Execution escaped by false confession* by friend (father's friend). *Esopete* pp. 137–39.

J1210–J1229. Clever person puts another out of countenance.

*J1215.2. *"Eat spiritual food,"* says monk to brother who criticizes working at earthly pursuits like gardening. Will not give him "earthly" food. *a.b.c.* 425; Tubach 5386.

J1217.2. *Simple man puts philosopher out of countenance* by telling him that wisdom came before learning. *a.b.c.* 392.

*J1217.3. *Worldly man asks his brother, a monk, for money.* Cannot ask other brother who is recently dead because he is dead to world. Monk responds he is even more dead to world. *Espéculo* 477.376–77.

*J1217.4. *Saint's father leaves him large inheritance.* Saint says it is impossible because he died (withdrew from world) before his father. *Espéculo* 478.377.

J1250–J1499. Clever verbal retorts (repartee).

J1260. Repartee based on church or clergy.

*J1261.4.1. *Moribund refuses sacrament* because those offering it are not his peers. *a.b.c.* 153.

*J1261.11. *Celibate acquiesces passively to widow's sexual advances.* Claims to be free of guilt because she was active not he. *Esopete* p. 165.

*J1261.12. *Bishop abstains from eating meat.* Parishioner questions his sincerity: "You are eating my flesh and blood by stealing the cow that feeds me." *Espéculo* 68.46–47.

*J1261.13. *Saint, served meat, tells bishop he has not eaten dead animals since he entered religious life.* Bishop responds: "Since I entered religious life, I have not slept, nor have I permitted anyone who complained about me to sleep." *Espéculo* 504.397.

J1262.4. Levity regarding biblical passages.

*J1262.3.1. *"Give and you shall be given."* Monks ask that two servants who had been dismissed be returned to restore prosperity. They are named "Give" (*Dad*) and "Given" (*Dado*). *Espéculo* 241.162.

J1262.5.2. *Parishioner hears preacher say that alms are returned "100 to 1."* Gives cow expecting to receive 100. *a.b.c.* 139; Tubach 176, 4089.

*J1262.5.3. *Saintly man's steward dispensed five coins instead of ten to beggar.* Because God returns hundredfold, steward must repay five hundred coins. *a.b.c.* 140; Tubach 176, 4089.

*J1262.5.3.1. *Merchant gives wealth to God because he will be rewarded hundredfold.* Digs and finds gold worth three hundred silver pounds. *Espéculo* 244.164.

J1262.6. *"You don't blame a toolmaker for making all manner of tools,* both harmful and helpful, so why blame God for making bad beasts as well as good ones?" *a.b.c.* 56.

*J1262.7.1. *"Think about Judgement Day just as criminal thinks about execution day,"* says abbot to monks. *a.b.c.* 70; *Espéculo* 194.134–35; Tubach 1229.

*J1262.10. *"If you cannot see the soul in the living man,* how can you expect to see it in the dead body?" says wise man to atheist. *a.b.c.* 24.

J1263. Repartee concerning clerical abuses.

*J1263.1.5. *Devil sends archbishop letter* saying that all ignorant, stupid priests had been sent him by devil. *a.b.c.* 196.

*J1263.1.6. *Devil leaves message on scholar's hand.* Greets church officials whose behavior sends so many to inferno by example. *Espéculo* 470.371.

*J1263.1.7. *Devil marks messenger's face.* Carries message of clerical ignorance. Marking cleansed by holy water. *a.b.c.* 196; Tubach 3032.

J1263.4. Repartee concerning clerical luxury.

J1263.4.2. *Man calls St. Peter and St. Paul fools* for enduring poverty if rich abbots can reach heaven too. *a.b.c.* 152; *Espéculo* 472.371–72; Tubach 3716.

*J1263.5.4. *Saintly man's steward told to give beggar three coins, holds one back*; then charitable men give them two hundred coins. Saint says: "Accept these coins, but know that you took a hundred from me when you held back one from beggar." *a.b.c.* 141; *Espéculo* 240.161.

J1269. Repartee based on church or clergy: miscellaneous.

*J1269.14. *Holy man sees sinner.* "He today, I tomorrow." *a.b.c.* 228.

J1269.16. *"Have you given up as much as I?"* Previously wealthy monk, criticized for sleeping in comfortable bed, responds. *a.b.c.* 258; Tubach 539.

J1280. Repartee with ruler (judge, etc.).

J1281. *Man cries out "Tyrant!"* He is answered: "If I were a tyrant, you would not say so." *a.b.c.* 346; *Castigos* MS A BNM 6559 31.147 (ADMYTE 0 96v); *Glosa* 1.2.14.133; Tubach 5011.

*J1281.1. *Caesar proves he is no tyrant* by letting courtiers insult him for his baldness, his humble lineage. *a.b.c.* 346; *Glosa* 1.2.14.132–33; *Castigos* MS A BNM 6559 31.148 (ADMYTE 0 95r).

*J1281.1.2. *Empress offers judge great honors* if he will make false judgement. He replies: "I do not want honors at the price of the truth." *Espéculo* 396.292.

*J1281.2. *King retorts to insulting ambassador* who had said he should be hanged. He tells him he is better than those who sent him to insult him. *a.b.c.* 345; *Castigos* MS A BNM 6559 31.148 (ADMYTE 0 96r).

*J1281.3. *"Friend, if I am a dwarf, then I have need of good stilts,"* responds Julius Caesar to a jeerer who thought to insult him. *Castigos* MS A BNM 6559 13.118, 82.215 (ADMYTE 0 96v); *Glosa* 2.1.13.65.

*J1281.3.1. *Caesar hears insult without anger.* Said to be baker's son. *Castigos* MS A BNM 6559.31.147 (ADMYTE 0 95r); *Glosa* 1.2.14.133.

*J1281.3.2. *Scipio told he is no warrior.* "My mother bore me to be emperor, not warrior." *Castigos* MS A BNM 6559 31.147 (ADMYTE 0 96r); *Glosa* 1.2.14.133.

*J1281.3.3. *Vespasian told that foxes can shed coat but not heart.* The emperor can shed neither. "To such men we owe laughter, to ourselves correction and to evil ones punishment." *Castigos* MS A BNM 6559 31.147 (ADMYTE 0 96r); *Glosa* 1.2.14.133.

*J1281.4. *"Move along where the king won't hear you."* King, sitting behind curtain, hears men reviling him. Lets them know he has heard. *a.b.c.* 341; *Castigos* MS A BNM 6559 31.147 (ADMYTE 0 95v); *Glosa* 1.2.14.133–34; Tubach 2908.

*J1281.5. *Alexander asks desert philosophers what gift he might give them.* They reply "Immortality." He, as a mortal cannot grant them this. They reply: "If you are mortal, why do you do so many evil things?" *Espéculo* 385.282–83.

*J1281.6. *"I would rather that you smelled of other things than unguents and scents."* Ruler with sensitive nose denies important post to noble youth. *a.b.c.* 323.

*J1281.7. *King invites enemy to dinner.* Serves him dish prepared with flesh of guest's sons. Asked if meal was good, says: "In the king's house all meals are pleasing." *Castigos* MS A BNM 6559 13.118 (ADMYTE 0 52v).

J1281.8. *Flatterers tell Alexander he is son of Jupiter.* He replies: "This arrow wound proves I am mortal." *Castigos* MS A BNM 6559 (ADMYTE 0 111r).

*J1283.1. *Alexander and gift.* Gave man a city. Man protested he was unworthy. "If you do not merit it, then it is not fitting for me to give it to you." *a.b.c.* 97; *Castigos* MS A BNM 6559 14.119; *Glosa* 1.2.17.155; *Çifar* p. 99; cf. Tubach 100.

*J1283.2. *King excuses self from giving money to friend.* Friend first asks for large amount, and king tells him it is too much for a friend to ask. When man asks for lesser amount, king tells him it is a sum not fitting for a king. *a.b.c.* 321; *Çifar* p. 99.

J1289.10. *King will destroy city.* Annoyed by plea of philosopher, says he will do nothing philosopher asks. Philosopher asks him to destroy city. City is saved. *a.b.c.* 233; Tubach 105.

*J1289.10.1. *Noble will destroy monastery if son does not return to secular life.* Son agrees, provided that father will agree to change law that sons and fathers must meet the same end. Father enters monastery. *Espéculo* 387.283–84; cf. Tubach 4183.

*J1289.21. *Caesar offers to send lawyer* to defend veteran soldier. Soldier says: "When I was your soldier I fought for you, I did not send in a substitute." Caesar appears in court for him. *a.b.c.* 319; Tubach 4181.

*J1289.22. *Emperor asks pirate*: "Why are you a pirate?" Responds: "I am only doing what you do on a larger scale." *a.b.c.* 42; *Castigos* MS A BNM 6559 31.137 (ADMYTE 0 95r); *Glosa* 1.2.10.110–11; Tubach 113.

*J1289.23. *Only booty he had earned from African military campaign* was his nickname, says Scipio Africanus when accused of having profited from African campaign. *a.b.c.* 255; *Glosa* 1.1.7.38.

*J1289.24. *Knight cuts horseshoe with sword.* Duke demands knight's sword but is unable to cut even a nail with it. Knight says: "Sir, I gave you the sword, not the strong arm." *Espéculo* 560.453–54; Tubach 4694.

*J1289.25. *"My tongue does not belong to you,"* retorts condemned man to king as he bites it out and flings it at king. *Castigos* MS A BNM 6559 31.148 (ADMYTE 0 96r); *Glosa* 1.2.14.134; cf. Tubach 4911.

J1289.26. *Physician threatened with death* by tyrant. "When you harm God's creatures, remember that only God can cure you." *a.b.c.* 373.

*J1289.27. *Theodosius condemned to be crucified.* "It does not frighten me. I can die on earth or up in the air." *Glosa* 1.2.14.134; *Castigos* MS A BNM 6559 31.148–49 (ADMYTE 0 95v).

J1310. Repartee concerning wine.

*J1319.2. *Mouse in wine vat.* Promises cat anything if he will save him. Breaks promise, telling cat, "I was drunk when I promised." *Gatos* 56; Tubach 3426.

J1320. Repartee concerning drunkenness.

*J1320.0.1. *Drunken man taunts bishop with invitation to eat* on fast day. Bishop replies: "You will dine today in hell." Man dies. *Espéculo* 10.8.

*J1325. *Why English are short lived.* Drink more in four years than others do in twenty (rather than eat). Teacher explains: "God did not want to deprive others of sustenance so deprived them of food." *Espéculo* 196.137.

J1340. Retorts from hungry persons.

J1341.5. *Hungry apprentice attracts master's attention* by saying he is insane. *a.b.c.* 102; *Disciplina* 20.76–78; *Esopete* pp. 151–52; Tubach 2753.

J1369. Rude retorts: miscellaneous.

*J1369.6. *"Cursed be the words of your mouth,"* retorts precentor to false flatterer who has said "blessed be the words of your mouth." *a.b.c.* 9; Tubach 2078.

J1370. Cynical retorts concerning honesty.

*J1374. *Philosopher sees bailiffs leading thief to gallows.* He says: "I see greatest thieves leading a lesser one to the gallows." *Espéculo* 66.46.

J1390. Retorts concerning thefts.

*J1397.1. *Owner of sheep rebukes neighbor.* Man asks neighbor what happened to sheep when he chased the wolf that had stolen it. Neighbor says he caught wolf but ate the sheep instead of returning it to owner who says: "You are as bad as the wolf." *Çifar* p. 60.

J1420. Animals retort concerning danger.

J1421. *Peace among the animals* (Peace fable). Fox tries to beguile cock by reporting a new law establishing peace among animals. Dogs appear; the fox flees. "The dogs have not yet heard of the new law." *Esopete* pp. 63–64; Tubach 3629.

J1430. Repartee concerning doctors and patients.

*J1432.1. *"It hurts where you touch me,"* says sick ass to wolf as his doctor. *Esopete* p. 78.

J1434. *Strenuous cure for madness.* Doctor throws patient into a pit of water. Servant warns hunter (a person who engages in a mad activity) to flee before master throws him into the pit also. *Esopete* p. 152.

*J1434.1. *"I am well. Take me out of the pit."* So says patient put in pit of water as cure for insanity. *Esopete* p. 152.

J1440. Repartee: miscellaneous.

*J1440.1. *Man considering taking holy orders* told to be like an ass: obedient. *a.b.c.* 374; Tubach 390.

J1442.1. *Cynic wants sunlight* (Socrates to royal hunters) or (Alexander to Diogenes): "What can we do for you?" "Get out of my sunlight. Don't take away from me what you can't give me." *a.b.c.* 348, 427; Tubach 1673.

J1442.1.1. Plato says he is ruler's superior because he is guided by reason and ruler is guided by will. *a.b.c.* 259.

*J1442.14. "I know where my shoe pinches," says man rebuked for leaving his wife whom all regard as good. *a.b.c.* 371 (not in Paris MS); Tubach 4339.

*J1442.15. "Thanks for your kind words, but may your deceitful eyes go blind." So says wolf to shepherd who hid him from hunter but winked in hunter's direction to betray him. *Esopete* p. 75.

J1454. The lion and the statue. A man points out the statue to show the supremacy of man. The lion: "If it had been a lion sculptor, the lion would have been standing over the man." *Esopete* pp. 78–79.

J1473.1. The greedy dreamer. Shepherd dreams he is offered a price for his sheep. In dream demands an even higher one. Wakes, finds he was dreaming and is willing to accept the lower one. *Disciplina* 31; Tubach 1788.

*J1476.1. The earthen pot humbled. Rain water: What is your name? Pot: A fine pot made for years of service. River: You shall soon be mud again. *Esopete* p. 128.

J1488. What the bear whispered in his ear. Paid guide climbs tree and leaves traveler to mercy of bear. Traveler feigns death, and the bear sniffs him and leaves. The guide: "What did the bear say to you?" He said, "Never trust a coward like you." *Esopete* pp. 121–22.

*J1489. Evil king finds sentry asleep. Sentry says he was not asleep: "I was thinking that the magpie has as many white feathers as black." Is spared because it is so. Caught again he replies: "I was thinking that the vixen has as many bones in her tail as in her spine." Is spared because it is so. Caught a third time he says: "I was thinking you are the devil's man, and he will come and get you." That day devils come and carry off evil king. *a.b.c.* 114.

J1494.1. Lame knight says he is better soldier. Will stand and fight, not flee. *Glosa* 1.2.13.125.

J1500–J1649. Clever practical retorts.
J1510. The cheater cheated.

*J1510.1. Fraudulent claim by stag made in presence of wolf whose presence intimidates sheep into acknowledging debt. Repayment scheduled for when wolf will not be present. *Esopete* p. 52.

*J1510.2. Usurers cheated. Warrior deposits sand-filled chests with usurers as surety for a loan. *CMC* vv. 80–212.

J1511. A rule must work both ways.

*J1511.9.1. Employer says she has eyes in buttocks to supervise clever slave's actions. He uncovers them while she sleeps. *Esopete* p. 16.

*J1511.21. Envious guest collects all bones from meal and heaps them on plate of favored newcomer, leaving his own plate empty. Calls attention to newcomer's greed. Newcomer retorts: "I have done what is natural. I have eaten the meat and left the bones. My companion has behaved like a dog. He has eaten both meat and bones." *Disciplina* 21.

*J1512.2. *To return the eye to the one-eyed person.* "Let me have your other eye so that I can see whether the one I bring you matches." *Sendebar* Day 8, Tale 22.

J1521. Swindler's plan foiled.

*J1521.1.1. *Peasant kills fox who betrayed wolf* in order to get wolf's food supply. *Esopete* p. 63.

J1522. Rebuke to the stingy.

*J1522.3. *Gemstone merchant hires artisan* to polish stones. Artisan sees stringed instrument. Merchant tells him to play it. End of day, merchant denies him his pay. Answers: "You told me to play it." *Calila* p. 113; *Exemplario* 9r.

J1528. Dream interpretation answered by new interpretations.

*J1528.1. *Malicious interpretation of royal dream* corrected by new interpretation by philosopher. Revised prophecies come true. *Calila* p. 286.

J1530. One absurdity rebukes another.

J1531.2. *The iron-eating mice.* Rogue claims that mice have eaten the iron entrusted to him by dupe. Dupe abducts rogue's son; says that a falcon carried him off. Explains that in land where mice eat iron, falcons can carry off children. Rogue returns iron; dupe returns son. *Calila* p. 175; *Exemplario* 19r; *Esopete* p. 167; cf. K1667.

*J1531.4. *Husband paints lamb on wife's abdomen* to ensure her chastity during his absence. Returns after long absence to find that her lover has repainted it; it is now a full-grown ram. *LBA* cc. 474–87.

*J1539.2.1. *Aesop's master steals pig's foot from pot* to incriminate him. Aesop and master both replace stolen pig's foot in pot. Too many in pot. *Esopete* p. 10.

J1540. Repartee between husband and wife.

J1546. *Woman curious about senate's secret deliberations.* Son (husband) tells her they have decided that each man may have many wives. Gullible woman believes it. *a.b.c.* 394; Tubach 5269.

J1550. Practical retorts: borrowers and lenders.

*J1552.5. *Holy man allows borrowers of bread to repay* what they owe on honor system. Violator who has not ever repaid finds storehouse empty. *a.b.c.* 310; *Espéculo* 233.157–58.

J1565. Inappropriate hospitality repaid.

J1565.1. *Fox and crane invite each other.* Fox serves the food on a flat dish so that the crane cannot eat. Crane serves his food in a bottle. *Esopete* p. 52; Tubach 2170.

J1565.2. *Bees serve honey for dinner to beetles* who eat very little. Beetles invite bees and serve them animal dung. Bees do not eat. *Gatos* 34.

J1566.1. *Philosopher spits in king's beard* because no place in elegant palace is suitable for spitting. *a.b.c.* 188; Tubach 525.

J1577. *Deceptive invitation to a feast.* Vulture invites birds to dinner and eats them (lion and foxes). *Esopete* p. 78; cf. Tubach 2169.

J1580. Practical retorts concerning almsgiving.

*J1580.0.1. *Saint leaves possessions to poor.* Tells his two unmarried sisters: "God who made you will provide for you just as he did for me." *Espéculo* 43.29–30.

*J1592. *Impoverished scholar gives knowledge in form of grammar lesson instead of alms. a.b.c.* 131; Tubach 173.

J1600. Practical retorts: miscellaneous.

*J1600.1. *Who lost the sword?* Man asks sword who lost it. Sword: "What matters is how many men I have lost." *Esopete* p. 79.

J1607. *The testament of the dog.* The owner of a dog has him given a Christian burial. Hearing protests, the bishop thereupon pretends that the dog has left the church a large legacy. *Esopete* pp. 152–53; cf. Tubach 4949.

J1608.1. *Fox asks mule about its identity,* its parentage, its name. Mule says its father wrote information on hoof. Fox sees through trick. *Esopete* p. 85; Tubach 3432.

*J1623.1. *Drunkard cured of seeing double.* Returns home drunk, sees wife and his two children. Accuses her of infidelity because sees four children. Kills her and children. Sober, he kills self. *Espéculo* 198.138.

*J1623.2. *Drunkard returns home.* Demands that wife undergo ordeal by burning metal. She agrees but tells him he must hand her the red-hot poker. Pain restores him to sobriety. *Espéculo* 200.139–40; cf. Tubach 59.

J1634. *To follow the king.* In order to test a favorite, king says he will retire from world and offers him the regency. On advice from philosopher, favorite says that he will accompany king into retirement. *a.b.c.* 215 (not in Paris MS); *Lucanor* Ex. 1; *Barlaam* pp. 25–29.

J1647. *Priest asked to preach short sermon* says, "He who is of God hears his word, therefore you are not of God." *a.b.c.* 362; Tubach 4244.

*J1647.1. *Preacher tells king who is too busy hunting* to hear sermon that sermons are for those who will listen and benefit from them. *Çifar* p. 75.

J1650–J1699. Miscellaneous clever acts.

J1661. Deductions from observations.

*J1661.1.2.2. *Deduction that prince (king's son) is not his.* Sickened by cooked meat. Queen's lover ate only raw meat. *a.b.c.* 175; Tubach 500.

*J1661.1.2.3. *Deduction that king is illegitimate.* His nature is revealed by his behavior. He rewards favorites with bread, therefore he is son of a baker. *a.b.c.* 313; Tubach 500.

J1661.1.5. *Deduction that horse was reared on milk of a she-ass.* Horse is observed to shake ears like an ass. *a.b.c.* 313; Tubach 2611.

J1661.1.6. *Deduction by feeling stone to test value.* Warmth of stone shows that it contains a worm. *a.b.c.* 313; Tubach 5391.

J1662. *Cat's only trick.* She can climb tree to escape hunting dogs, but fox, who brags about knowing many tricks, is captured. *Gatos* 40; *Esopete* pp. 87–88; *Espéculo* 24.16; Tubach 2180.

J1675. Clever dealings with a king.

J1675.0.1. *Knight hailed before king for beating blasphemer.* Tells king just as he would fight to protect king's name, so would he fight to protect the name of the King of Kings. *a.b.c.* 53.

J1700–J2799. FOOLS AND OTHER UNWISE PERSONS
J1700–J1729. Fools (general).
J1730–J1749. Absurd ignorance.

J1733. *Why the pigs shriek.* The sheep does not understand why the pig being carried to slaughter shrieks. *Esopete* p. 11; Tubach 3775.

J1744. Ignorance of sexual relations.

*J1744.2. *Naive new bride compares husband's penis* with that of an ass and finds him wanting. *Esopete* pp. 165–66.

*J1745.1.1. *Absurd ignorance of sex.* Pious maiden (nun) convinced by go-between that God does not see what is done at night. Spends night with go-between's customer. *a.b.c.* 108; Tubach 1436.

*J1745.3. *Foolish young woman sees copulation between youth and ass.* Told he is giving beast sense, she asks for same treatment. *Esopete* p. 24.

*J1745.4. *Sheltered prince shown all forms of human and animal life* for first time was told that young women are devils who deceive men. Asked what he liked best, chose the "devils." *Barlaam* pp. 261–63.

*J1745.5. *Inexperienced young monk (never having seen a woman)* is told that women are goats. Obsessed by what he had seen through window is unable to eat (meat) because he felt so sorry for the poor goat. *a.b.c.* 300.

J1750–J1849. Absurd misunderstandings.
J1750. One animal mistaken for another.

*J1756.2. *Horse thief mistakes lion for horse* and mounts him and rides until daybreak. *Sendebar* Day 6, Tale 14.

J1760. Animal thought to be an object.

J1761.3. *Firefly thought to be a fire.* Bird who tries to keep monkeys from this error is killed by them. *Calila* p. 170.

J1772. One object thought to be another.

*J1772.15. *File thought to be food. Esopete* p. 65.

J1780. Things thought to be devils, ghosts, etc.

*J1781.4. *Man thought to be devil (storm) by lion.* Man rides lion all night, thinking it to be a horse. *Sendebar* Day 6, Tale 14.

J1790. Shadow mistaken for substance.

J1791.3. *Diving for cheese.* Animal sees moon reflected in water and thinking it cheese, dives for it. *Disciplina* 23; *a.b.c.* 363; Tubach 1699.

J1791.4. *Dog drops meat (cheese) for the reflection.* Crossing a stream with meat in his mouth, he sees his reflection; thinking it another dog with meat, he dives for it and loses his meat. *Esopete* p. 34; *Exemplario* 9v; *Calila* p. 114; *LBA* cc. 226–29; *Espéculo* 41.a.28; Tubach 1699.

J1791.8. *Duck dives for star, thinking it is fish.* The next day when she sees fish, she lets it escape. *Calila* p. 155.

J1792. Picture mistaken for original.

J1793. *Mask mistaken for face. Esopete* p. 53.

J1810. Physical phenomena misunderstood.

*J1810.0.1. *Bird mistakes falling of leaf* for falling of sky. Frightened. *Gatos* 3.

J1812.2. *Hares think sound of waves is great danger to them. LBA* cc. 144–50.

J1820. Inappropriate action from misunderstanding.

*J1820.1. *Satyr drives man away* because he blows on hands to warm them and on wine to cool it. *Esopete* pp. 126–27.

*J1821.2. *Birds see watery eyes of hunter and think he weeps for them* in pity. *Esopete* pp. 76–77; *Gatos* 4.

*J1849.5. *Abbot sends monk for manure;* he returns because a lioness lives where the manure is. Told to rope her and bring her here. Credulous monk tries, and she resists until he tells her that abbot had sent him. Abbot says: "Just as you are witless, you have captured a witless beast." *a.b.c.* 317; *Espéculo* 415.313–14; Tubach 3075.

*J1849.6. *Goose too heavy to fly well asks crow to help.* Crow tries to lift him but cannot and accuses goose of resisting. *Gatos* 38.

J1850–J1999. Absurd disregard of facts.

J1853.1.1. *Money from the broken statue.* Fool sells goods to a statue, and when it will not pay him, knocks it to pieces. He finds a treasure inside. *Esopete* p. 110.

J1880. Animal or objects treated as if human: miscellaneous.

J1881.2. Animal sent to go on errand by itself.

J1881.2.2. *Peasants must make overdue payment.* They tie money to the neck of a fleet-footed animal, a hare, telling it to take it to creditor. *Gatos* 44.

J1891. Object foolishly blamed.

*J1891.4. *Blacksmith not to be blamed* because tools can cause damage. *a.b.c.* 56.

J1900. Absurd disregard or ignorance of animal's nature or habits.

J1909.1. *Fisherman fails to make fish dance to his flute.* Later they jump about without the aid of his flute. *Esopete* p. 110; cf. Tubach 2053.

*J1909.1.2. *Hyena (jackal) captured by peasants.* Good peasants plead for his safety and feed him in pit where he is captive. He escapes, takes revenge on those who wanted to kill him. *Esopete* p. 76.

J2050–J2199. Absurd shortsightedness.

J2061. Castle-in-air shattered by lack of forethought.

J2061.1. *Air-castle.* Jar of honey suspended over hermit's head. He dreams of selling honey and through successive transactions becoming tremendously wealthy. In dream he will punish disobedient offspring. Raises stick and shatters jug of honey. *Calila* p. 264; *Exemplario* 66r–66v; Tubach 3286.

*J2061.3.1. *Air-castle.* Jar of honey to be sold. Woman on way to market to sell honey laughs with joy at future wealth and knocks jar off head. *Lucanor* Ex. 7; Tubach 80.

J2066. Foolish waiting.

J2066.4. *Wolf scorns salt meat* in false expectation of other food. *LBA* cc. 766–79; *Esopete* pp. 91–93.

J2066.5. *Wolf waits in vain for nurse (mother) to throw away child.* She has threatened to throw the child to the wolf. *Esopete* p. 119.

J2070. Absurd wishes.

J2071. *Three foolish wishes.* Three wishes will be granted: used up foolishly. Wife tells man to wish for many women. Unhappy with many women, she advises him to wish that God free him from women. Wish granted. He is alone. Then must use third wish to restore his wife. *Sendebar* Day 7, Tale 17; Tubach 5326.

*J2072.5.1. *Short-sighted wish.* Camel wishes for horns. Punishment: his ears are cropped instead. *Esopete* p. 121; Tubach 838.

*J2072.5.2. *Short-sighted wish.* Bees wish for lethal sting. Punishment: their sting is suicidal instead. *Esopete* p. 112.

J2074. *Twice the wish to the enemy.* (The covetous and the envious.) *A* can have a wish, but *B* will get twice the wish. *A* wishes to lose an eye so that *B* may be blind. *a.b.c.* 217; *Esopete* p. 125; *Espéculo* 328.228–29; *Alexandre* cc. 2360–65; Tubach 560.

J2080. Foolish bargains.

*J2084. *Buyer of sandalwood* burns a small bit to convince seller that it is worthless in his town. Will take it for whatever seller will ask. Seller learns it is worth weight in gold. Seller asks impossible task or return of merchandise. *Sendebar* Day 8, Tale 22.

J2092. *The trusted porters.* Man finds treasure but is robbed by porters he has hired to free him from trouble of carrying it. *Calila* pp. 91–92; *Exemplario* 2r.

J2100. Remedy worse than disease.

J2102.3. *Bald man aims at fly.* Hurts his head. *Esopete* p. 52; Tubach 458.

*J2102.3.1. *Heretic aims at fly* that lights on head. Hits it so many times that heretic dies. *Gatos* 6.

J2103. Expensive extermination of rodents.

J2103.1. *The cat to guard the cheese.* Man puts cat in chest to keep mouse from eating cheese. Cat kills mouse and then eats cheese. *Gatos* 16; *Espéculo* 65.45–46; Tubach 886.

J2107. *Taming the bull* by cutting off its horns. It makes him more violent. *Esopete* p. 126.

J2112.1. *Young wife plucks husband's grey hairs.* Old wife his black. Soon all are gone. *Esopete* p. 113; Tubach 2401.

*J2119.1.2. *Man asked friend for advice for eye pain.* Take them out and put them in your pocket. *a.b.c.* 76; Tubach 1952.

J2120. Disregard of danger to objects (or animals).

J2129.3. *Getting all the eggs at once.* Hen lays golden eggs; is killed. *Alexandre* c. 143.

J2130. Foolish disregard of personal danger.

*J2131.1.2. *Blind men given pig* on the condition they beat it to death with sticks. They beat each other instead. *a.b.c.* 64; Tubach 698.

*J2121.1.4. *Numskull deceived into removing eyes* to cure headache. *a.b.c.* 76; Tubach 1952.

*J2131.5.8. *Disregard of danger.* Lamb disregards danger of seeking refuge among wolves when fleeing dogs. *Alexandre* c. 1780.

J2132.5. *Animal allows self to be tied* to another's tail and is dragged to death. *Esopete* pp. 24, 34; Tubach 3425.

J2133. Numskull falls.

J2133.9. *Blind men fall into abyss.* A blind man, accepting as his guide another blind man, falls with him into abyss. *Lucanor* Ex. 34; Tubach 701.

J2135. Numskull starves self.

*J2135.1.1. *Members to starve belly.* This brings about death of entire body. *Esopete* p. 66; Tubach 570.

J2136. Numskull brings about own capture.

J2136.5.1. *Thief stops to admire beautiful things* before stealing them. Caught. *a.b.c.* 101; *Disciplina* 30; Tubach 4782.

*J2136.5.10. *Careless thief in poor man's house* steals last bit of poor man's flour. Putting it under his cape he drops goods stolen elsewhere. Poor man attacks thief who leaves without cape and stolen items. *Exemplario* 4r–4v; *Calila* pp. 96–97.

J2137. Death through lack of foresight.

J2137.1. *The louse invites the flea.* The flea bites the man and jumps away. The bed is searched, and the louse killed. *Calila* p. 152.

J2137.5. *Sheep killed by butcher,* who they are persuaded will spare them. They betray each other. *Esopete* p. 76.

*J2137.5.1. *Young rams butchered* because they did not heed advice of elders. *Esopete* p. 78.

*J2137.8. *Tiger as proposed defender* of other animals is unexpectedly wounded by well-hidden hunter's arrow. *Esopete* p. 123.

*J2159.1. *Man inattentive to the danger of drowning* persists in crossing river overburdened by load of precious stones. Drowns. *Lucanor* Ex. 38.

*J2159.2. *Man loads self* with such heavy burdens that the weight causes his death. *a.b.c.* 260 (not in Paris MS); Tubach 2135.

J2160. Other shortsighted acts.

J2172. Shortsightedness in caring for livestock.

J2172.1. *The shepherd who cried "Wolf"* too often. When the wolf really comes, no one believes him. *Esopete* p. 111.

J2175. Shortsightedness in dealing with children.

J2175.4. *Man lets son play in river.* Son drowns, and man drowns trying to save him. *Sendebar* Day 2, Tale 3.

J2190. Absurd shortsightedness: miscellaneous.

J2199.4.1. *Fool protects shoes.* Treads on thorns to protect shoes and hurts feet. *a.b.c.* 37; Tubach 4351.

*J2199.5. *Greedy husband supplies wife* to an inexperienced fat prince because he believes him to be impotent. When the prince and the woman evidently enjoy each other, the husband kills himself. *Sendebar* Day 4, Tale 9.

J2200–J2259. Absurd lack of logic.

J2211. Logical absurdity based upon certain false assumption.

*J2211.5. *Man shows lion a picture of a lion overcome by a man.* Lion not convinced. Later in amphitheater he defeats the man. *Esopete* pp. 78–79.

J2238. *Book gives wisdom.* A man believes himself wise because he has a book that he uses but does not understand. *Calila* pp. 92–93.

*J2238.1. *Fool asks for rhetorical rule.* Given Ciceronian rule, memorizes it, and recites it to audience instead of applying it. *Exemplario* 2r; *Calila* p. 92.

J2260–J2299. Absurd scientific theories.

J2273. Absurd theories concerning the sky.

J2273.1. *Bird thinks sky will fall if it does not support it.* Leaf falls on feet and frightens it. *Gatos* 3.

J2300–J2349. Gullible fools.

*J2301.4. *Gullible husband* and wife both believe evil old woman. *a.b.c.* 370 (not in Paris MS); *Lucanor* Ex. 42; Tubach 5361.

*J2301.4.1. *Gullible husband* believes wife's account of an admonitory dream. Her actions have saved him. *Sendebar* Day 6, Tale 16.

*J2301.4.2. *Gullible husband.* Heron finds spot where fish abound. Wants it all to himself and his family. Heron wife tells her friend (a curlew) to pretend to be willing to share another such spot with husband. Husband invites curlew. *Calila* p. 339.

*J2301.4.3. *Husband hides under wife's bed.* She spends night with lover and tells lover how much she loves husband. In morning, gullible husband commiserates with her over her sleepless night and urges her to stay in bed. *Calila* p. 241.

*J2301.4.4. *Husband's good eye treated so that lover can depart.* Had returned with one eye wounded. *a.b.c.* 161; *Disciplina* 9; *Esopete* pp. 147–48; *Talavera* 2.10.188; cf. Tubach 1943.

*J2301.4.5. *Wife outwits husband* with extended sheet. Enables lover to leave house unseen. *a.b.c.* 162; *Esopete* p. 148; *Disciplina* 10.

*J2301.4.6. *Wife entertains lover during husband's absence.* Husband returns and mother-in-law (guardian) counsels lover to pretend he is fugitive from street ruffians. *Disciplina* 11; *Esopete* pp. 145–46; Tubach 4692.

*J2301.4.7. *Husband locked out.* Wife tricks husband into thinking she has drowned in well. He leaves, and she locks him out. *a.b.c.* 303; *Disciplina* 14; *Talavera* 2.1.147 n. 36; Tubach 5246.

*J2301.4.8. *The husband temporarily blinded* so that lover can leave unseen. Wife sprays his eyes with mother's milk. He hears noise; she tells him it is the cat. *Talavera* 2.10.188; cf. Tubach 1943.

*J2301.4.9. *Wife's lover under bed.* Husband returns home. She has husband turn round to brush hair off his clothes. He hears lover leave; she tells him it is the cat. *Talavera* 2.10.188–89.

MOTIF INDEX OF

*J2301.4.10. *Wife's lover under bed.* Husband returns home. Wife tips over candle, extinguishing it. Sends husband out for light. *Talavera* 2.10.189.

*J2301.4.11. *Wife's lover behind curtains.* Husband returns home. Wife shows husband a new kettle she says has holes in it. Holds it in front of his eyes, slaps it loudly. Husband neither sees nor hears lover leave. *Talavera* 2.10.189.

*J2301.4.12. *Husband paints lamb on wife's stomach before leaving on trip.* Stays away years; returns to find ram portrayed (painted by lover in his absence). Wife retorts: lamb had matured with the years. *LBA* cc. 474–85.

*J2304. *Gullible priest* believes tricksters who tell him that deer (bought for sacrifice) is dog. *Calila* p. 236; *Esopete* pp. 167–68; Tubach 2975.

J2312. *Naked person made to believe he is clothed.* Tricksters pretend to make clothes for the emperor. Cloth is visible only to those of legitimate birth. None at court are willing to admit they cannot see it. Finally a slave who has nothing to lose tells emperor he is naked. *Lucanor* Ex. 32; cf. Tubach 3577.

*J2314.1. *Gullible hermit* believes apparition who tells him devil will come to him in shape of aged man holding a scythe. Mistakes father for devil and kills him. *a.b.c.* 87; Tubach 2570.

J2315.2. *Gullible husband made to believe he has cut off his wife's nose.* Barber's wife, whose nose has been cut off when she took friend's place, returns home. Her husband made to believe that he has accidentally cut off her nose when he threw razor at her. *Calila* pp. 139–41; *Exemplario* 14v–15r.

*J2326.2.1. *Gullible king* believes false dream interpretation by his enemies. He is to kill family, relinquish sword and battle elephant. *Calila* p. 282; *Exemplario* 72r–72v.

J2338.1. *Cuckold made to believe that God is donor of fine things* that wife's lover has given them. *Esopete* p. 149.

*J2339. *Trickster fox* convinces wolf to ask mule its identity, its parentage, its name, knowing that mule will say that the information is on hoof. Wolf kicked. *Esopete* p. 85; Tubach 3432.

*J2342.6. *Wife convinces husband that he is guilty of breaking mutual fidelity pact,* when she is found in compromising situation. *Sendebar* Day 4, Tale 10.

J2350–J2369. Talkative fools.

J2357. *Tortoise disregards warning and speaks.* Loses grip on stick that holds it aloft as helpful birds carry it through the air. *Calila* p. 165; *Exemplario* 22v–23r; Tubach 1832.

J2370–J2399. Inquisitive fools.

J2378. *What will the robber do?* A man curious as to what a robber will do waits to intervene and falls asleep. *Calila* pp. 93–94; *Exemplario* 2v.

J2400–J2449. Foolish imitation.
J2410. Types of foolish imitation.

J2412.1. *Hot onion to the eye.* Doctor had cured his sore foot with this remedy. *a.b.c.* 283; Tubach 3530.

J2413.1. *Ass tries to caress master like the dog.* He is driven off. *Çifar* pp. 33–34; *Esopete* p. 38; *LBA* cc. 1401–8; Tubach 372.

J2413.3. *Daw tries to carry off sheep like eagle.* Fails, claws are caught in fleece. *Esopete* p. 109; Tubach 2346 (raven and fat goose).

*J2413.5.1. *The young fox tries to imitate a wolf* who has pulled down a colt. He tries to pull down a mare (but he) cannot get loose and is carried to owner who kills him. *Esopete* pp. 96–98.

J2415. Foolish imitation of lucky person.

*J2415.1.3. *Good poet justifies his low birth.* Tells king that a rose grows among thorns as he did among humble persons. King sends him away with many gifts. Bad poet justifies self because of high birth. Unrewarded, imitates other poet; tells king that rye grows among wheat. King sends him away without gifts. *Disciplina* 3.

*J2415.3.1. *Crow wants to imitate ringdove.* Seeks friendship of mouse. Denied because it is crow's nature to hunt mice. *Exemplario* 42v; *Calila* pp. 205–6.

*J2415.8. *Man hides in tree to overhear animal's secrets,* as had his companion who had reaped great rewards from king for revealing them. Is mistaken for companion and is killed by animals for having revealed secrets. *Gatos* 28.

*J2416.1. *Humble man becomes king.* Tries to eat like a king. Falls ill. *a.b.c.* 81; Tubach 3843.

J2450–J2499. Literal fools.
J2460. Literal following of instructions.

*J2461.1.9. *Literal fool.* Monk sent to fetch manure complains that the pile is near a lioness's den. Impatient abbot tells him to fetch lioness too. Monk does so. *a.b.c.* 317; Tubach 3075.

J2466. Literal following of the count.

J2466.1. *Man drags heavy sack symbolic of sins.* A man cannot remember the number of his sins. Puts a pebble in a sack for each. Comes to confession with three sacks of pebbles. *a.b.c.* 1; Tubach 4413.

J2469.1. *A lentil in the soup.* "You said you wished a lentil soup; so I put one in. If you had wished more lentils, you should have said so." *Esopete* p. 10.

*J2469.1.1. *Food for master's most dearly beloved* given to pet rather than to wife by literal-minded slave. *Esopete* pp. 11–12.

*J2469.1.1.1. *Literal obedience.* Slave tells master he should have specified exactly what sort of water he wanted and in what sort of vessel. Brings foul water in wrong vessel. *Esopete* p. 10.

*J2469.1.2. *Instructions followed literally.* Master sends to know if bathhouse is crowded. Slave reports only one man present. All others had stumbled over obstruction at entrance. Only one man acted to avoid danger. Others did not act like men. Tells master only one man is there. *Esopete* p. 14.

*J2469.5.3. *Literal obedience.* Slave told that mistress's buttocks have eyes, bares them while she sleeps so she can watch food on table. *Esopete* p. 16.

*J2469.5.4. *Literal obedience.* Slave told to admit only wise men. Admits only one who does not fall into his verbal trap. *Esopete* p. 16.

*J2469.6. *Literal fool calls servant "devil,"* thereby calling upon a real demon, and orders him to loosen his boots. Real demon dissolves laces. *a.b.c.* 113; Tubach 1605.

*J2469.7. *Literal fool denies God.* Devil's power is greater than God's because devil put stone in his path. He is punished with paralysis and blindness. *Cantigas* 407.

J2470. Metaphors literally interpreted.

J2475. *"Greasing the judge's palms."* Woman misunderstands instructions to grease bishop's hands. Literally applies oil to them. *a.b.c.* 95; Tubach 2421.

K. DECEPTIONS

K0–K99. CONTESTS WON BY DECEPTION

*K97.3. *Battle won by deception.* Dead hero's corpse arranged in saddle with mighty sword in hand to lead troops against enemy. *Abreviada* 2.150–60.

K100–K299. DECEPTIVE BARGAINS

*K171.0.3. *Wheat crop divided unfairly.* Trickster covers partner's smaller share "to protect it." Partner returns the favor, moving sheet to larger share. Trickster gets the smaller share. *Calila* p. 95; *Exemplario* 3r–3v.

K171.1. *Deceptive crop division: above the ground, below the ground.* Truth takes the roots of jointly owned tree and Lies takes the trunk and branches. *Lucanor* Ex. 26.

K171.5. *Deceptive division of animals.* Evil tells Good to take the lambs; he will take the milk and wool; Evil will take piglets and give Good the milk and wool of pigs. *Lucanor* Ex. 43.

*K171.5.1. *Deceptive division of vegetables.* Evil takes turnip roots; Good the leaves. Evil takes leaves of cabbage, leaving roots to Good. *Lucanor* Ex. 43.

K171.7. *Deceptive division of shared wife.* Evil takes lower half of wife; Good takes upper half. Child begotten by lower half not permitted to nurse the top half, which belongs to Good. *Lucanor* Ex. 43; Tubach 1921.

*K171.10. *Who will inherit apple tree?* Eldest son will choose all that is straight and twisted; the second will choose all that is green and dry; the youngest will choose roots, trunk, and branches. *Esopete* pp. 94–96.

*K171.11. *Who will inherit goat?* Eldest wishes that goat be so large that it might be able to drink the seas dry; the second wishes that all the rope and wood in the world would not be enough to tie it; the youngest wishes that it be so large that an eagle in flight will see only the goat from on high. *Esopete* pp. 94–96.

*K171.12. *Who will inherit the mill?* The greatest liar. The eldest is so lazy that water that drips in his ear has caused his brains to leak out. *Esopete* pp. 94–96.

K185. Deceptive land purchase.

K185.1. *Deceptive land purchase: ox-hide measure.* Dido orders it to be cut in thin strips to outline large territory (Dido). *Ilustres mujeres* 40.47r–49r; *PCG* 53.34–5; *Abreviada* 1.16.

K191. *Peace between sheep and wolves.* As condition for peace wolves demand that sheep send away dog guards. When unprotected, wolves kill sheep. *a.b.c.* 415; *Esopete* pp. 2, 19, 65; Tubach 5357.

K192. *Man helps horse against stag.* Horse must agree to be saddled and bridled. Man then refuses to release him. *Esopete* pp. 77–78; Tubach 2619.

K200–K249. Deception in payment of debt.

K218.4. *Devil cheated of promised soul* by intervention of Virgin Mary. *Castigos* MS A BNM 6559 82.215.

K220. Payment precluded by terms of the bargain.

*K227. *Price of horse and falcon to be doubled each day.* When payment is due, payment is impossibly high. *PCG* 709.410; *Abreviada* 2.254.

K230. Other deceptions in the payment of debt.

*K231.2.2. *Gem merchant hires assistant who sees harp.* Asked to play it. Spends day playing harp. Merchant refuses payment but is reminded that he had requested music. *Calila* p. 113; *Exemplario* 9r.

K231.3. *Refusal to make sacrifice after need is past.* Woman in labor promises to keep feast day. After she gives birth, she works on feast day and is paralyzed. *a.b.c.* 165; cf. Tubach 4138.

K236. Literal payment of debt (not real).

*K236.5. *Money in the stick.* Before swearing, debtor (ostensibly to free hands) hands a stick containing repayment of loan to lender. Swears he has repaid loan. Retrieves stick. *a.b.c.* 234; Tubach 3469.

K264. Deceptive wager.

*K264.3. *Combat between wolf and hare.* Hare bets he will defeat wolf. He outruns wolf, until exhausted wolf can run no more. Wolf asks him why he hadn't stood and fought. Fleeing is his way of fighting. *Gatos* 58.

K265. Other deceptions: miscellaneous.

*K267. *Woman mixes husked and unhusked barley together.* Only she knows that dog has urinated on husked grain. *Calila* p. 212 n. 116.

K300–K499. THEFTS AND CHEATS

K305. Contest in stealing.

K305.2.1. *Friends enter into stealing contest.* Friend marks own share;

MOTIF INDEX OF

other friend changes mark. Thieving friend steals own share. *Calila* pp. 95–96; *Exemplario* 3r–3v.

K330. Means of hoodwinking owner or guardian.

*K331.1.1. *Dog hoodwinked into letting wolf kill sheep.* Made to think that shepherds will feed him more if he appears weak. *Esopete* pp. 93–94.

K334.1. *Raven (crow) with cheese in its mouth.* The fox flatters it into singing so that it drops the cheese. *a.b.c.* 11; *LBA* cc. 1437–43; *Esopete* p. 37; *Lucanor* Ex. 5; Tubach 2177.

*K334.1.1. *Small dog gives bed to larger dog who speaks sweetly to her.* Large dog keeps bed. *Esopete* p. 35.

*K335.1.0.2. *Frightened thief leaves sheet behind.* He extends sheet to catch few wheat grains in poor man's house. Chased away, leaves sheet behind. *Calila* pp. 96–98.

*K335.1.0.3. *Thief comes to rob poor man.* Finds only a bit of flour. Poor man, enraged, attacks thief, who leaves behind spoils from other houses. *Exemplario* 4r–4v.

*K344.1.5. *Owner persuaded that deer (goat) is worthless dog* by tricksters. *Calila* p. 236; *Exemplario* 55r; *Esopete* pp. 167–68; Tubach 2975.

K345. Sympathetic helper robbed.

K345.2. *Thief sent into well by trickster.* A weeping boy tells a passing thief that he had lost a silver cup in well. The thief takes off his clothes and goes after the cup, intending to keep it. He finds nothing. When he comes up child has stolen his clothes. *Esopete* p. 125.

K346. *Thief trusted by cleric* to guard goods steals them and runs off. *Calila* p. 138; *Exemplario* 13v.

K354. Trickster asks hospitality; expels owner.

*K354.2. *Alexander, disguised as knight,* steals host's golden flatware. Caught. Says that in Alexander's court it is customary to give flatware to guests. Shames royal host. *a.b.c.* 34; Tubach 112; cf. U45.

K400. Thief escapes detection.

K401.1.1. *Trail of stolen goods made to lead to victim.* Heron counseled by crab to free itself from snake's depredation: leave trail of fish leading to snake's nest. Mongoose follows trail, kills snake and her young, and then kills heron and her young. *Calila* p. 173.

K401.2. *Stolen goods taken to dupe's house.* Book hidden in bedchamber. Dupe is accused, *a.b.c.* 117; Tubach 2431.

K401.2.2. *Crow drops necklace in* snake's hole. Leads hunters there. *Calila* p. 145; *Exemplario* 15v.

K402.3. *The ass without a heart.* Jackal (fox) tells sick lion that ass's heart and ears are a cure for illness. Brings him an ass, who escapes. Lion recaptures and kills ass. Jackal eats ears and heart; tells lion that ass had neither ears nor heart. *Calila* pp. 259–61; *Exemplario* 64v–65v; *LBA* cc. 892–906; Tubach 717.

K420. Thief loses goods or is detected.

K427.1. *Clever animal betrays thief.* Horse catches arm of thief and holds on until help comes. *a.b.c.* 242; Tubach 2608.

K439. Thief loses goods or is detected: miscellaneous.

K439.3. *Thief tricked into robbing self.* Has covered companion's goods with a sheet to mark them. Companion misunderstands, switches the sheet to protect the other's goods. *Calila* pp. 95–96; *Exemplario* 3r–3v.

K440. Other cheats.

*K441.3.1. *Lawyer takes two fees in a single case.* Higher fee wins greater support. *a.b.c.* 309; cf. Tubach 2851.

K444. *Dream bread: the most wonderful dream.* Three pilgrims (two townsmen and a rustic) agree that the one who has the most wonderful dream shall eat the last loaf. Rustic eats it and in morning tells others he had dreamt they were dead. *a.b.c.* 98; *Esopete* p. 142; *Disciplina* 19; *Espéculo* 532.420–21; Tubach 1789.

K445. *The emperor's new clothes.* Tricksters pretend to make clothes for the emperor. Cloth is visible only to those of legitimate birth. None at court are willing to admit they cannot see it. Finally a slave who has nothing to lose tells emperor he is naked. *Lucanor* Ex. 32; cf. Tubach 3577.

K451.3. *Concealed confederate as unjust witness.* Rogue and dupe hide money under a tree. Rogue steals it; accuses dupe of theft; enlists confederate to hide in tree hollow to testify against dupe. Judge sets fire to tree smoking out confederate. *Calila* p. 171; *Exemplario* 26v–27r.

K475. Cheating through equivocation.

*K475.4. *Saintly bridegroom determined to remain chaste* tells new bride he is going to the Holy Sepulcher, the name of a nearby church. He leaves for the Holy Land. *San Alejo* p. 101.

K476. Cheating by substitution of worthless articles.

*K476.1.3. *Gold deposited with monk (Julian the Apostate) for safekeeping.* He replaces gold with ashes and flees. *Espéculo* 54.37–38.

K476.2. *False articles used to produce credit.* Chests filled with stones left as deposit. *a.b.c.* 163; *Esopete* pp. 139–41; *Disciplina* 15; *CMC* vv. 65–212; cf. Tubach 965.

K477. Attention secured by trickery.

*K477.4. *Entry into enemy's camp by pretending to be angered by mistreatment at hands of own camp.* Crow, battered and bloody, offers services to owls. *Calila* pp. 224–52; *Exemplario* 53v–56v; *Lucanor* Ex. 19; Tubach 1358.

K500–K699. ESCAPE BY DECEPTION

K510 Death order evaded.

*K511.1.1. *Death avoided by trickery.* Alexander vows to sacrifice first thing seen. Man on ass convinces him that ass is seen first. *a.b.c.* 118; Tubach 131, 3289.

K512. Compassionate executioner.

*K512.0.1.1. *Compassionate executioner* spares calumniated wife and abandons seven princelings instead of killing them. *Ultramar* I.1.55.92.

MOTIF INDEX OF

*K512.0.1.2. *Compassionate executioner.* Spares young woman. Uses dog's heart as proof. *Ultramar* I.2.43.562.

*K512.0.3. *Compassionate executioner.* Servants charged with killing the infant hero are touched by his beauty and leave him in care of shepherds. *Alexandre* cc. 355–56.

K512.1.1. *Compassionate executioner.* King's counselor spares life of king's favorite wife condemned to death hastily. Shows king bloody sword as proof of execution. *Calila* p. 280; *Exemplario* 72v.

*K512.5. *Compassionate executioner hides victim* in tomb instead of killing him. *Esopete* p. 20.

*K513. *Execution of three knights.* Three sentenced to be hanged: compassionate one falsely reported he had killed first one; second one did not bring the alleged assassin to justice; the third did not obey orders to kill the first. *a.b.c.* 222; *Glosa* 3.2.22.204; Tubach 4229.

K520. **Escape from danger by disguise, shamming, or substitution.**

K521.4.1. *Disguise in clothes of other sex* so as to escape (Wives of the Minias). *Ilustres mujeres* 29.36r–37v; *Alexandre* cc. 410–16; *PCG* 718.420–21.

K521.6. *Abbot escapes from lover's suspicious husband* in disguise of priest. *Sendebar* Day 8, Tale 22.

K522.4.1. *Trout pretends to be dead.* Floats on surface; thrown on bank near water is able to escape to safety. *Calila* p. 149; *Exemplario* 18r.

*K523.1.1. *Hermit leaves cave to pray for soul of dead youth.* Feigns madness in order to be permitted to return to isolation of cave. *a.b.c.* 405.

*K525.11. *Escape by substituting sand for treasure.* Dido throws overboard sacks filled with sand to fool pursuers. *PCG* 52.33–34.

K527. **Escape by substituting another person in place of intended victim.**

*K527.3.1. *Exchange of clothes between rich man and poor man.* Rich man intent on giving up worldly life gives rich garments to poor pilgrim. *San Alejo* p. 101.

K528.2. *Escape by substituting self for another condemned to die.* Holy man substitutes self for deacon held by enemy. *a.b.c.* 295; Tubach 4153.

K544. **Escape by fooling captor.**

K544. *Monkey escapes death; it is custom to leave heart at home.* Monkey responds to request for his heart (as remedy for turtle's ailing wife) that he has left it at home. *Calila* p. 258; *Exemplario* 64r.

K550. **Escape by false plea.**

K551.4. *Escape by pretending to go for bath.* Woman avoids sexual act by saying she must bathe first. *Sendebar* Day 1, Tale 1.

*K551.29. *Wolf is persuaded to kill ass where neighbors will not see* to save him embarrassment. *Esopete* pp. 88–89.

*K551.30. *Flea pleads for liberty* because biting is his nature. Plea is unheeded. *Esopete* p. 113; Tubach 2081.

K558. *Man allowed to pick out tree to be hanged on.* Cannot find one to his liking. *a.b.c.* 130; Tubach 4790.

*K558.3. *Sentenced to have his eyes taken out,* asked if he could select the instrument. Favor granted, but then he could not find a nail that suited him. *a.b.c.* 151; Tubach 1947.

K561. Escape by persuading captor to talk (sing).

*K561.0.2. *Attempted escape* by persuading captor that animal was only joking fails. *Esopete* pp. 88, 98.

K561.1. *Animal captor persuaded to talk and to release captive.* Usually cock and fox, fox and wolf, or mouse and cat. *Esopete* p. 86.

K561.1.1. *Cat and cock debate usefulness to household.* Cat: "Even so, I do not intend to fast." *Esopete* p. 110.

*K561.1.1.1. *Weasel pleads that she has kept man's house free of mice.* Is killed anyway. *Esopete* p. 54; Tubach 5228.

K561.2. *Sheep (goats) persuade wolf to sing.* LBA cc. 766–79; *Esopete* pp. 91–93.

*K574. *Escape from invasion* by convincing Alexander his campaigns will bring him enemies. *a.b.c.* 6; Tubach 139.

K579. Escape by false plea: miscellaneous.

K579.5.1. *Wolf acts as judge* before eating the rams. They are to go to the end of the field and run to him. They run at him and kill him. *LBA* cc. 766–79; *Esopete* pp. 91–93.

K600. Murderer or captor otherwise beguiled.

*K601.3. *Dove tells marauding fox she will not throw chicks down for her to eat.* Fox must climb tall tree to get them. Fox does not climb tree. *Calila* p. 352.

K604. *The three teachings of the bird.* In return for release from captivity, the bird gives the man three teachings. These usually mock the man for having released what he had. *a.b.c.* 124; *Disciplina* 22; *Çifar* p. 76; *Esopete* pp. 142–43; *Barlaam* pp. 92–94; Tubach 322.

K640. Escape by help of confederate.

K640.1. *Escape by help of son-in-law as confederate.* *Lucanor* Ex. 25.

K650. Other means of escape.

K651 *Fox escapes from well.* Persuades wolf to descend into well in one bucket thereby rescuing fox in other. *Esopete* pp. 144–45; *Disciplina* 23; *Gatos* 14; Tubach 5247; cf. Tubach 2175.

K652. *Fox climbs from pit on wolf's back.* *Esopete* p. 109; Tubach 5247.

K700–K799. CAPTURE BY DECEPTION

K713. Deception into allowing self to be fettered.

K713.1.2. *Animal allows self to be tied to another for safety.* Carried to his death. *LBA* cc. 407–16; *a.b.c.* 358; *Esopete* pp. 24, 34, 86–87; Tubach 3425.

*K713.1.2.1. *Animal allows self to be tied to another* to gain importance. Wolf persuaded by captive ass to permit ass tied to him to follow him as his slave. Ass leads wolf to man. *Esopete* pp. 88–89.

*K721.2. *Cock persuaded to descend from tree* to receive kiss of fealty from deceitful fox. Eaten. *Esopete* pp. 63–64; Tubach 3629.

K730. Victim trapped.

K730.3. *Leopard traps lion* by having two doors to cave, one large one, one small. Lion enters large entrance, and leopard leaves by small one and attacks back of lion. *a.b.c.* 210; Tubach 3014.

K746. *Birds allow selves to be captured in net* because of greed for food. *Castigos* 1.36.

*K746.1. *Fish swallow hook* because of greed for bait. *Castigos* 1.36.

*K747. *Fleeing man's hair* caught in tree limb. *Castigos* MS A BNM 6559 (ADMYTE 0 80v); *Glosa* 1.1.11.59–60.

K800–K999. KILLING OR MAIMING BY DECEPTION
K810. Fatal deception into trickster's power.

K810.1. *Fox lures wolf into lion's power* telling lion that wolf's skin is cure for illness. Wolf had told lion same story about skin of fox. *Esopete* pp. 90–91.

*K810.1.1. *Agreement between lion and man* not to touch one another. Man ensnares lion and clubs him to death. *Esopete* pp. 98–100.

*K810.1.2. *Fox lures wolf (with story that moon's reflection is a cheese)* into well and leaves him there. *a.b.c.* 363; *Esopete* pp. 144–45; *Disciplina* 23; see J1791.3.

*K811.3. *Cruel king lured into enemy's power* by invitation to false execution of count's daughter. He speaks imprudently to crowd and is stoned to death. *Çifar* pp. 99–100; *Castigos* MS A BNM 6559 31.148 (ADMYTE 0 96r).

K812.2. *Men lured to their death when their fields are set on fire.* Samson defeats them. *Castigos* MS A BNM 6559 22.138.

K813.1. *Curlew (whimbrel) leads lover to cave* where a jackal (lion) kills and eats her. *Calila* p. 350; *Exemplario* 90r.

*K813.3. *Curlew convinces heron's wife to feed mate a fish with stick hidden in it.* Husband dies. *Calila* p. 350; *Exemplario* 90r.

K815. Victim lured by kind words.

K815.2. *Spider invites wasp to rest* on her "white curtain." Wasp caught in web is eaten. *Gatos* 29; Tubach 4571.

K815.3. *Dogs listen to wolves' hypocritical words.* Are killed. *Esopete* pp. 2, 19, 65.

*K815.4.1. *Vulture's birthday party.* Vulture invites other birds to party and eats them. *Esopete* p. 78.

K815.7. *Cat acts as judge between sparrow and hare.* Eats them both. *Calila* p. 232; *Exemplario* 53v.

K815.8. *Hawk persuades doves to elect him king.* Kills them. *Esopete* pp. 49–50; cf. Tubach 1755, 3554.

K815.13. *Cat makes truce with mice.* When time is up mice still do not leave. Cat eats them. *Calila* p. 347.

K815.14. *Fish tricked by crane into letting selves be carried from one pond to another.* The crane eats them. *Calila* p. 143; *Exemplario* 16r–16v.

*K815.20. *Fox tricks wading bird and kills him.* Asks him to show how he protects self from cold. Puts head under wing and fox kills him. *Calila* p. 353; *Exemplario* 92r.

*K815.21. *Fox tricks cock by gnawing tree trunk and slapping tail against it.* Cock, convinced it is not safe, moves to other trees and is caught. *Lucanor* Ex. 12.

K824. *Sham doctor kills patient.* Told to mix medicine for an ailing princess, unwittingly includes a fatal poison in his concoction. King orders him to drink his own medicine. *Calila* p. 192; *Exemplario* 35v.

*K824.2. *Devil tells monk to fast for 8 or 9 days.* Almost dies. *a.b.c.* 4; *Espéculo* 7.6–7; Tubach 1529.

K827. Dupe persuaded to relax vigilance, seized.

K828.1. *Fox in sheepskin gains admission to fold and kills sheep. Gatos* 25.

K828.2. *Fox, feigns illness, admitted to hen roost;* kills the hens. *Gatos* 24.

*K828.4. *Brigands wear monk's garb to deceive traveling merchants.* Merchants permit them to join their party and are robbed and killed. *Gatos* 26.

K870. Fatal deception by narcotic (intoxication).

K871.1. *Slaughter of drunken enemies in banquet hall.* Food and doctored wine left for them after feigned retreat. *a.b.c.* 420; *Ilustres mujeres* 47.54v–55v (Tamires); Tubach 5304.

K872. *Judith and Holofernes.* Woman chosen to sleep with intoxicated general kills him in bed. *Castigos* MS A BNM 6559 83.217.

K910. Murder by strategy.

*K911.6. *Young king feigns illness to lure traitors to his chambers.* His courtiers kill them. *Çifar* p. 80.

K940. Deception into killing own family or animals.

K943. *Hermit (deceived by devil) kills his own father,* supposing him to be the devil. *a.b.c.* 87; Tubach 2570.

K950. Various kinds of treacherous murder.

K952.1. *Animal killed from within.* Hydrus (fabulous water serpent) enters crocodile's mouth while it sleeps, bites its heart, and kills it. *Gatos* 13; see Tubach 1326.

*K953.3.5. *Crab learns crane intends to kill him.* Squeezes bird's throat and kills him. *Calila* p. 143.

K959. Other kinds of treacherous murder.

*K959.7. *Mother-in-law orders son-in-law to be shut in wine cellar* and murdered there. *a.b.c.* 272; Tubach 2737.

K960. Other fatal deceits.

K961. *Flesh of certain animal alleged to be only cure for disease;* animal to be killed. *Esopete* pp. 67, 90–91; *Calila* pp. 259–61; *Exemplario* 64v–65v.

K961.1. *Cure for illness is monkey's heart.* Monkey and tortoise friends. Wife wants tortoise to abandon friend and return to her. Tortoise told that cure for wife's illness is monkey's heart. *Calila* p. 253; *Exemplario* 63v.

K961.1.1 *Tit for tat. Wolf tells sick lion that fox does not esteem him.* Fox overhears it. Later fox tells lion that only cure lies in his wrapping himself in the wolf's skin. Wolf is killed. *Esopete* pp. 90–91.

K962. *Camel induced to offer self as sacrifice.* Other animals pretend to offer themselves to the lion as food. Lion convinced of their unwholesomeness, eats the camel. *Calila* p. 158; *Exemplario* 20r–20v.

K975. *Secret of strength treacherously discovered.* Samson tricked to reveal it. *Castigos* MS A BNM 6559 22.138 (ADMYTE 0 80r).

K978. *Uriah letter.* Man carries written order for his own execution. *LBA* cc. 258–59; *PCG* 738.435; *Abreviada* 2.282.

K978.1.2. *King sends woman's husband to battle in order to be able to seduce her.* (See K978, *Uriah letter.*) *Sendebar* Day 1, Tale 1; *Lucanor* Ex. 50; Tubach 1453; *Talavera* 1.17.101–2.

K1000–K1199. DECEPTION INTO SELF-INJURY
K1010. Deception through false doctoring.

K1011. *Eye remedy.* Under pretense of curing eyesight, crow blinds eagle. *Gatos* 31; Tubach 3530.

K1011.1. *Fool tricked into curing headache* by removing his eyes. *a.b.c.* 76.

K1021. *The tail fisher.* The bear is persuaded to fish with his tail through a hole in the ice. When he is attacked and tries to escape, he loses his tail. *Esopete* pp. 90–91; Tubach 2074.

K1022.1. *Wolf overeats in the cellar (larder).* Cannot escape through narrow opening. *Esopete* pp. 93–94; *Espéculo* 11.8; Tubach 4092, 5346.

K1040. Dupe otherwise persuaded into voluntary self-injury.

K1041. *Borrowed feathers.* Dupe lets self be carried aloft by bird and dropped. *Esopete* pp. 37, 119.

K1054. *Thief tricked into trying to climb down moonbeam.* Man hearing a robber enter house tells his wife to ask him where he found his wealth. He answers that he said magic words and climbed down a moonbeam and climbed up again to enter through a window. Thief tries it and falls. *a.b.c.* 77; *Disciplina* 24; *Calila* pp. 109–11; *Exemplario* 8r–8v; Tubach 4778.

*K1075.1. *Fox tricks wolf into asking questions* of mule who kicks him to death. *Esopete* p. 85; Tubach 3432.

K1080. Persons duped into injuring each other.

K1081. *Blind men duped into fighting each other.* Given sticks and a pig, told to kill it. They hit each other when pig escapes. *a.b.c.* 64; Tubach 698.

*K1084.4.1. *Calumniators cause king of carnivores and king of herbivores to fight.* Both lose power. *Lucanor* Ex. 22; *Calila* p. 168; *Exemplario* 13r.

K1085. *Woman makes trouble between husband and wife.* Tells wife to increase her husband's love by cutting a hair from his beard. Also tells husband that wife will try to cut his throat. *a.b.c.* 370 (not in Paris MS); *Esopete* pp. 149–151; *Espéculo* 463.362; *Lucanor* Ex. 42; Tubach 5361.

K1110. Deception into self-injury.

*K1111.4. *Deception into self-injury.* Lamb, fleeing dogs, seeks refuge among wolves. *Alexandre* c. 1780.

K1121.1. *Lion (wolf) as sham doctor* approaches too near to horse (to loosen smith's nail in hoof); kicked in face. *Esopete* p. 61; cf. *Esopete* pp. 85, 91–93; *LBA* cc. 298–303; Tubach 2605.

K1121.2. *Sow kicks wolf into stream* when he comes to baptize her pigs. Thus she saves them from him. *LBA* cc. 766–79; *Esopete* pp. 91–93; Tubach 4554.

K1200–K1299. DECEPTION INTO HUMILIATING POSITION
K1210. Humiliated or baffled lovers.

K1211. *Virgil in the basket.* A man who is to be pulled up to his lover's window is left hanging in the basket in the public gaze. *LBA* cc. 261–68; *Talavera* 1.17.100–1.

*K1211.1.2. *Man caught in a net.* Descending from tower where he had been with a woman, is caught and left suspended for all to see. *Talavera* 1.17.03.

K1215. *Aristotle and Phyllis: philosopher as riding horse for woman.* Philosopher warns against uxoriousness. In revenge, woman tricks philosopher into letting her ride him on all fours. Husband comes and sees them. *Talavera* 1.17.99–100; Tubach 328.

K1227. Lover put off by deception.

*K1227.4.2. *Clever woman tells amorous youth to strip off clothes, then shouts for neighbors.* Tells him to lie down, puts chunk of bread in mouth, douses him with water, and tells neighbors he had choked. Proves to him he knows nothing of womanly guile. *Sendebar* Day 8, Tale 18.

K1240. Deception into humiliating position: miscellaneous.

K1265. *Parsimonious employer falsely reported insane* when does not feed apprentice. No one will believe him. *a.b.c.* 102; *Disciplina* 20; *Esopete* pp. 151–52; Tubach 2753.

*K1290. *The dog and the sheep.* Dog accuses sheep of having taken bread from him. Sheep convicted. *Esopete* p. 34.

K1300–K1399. SEDUCTION OR DECEPTIVE MARRIAGE
K1315. Seduction by impostor.

K1315.1. *Seduction by posing as a god.* Woman tricked into offering self to god by deceitful priests in service of seducer. *a.b.c.* 385; Tubach 4221.

K1317. Lover's place in bed usurped by another.

K1317.1. *Serving-man in his master's place.* Man devises disguise to enter woman's house safely. Servant uses disguise to lie with master's beloved. Master visits her, learns truth, beats servant, and destroys disguise. *Calila* p. 184; *Exemplario* 32v.

K1340. Entrance into woman's (man's) room (bed) by trick.

K1343.1. *Man drawn up into female bedchamber* in basket. *LBA* cc. 261–68; *Talavera* 1.17.100–1.

K1350. Woman persuaded by trick.

K1351. *Weeping bitch.* A procuress throws pepper in eye of bitch so that

MOTIF INDEX OF

she weeps. Procuress pretends to a virtuous woman that bitch is a woman transformed as punishment for failure to respond to her lover. Woman, fearful of similar transformation is persuaded. *a.b.c.* 234 (not in Paris MS); *Esopete* pp. 146–47; *Disciplina* 13; *Sendebar* Day 4, Tale 10; Tubach 661.

K1353.2. *Woman deceived into seduction.* Thinks that invader will spare her, but afterwards he discards her. *a.b.c.* 246; Tubach 1081.

K1397. *Lucretia seduced through threat.* Sextus says he will kill her and leave a naked slave in her bed to bring dishonor to her house. She yields. Later kills herself. *Ilustres mujeres* 46.52v–54v (Lucrecia); *a.b.c.* 62; *Jardín* pp. 257–58; *Glosa* 2.1.19.94; Tubach 3095.

K1500–K1599. DECEPTIONS CONNECTED WITH ADULTERY

K1510. Adulterous wife outwits husband.

K1511. *The husband locked out,* excessive precautions to assure wife's fidelity. Despite efforts, wife returns home late at night; her husband refuses to admit her. She threatens to throw herself in the well. Husband leaves house to see if she has drowned. She enters the house and bars him from house. *a.b.c.* 303; *Disciplina* 14; *Talavera* 2.1.147 n. 36; Tubach 5246; see T481.9.

K1512. *The cut-off nose.* Carpenter's wife has another woman, a barber's wife, take her place while she goes to her lover. Carpenter speaks to wife's friend, gets no answer and cuts off her nose. In the morning wife returns and still has nose. Husband made to believe it was restored miraculously. Barber's wife, whose nose has been cut off when she took friend's place, returns home. Her husband made to believe that he has accidentally cut off her nose when he threw razor at her. *Calila* pp. 139–41; *Exemplario* 14v–15r; see T481.10

K1514.1 *The husband in the chicken house (dovecote).* Husband returns unexpectedly and surprises his wife with her lover. She makes the husband believe he is pursued and hides him in the chicken house. *Esopete* pp. 148–49; see T481.11.

K1516. *Wife outwits husband with extended sheet.* Lover leaves house unseen. *a.b.c.* 162; *Esopete* p. 148; *Disciplina* 10; Tubach 4319; see T481.20.

K1516.1. *The husband's good eye treated* so that lover can leave house unseen. *a.b.c.* 161; *Disciplina* 9; *Esopete* pp. 147–48; *Talavera* 2.10.188; cf. Tubach 1943; see T481.12.

*K1516.1.2. *Wife's lover under bed.* Husband returns home. She has husband turn round to brush hair off his clothes. He hears lover leave; she tells him it is the cat. *Talavera* 2.10.188–89; see T481.14.

K1516.3. *Wife's lover under bed.* Husband returns home. Wife tips over candle extinguishing it. Sends husband out for light. *Talavera* 2.10.189; see T481.15.

K1516.7. *Wife washes husband's hair.* Lets lover escape while husband is thus blinded. *Talavera* 2.10.188–89.

K1516.8. *Wife shows husband new kettle to look for hole in it.* Holds it in front of his eyes, slaps it loudly. Husband neither sees nor hears lover leave. *Talavera* 2.10.189; see T481.16.

K1516.9. *Wife shows husband how full her breasts are of milk.* She squirts milk in his eyes and lets lover escape. *Talavera* 2.10.188; see T481.13.

K1517. Lover escapes by disguise.

K1517.1. *Two lovers are pursuer and fugitive.* Wife is visited by two lovers. When the husband arrives, one goes out with drawn sword and the other hides in house. She convinces her husband that she has given refuge to a fugitive. *Sendebar* Day 2, Tale 5; Tubach 4693; see T481.17.

K1517.1.2. *Wife entertains lover during husband's absence.* Husband returns and mother-in-law (guardian) counsels lover to pretend he is fugitive from street ruffians. *Disciplina* 11; *Esopete* pp. 145–46; Tubach 4693; see T481.18.

K1517.6. *Husband returns while abbot is in house.* Errant wife enlists aid of friar who brings extra habit next day. Abbot escapes wearing friar's habit. *Sendebar* Day 8, Tale 22; see T481.19.

K1518. *The enchanted pear tree.* Wife and lover are up in tree. Blind husband hears them and prays to Jupiter for restoration of sight. Prayer is answered. Wife convinces cuckold that her adultery convinced Jupiter to grant his wish. *Esopete* p. 147; Tubach 3265; see T481.21.

*K1518.1.1. *Husband made to believe that birth of child to wife who has committed adultery* is a gift from God. *Esopete* p. 149; cf. Tubach 971.

K1521. Lover successfully hidden from husband.

K1532. Gullible husband under bed.

K1532.1. *Wife, in bed with lover,* knows that husband is hiding under bed. Tells lover how much she loves husband. *Calila* p. 241; *Exemplario* 57r; *Esopete* p. 168; see T481.22.

K1536. *Wife drugs husband's wine* and has husband made monk while he is unconscious, so as to get rid of him. *a.b.c.* 304; Tubach 1803.

K1543. *The marked cloth in the wife's room.* A go-between obtains a woman for a client by leaving a marked cloth in woman's house. Husband beats woman; she leaves and is tricked into thinking that sex with the go-between's client will help her solve her problem. Go-between tells husband that she had left the cloth in his house, and husband is deceived. *Sendebar* Day 5, Tale 13.

*K1544.2. *Husband unwittingly instrumental in wife's adultery.* Greedy husband supplies his wife to an inexperienced fat prince because he believes him to be impotent. When the prince and the woman evidently enjoy each other, the husband kills himself. *Sendebar* Day 4, Tale 9.

*K1544.2.1. *Husband unwittingly instrumental in wife's adultery.* Believes that wife will spend night with god, Anubis, not with trickster posing as god. *a.b.c.* 385; Tubach 4221.

*K1544.2.2. *Husband unwittingly instrumental in wife's adultery.* Wife's lover (an apothecary) substitutes earth for needed medicine. Wife returns with packet; tells husband she was run down by a horse on way and lost money. Used a sieve to find missing money and could not find it. Husband replaces money. *Exemplario* 28v.

K1580. Other deceits connected with adultery.

*K1584.1 *Maidservant is go-between for knight who wants to seduce another's wife.* Convinces wife to don magic slippers sent by suitor. *Cantigas* 64.

K1600–K1699. DECEIVER FALLS INTO OWN TRAP

K1612. *Message of death fatal to messenger.* Man is sent to kiln where attendants have been instructed to throw the first arrival into oven. Intended victim stops to pray and is delayed. Messenger sent to inquire about execution is first arrival and is burned instead. *a.b.c.* 8.

K1613. *Poisoner poisoned with own poison. Calila* p. 192; *Exemplario* 35v.

K1613.1. *Person trying to blow poison into another's nose accidentally poisoned.* Victim sneezes and poison enters throat of poisoner. *Calila* p. 138.

*K1613.6. *Man, posing as physician,* mixes a fatal poison in medication for princess. She dies and king orders him to drink his own medicine. *Calila* p. 192.

K1626. Would-be-killers killed.

*K1632.1. *Animal victim of own ruse.* Heron leaves trail leading mongoose to snake's nest. Snake killed but heron and young also killed. *Calila* p. 173.

K1635. *Partnership between partners Evil and Good.* Evil cheats his partner. Takes lower half of wife; Good takes upper half. Child begotten by lower half not permitted to nurse from top half, which belongs to Good. *Lucanor* Ex. 43; cf. *Lucanor* Ex. 26.

K1667. *Dishonest banker deceived into delivering deposits by making him expect even larger.* Refuses to return traveler's money chest. Traveler sends friends with ten chests filled with stones to make false deposit. In order to make the impression of honesty in the presence of new depositors, banker agrees to return traveler's money chest. *a.b.c.* 163; *Disciplina* 15; *Esopete* pp. 139–40; Tubach 3355, 4969.

*K1667.2. *Money lenders deceived* into accepting chests filled with sand as surety for loan. *CMC* vv. 65–212.

K1681.1. *Originator of death first sufferer.* Inventor of death machine is first to use it. Cruel tyrant orders him to be first victim. *a.b.c.* 316; cf. Tubach 3134.

*K1684.1 *Rich man wants relic of St. Augustine.* Guardian of relics gives him finger, saying it was Augustine's. God impressed by rich man's faith and good works, substitutes a real relic. Guardian denies its authenticity and is punished. *a.b.c.* 103.

K1700–K2099. DECEPTIONS THROUGH SHAMS

K1710. Ogre (large animal) overawed.

K1715.1. *A weak animal shows a powerful one his reflection and frightens him.* Tells him that this animal is threatening to kill him (usually hare and lion). *Calila* p. 146; *Exemplario* 17r–17v.

K1716. *Hare as ambassador of the moon.* Hare tells elephants that moon disapproves of their mistreatment of weaker animals. Shows elephant king moon's reflection in spring. Elephant drinks from spring, disturbs water, and believes that moon is angry. *Calila* p. 230; *Exemplario* 52v.

K1771. Bluffing threats.

*K1771.10. *Cleric threatens devils with imprisonment in flask* if they do not obey him. *Cantigas* 125.

*K1775. *Bluff: insult repeated as harmless remark.* The trickster makes an insulting remark, but when called on to repeat what he said, he changes it so as to turn aside wrath. *Esopete* pp. 88, 98.

*K1784.3. *Sandpipers and sea.* Sea washes away fledglings. Sandpipers enlist aid of the king of the birds (*falcón oriol*) to confront the sea who relents and returns young to their parents. *Calila* p. 164; *Exemplario* 22v.

K1800–K1899. Deception through disguise or illusion.

K1810. Deception through disguise.

*K1810.2.1. *Ram wears mastiff's skin* to protect herd from wolves. Detected. *Esopete* p. 98.

*K1810.2.2. *Cat who had killed all but one mouse* in monastery wears monks' robes, takes place at monks' table to catch big mouse. Mouse believes cat to be merciful now that he is monk. Cat eats mouse. *Gatos* 9; Tubach 888.

K1811. Gods in disguise visit mortals.

*K1811.0.3. *Christ in guise of poor man* comes to saint's household. Is fed. *a.b.c.* 136.

*K1811.0.4. *Angel in guise of beggar comes to saint.* Given money and valuables. *a.b.c.* 137.

*K1811.4.3. *Abbot deceived by devil disguised as angel.* Told to create divisive rules in monastery. *a.b.c.* 4; Tubach 19.

*K1811.6. *Angel appears to saint* as man who has lost everything in shipwreck; is given alms. Later comes to him as his guardian angel. *a.b.c.* 137.

K1815. Disguise.

K1815.1.1. *Pious pilgrim dies unknown in his father's house,* until letter clutched in hand is read. *San Alejo* pp. 78–79.

*K1815.3. *Calumniated courtier advised by his counselor* to dress as pilgrim to convince king of his loyalty and willingness to accompany him on retreat from world. *a.b.c.* 215 (not in Paris MS); *Lucanor* Ex. 1; *Barlaam* pp. 25–29.

K1832. *Disguise by changing voice.* Wolf tries to fool kids by assuming mother goat's voice. Fails. *Esopete* p. 51.

MOTIF INDEX OF

K1837.7. *Woman (St. Eugenia) living disguised as man* and unrecognized in a monastery becomes abbot. *a.b.c.* 158; Tubach 1915.

*K1837.8.2. *Widowed queen masquerades as son who is heir to throne ruling in his stead.* Once in power, drops imposture and rules on her own. *Ilustres mujeres* 2.6r–8r (Semiramis); Tubach 4224.

K1840. Deception by substitution.

K1841. Virgin Mary substitutes for a mortal.

K1841.3. *Virgin Mary takes place of woman* whose husband had pledged her to devil. *a.b.c.* 268; *Cantigas* 216; *Castigos* MS A BNM 6559 83.216; Tubach 5283.

K1860 Deception by feigned death (sleep).

*K1867.1.1. *Cat feigns death* in order to catch mice. Detected. *Esopete* pp. 110–11; cf. Tubach (fox feigns death) 2176.

K1900–K1999. Impostures.

K1911. The false bride.

K1911.3.7. *False bride detected* when her mother comes to see her. She does not have joined toes of real bride. *Ultramar* I.2.43.566

K1955. Sham physician.

*K1955.0.1. *Sham physician.* Wolf offers to help pregnant sow. Detected. *Esopete* p. 50; Tubach 4554.

*K1955.0.2. *Sham physician.* Lion offers to cure horse. Is kicked. *Esopete* p. 61; Tubach 2605.

*K1955.0.3. *Sham physician.* Wolf visits sick ass. "Where does it hurt?" "Where you touch me." *Esopete* p. 78.

*K1955.0.4. *Frog attempts to be a great physician.* Shamed by fox. *Esopete* p. 120; Tubach 1692.

*K1955.2.2. *Crow offers to cure eagle's eyes.* Applies onion juice, blinds it, eats its young. *Gatos* 31; Tubach 1833.

*K1955.10. *Sham physician* tells emperor he has universal cures: an herb to drink, an unguent, and a powder for baths. Needs two hundred camels to fetch herbs from a distant place. Must go alone. *Çifar* pp. 127–28.

K1961. Sham clerical person.

K1961.2.1. *Woman in disguise becomes pope* (Pope Joan). *Ilustres mujeres* 101.103r–103v; Tubach 2813.

*K1961.6. *Wolf as monk.* Wolf attired as monk says "cordero" or "carnero" instead of "paternoster." *Gatos* 19; Tubach 5338.

*K1961.7. *Cat as monk.* Wears monks' robes, takes place at monks' table to catch big mouse. Mouse believes cat to be merciful now that he is monk. Cat eats mouse. *Gatos* 9; Tubach 888.

K1962. False prophet.

K1962.1. *Mohammed trains dove to eat grains of wheat placed in Mohammed's ear.* Tells people that dove is God's messenger. *Castigos* 21.128; Tubach 1762.

*K1962.2. *Mohammed convinces new wife* that palsy is message from the angel Gabriel. *Castigos* 21.130.

*K1962.3. *Mohammed took servant's wife.* Told all that the angel Gabriel had sent her to him. *Castigos* 21.131–32.

*K1966.2. *Alchemist.* Trickster convinces king he can transform lead into gold. Needs ten camels loaded with silver to purchase needed ingredients. *Çifar* pp. 128–29; *Lucanor* Ex. 20; Tubach 89.

K2000–K2099. Hypocrites.

K2010.3. *Wolves sign false truce with sheep.* Dogs to be dismissed. After the dogs have been dismissed, the wolves devour the sheep. *Esopete* pp. 2, 19, 65; Tubach 5357.

K2030. Double dealers.

K2031.1. *Dog at master's table* is friendly to guests. On the street growls at them. *a.b.c.* 208; Tubach 1703.

*K2031.2. *Snake helps man and then harms him.* Farmer tramples snake. Snake prophesies weather, and man finds his advice profitable. When man sends child to reward snake, the reptile kills child. *Esopete* pp. 89–90; Tubach 4251.

*K2031.3. *Bat tries to be bird, then to be quadruped.* *Esopete* p. 62; Tubach 501.

K2041.1. *Double-dealing physician* offers to poison king if king's enemy will pay him. Enemy refuses and sends him as prisoner to king. *Glosa* 1.2.12.122; *a.b.c.* 315; Tubach 3761.

K2042. *Crow goes to owls saying crows have cast him out.* Having learned secret hiding places of owls, returns to crows and leads them to victory over owls. *Calila* p. 237; *Exemplario* 53v–56v; *Lucanor* Ex. 19; Tubach 1358.

K2052. False modesty.

K2052.1. *Bride insists upon wearing chemise to bed.* Husband must wear underclothes. *Castigos* MS A BNM 6559 (ADMYTE 0 17r).

K2058. Pretended piety.

*K2058.3. *Elderly monk about to die,* admits that he had always eaten when they thought he had been fasting. *a.b.c.* 438; *Espéculo* 8.7; Tubach 1850.

*K2058.4. *Hypocritical cleric participates passively in sexual acts* with widow. Exculpated because he did nothing actively. *Esopete* p. 165.

K2060. Detection of hypocrisy.

K2061.1. *Wolf acts as shepherd: plan detected.* Wolf to guard sheep while shepherd is away kills and eats them. On return, shepherd sees wolf's tooth marks in skins. *Gatos* 21; Tubach 5343.

K2061.1.1. *Wolf proposes abolition of dog guards for sheep.* Plan detected too late. *a.b.c.* 415; *Esopete* pp. 2, 19, 65. Tubach 5357.

*K2061.1.2. *Shearer pretends that wolf has eaten woman's sheep.* She prays to Virgin Mary and then hears sheep bleat revealing its presence. *Cantigas* 147.

K2061.4. *Wolf tries to entice goat from high place*: plan detected. *Esopete* pp. 125–26; cf. Tubach 2309.

K2061.6. *Wolf offers to act as midwife for sow.* Plan detected. *LBA* cc. 766–79; *Esopete* p. 50; Tubach 4554.

K2061.9. *Cat hangs on wall* pretending to be dead. Mice detect plan. *Esopete* pp. 110–11.

K2062. *Thief tries to feed watchdog and stop his mouth.* Dog detects plan. *Esopete* p. 50; *LBA* cc. 166–80.

*K2064.1. *"Holy" hermit revealed as sinner.* Is owner of blasphemous portrait of Jesus hidden in secret chamber. *Talavera* 4.1.262–67.

K2090. Other hypocritical acts.

*K2094.1. *Dogs are hypocrites.* Beg for morsels at table but are indifferent when there is no food. *a.b.c.* 208; cf. Tubach 1703.

K2100–K2199. FALSE ACCUSATIONS

K2101. *Falsely accused minister reinstates himself* by his cleverness. He follows advice of his own adviser and deceives king. *a.b.c.* 75; *Barlaam* pp. 26–31; *Lucanor* Ex. 1.

*K2101.1. *Falsely accused royal physician* vindicated by royal trust. *Alexandre* cc. 902–13; *Glosa* 1.2.13.124; Tubach 134.

*K2101.2. *Falsely accused minister reinstated* because of devotion to Virgin Mary. King's investigator proves him innocent. *Cantigas* 97.

*K2103. *Letter said to have been written by priest is false evidence of treason.* Virgin Mary's intervention proves his innocence. *Cantigas* 206, 265; *a.b.c.* 273, 391; Tubach 2419.

*K2103.1. *Woman vendor falsely accused of stealing ring left in pawn for merchandise.* Accuser lost it in river; recovered in fish's belly. *Cantigas* 369.

*K2105. *Boy substitutes crow's egg for stork's.* Mother stork accused of adultery is stoned by other fledglings. *a.b.c.* 13.

K2110. Slanders.

*K2110.2. *Son, denied horse by mother,* accuses her of infidelity to his father. She is freed from prison by intervention of wise man at court. *Abreviada* 2.333.

K2111. *Potiphar's wife.* Empress demands sex from courtier. Spurned, accuses him of rape. *a.b.c.* 365; *Sendebar* pp. 74–76.

K2111.5. *Mother importunes son sexually.* Denied, she falsely accuses him of trying to rape her. *a.b.c.* 172; Tubach 2734.

K2111.6. *Young woman falsely accuses saint* of having fathered her child. *a.b.c.* 89; *Espéculo* 436.330–31; Tubach 648.

*K2111.6.1. *Widow falsely accuses St. Eugenia of rape* (thinking she is man). *a.b.c.* 158; Tubach 1915; cf. Tubach 3380.

K2112. Woman slandered as adulteress.

*K2112.0.1. *Woman falsely accused of adultery by her husband.* Prayer for sign that husband lied is answered; he develops leprosy as punishment for calumny. *Lucanor* Ex. 44.

*K2112.0.2. *Susanna and the elders.* Lustful elders accuse woman falsely of adultery. Prophet Daniel proves they have lied. *Glosa* 2.2.6.148; *Castigos* 9.69; Tubach 4684.

*K2112.0.3. *Woman falsely accused of adultery* by husband. Knives fail three times to cut her throat. After fourth stroke, apparently dead, is revived magically and freed. *a.b.c.* 14; Tubach 4697.

K2112.2. *Woman bathes leper and puts him in her bed.* Husband returns. Accuses her, but finds nothing but fragrant roses in bed. *Espéculo* 304.210–11; Tubach 3020.

K2115. *Animal-birth slander.* Evil mother-in-law writes to absent son, telling him his wife has given birth to seven hounds. *Ultramar* I.1.53.89.

*K2116.5.1. *Man falsely accused of having murdered unfaithful wife.* Flees to pray to Virgin Mary. She delivers him from pursuers. *Cantigas* 213.

K2117. *Calumniated wife: substituted letter (falsified message).* Evil mother-in-law substitutes letter for one announcing birth of children for one that says wife has given birth to seven hounds. *Ultramar* I.1.53.89.

K2117.1. *Husband's letter ordering that calumniated wife be treated well is altered* by evil mother-in-law to say that wife and her sons are to be killed. *Ultramar* I.1.53.90.

K2130. Trouble-makers.

K2131.2. *Envious jackal makes lion suspicious of his friend, the bull.* Lion kills bull. *Calila* p. 124; *Exemplario* 11r; *Lucanor* Ex. 22.

*K2131.6. *Monk accuses another to abbot.* Told to attend to own faults. *a.b.c.* 88; Tubach 3389.

*K2131.7. *Two female captives deprived of clothing.* One woman finds bit of cloth to cover herself. Second complains; captor reproaches her. She must look to her own shame, not that of another. *Calila* pp. 194–95; *Exemplario* 37r.

K2141. *Jealous courtiers shake lion king's confidence in his counselor,* the virtuous jackal, by accusing the non-meat-eating jackal of stealing meat from lion. *Calila* pp. 306–10; *Exemplario* 79r–80v.

*K2141.1. *Jealous courtiers accuse king's favorite of disloyalty.* He is advised to pretend that he is ready to give up wealth and accompany king on a retreat (pilgrimage) to prove loyalty. *a.b.c.* 75, 215 (not in Paris MS); *Barlaam* pp. 25–29; *Lucanor* Ex. 1; *Voragine* 2.180.356–57.

K2150. *Stepmother (king's favorite wife)* accuses prince of attempted rape. Innocent made to appear guilty. *Sendebar* pp. 74–76.

K2155. *Silver goblet planted in luggage of man.* Made to look guilty of theft. *a.b.c.* 38; *Cantigas* 175; *Santiago* 5.57–61; *Esopete* p. 23; cf. Tubach 3796.

*K2155.1.2. *Envious monk hides book in another's bed* and accuses him of theft. *a.b.c.* 117; Tubach 2431 b).

*K2155.1.3. *Meat belonging to lion* left in quarters of fasting jackal. *Calila* p. 309; cf. Tubach 2431 b).

*K2155.4. *Innocent woman made to look like murderer.* Told to hold razor to husband's throat to cut a hair. *a.b.c.* 370 (not in Paris MS); *Lucanor* Ex. 42; *Esopete* pp. 149–50; Tubach 5361.

K2155.5. *Crow leads hunters to serpent's nest,* dropping jewels in nest to attract men. *Calila* p. 145; *Exemplario* 15v.

MOTIF INDEX OF

*K2156.1. *Innocent man accused of treason* because of falsified letters purportedly written by him. *Esopete* p. 20; *a.b.c.* 273.

*K2176. *Monk spends nights with prostitutes to reform them.* Accused falsely of fornication, but after his death, truth revealed. *a.b.c.* 229.

K2200–K2299. VILLAINS AND TRAITORS

K2210. Treacherous relatives.

K2213.1. *Matron of Ephesus (Vidua).* A woman mourns night and day by her husband's grave. A knight guarding a hanged man is about to lose his life because of the corpse he has stolen from the gallows. Grieving widow offers him her love and substitutes her husband's corpse on the gallows so that knight can escape. *Esopete* p. 64; Tubach 5262.

K2214.1. *Treacherous daughters (sons)* afflicted with terrible illness. *a.b.c.* 260.

K2217. *Treacherous uncle* tried to subvert young king's power. *Çifar* p. 79.

K2217.1. *Treacherous nephew kills uncle for money. a.b.c.* 120; Tubach 5020.

K2218. *Treacherous mother-in-law accuses innocent wife.* Puts Moorish slave in wife's bed. *Cantigas* 185.

*K2219. *Treacherous sons* beaten by father for returning territory to enemy. *Glosa* 1.2.12.120.

K2230. Treacherous lovers.

K2232.1. *Treacherous lover (man) betrays woman's love and deserts her.* Eneas leaves Dido fearing disclosure of his part in Trojan losses. *Castigos* 40.185–86.

K2240. Treacherous officers and tradesmen.

K2241. *Treacherous innkeeper.* Steals pilgrim's goods. Santiago restores goods. *Santiago* 6.61–64.

*K2241.1. *Treacherous innkeeper plants evidence of theft in baggage of guest.* Treachery detected. *Santiago* 5.56–61; *a.b.c.* 38.

*K2242.1. *Treacherous steward.* King's steward, in charge of treasury, takes double his fee and becomes rich. King names others to guard against losses. They too steal from treasury. *Çifar* p. 106.

*K2242.2. *Treacherous steward* who kills Jew under royal protection is executed. *a.b.c.* 167; Tubach 2799.

*K2242.3. *Treacherous steward* mismanaged estate of absent employer. *a.b.c.* 219.

K2246. *Treacherous prince.* King sells privilege of judging crimes to another who sells justice. Those who were misjudged rebel and king repents. *Çifar* p. 107.

K2248.0.1. *Treacherous ministers.* Advised high taxes and debased coinage. *Çifar* p. 105.

K2250. Treacherous servants and workmen.

*K2255.3. *Drover left behind to care for wounded bull.* Tires of task and abandons it; tells master bull has died. *Calila* p. 123; *Exemplario* 11r.

K2280. Treacherous churchmen.

*K2284.0.1. *Treacherous churchmen.* Pope is warned against peculations of cardinals. *Çifar* p. 107.

*K2284.0.2. *Treacherous believers in active ministry,* jealous of contemplative monk, kill his animal friend, a bear. *a.b.c.* 329; Tubach 519.

K2285.0.1. *Villains disguised as monks.* Brigands wear monk's garb to deceive traveling merchants. Merchants permit them to join their party and are robbed and killed. *Gatos* 26.

K2290. Other villains and traitors.

K2292. *Treacherous physician* offers to poison ruler to please ruler's enemy. *a.b.c.* 315; *Glosa* 1.2.12.122; Tubach 134.

K2294. *Treacherous host.* Pilgrim's wife dies in host's house. Host keeps all his possessions. At destination St. James tells him evil host's house will be burned. *Espéculo* 305.211–12; Tubach 3790.

K2300–K2399. OTHER DECEPTIONS

*K2310.1. *Hunter who has promised not "to touch" lion catches him in trap* and beats him to death with club. *Esopete* pp. 98–100.

K2315. *Peasant betrays fox by pointing.* The peasant has hidden the fox in a basket and promised not to tell. When the hunters come, he says, "The fox just went over the hill," but he points to the basket. *Esopete* p. 75.

K2350. Military strategy.

K2351.1. *Fire tied to foxes' tails* destroys enemy. *Glosa* 1.1.10.59; *Castigos* MS A BNM 6559 (ADMYTE 0 80r).

K2357. *Disguise to enter enemy's camp (castle).* Alexander enters Porus' castle disguised as a simple knight. *a.b.c.* 34.

K2365. Enemy induced to lift siege.

K2365.2. *Besieged citizens surrender city* to king who showers them with golden apples of great value. *a.b.c.* 309; Tubach 317.

K2365.3. *Enemy soldiers persuaded by show of great wealth to desert to visiting king's side.* Invited to dine, Alexander in guise of envoy, steals golden tableware. Says his king always lets guests take it away. Soldiers desert to his side. *a.b.c.* 34; Tubach 112.

*K2365.4. *Enemy lured into ambush.* Splendid banquet left unattended. Invaders attacked while eating. *a.b.c.* 209; Tubach 5304.

K2369.3.1. *Treacherous teacher delivers children of besieged city to enemy.* Enemy will not accept these hostages and returns them. Teacher punished. City gratefully surrenders to enemy. *a.b.c.* 256; *Glosa* 1.2.12.121; cf. Tubach 1082.

K2369.6. *Military strategy.* City won by diverting river that fed moat. Enemy soldiers march through empty river bed into the city. *a.b.c.* 340 (not in Paris MS); Tubach 4109.

*K2369.7.1. *King proposes sending poison to enemy.* Senators warn enemy. Would rather win in battle. *Glosa* 1.2.12.121.

K2370. Miscellaneous deceptions.

*K2372. *Abbot orders monks to insult young monk* to take his mind off his

lascivious thoughts. At end of year he is cured. *a.b.c.* 213; Tubach
3097.

L. REVERSAL OF FORTUNE

L0–L99. VICTORIOUS YOUNGEST CHILD

L10. Victorious youngest son.

*L10.3 *Youngest of three brothers is wisest.* One undertakes to maintain
the peace; second chooses to visit the sick; third chooses to withdraw
from the world. The first two could not fulfill their aims. They went
to the third who solved their dilemma with parable of powder in turbulent water. *a.b.c.* 82; cf. *Espéculo* 496.392; Tubach 803.

*L13.2. *Youngest son best fitted to reign.* Youngest son shows greatest willingness to learn and to serve. *Lucanor* Ex. 24.

L50. Victorious youngest daughter.

*L54.2. *Youngest of three daughters agrees to marry virtuous elderly warrior.*
Her sisters had rejected his suit earlier. *Lucanor* Ex. 27.

L100–L199. UNPROMISING HERO (HEROINE)

L114.1. *Lazy hero.* Least truthful son to inherit mill. Three sons lie
about their laziness. *Esopete* pp. 94–96; Tubach 3005.

L140. The unpromising surpasses the promising.

*L143.3. *Rich man poisons poor man's bees.* Poor man used last bit of oil
and vinegar to cure bees. *a.b.c.* 15; cf. Tubach 551.

L146.1. *Ape tries to flee with favorite child.* Neglected child saves self.
Favorite child is killed through mother's over-anxiety. *Esopete* p. 128;
Espéculo 41.27–28; Tubach 299.

L200–L299. MODESTY BRINGS REWARD

L211. *Modest choice: three casket type.* Objects from which choice is to be
made are hidden in caskets. The worst-looking casket proves to be
the best choice. Chests adorned with gold and precious stones contain putrefying remains; chest containing royal treasures covered with
pitch. *Barlaam* pp. 56–58; *Espéculo* 449.343–44; Tubach 967.

*L212.1.1. *Modest choice best.* Second royal wife gains favor over favorite
by choosing reward of splendid clothes rather than crown. *Calila* p.
280; *Exemplario* 72r.

L213. *Youth chooses poor bride rather than rich one.* Will live like a poor
man with family. Her father reveals great treasure. *a.b.c.* 286 (not in
Paris MS); *a.b.c.* 387 (not in Paris MS) (tale not given); *Barlaam* pp.
140–43; Tubach 3841.

*L213.3. *Father will choose poor husband for daughter over rich one.* Better
for a man to need money than for money to need man. *a.b.c.* 422;
Lucanor Ex. 25; Tubach 1444.

L300–L399. TRIUMPH OF THE WEAK

*L302. *Poorly armed animal overcomes stronger one by chance.* Evil falcon demands that nightingale sing for him to save offspring. Displeased, he begins to eat them. Hunter captures falcon. *Esopete* pp. 62–63; Tubach 4388.

L310. Weak overcome strong in conflict.

L311. *Weak (small) hero overcomes large fighter.* David and Goliath. *Castigos* 10.77, 36.172.

L315. Small animal overcomes large one.

L315.2. *Mouse torments bull who cannot catch him. Esopete* p. 127.

L315.3. *Fox burns tree in which eagle has nest.* Revenges theft of cub. *Esopete* p. 37; Tubach 2181.

L315.7. *Dungbeetle keeps destroying eagle's eggs.* Eagle at last goes to sky and lays eggs in Zeus's lap. The dungbeetle causes Zeus to shake his apron and break the eggs. *Esopete* p. 109.

L315.9. *Eagle threatens falcon who has caught a heron.* Falcon must attack and defeat eagle to retain its prey. *Lucanor* Ex. 33.

L350. Mildness triumphs over violence.

L350.1. *Mildness triumphs over violence.* Queen advises husband to use kindness (in manner of physicians) to enemies. *Çifar* pp. 124–25; *a.b.c.* 302; *Castigos* MS A BNM 6559 (ADMYTE 0 115r); *Glosa* 1.2.27.204; cf. Tubach 5381.

*L350.1.1. *Mildness triumphs over violence.* King must be physician to subjects, feeding the thin, withholding food from the obese, cutting where necessary, easing pain, and applying remedies. *Castigos* 37.160.

L350.2. *Holy man uses kind words to pagan priest* who has just hit a Christian. Pagan repents and is converted. *a.b.c.* 218.

L361.1. *Sinner given grave penance kills priest.* Next priest gives mild penance and succeeds where others failed. *a.b.c.* 299 (not in Paris MS); Tubach 3674.

L390. Triumph of the weak: miscellaneous.

L391.1. *Reed pricks dog and drives him away when he urinates on it. Gatos* 47; Tubach 812.

L392. *Mouse stronger than sun, wind, and mountain: rat-maiden. Calila* p. 244; *Exemplario* 58v; Tubach 3428.

L392.1. *Mosquitoes and horseflies sting Pharaoh.* Show they are stronger than person who cannot escape them. *Castigos* MS A BNM 6559 75.206.

*L396. *Sheep successfully resists deer's fraudulent claim of a debt.* Refuses payment because promise to pay made in presence of wolf. *Esopete* p. 52.

L400–L499. PRIDE BROUGHT LOW

L410. Proud ruler (deity) humbled.

L410.1. *Proud king humbled.* Realizes that pomp, possessions, power are of short duration. All that he rules will be turned to dust. *a.b.c.* 361; *Castigos* MS A BNM 6559 (ADMYTE 0 88v).

MOTIF INDEX OF

*L410.1.1. *Proud king requires subjects to worship him.* Wounded in battle, aware of his mortality, repents. *a.b.c.* 215.

L410.1.2. *Proud king punished for bestial acts.* Forced to live naked in wild like a beast. *Castigos* 9.71.

L411. *Proud king displaced by angel.* (King in the bath.) While king is in bath an angel in his form takes his place wearing his clothes. The king, wearing rags, is rejected by all until he repents of his excessive pride. *Lucanor* Ex. 51.

L413. *Golden grave of Alexander.* Philosophers say that his power and treasures no longer matter. *Disciplina* 32.

L414. *King vainly forbids tide to rise.* When he almost drowns, he discards his crown and acknowledges his weakness. *Castigos* MS A BNM 6559 28.143 (ADMYTE 0 88r); *Glosa* 1.1.9.47; Tubach 4863.

L416.1. *Proud king humbled when imprisoned* by enemies but laughs at the pursuit of worldly goods. *a.b.c.* 418.

*L416.2. *Rulers of great city inattentive to defenses.* Enemy diverts river that feeds moat and destroys city. *a.b.c.* 340 (not in Paris MS); Tubach 4109.

*L416.3. *Enemy arrogantly threatened Christians with destruction.* Christian army triumphs. Defeated enemy's son imprisoned, tortured, and killed. *a.b.c.* 416.

*L416.5. *Knight abuses servant, punching and kicking him.* Servant, a frequent pilgrim, calls out to Santiago who saves him. *Santiago* 13.75–76.

L420. Overweening ambition punished.

*L420.0.2. *Emperors of Persia, Greece and Rome aspired to be gods.* Many lived like sinners. *a.b.c.* 360; Tubach 2323.

L421. *Attempt to fly to heaven punished.* Car supported by eagles. *Alexandre* cc. 2499–2500.

L424. *Man who has never known unhappiness* is swallowed up by earth with all his household. *a.b.c.* 287; Tubach 3938.

L430. Arrogance repaid.

L435.1.1. *Self-righteous monk rebuked by abbot* for attacking others for sin without looking at his own sins. *a.b.c.* 88; Tubach 3389.

L450. Proud animal less fortunate than humble.

L451. *Town mouse and country mouse.* Wild animal finds his liberty better than tame animal's ease. *Esopete* pp. 36–37; Tubach 3281.

L451.3. *Wolf prefers liberty* and hunger to dog's servitude and plenty. *Esopete* pp. 65–66; *a.b.c.* 245; Tubach 5337.

L452.2. *Ass jealous of war-horse* until he sees him wounded. *LBA* cc. 237–45; *Esopete* p. 62; cf. Tubach 2615.

L460. Pride brought low: miscellaneous.

L461. *Stag scorns his legs but is proud of his horns.* Caught by his horns in trees. *Esopete* p. 63; *Gatos* 12; Tubach 4589.

*L461.1. *Goat, having seen the reflection of his horns in water,* believes self capable of fighting wolf. Meanwhile, wolf approaches from behind and seizes the goat. *Esopete* p. 88; cf. Tubach 4589.

L491. *One out of twelve monks proudly refused to eat meat.* Asked for bread. Next day leftover meat was fine white bread; leftover bread was mass of frightful worms. *Espéculo* 516.407.

*L491.1. *Monks told that food eaten by all others, and charity lead to good life.* Must avoid attention to own possessions. *Espéculo* 517.407–8.

*L491.2. *At mealtime monk called for salt because he did not eat cooked food.* Sent to eat in own cell. *Espéculo* 518.408; Tubach 36, 4138.

*L492. *Visiting monk complained about wine served to him.* Went to a cave that collapsed. Found half-dead in debris. Abbot orders cave to be maintained as warning against singularity. *Espéculo* 519.408–9.

*L493. *Saint leaves off wearing hair shirt.* Dresses as other members of order. *Espéculo* 520.409.

*L493.1. *Saint on deathbed.* Tells brothers he had never exercised his own will. *Espéculo* 521.409.

*L494. *Monk so committed to maintain silence* refused to confess except by gestures. Admonished, he left order. *Espéculo* 522.409–10.

M. ORDAINING THE FUTURE

M0–M99. JUDGEMENTS AND DECREES

*M2.2. *Inhuman decision of king.* Man pleads that king spare one of his sons. King kills all three. *Castigos* MS A BNM 6559 13.118 (ADMYTE 0 52v); Tubach 1494.

*M2.3. *Courtier advises king to drink less.* Angry king proves sobriety by shooting arrow into courtier's son's heart. *Castigos* MS A BNM 6559 13.118 (ADMYTE 0 52v).

*M2.4. *King invites enemy to dinner.* Serves him dish prepared with flesh of guest's sons. Has severed heads brought to table. *Castigos* MS A BNM 6559 13.118 (ADMYTE 0 52v).

*M2.5. *Enemy captive shown severed heads* of seven sons. *PCG* 743.441–42.

M10. Irrevocable judgements.

M13. *Sentence applies to king's own son.* Those caught in adultery are to have eyes put out. When king's son is found guilty, king has one of his own eyes and one of his son's eyes put out to satisfy law. *a.b.c.* 224; *Castigos* MS A BNM 6559 9.105–6; Tubach 1944.

M14. *Irrevocable judgement of king upheld.* King leaves laws that must be kept until he returns. He dies and orders that his bones be cast into the sea. *a.b.c.* 243; *Glosa* 3.2.24.219; Tubach 3101.

M50. Other judgements and decrees.

*M57. *Even one involuntary act of charity outweighs lifetime of sins.* Miserly man has neither stick nor stone, so throws loaf of bread at beggar. Sees that it balances out evil lifetime, sells all, and gives to poor. *a.b.c.* 135; *Espéculo* 239.160–61.

*M58. *One generous act sufficient* to ensure salvation for saint. Gave away good deeds to another. *a.b.c.* 138.

M100–M199. VOWS AND OATHS
M100. Broken oaths.
M101.4. *Woman vowed to keep St. Francis' day to ensure a successful parturition.* She broke vow by working on that day, and her hand withered. *a.b.c.* 165; cf. Tubach 4138.

*M101.4.1. *Woman breaks vow not to eat meat.* She has bone in throat for eight days. Virgin Mary cures her, and she renews vow. *Espéculo* 562.456; Tubach 727.

*M101.4.2. *Ailing cleric promises to join order if prior cures him.* Cured, he breaks vow three times. Third time, devils come for him, and he dies. *Espéculo* 563.456–57.

*M101.4.3. *Woman neglects promise to make pilgrimage, son dies.* Prays to Virgin Mary, who resuscitates child dead for four days. *Cantigas* 347.

*M102. *Thief swears innocence with oath to God and Virgin Mary.* Caught soon after stealing again; is hanged. *Cantigas* 392.

M120. Vows concerning personal appearance.
*M121.1. *Vow not to cut beard* until hero's exile is terminated. *CMC* vv. 1240.

*M121.2. *Vow not to cut beard or hair* until king has found good husband for daughter. *Apolonio* cc. 550.

M122. *Vow: queen not to bind hair* till enemy is conquered (Semiramis). *Ilustres mujeres* 2.6v–8r; *Jardín* p. 247; Tubach 4224.

M161. Vow never to flee in fear of death.
*M161.7. *Refusal to accept conquest.* Women of conquered town kill their children and themselves after men have been killed by enemy. *Ilustres mujeres* 80.82v–83v (Wives of the Cimbros).

M177. Vow to change religion.
*M177.1.1. *King swears to become Christian* after saint cures him. *Castigos* 10.76.

M183. Religious vows.
*M183.5. *Nuns vow not to ever leave convent.* Great fire approaches, and archbishop urges them to break vow in order to save their lives. They stand firm and fire ceases. *Espéculo* 561.455–56.

M200–M299. BARGAINS AND PROMISES
M201. Making of bargains and promises.
*M201.0.1.2. *Hermit makes bargain with God.* Asks for wealth for a man who had sheltered him. Must promise he will use it well. *Espéculo* 64.45.

*M201.0.3. *Prince makes bargain with Virgin Mary.* He will light candles and praise her name if she helps him find his lost hawk. Hawk magically appears in his hand. *Cantigas* 44.

*M201.0.4. *Warrior promises Virgin Mary to pay for 1,000 masses* after he succeeds in his future military campaigns. *CMC* vv. 221–25.

M202. Fulfilling of bargain or promise.

*M202.0.2. *Pilgrim promises woman to bring back image of Virgin Mary from Holy Land.* Virgin Mary protects him from lion, from thieves, from shipwreck. On return, Virgin Mary forces him to keep promise. *Cantigas* 9.

M202.2. *Captive keeps word to return to enemy* if mission to his people to arrange exchange of prisoners fails. He had counseled against exchange. *a.b.c.* 377; *Çifar* p. 105; *Glosa* 1.2.12.118.

M203.1. *King's promise irrevocable.* King punishes his steward who had robbed a Jew to whom king had promised safe conduct through a wood. *a.b.c.* 167; Tubach 2799.

*M203.4. *King's promise irrevocable.* Promises to do nothing that philosopher requests. Clever philosopher asks him to destroy city. King must refuse to destroy city. *a.b.c.* 233; Tubach 139.

*M203.5. *King's promise irrevocable.* Alexander vows to sacrifice first thing he meets. It is a man riding an ass. Man pleads that ass preceded him. King amused, man spared. *a.b.c.* 118; Tubach 131, 3289.

M205. Breaking of bargains or promises.

*M205.0.2. *Fox promises to pay boatman for passage.* Payment is a slap in face with wet tail. *Gatos* 49.

*M205.0.3. *Mouse in wine vat.* Promises cat anything if he will save him. Breaks promise, telling cat, "I was drunk when I promised." *Gatos* 56; Tubach 3426.

*M205.0.4. *Hawk (crow) breaks promise to spare nightingale's (dove's) young* if she sings for him. He kills them because song was not good enough. Hunter snares falcon. Breaking promise punished. *Esopete* pp. 62–63; *Gatos* 41; *Espéculo* 71.47–48; Tubach 4388.

*M205.1.3. *Man in storm at sea promises St. Michael a calf if he is saved.* Three times when sea has calmed he refuses to keep promise. Third time he is drowned along with his calf and his cow. *Espéculo* 551.444; Tubach 1297.

M205.2. *Curse as punishment for broken promise.* Youth broke promise to a woman friend. Devils appeared to torment him until he confessed and kept his promise. *Espéculo* 284.191.

*M205.2.1. *Pilgrims promise to take care of each other until they reach goal.* All break promise save one who had refused to pledge. Santiago appears to keeper of pledge, helps him, and sends word that breakers of promise must atone. *Santiago* 4.53–56.

*M205.5. *Dragon (monster) does not give promised wealth to rescuer.* Threatens to eat him. Rescuer returns him to previous peril on advice of fox as judge. *Esopete* pp. 86–87; cf. Tubach 4254.

*M205.6. *Mother breaks promise to Virgin Mary.* Child dies but is brought back to life through mother's prayers to saint. *Cantigas* 43.

*M205.7. *Woman who had promised not to sew on the Sabbath broke promise.* Punished by losing use of hands. Sent to Chartres to be cured by Virgin Mary. *Cantigas* 117; cf. Tubach 4138.

*M205.8. *Leatherworker broke promise not to work on feast day.* Punished by swallowing needle that sticks in throat. Virgin Mary cures him at altar where he coughs up needle. *Cantigas* 199; cf. Tubach 4138.

M210. Bargain with devil.

M211. *Bargain with devil.* Virgin Mary brings man pact he signed with devil and frees him from devil's power. *a.b.c.* 261; *Milagros* 24; *Cantigas* 3; *Espéculo* 361.264–65; *Talavera* 1.13.91; *Castigos* MS A BNM 6559 82.215; Tubach 3572.

M211.1. *Drunken man unwittingly sells soul to devil.* Penniless, he enters tavern and sells soul to stranger. Stranger says he owns body too, just as buyer of horse owns halter. Man disappears forever. *Espéculo* 197.137–38; *Castigos* MS A BNM 6559 89.225–26; Tubach 4540.

*M211.10. *Devil will make man rich.* After he appears to him three times, man will surrender his soul. Three times in lifetime devil disguised as poor man visits him. Returns to carry him off. *Espéculo* 186.126–27.

M212.2. *Devil at gallows repudiates bargain with robber.* Devil helped thief in exchange for soul. Thief on gallows told to stand on devil's shoulders. Devil slips out from weight, and thief is hanged. *LBA* cc. 1454–79; *Lucanor* Ex. 45; *Espéculo* 185.126; cf. Tubach 2235.

M217. *Devil bargains to help man win woman.* Monk (servant) desires daughter of pagan priest (nobleman). Required to deny Christ. Repents. *a.b.c.* 23, 106; *Espéculo* 187.127–29; Tubach 3566.

*M217.1. *Man makes pact with devil.* Will deny Jesus and Virgin Mary and will be guaranteed worldly success. *Cantigas* 281; *Milagros* 24.

M242. Bargains and promises between mortals and supernatural beings.

*M242.4. *Man, whose granary was burning,* promised God he would give grain to poor if fire were extinguished. Breaks promise. *Gatos* 57.

*M242.5. *Woman promises Virgin Mary she will make her a wimple* if the Virgin will cure her silkworms. Forgot promise, but silkworms magically worked on wimple for her. *Cantigas* 18.

*M242.6. *Peasant promises calf to Virgin Mary* if she will protect it from wolves and thieves. Breaks promise. Calf breaks free and runs to her church. *Cantigas* 31.

*M244.3. *Captured bird promises to give captor three counsels* in exchange for freedom. *Esopete* pp. 142–43; Tubach 322.

M250. Promises connected with death.

M251.1. *Dying monk promises there will be room for his pupil in his grave.* When grave is opened, it is too small to accommodate two bodies. Monk's body turns on its side to make room. *a.b.c.* 399; Tubach 1271.

*M253.1. *Dying man promises friend he will return to tell him about otherworld.* Suffers torment in purgatory because of his obligation. *Espéculo* 286.192.

M256. Promise to dying man broken.

*M256.2. *Pilgrims to Santiago de Compostela break promise to help dying* *companion.* Other man stays with him. Santiago carries body to his church; rewards faithful one and denies benefits of pilgrimage to others. *Espéculo* 285.191–92.

M300–M399. PROPHECIES

M302. Means of prophesying.

*M302.4.2. *At birth, stars say prince* will live long life but at twenty will experience troubles with father (threat of death to self or to father). *Sendebar* p. 67.

*M302.4.3. *Stars say prince* must be silent for seven days. *Sendebar* p. 73; Tubach 4703.

*M302.4.4. *At birth stars say prince* must not see either sunlight or fire. If he were to see it he would be blind. *Barlaam* pp. 262–63.

M310. Favorable prophecies.

M312.0.2. *Prophecy: future greatness as rhetor* prophesied by bees leaving honey on lips of child. *a.b.c.* 180.

M312.0.2.1. *Prophecy: future wealth of child* prophesied by ants leaving grains of wheat on lips. *a.b.c.* 180; Tubach 293.

M312.0.2.3. *Prophecy: future greatness of unborn child* prophesied by egg magically caused to bring forth chick with mature comb. *a.b.c.* 180.

M312.0.4. *Prophecy: pregnant woman's dream* foretells child's future greatness. *a.b.c.* 180; cf. Tubach 647.

*M312.0.4.1. *Prophecy: pregnant woman's dream* while pregnant. Baby daughter's heirs will found a great line. Angel tells her in dream she must baptize immediately upon birth before nursing her. Baby must not drink any milk but her mother's. *Ultramar* I.1.84.169; Tubach 3283.

*M312.0.4.2. *Prophecy: pregnant woman's dream* prophesies that her lineage will be honored in Holy Land. A griffin and two eagles clear temple in Jerusalem of rats, bats, and owls that had nested on altars. Placed on a throne by them, a griffin pecks out her heart and entrails and encircles the city with them. *Ultramar* I.1.144.290–91.

*M312.0.4.3. *Prophecy: pregnant woman dreams* prophesy that one of her sons will be instrumental in avenging Jesus' death. *Armas* p. 122.

*M312.0.4.4. *Prophecy: pregnant woman's dream.* Son will kill father. *Ilustres mujeres* 23.29v–30r (Jocasta).

*M312.10. *Prophecy: angel Gabriel appears in hero's dream* prophesying future success. *CMC* vv. 405–9.

M314. Man will become king.

*M314.5. *Hermit's dream* prophesies that knight will become king. *Çifar* pp. 36–37.

*M314.6. *Knight dreams that exiled king will conquer occupied territory* and be its king. *Abreviada* 3.26.

M340. Unfavorable prophecies.

M341. Death prophesied.

*M341.0.4. *Prophecy of death.* Monk given names of those who will die soon, including his own. Fulfilled. *a.b.c.* 375.

*M341.0.5. *Prophecy of death.* Simple young monk, dying of pestilence, given letters by mysterious youth giving names of all who were to die of pestilence. *a.b.c.* 402; Tubach 1475 b) 1.

*M341.0.6. *Prophecy of death.* Simple man returns from heaven knowing who in household will die of pestilence. *a.b.c.* 383.

*M341.0.7. *Prophecy of death.* Captive bishop confirms king's prophetic dream. *a.b.c.* 61.

M341.1. *Prophecy of death.* Bishop's death foretold (thirty days) if he refuses to remove sinner's body from church. Refuses and dies. *a.b.c.* 353; Tubach 1267.

*M341.1.1.1. *Prophecy of death.* God appears to deacon in dream. He must tell bishop he will die on the Day of the Apostles. *a.b.c.* 65.

*M341.1.5.3. *Prophecy of death.* Image of infant Jesus tells young boy he will join him in heaven tomorrow. *Cantigas* 353.

M341.2. Prophecy: death by particular instrument.

M341.2.4. *Prophecy: five-fold death.* Prince to die from stoning, burning, falling off a cliff, hanging, and drowning. It so happens. *LBA* cc. 123–65.

M342. Prophecy of downfall of kingdom.

M342.1. *Prophecy of downfall of king.* King sends emissaries to philosopher who tells them that they may return because cruel king has been replaced. *Disciplina* 25.

*M342.1.1. *Prophecy of downfall of king.* Dream interpreted falsely by his enemies to say that king must kill family and advisers and bathe in their blood to avoid losing his realm. *Calila* p. 280; *Exemplario* 72v.

*M342.1.2. *Prophecy: enemies will attack duke and his forces.* Duke dreams of being in a magic forest, attacked by four lions, three fierce bears, and two flying dragons, followed by ferocious dogs. Wife interprets it a warning that his enemies were coming to attack him. *Ultramar* I.1.112.231–32.

*M342.1.3. *Prophecy of downfall of emperor* who persecuted Christians. Will lose battle and will die. *Espéculo* 221.150.

*M342.3. *Monk sees vision of king* swallowing one leg of image of Christ crucified and trying to eat the other: one leg is the clergy; other one, the people. King does not heed vision, is assassinated while hunting. *Espéculo* 218.148–49.

M351. *Prophecy that youth will abandon his religion* and become Christian. *Barlaam* p. 22.

*M356.6. *Wise men sent to hear sage's prophecy.* Kingdom to be destroyed; evil king to die to be replaced by a just one. Wise men return to find it fulfilled. *a.b.c.* 379.

M360. Other prophecies.

M362. *Prophecy: death of ruler to insure victory.* Battle will be won by side whose king dies. *Castigos* MS A BNM 6559 10.110; *Glosa* 1.2.12.119.

M363. Coming of religious leader prophesied.

M363.1. *Coming of Christianity prophesied.* Alexander the Great told high priest of Jerusalem that he saw the face of God in priest's face. *Espéculo* 220.150.

M364.7.2.1. *Story of Genesis* and "In the beginning was the word" prophesied by pagan. *a.b.c.* 244.

M370. Vain attempts to escape fulfillment of prophecy.

*M370.2. *Prophetic dream of bishop's death fulfilled.* Man witnesses solemn trial; bishop condemned. Dreamer goes to palace and finds bishop dead. *Espéculo* 468.369–70.

*M370.3. *Prophetic dream of pope's death fulfilled.* Cardinal and two holy women witnessed solemn trial where Jesus Christ found him guilty. Pope found dead next day. *Espéculo* 469.370.

M372. *Confinement in tower to avoid fulfillment of prophecy.* No one to approach prince until he reaches young manhood. *Barlaam* pp. 34–35.

*M372.2. *Prophecy: weaver's son to be royal bailiff.* Despite paternal pressure, child chooses studies over weaving. *Poridat* 45–46.

*M372.3. *Prophecy: princeling to be blacksmith.* Despite paternal efforts, child refuses studies in favor of labor. *Poridat* 46.

*M375.2.1. *Slaughter of unborn and newborn children* to avoid fulfillment of prophecy that one of them would be king of Rome. *a.b.c.* 180.

M400–M499. CURSES

M410. Pronouncement of curses.

*M411.1.3. *Mother curses children* who have mistreated her. *a.b.c.* 260; Tubach 1440 c).

M411.8.2. *Hermit curses men who kill* his companion-bear. They die of a dreaded illness. *a.b.c.* 329.

M420. Enduring and overcoming curses.

*M423.1. *Mother's curse lifted* by prayer and reverential penitence. *a.b.c.* 260; Tubach 1440 c).

M470. Curses on objects or animals.

M474. *Curse on land.* Man whose land bordered church lands cultivated church lands. His oxen broke their yokes and ran wild. He died within ten days. *Espéculo* 219.149.

N. CHANCE AND FATE

N0–N99. WAGERS AND GAMBLING

N0. Wagers and gambling.

N1.2.1. *The miracle of broken die* saves soul of gambler, allowing saintly man to win. *a.b.c.* 252; Tubach 2239.

*N.1.2.1.1. *The miracle of broken die makes man winner.* Virgin Mary helps him win over opponent because he had promised property to her if he won. *Cantigas* 214; cf. Tubach 2239.

N10. Wagers on wives, husbands, or servants.

N12. *Wager on wife's obedience. Lucanor* Ex. 27; cf. Tubach 4354.

N50. Other wagers.

*N67.1. *Wager: stingy man can be forced to give alms.* Pauper taunts him; angered miser, not able to find stick or stone to throw, throws a loaf of bread at beggar. *a.b.c.* 135.

*N68. *Wager based on reductio ad absurdum of task.* When an impossible task is given, the hero responds with a countertask so absurd as to show the manifest absurdity of the original task. Wager: drink the seas dry: counterwager stop up all the rivers. *Esopete* p. 15; *Sendebar* Day 8, Tale 22.

N100–N299. THE WAYS OF LUCK AND FATE

N110. Luck and fate personified.

N111. *Fortuna.* Luck (fate) thought of as a goddess. *Talavera* 4.2.276–98; *Compendio* pp. 251–73; cf. Tubach 2154, 2155, 2156.

N120. Determination of luck or fate.

*N126.3. *Queen casts lots* to foresee future events in realm. *Ultramar* I.1.166.323.

N130. Changing of luck or fate.

N134.2. *Corpse brings bad luck to ship.* Cast overboard. *Apolonio* cc. 273–83.

N140. Nature of luck and fate: miscellaneous.

N142. *Destiny (fate) better than work, show, or intelligence.* Laborer makes very little by his work; handsome nobleman more by pleasing a woman; merchant more by speculation; prince most of all because of his royal heritage. *Calila* p. 324; *Exemplario* 83v–84r.

N146. Man not fated to die cannot be killed.

*N146.1. *Christian captured by Moors sentenced to death.* Stoned, throat cut, but does not die. Calls upon Virgin Mary to send for priest so he can confess. Then he dies. *Cantigas* 124.

N170. The capriciousness of luck.

N172. *Prodigal son favored over faithful son. Barlaam* pp. 102–3.

*N174.1. *Emperor, afraid of lightning, constructed underground retreat.* Left it only on fine days, but storm overtook him and killed him. *Çifar* p. 27.

*N178.1. *Broken leg saves man from fatal fight.* King has ordered that he be killed in a fight. He breaks leg and cannot go to palace that day. King forgives him when learns of his innocence. *Lucanor* Ex. 18.

*N181.1. *Rich man tells poor man that he is rich because he finds money on the way to church.* Poor man goes and gets both spiritual and temporal sustenance. *Espéculo* 228.152–53.

N200. The good gifts of fortune.

N211.1. *Lost ring found in fish.* Returned to queen who uses it to prove her fidelity to husband. *Espéculo* 125.83; Tubach 4102.

*N212.2. *Money will go to its destination.* Man told that money he found belongs to another. Hollows out tree trunk; puts money inside and throws it into sea. Trunk washes up at door of rightful owner who uses it for firewood; gold begins to melt. His wife finds trunk and hides it. First man is beggar now, and wife of rightful owner bakes bread with money inside; gives it to first man. He sells bread to fishermen who begin to feed it to horses. Wife gives them oats for her bread. Money has returned to owner. *Espéculo* 58.41; Tubach 4954.

N250. Persistent bad luck.

*N252.2. *Messenger announces misfortune to holy man.* Someone has set fire to his crops. He accepts his luck. *a.b.c.* 343.

*N252.3. *Servant (messenger) reports successive misfortunes* to master who has said he does not need to hear bad news. *a.b.c.* 195; *Disciplina* 27; Tubach 1705.

N253. *Safety in shadow of wall.* After escaping a series of misfortunes, man is apparently safe when sheltering wall falls on him and kills him. *Calila* p. 124.

N255. Escape from one misfortune into worse.

N255.2. *Ass gets progressively worse masters.* Finally farmer beats him while alive and will not spare his hide even when he is dead. *Esopete* pp. 66–67; Tubach 387.

N270. Crime inevitably comes to light.

*N275.5.2. *Sheep thief confesses* in church when bishop orders belly of thief to bleat. *a.b.c.* 179; Tubach 4317.

N300–N399. UNLUCKY ACCIDENTS

N330. Accidental killing or death.

N332.3. *Serpent carried by bird* lets poison drop into milk and poisons drinkers. *Sendebar* Day 8, Tale 19.

N333. Aiming at fly has fatal results.

N333.1. *Heretic killed by hitting fly* on his face. *Gatos* 6; *Esopete* p. 52; Tubach 2103.

N340. Hasty killing or condemnation (mistake).

N340.2. *King hastily has thousands put to death* for stoning his judges. *Castigos* MS A BNM 6559 10.107–8; *Glosa* 1.1.13.67–68; Tubach 1494.

*N340.2.1. *King wrongly advised to kill* wife, son, counselor, philosopher, war elephants, charger and to bathe in their blood to avoid destruction of realm. He does not. *Calila* p. 280.

N340.3. *Woman wrongly judged to be drunk* when seen to drink a full glass of wine. *a.b.c.* 51.

N341. *Emissary of evil noble killed* in place of intended victim of ambush. *a.b.c.* 8.

N346. *Pigeon hastily kills mate* for stealing wheat stored in nest. It has dried out and appeared to be less. With moisture it swells, and pigeon kills self in remorse. *Sendebar* Day 6, Tale 16; *Calila* p. 291. *Exemplario* 73r.

N347.1. *Cleric accidentally suspected of crime* had wandered into a tavern and was arrested among a group of spies. Executed despite innocence. *a.b.c.* 349 (not in Paris MS); *Disciplina* 7; *Espéculo* 533.421; Tubach 2431.

N347.2. *Holy man enters brothel to reform prostitutes.* Accused of loose behavior. *a.b.c.* 229.

N350. Accidental loss of property.

*N352.1.1. *Eagle carries off official's ring* and drops it in slave's lap. *Esopete* pp. 17–18.

N380. Other unlucky accidents.

N381. *Drop of honey* causes chain of events. Hunter drops honey in a shop; bee lights on honey; storekeeper's cat kills bee; hunter's dog kills cat; storekeeper kills dog; hunter kills storekeeper; villagers and neighbors of storekeeper kill hunter; villagers and neighbors of hunter come, and the two groups kill each other. *Sendebar* Day 3, Tale 7.

N383.2.1. *Man is sickened when he realizes* he has eaten bread from flour used for abscess plaster. *Sendebar* Day 2, Tale 4.

N388. *Blind men accidentally hurt each other* (trying to kill pig). *a.b.c.* 64; Tubach 698.

N400–N699. LUCKY ACCIDENTS

N410. Lucky business ventures.

N411.5. *Seller of sandalwood learns its value* in land lacking sandalwood. *Sendebar* Day 8, Tale 22.

N440–N499. Valuable secrets learned.

N451.1. *Secrets of animals (dwarfs) accidentally overheard from tree.* Animal tells others that it will help him rid themselves of man. Man in tree overhears and shoots the speaker. *Esopete* p. 123.

N455.2.1. *Cheaters' secrets overheard* and used in court against them. *Sendebar* Day 8, Tale 22.

N500–N599. Treasure trove.

N510. Where treasure is found.

N511.1.6.1. *Treasure found in ruined wall.* Stonecutter rewarded for hospitality, finds a treasure when he tears down old wall. *Espéculo* 64.45.

*N511.1.9.1. *Treasure buried under roots of tree.* Grateful doves lead monk to spot. *Calila* p. 334.

N514. Treasure hidden in religious shrine (object).

*N514.3. *Treasure found in broken statue.* Man, angry at religious statue, smashes it against wall. Finds hidden gold. *Esopete* p. 110.

N530. Discovery of treasure.

*N531.6. *Virgin Mary appears in dream to king.* Tells him where he will find buried treasure. *Cantigas* 348.

*N534.7.2. *Hermit digs in mouse's hole* and finds hidden coins. *Calila* p. 210; *Exemplario* 46r.

N535.1. *Treasure indicated by stone cross on palace floor.* Cross dug up reverently; treasure found beneath it. *a.b.c.* 144; Tubach 4950.

*N535.2. *Treasure indicated by shadow of extended figure of statue.* a.b.c. 241; Tubach 2720, 4611.

*N535.3. *Eagle carries off official's ring* and drops it in slave's lap. *Esopete* pp. 17–18.

N538.1. *Treasure pointed out by soul* that has left body in dream. *a.b.c.* 142.

*N545.1.1. *Eagle leads rescuer to site of great treasure.* a.b.c. 207.

N590. Treasure trove: miscellaneous.

*N592. *Golden tablets unearthed* bearing message warning of the sin of avarice. *a.b.c.* 35; Tubach 4175, 4702.

N600–N699. Other lucky accidents.

N635. *The triple tax.* Poet is given by king the right to demand a coin from hunchbacks to enter city; from persons with head lice; from persons with scabies; from one-eyed persons, from those with hernias. He demands coin from hunchback who protests. In tussle, hunchback is revealed to suffer all infirmities. With revelation of each, poet demands another coin. *a.b.c.* 84; *Esopete* pp. 143-44; *Disciplina* 6; *Espéculo* 489[1], 386; Tubach 4892.

N685. *Fool passes as wise man* by remaining silent. *a.b.c.* 408.

*N699.3.1. *Accused man interrupts trip to pray.* Avoids ambush. *a.b.c.* 8.

P. SOCIETY

P0–P99. ROYALTY AND NOBILITY

P10. Kings.

P11. Choice of kings.

*P11.0.2. *Choice of king through force.* Man is forced to accept office. *Barlaam* p. 321; *Castigos* 11.112.

*P11.7. *King chosen for a year* provides for future. Knowing that the custom is that he is to be deposed in a year, he sends provisions to a safe place out of the kingdom. *Lucanor* Ex. 49; *a.b.c.* 366; *Barlaam* pp. 121–23; *Espéculo* 243.163; Tubach 2907.

*P11.8. *Gods tell people to choose king* whom they find eating from an iron table. Choose a farmer they see eating on a metal plough blade. *a.b.c.* 384.

P12. Character of kings.

P12.5. Good king never retreats in battle.

*P12.5.0.1. *Hero-king's (Cid) body* on his charger leads troops to victory in battle. *PCG* 2.956.636–38.

P12.9. *Nobility of character a mark of kings.* King (Alexander, Scipio Africanus) shows nobility by sending women captives back unharmed. *a.b.c.* 83; *Castigos* MS A BNM 6559 23.140 (ADMYTE 0 82v); Tubach 3971.

*P12.9.1. *Roman consul invites captive enemy* to join him in deliberations. *a.b.c.* 211; Tubach 1900.

*P12.10.1. *Caesar was generous to heirs of his enemy. a.b.c.* 211.

*P12.15. *Great king accepts explanation* that great power is temporary and hollow. *a.b.c.* 361.

*P12.16. *Just king accepts explanation* that people who had criticized him were drunk. Truthful admission cools his anger. *a.b.c.* 419.

P13. Customs connected with kings.

P13.9.1.1. *King deserves great privileges.* Alexander sought advice from Parmenyon. Told by Parmenyon: "If I were Alexander I would accept." Replies: "I am not Parmenyon, but Alexander and deserve greater gift." *a.b.c.* 257; *Glosa* 1.2.19.168–69; Tubach 90.

P14. Particular practices of kings.

P14.19. *King goes at night to observe his subjects.* Hears them say he is greatest fool in land because he gave trickster wealth to fetch secret ingredient to change lead into gold. *Çifar* p. 129; *Lucanor* Ex. 20.

*P14.24. *King never permits execution of those sentenced to death.* Killing human beings wrong. *a.b.c.* 397.

*P14.25. *King does not permit anyone to ask him why he never laughs.* Penalty is beheading. *Çifar* p. 130; Tubach 4994.

*P14.26. *King spares life* of respected stranger who violates prohibition. *Çifar* p. 130.

P15. Adventures (deeds) of kings.

P15.1.2. *King pardons person who has mistaken a remarkably beautiful courtier* in his entourage for him. *a.b.c.* 314; Tubach 2910.

*P15.1.3. *Emperor pardons defeated king.* It is honorable to defeat enemy and then to pardon him. *a.b.c.* 125.

P15.6. *Alexander descends to bottom of sea* in glass barrel with rooster to tell time. Learned tactics from fish. *Castigos* MS A BNM 6559 33.153 (ADMYTE 0 104v); Tubach 123.

P16. End of king's reign.

*P16.1.3.1. *Evil king who had abused power* destroyed by divine instigation. Consults philosophers. They recommend that he send for advice to a wise man, Mariano. *a.b.c.* 379; *Disciplina* 25.

*P16.1.5. *King retires from world.* Abdicates in favor of son. Son abuses power. King returns to defeat tyrant (takes out his eyes and imprisons him). Crowns younger son. *a.b.c.* 22.

*P16.1.6. *Pious king abdicates to retreat to ascetic life.* Leaves kingdom to advisor. *Barlaam* pp. 319–22.

P17. Succession to throne.

*P17.11.1. *Rustic healer made adviser to ruler.* Poisons him, seizes power, and rules cruelly. *a.b.c.* 384.

P19. Other motifs associated with kings.

*P19.3.1. *King grants all wishes of those who come to him.* They must not leave unhappy. *a.b.c.* 364.

P19.4.2. *King inadvertently disobeys law.* Enters court armed; kills self. *Glosa* 1.2.11.114; *Castigos* MS A BN 6559 (ADMYTE 0 31v).

P20. Queens.

*P29.4. *Queen insists that frivolous idle woman who disdains spinning learn to spin* or that she not appear at court. *Castigos* 6.59.

P50. Nobility.

*P50.0.2. *King and vassals*: lion king sets out to avenge mistreatment of vassals. *Esopete* pp. 98–100.

P100–P199. OTHER SOCIAL ORDERS

P110. Royal ministers.

P111. *Banished minister* found indispensable and recalled. *Esopete* p. 21.

*P111.1. *Minister who spared life of king's favorite wife* pardoned and restored to office. *Calila* p. 280.

P150. Rich men.

P152. *Rich man sees that his wealth will not help him gain eternal life.* Enters religious order. *Espéculo* 39.26–27.

P200–P299. THE FAMILY

P210. Husband and wife.

*P214.2. *Wife kills self* when abandoned by husband (to join dead husband). *Castigos* 40.185–86; *Ilustres mujeres* 40.47r–49r (Dido).

P230. Parents and children.

*P230.4. *Parents must chastise son when young.* Lesson from tale of farmer who yokes a calf and an ox to tame the calf. *Esopete* pp. 64–65.

*P231.3. *Mother love.* Noble woman insists on nursing her own children. Will not permit them to have wetnurse. *Castigos* MS A BNM 6559 (ADMYTE 0 7r).

*P231.4.1. *Mother (Empress Irene) orders that son's eyes be put out. a.b.c.* 295 (not in Paris MS).

P232. Mother and daughter.

*P232.3. *Daughter who had offended mother* during lifetime is punished in afterlife. *Espéculo* 440.334.

*P232.4. *Mother curses children who mistreated her.* Treacherous daughters and sons afflicted with terrible illness. Cured by saint. *a.b.c.* 260; Tubach 1440 c).

*P232.5. *Devils torment daughter who had verbally abused her mother.* *a.b.c.* 336.

P233. Father and son.

*P233.2.2. *Poor widow tells emperor his son had killed hers.* He gives his son in exchange. *Espéculo* 348.247–48; *Abreviada* 1.206; Tubach 4989.

P233.8. *Prodigal son returns. Barlaam* pp. 102–3.

*P233.9.1. *Duke's son chastises father for licentious ways.* Will only acknowledge him because of mother's honor. Chooses not to inherit dukedom. *Castigos* 1.41–42; Tubach 362.

*P233.9.2. *Evil king defeated by enemies flees.* His own son imprisons him, tortures him, and kills him. *a.b.c.* 416.

*P233.9.3. *Son mocks father when he sees him drunk and naked* (Noah). *a.b.c.* 421.

*P233.12. *Father dies in his son's stead.* Justice demanded that one die. *a.b.c.* 339; Tubach 2005.

*P233.13. *Santiago rewards pilgrimage of father.* Sustains falsely accused son on gallows until innocence is proved. *a.b.c.* 38; *Santiago* 5.56–61; Tubach 3796.

*P233.14. *Sentence applies to king's own son.* Those caught in adultery are to have eyes put out. When king's son is found guilty, king has one of his own eyes and one of his son's eyes put out to satisfy law. *a.b.c.* 224; *Castigos* MS A BNM 6559 (ADMYTE 0 31*v*); Tubach 1944.

*P233.15. *Son on gallows bites his mother's (father's) nose off:* punishment for lack of discipline in youth. *a.b.c.* 338; *Çifar* pp. 82–83; *Esopete* pp. 112–13; *Castigos* 1.41; *Glosa* 2.2.2.129–30; *Espéculo* 287.196–98; Tubach 3488.

*P233.15.1. *Three sons condemned to hang.* Parents had not stopped them from their evil ways. *Espéculo* 289.198–99; see Q586.

*P233.16. *Spoiled child blasphemed God,* and when a pestilence came he fell ill. In a delirium, saw devils coming for him. He died, and so did his father. *a.b.c.* 52; *Espéculo* 79.52; Tubach 684.

*P233.16.1. *Father lets son play in river.* Son drowns, and man drowns trying to save him. *Sendebar* Day 2, Tale 3.

*P233.17. *Test of paternity.* Shooting at father's corpse. Youngest of supposed sons refuses to shoot and is judged the only genuine son of dead emperor. *a.b.c.* 174; Tubach 1272.

*P233.18. *Man cruel to his father,* told by his own son that he will be mistreated in his old age. *a.b.c.* 337; *Espéculo* 439.333–34; Tubach 2001.

*P233.19. *Father and sons.* Father leaves will saying that treasure is buried in vineyard. At his death, sons dig up vineyard; learn that treasure is cultivations of land. *Esopete* pp. 113–14.

P234 Father and daughter.

*P234.3. *Daughter suckles imprisoned parent* denied food by jailers. *Ilustres mujeres* 65.69*r*–70*r* (unknown young Roman woman); *a.b.c.* 171, 173; *Glosa* 2.2.4.137–38; Tubach 3969.

*P234.4. *Father ties infant daughter to lance.* Throws her across stream to save her from pursuers. *Ilustres mujeres* 37.43*r*–45*r* (Camilla).

*P234.5. *Daughter saves father from attacker. Ilustres mujeres* 62.67*r* (Claudia).

*P234.6. *Daughter saves father from death sentence. Ilustres mujeres* 15.22*r*–23*r* (Hypsipyle).

P236. Undutiful children.

P236.2. *Satiric legacy.* Supposed chest of gold induces children to care for aged father. *a.b.c.* 126; Tubach 965.

*P236.8. *Undutiful children.* Dying father hears children crying out, "Where will we go, what will we do when our father dies?" He reminds them they will enjoy the wealth he has amassed. He asks why are they not concerned with what will happen to him. *Espéculo* 389.284–85.

P250. Brothers and sisters.

P251.3.1. *Hostile brothers* come to each other's aid when threatened by outsider. *a.b.c.* 311.

P251.5.5. *Brother unjustly imprisoned by brother.* PCG 825.502–3.

*P253.1. *Sister kills her brother (husband)* to wrest throne from him. *Ilustres mujeres* 89.88r–90r (Cleopatra).

P260. Relations by law.

*P266. *Daughter-in-law* stays in husband's family's household after he has abandoned her. *San Alejo* p. 89.

P300–P399. OTHER SOCIAL RELATIONSHIPS

P310. Friendship.

P315. *Friends offer to die for each other.* Each falsely confesses to crime to save the other. Neither guilty. *Disciplina* 2; *Çifar* pp. 9–11; *Esopete* pp. 137–39; *Glosa* 1.2.28.211; Tubach 2208, 2215.

P317.1. *Plato refuses to believe that Xenocrates has spoken ill of him. a.b.c.* 20, 168; *Glosa* 1.2.13.124–25; Tubach 2211, 3820.

*P317.1.1. *Alexander takes supposedly poisoned medicine* showing confidence in physician friend. *a.b.c.* 168; *Glosa* 1.2.13.124; Tubach 134, 1401.

P320. Hospitality.

*P324.2.1. *Host treats guest with excellent food.* Guest had imbibed foul water before entering. Vomits and is unable to eat. *Espéculo* 36.25–26.

*P324.4. *Saint eats gluttonously* to please guests. Repents next day. *Espéculo* 298.208.

*P324.5. *Saint has only bacon to give guest during Lent.* Both partake as sign of hospitality. *Espéculo* 297.207–8; cf. Tubach 3243.

P325. *Host surrenders wife to guest* who unwittingly falls in love with the wife. The host, on being informed, out of pure generosity repudiates wife and has her marry the guest. *Esopete* pp. 137–39; *Disciplina* 2; *Çifar* pp. 9–11.

P340. Teacher and pupil.

*P344. *Teacher gives pupil Ciceronian rule for rhetoric.* Student memorizes rule and recites it instead of applying it. *Exemplario* 2r; *Calila* p. 92.

*P344.1. *Teacher writes all worldly wisdom on walls* and confines pupil to room to learn it in short time. *Sendebar* p. 72.

P360. Master and servant.

P361. *Faithful servant dies instead of master.* Puts on master's clothes and ring; throat is slit. *a.b.c.* 166; *Glosa* 2.3.15.304; Tubach 2209.

*P361.1.4. *Servant kills master to save him from dying at enemy's hands.* Kills self. *Glosa* 2.3.15.304.

*P361.8.1. *Faithful servant undergoes torments in master's place. a.b.c.* 166.

*P361.10. *Servant deceives invading enemy.* Pretends he has thrown cruel master on pyre. Saves him. *Glosa* 2.3.15.304.

*P361.11. *Servants deceive enemy; they are carrying off mistress* to kill her for cruelty. Save her. *Glosa* 2.3.15.304.

*P361.12. *Servant asked to help kill king by prince.* Supplies harmless substance instead of poison. *Glosa* 2.3.15.305.

P400–P499. TRADES AND PROFESSIONS

P435. Usurer.

*P435.3. *Ass carries usurer's body to the gallows* instead of to the church. *Espéculo* 567.461–63; Tubach 375.

*P435.4. *Corpse of usurer rises up,* destroys church furnishings, beats monks, kills one, because his soul was suffering torments despite promises that soul would be prayed out of hell. *a.b.c.* 149; Tubach 5031.

*P435.5. *Church built by usurer's money made to collapse* by devil. *a.b.c.* 148; cf. Tubach 1053.

*P435.6. *Usurer and his descendants punished in hell,* ten generations who had benefited arranged on a ladder. *a.b.c.* 385 (not in Paris MS); cf. Tubach 5027, 5062.

*P435.7. *Saint who accepted alms from usurer* punished in hellfire by burn on his cheek. *Espéculo* 12.9–10.

*P435.8. *Usurer gave abbot money to pray for him.* God said all but one coin had been earned dishonestly. Accepted only one coin on altar. *a.b.c.* 132.

*P435.9. *Punishment from otherworld:* leprosy, erysipelas, and poverty. Executors of usurer's will do not make restitution of his ill-gotten wealth. *Espéculo* 262.176–77.

*P435.10. *Usurer's soul condemned* to eternal torment despite generosity to monastery. Returns and attacks monks. *a.b.c.* 149.

*P435.11. *Man who deserted his usurer father and brother sees them roasting in hell* and blaming each other for their plight. *a.b.c.* 430; Tubach 5027.

*P435.12. *Usurer leaves wealth to friends and family.* Leaves nothing for his soul. Acknowledges the omission to priest and then dies. *Espéculo* 659.462–63; Tubach 5050.

*P435.13. *Dying man (usurer) reproaches soul for desire to leave him* despite his great wealth and comfort. *Lucanor* Ex. 4; *Espéculo* 568.462.

*P435.14. *Dead moneylender's heart found in strongbox.* Saint tells mourners at funeral of moneylender. *Lucanor* Ex. 14; Tubach 2499.

*P435.15. *Hero (Cid) deceives moneylenders.* Gives them chests filled with sand as surety for loan. *CMC* vv. 65–212.

P446. Barber.

P446.2. *Distrust of barbers.* Barber sees inscription over door: "Whatever you do, do wisely, and think of the consequences." He is hired to cut king's throat, drops razor, and confesses. *a.b.c.* 69.

P446.2.1. *Distrust of barbers.* King to avoid possible assassination singes beard rather than have barber shave him. *Castigos* MS A BNM 6559 25.141 (ADMYTE 0 84v).

P448. Butcher.

P448.1. *Sheep killed by butcher*, who they are persuaded will spare them. They betray each other. *Esopete* p. 76.

P458. Woodsman.

P458.1. *Trees not to supply wood for woodsman's axe handle. Esopete* p. 65; Tubach 444.

*P458.2. *Water spirit returns* silver axe to woodchopper in place of the one he has lost. *Esopete* p. 112.

P460. Other trades and professions.

P462. Stonecutter.

*P462.1. *Treasure found in ruined wall.* Stonecutter rewarded for hospitality, finds a treasure when he tears down old wall. *Espéculo* 64.45.

P463. Baker.

*P463.1. *Sultan is recognized as son of baker* because his reward to philosopher is loaves of bread. *a.b.c.* 313; Tubach 500.

*P463.2. *Unreasonable threat of punishment* to cook, to baker, and to host's wife to frighten guest. *Esopete* pp. 13–14.

*P463.3. *Bakers use matter from abscess* in bread dough. *Sendebar* Day 2, Tale 4.

*P463.4. *Prince whose father was really the court baker* (cook) advised to remember both his royal and his humble heritage. *a.b.c.* 189.

P464. Shepherd.

*P464.1. *Shepherd who cried "Wolf"* too often. When the wolf really comes, no one believes him. *Esopete* p. 111.

P465. Lawyer.

*P465.1. *Dying lawyer offers self to God.* God says he must be judged. Refuses to be judged by his equals and so dies without communion and confession. *Espéculo* 19.14; cf. Tubach 2991.

*P465.2. *Widow gives lawyer a cart as fee.* Adversary gives him ox to pull it. She loses case and says: "The cart does not go well." He replies that it needs an ox to pull it. *Espéculo* 23.16.

*P465.3. *Man's lawyer is bribed to lose a lawsuit.* Appears in court saying he has "esquinança" ('quinsy') and cannot speak. His client says he does not have "esquinança" but rather "argençia" ('money disease'). *a.b.c.* 309.

*P465.4. *Dying lawyer says: "I appeal."* Asks for defense. Dies without confession and goes to hell. *Espéculo* 21.15; Tubach 2991.

*P465.5. *Nose cut off as punishment for theft.* Lawyer stole land from church. Saint appears and tells him to return it. Third time cuts off nose as sign of perjury and theft. *Espéculo* 458.357–58.

*P465.6. *Lawyers bathe in special hell's fire. a.b.c.* 12.

P466. Doctors.

*P466. *Doctor prescribes same remedy* for a sore eye that he had used to cure his own sore foot. Patient blinded. *a.b.c.* 283.

P482. Painter.

P482.1.1. *Devil pulls scaffold from under painter's feet.* Virgin rescues him. *a.b.c.* 263; Tubach 3573.

P500–P599. GOVERNMENT
P510. Law courts.
P511. Criminal to choose method of execution.

P511.2. *Sentenced to have eyes taken out*, is granted favor of selecting instrument. Is unable to find suitable nail. *a.b.c.* 151; Tubach 1947.

*P511.3. *Man to choose tree for his hanging* is unable to find suitable tree. Is not executed. *a.b.c.* 130; Tubach 4790.

P520. Lawsuits.

*P521.1. *Lawsuit between wolf and fox.* Ape is judge; greyhound lawyer for wolf; sheepdog lawyer for fox. *LBA* cc. 321–71.

*P521.2. *Fraudulent claim by stag* made in presence of wolf whose presence intimidates sheep into acknowledging debt. Repayment scheduled for when wolf will not be present. *Esopete* p. 52.

P522. Laws.

*P524.3. *High-born woman pledges son as security with usurer.* Unable to repay, calls on Virgin Mary, who helps her rescue him. *Cantigas* 63.

P525. Contracts.

*P525.4. *Borrower offers Virgin Mary and Christ as guarantors of repayment of debt.* Repayment put in sea, miraculously reaches Jewish creditor on time. *Milagros* 23; cf. *Castigos* 7.64; *Cantigas* 25; Tubach 2797.

P530. Taxes or tributes.

*P532.1. *Unpaid tithes* result in pestilence or crop failures. *Espéculo* 171.115.

P550. Military affairs.
P555. Defeat in battle.

P555.0.1. *Defeated soldier* tells emperor that battle was lost because of emperor's impiety. *Espéculo* 217.148.

P600–P699. CUSTOMS

P612. *Trumpet blown before house of one sentenced to death. a.b.c.* 192, 292; *Barlaam* p. 55; *Espéculo* 192.133–34, 294.202–3; Tubach 4994.

P672. *Pulling a man's beard as an insult. CMC* vv. 3280–90.

*P672.1.5. *Jew touches dead hero's beard.* Corpse unsheathes sword to punish him. *PCG* 2.961.642–43.

*P672.6. *Insult:* throwing blood-filled object (cucumber) at another is cause of dishonor. *Abreviada* 2.281.

P690. Political customs.

*P691. *Women punished to appease Neptune.* Not to vote, not to take part in public councils, not to give their name to offspring. *Jardín* pp. 243–44; Tubach 3462.

P700–P799. SOCIETY: MISCELLANEOUS

P711.7. *Man rises from sick bed* to battle for his country. *Castigos* MS A BNM 6559 57.184.

P711.9. *Patriotism:* agreement that battle will be won by those whose leader is killed in battle. Duke disguised as pilgrim joins battle and is killed. *a.b.c.* 340; *Castigos* MS A BNM 6559 57.184, MS A BNM 6559 10.110; *Glosa* 1.2.12.119.

Q. REWARDS AND PUNISHMENTS

Q10–Q99. DEEDS REWARDED

Q20. Piety rewarded.

*Q20.3. *Emperor of great piety,* vowed never to take the life of another being. Forgave his enemies and ruled in peace. *a.b.c.* 68.

*Q20.3.1. *Compassionate ruler forgives friends* who have offended him. Treats them with love. *a.b.c.* 67.

*Q20.3.2. *Compassionate emperor told to bathe in pool of infant blood* as cure, takes pity on mothers and refuses. God rewards him with cure (Constantine). *PCG* 316.183–86; *Abreviada* 1.342.

*Q20.4. *Pious holy man preaches the word of God,* after God restored his sight. Mission completed, he returns, and his soul is transported directly to heaven. *a.b.c.* 27.

*Q20.5. *Militant pope fought to defend church land.* God sends wind to open church doors to reward his piety. *a.b.c.* 33; Tubach 2370.

*Q20.6. *Cleric overwhelmed by sins confesses in writing.* Great contrition causes written words to be magically erased. *a.b.c.* 72; Tubach 1202.

Q21. Reward for religious sacrifice.

*Q21.0.1. *King rewards his son's piety* and prudence. Youth had given all his wealth to poor where it would always be safe. *Disciplina* 29; Tubach 4963.

*Q21.0.2. *Bishop told he would die prayed from tierce to nones.* Rewarded for his piety. *a.b.c.* 65.

Q21. Reward for religious sacrifice.

Q21.1. *Old woman gives her only cow believing she will receive a hundred in return from God.* A bishop hearing her faith sends her a hundred. *a.b.c.* 139; Tubach 4089; cf. Tubach 176.

*Q21.2. *Saint gives all his good deeds to a sinner.* Sinner will be pardoned. Devils come to get saint but sacrifice saves him. *a.b.c.* 138.

Q28. Reward for pilgrimage.

*Q28.1. *Pilgrim goes directly to holy places* while companions seek lodging. While at worship, his horse found him lodgings and awaited him there. *Espéculo* 231.154–55.

*Q28.2. *Reward for pilgrimage.* Old woman falls ill on way to Holy Land and dies. Celestial light descends, and she ascends to heaven. *Espéculo* 143.98–99.

*Q28.3. *Reward for pilgrimage.* Sick man, fearful of purgatory, told to make pilgrimage. Dies and goes directly to heaven. *Espéculo* 144.99.

*Q28.4. *Reward for pilgrimage.* Frequent pilgrim to Santiago de Compostela calls on saint for help in fight. Victorious, he is asked by opponent to call upon saint to cure broken limb. *Santiago* 13.75–76.

Q39. Piety rewarded: miscellaneous.

*Q39.2. *Reward for church attendance to holy man.* Elected bishop. *Espéculo* 229.153.

*Q39.3. *Virgin Mary promises young woman that she will be rewarded if she does not dance* or engage in frivolous behavior. She joins Virgin and other maidens in heaven. *a.b.c.* 85; Tubach 1424.

Q42. Generosity rewarded.

Q42.8. *Holy man gives credit for good deeds to dying woman* (man) so that she can go to heaven. He is rewarded. *Espéculo* 83.56; *a.b.c.* 138.

*Q42.8.1. *Abbot awards good deeds to knight.* When knight dies he goes to heaven; abbot is rewarded. *Espéculo* 84.56–57.

*Q42.10. *King gives clothes to leper* and lifts him into his saddle. Leper asks king to blow his nose for him. King does so and finds a huge ruby in his hand. Leper disappears magically. *Castigos* 7.61–62; cf. Tubach 3489.

Q44. Reward for almsgiving.

Q44.1. *Shepherd sent away from monastery for excessive almsgiving* restored after wolves eat monastery's sheep. *a.b.c.* 143.

Q44.2. *Steward pardoned for short accounts* when it is learned that he has given the money to the poor where it is safe from thieves. *a.b.c.* 145 (not in Paris MS); cf. Tubach 4963.

*Q44.5. *Emperor rewarded for almsgiving.* Great treasure unearthed beneath floor of palace. *a.b.c.* 144; Tubach 4950.

*Q44.7. *Bread shared with poor* replenished magically by God. *a.b.c.* 146, 147; Tubach 766, 2566.

Q45. Hospitality rewarded.

*Q45.0.1. *Poor fisherman who had shared his only garment with shipwrecked man* is rewarded richly. *Apolonio* cc. 632–37.

Q45.1. *Angel entertained unawares.* Hospitality to disguised saint (angel, god) rewarded. *Esopete* p. 3; *Castigos* MS A BNM 6559 54.181; cf. Tubach 2533, 3653.

Q51. Kindness to animals rewarded.

*Q51.3. *Holy man cures hyena cubs.* She rewards him with sheep skins and food. *a.b.c.* 50; Tubach 2714.

Q60. Other good qualities rewarded.

Q61. *Self-abnegation* rewarded. Man who declares self unworthy to look heavenward pardoned. *Castigos* MS A BNM 6559 87.223.

*Q62.1. *Youth invents false report of senate proceedings* to keep secret true proceedings. Senate rewards him with permanent permission to attend. *a.b.c.* 394; Tubach 5269.

Q69. Obedience rewarded.

*Q69.1. *Obedience rewarded.* Scribe called by abbot interrupts work. Returns to find it miraculously completed in gold. *Espéculo* 417.314.

Q72. Loyalty rewarded.

Q72.1.1. *Captured knight asked by captor what fate he merits.* He asks for death because he will never be disloyal to his master. Captor frees him. *a.b.c.* 79; *Glosa* 2.3.15.303.

Q80. Rewards for other causes.

*Q85.1. *Reward for graceful answer.* Lowly poet tells king that a rose grows among thorns as he did among humble persons. King sends him away with many gifts. *Disciplina* 3.

Q86.1. *Reward to ant for industry.* Ant has food all winter because she keeps it safe and dry by airing it in the sun. *Lucanor* Ex. 23; Tubach 265.

Q94. Reward for cure.

*Q94.1. *Truthful man reveals secret cures to king.* Magic spring cures blindness; bread partially eaten by fox restores princess's voice. Rewarded with many gifts and great wealth. *Gatos* 28.

Q100–Q199. NATURE OF REWARDS

Q110. Material rewards.

*Q111.9. *In exchange for restoration of lost riches,* husband agrees to deliver his wife to devil. *a.b.c.* 144.

*Q111.10. *Finder of great treasure, is rewarded* by community; they make statue of gold, silver, and jewels in his honor. *a.b.c.* 241; Tubach 2720; cf. Tubach 4611.

Q112.0.5. *Kingdom and hand of princess* reward for virtuous life. *Castigos* 1.41.

Q121. Freedom as reward.

*Q121.2. *Freedom as reward.* Captive interprets king's dream. Reward is his freedom and that of all the other captives. *a.b.c.* 61; cf. Tubach 1785.

Q140. Miraculous or magic rewards.

Q141.1. *Monks who always shared with the poor receive miraculous supplies* of flour and bread. *a.b.c.* 146, 147; Tubach 766.

Q147.1. *Body of saint miraculously rolls over in grave to make room for his pupil* to whom he had promised interment with him. *a.b.c.* 399; Tubach 1271.

Q147.2. *Magic wind blows open locked doors of church* to show that pope deserves to be buried there. *a.b.c.* 33; Tubach 2370.

Q150. Immunity from disaster as reward.

*Q151.8.1. *Life spared as reward for bravery and constancy.* Captive tells captor that death or release are the same to him. In either case he would be lost to his master. *a.b.c.* 79.

Q151.11. *Man rewarded by God for good deed.* Daniel unharmed by seven lions. *Castigos* 9.69–70.

Q170. Religious rewards.

Q171. *Immunity from punishment as reward.* Robber baron saved from devil by his daily devotion to Virgin Mary. *a.b.c.* 45.

Q172. Reward: admission to heaven.

*Q172.0.3. *Friar scribe's soul admitted directly to heaven* as reward for illuminating Virgin's name in three colors. *Cantigas* 384.

*Q172.0.4. *Angel promises admission to heaven to good monk* killed by a beast. *a.b.c.* 105.

*Q172.0.5. *Knight followed steps of Jesus in Jerusalem.* On Mount of Olives he was carried up to heaven. *a.b.c.* 434; Tubach 3797.

Q172.2. *Evil rich man on deathbed given chance to repent gives all his wealth to poor.* Is pardoned because of one act of charity. *a.b.c.* 135.

Q172.2.1. *The rich man's trial in heaven.* Piece of bread given to beggar is placed on scales. *a.b.c.* 135.

*Q172.2.1.1. *Evil rich man angrily throws a loaf of bread at a beggar.* On deathbed, is pardoned because of one act of involuntary charity. *a.b.c.* 135.

Q172.3. *Evil robber repents; is given chance.* He must embrace and live with next creature he encounters. It is a serpent whose venom kills him, but he goes to heaven. *Castigos* MS A BNM 6559 82.224.

Q200–Q399. DEEDS PUNISHED
Q211. Murder punished.

Q211.0.3. *Emperor carried off to hell* and plunged into boiling oil for many cruel murders. *a.b.c.* 114.

*Q211.0.4 *Herod punished for murders of innocents.* Castigos 9.71.

*Q211.0.5. *Greedy nephew murdered rich uncle.* Caught and killed. *a.b.c.* 120; Tubach 5020.

Q211.3. *Uxoricide punished.* Courtier kills wife, mistaking her for a young woman in the court who had sinned. *Castigos* 33.159.

*Q211.4.3. *Snake chases frog into man's house.* Tries to bite frog but bites man's child instead. Man puts curse on snake. He will be frog-king's mount forever. *Calila* p. 248.

Q212. Theft punished.

*Q212.5. *Thief caught when he steals from monastery garden.* His foot catches in fence, and he is caught; released. *a.b.c.* 178; Tubach 4782 b).

*Q212.6. *Monk attacked by marauding Goths robbed of horse.* Goths' horses will not cross river; they returned his horse and then he could continue journey. *a.b.c.* 191; Tubach 2636.

*Q212.7. *Theft of money offerings on altar punished by blindness and paralysis.* Moor's companions replace stolen money, and health is restored. *Cantigas* 329.

*Q212.8. *Theft of meal for fritters punished.* Tasting knife magically pierces mouth of thief. Prayers to Virgin Mary enable priest to remove it. *Cantigas* 157.

Q220. Impiety punished.

*Q220.2. *Monk tormented* with pains of all those for whom he had not prayed when alive. *Espéculo* 161.109.

*Q220.3. *Friar criticizes royal adoration of religious images* that neither speak nor move. Has bad luck for rest of life. *Cantigas* 297.

*Q220.4. *Cleric stole altar cloth to make underclothes for self.* Awakes with body contorted. Prays to Virgin Mary and is cured. *Cantigas* 327.

*Q220.5. *Pharaoh punished for disobedience to God's word.* Drowned in Red Sea. *Castigos* 9.70.

*Q220.6. *Nebuchadnezzar* punished for impiety. Condemned to wander naked, grazing like a beast. *Castigos* 9.71.

Q221.1. *Discourtesy to god punished.* Blasphemer rouses king's wrath. *Espéculo* 34.22–23.

Q221.3. Blasphemy punished.

*Q221.3.1. *Blasphemer extends right hand to blaspheme.* Cut off and hung at the door of the church. *Espéculo* 210.145–46.

*Q221.3.2. *Spoiled child blasphemed God* and when a pestilence came, he fell ill. In a delirium saw devils coming for him. He died, and so did his father. *a.b.c.* 52; Tubach 684.

*Q221.3.3. *Blasphemer punished by blood flowing from mouth* until death comes. *a.b.c.* 55; Tubach 681, 2240.

*Q221.3.4. *Nun said crazy things*; after church burial she was seen in a vision before altar. Punishment: cut in half; evil part burned. *a.b.c.* 247; Tubach 723.

*Q221.3.5. *Blasphemer's eye drops out on game board* as punishment for swearing on God's eyes. *a.b.c.* 55, 236; Tubach 681, 1949, 2240.

*Q221.3.6. *Blasphemer struck dead.* Horrible odor issues from his heart. *a.b.c.* 55; Tubach 681, 2240.

*Q221.3.6.1. *Gambler lost at dice in tavern and blasphemed against Virgin Mary.* Struck dead. *Cantigas* 72; Tubach 2240.

*Q221.3.6.2. *Woman gambler lost at dice, threw stone at image of Virgin Mary.* King ordered her dragged through streets. *Cantigas* 136; Tubach 5152.

*Q221.3.7. *Blasphemer, exposed buttocks to figure of Christ, paralyzed, save his tongue.* Power of speech retained to say "ave." *a.b.c.* 47.

*Q221.3.8. *Blasphemer punished; cursed the Virgin.* Tongue elongates, and he cannot speak. *a.b.c.* 52; Tubach 773.

*Q221.3.9. *Blasphemer doubts authenticity of Virgin Mary's slipper.* Suffers great pain and mouth is twisted. Slipper applied to afflicted area cures him. *Cantigas* 61.

*Q221.3.10. *Blasphemer carried off by demons* after denying Virgin Mary. *Cantigas* 238; *Jardín* p. 219.

*Q221.3.11. *Arian bishop blasphemed God.* Angel struck him dead with heavenly fire. *a.b.c.* 169.

*Q221.3.12. *Beguine commissions a blasphemous painting and hides it in a secret room.* Discovered. Hanged. *Talavera* 4.1.264–67.

Q221.5.1. *Disobedience to God punished.* Lot's wife transformed into pillar of salt. *Castigos* 50.212.

*Q221.9. *Punishment: cruel death.* Apostate emperor had stolen church property. *Espéculo* 209.145.

Q222. Punishment for desecration of holy places (images).

Q222.1.1. *Renegade priest killed for allowing Moors to desecrate Host.* Christian captive knight kills him. *Lucanor* Ex. 28.

Q222.2. *Punishment for desecration of figure of Christ.* Virgin Mary leads

MOTIF INDEX OF

mob to Jewish quarter where Rabbi of Toledo is found crucifying wax figure of Christ. Mob punishes him and the Jews of Toledo. *Milagros* 18.

*Q222.2.3. *Punishment for throwing image of Virgin Mary into sea.* Fish in sea disappear as long as statue is in sea. Fish appear again when statue restored to place. *Cantigas* 183.

Q222.3. *Foul portrayal of Jesus on cross* brings punishment to artist and to one who commissioned painting. *Talavera* 4.1.264–67.

*Q222.4.1. *Mayor takes church lands, falls ill,* and asks bishop to pray for cure in exchange for return of land. Reneges and falls ill again. Bishop refuses cure and is sent for forcefully. Mayor enters church and drops dead. *a.b.c.* 128.

Q222.5. *Punishment for desecration of church dedicated to Virgin Mary.* Men commit murder in her church; she sends Saint Marcial's (Saint Anthony's) fire (erysipelas) to punish them. *Milagros* 17.

*Q222.5.4.1. *Thieves trapped in hermit's cell.* Powerless to open door. *a.b.c.* 423.

Q223. Punishment for neglect of religious duties.

*Q223.1.1. *Neglect of religious duties.* Sickle suspended in church as reminder of farmer who used it on a feast day. It had adhered to his hand until he repented. *a.b.c.* 164; cf. Tubach 4138.

*Q223.1.2. *Neglect of religious duties.* A woman in labor suffered so much that she promised St. Francis that she would keep his feast day; forgot and her right arm was afflicted. *a.b.c.* 165; cf. Tubach 4138.

*Q223.1.3. *Leather worker broke promise not to work on feast day.* Punished by swallowing needle that sticks in throat. Virgin Mary cures him at altar where he coughs up needle. *Cantigas* 199; cf. Tubach 4138.

Q233.4. *Priest tends his vineyard, neglects hearing confession of dying parishioner.* *a.b.c.* 386.

Q223.6. *Woman who had promised not to sew on the Sabbath broke promise.* Punished by losing use of hands. Sent to Chartres to be cured by Virgin Mary. *Cantigas* 117; cf. Tubach 4135.

*Q223.6.1.1. *Failure to observe holiness of Sabbath punished.* Sinner crippled until confessed his sin. *Espéculo* 273.184, 274.184–85; Tubach 4135.

*Q223.6.2. *Failure to observe saint's day punished.* King who carved stick on saint's day reproached. Burned shavings on his own palm. *Espéculo* 276.185.

Q223.8. *Failure to do penance punished.* Angel gives ailing sinner three days to live. Must do penance and change ways. Spends one day in carnal pleasure and dies before able to do penance. *Espéculo* 354.252; Tubach 3684.

*Q223.8.1. *Penance postponed.* Man dies before he has chance to do penance. *Espéculo* 407.303–4; Tubach 3668.

*Q223.8.2. *Failure to do penance punished.* Sinner repents too late. Devils come and take his soul. *Espéculo* 452.351–52; Tubach 3662.

Q223.9.1. *Failure to fast punished by dragon* who will carry off monk's soul to hell. *a.b.c.* 438; *Espéculo* 8.7; Tubach 1850.

*Q223.9.1.1. *Failure to fast punished* by serpents and demons who torment with flames and beatings. *Espéculo* 9.7–8.

Q225. Punishment for scoffing at religious teachings.

Q225. *Scoffer punished.* Man says he prefers braying of asses to clerical preaching. Many asses come to his interment, attack his corpse, knock it to ground, and kick it. *Espéculo* 224.151; Tubach 620.

*Q225.0.1. *Scoffer punished.* Man says he prefers baying of greyhounds to preaching. Two greyhounds in his bed attack him and tear him to pieces. *Espéculo* 227.152; cf. Tubach 620.

Q225.1. *Heresy (Arian) punished.* Arius made to excrete his entrails. *a.b.c.* 187.

*Q225.4. *Jews punished for breaking God's commandments. Castigos* 50.212–13.

*Q225.4.1. *Punishment for denying Christian God.* Persecutor of Christians struck down. *Espéculo* 223[1].151.

*Q225.5. *Neglect to attend church punished.* Blacksmith in monastery neglected his religious duties. Sees place in hell reserved for him. *Espéculo* 230.153–54.

Q227. Punishment for opposition to holy man.

*Q227.4. *Opposition to holy man punished.* Man who stole his horse was magically detained at river. Could not cross until he returned stolen mount. *a.b.c.* 191; Tubach 2636.

Q227.5. *Woman punished for slander against bishop.* She cannot give birth to her child until she admits she accused bishop falsely. *a.b.c.* 89, 285; Tubach 648.

Q232. Punishment for change of religious faith.

*Q232.1.1. *Christian who became Arian to please king ordered killed* for lack of constancy in own faith. *a.b.c.* 169.

Q233.1. *Punishment for exchanging his soul for marriage with beloved.* Unable to attend church. *a.b.c.* 23; Tubach 3566.

Q233.1.2. *Punishment for exchanging soul for worldly success.* Unable to enter church. *Cantigas* 281.

*Q235.2. *Disobedience punished.* Cleric suffers damnation for not having obeyed without complaint. *Espéculo* 418.314–15.

Q240. Sexual sins punished.

*Q241.3. *Woman damned forever for one adulterous act.* None of her good works nor son's prayers could save her. *Espéculo* 27.19.

Q241.4. *Male storks punish their adulterous mates.* Offspring of adultery also punished. *Castigos* MS A BNM 6559 83.208; *Glosa* 2.1.8.40; Tubach 4640.

Q242. *Incest punished.* Suffer in this life and in next. *Castigos* 1.40–41.

Q242.2. *Father-daughter incest punished.* Father and daughter struck down by lightning. *Apolonio* c. 248.

*Q242.5. *Brother-sister incest punished.* Woman bitten by poisonous spider. *Castigos* MS A BNM 6559 82.216.

Q243. Incontinence punished: miscellaneous.

*Q243.0.1. *Punishment by extinction of royal line* for cohabiting with a Jewish woman from Toledo. Wounded in battle. Loses battle. *Castigos* 21.133.

*Q243.0.1.1. *Punishment for taking heathen wives.* *Castigos* 20.133.

*Q243.0.3. *Punishment for excessive carnality.* Deluge to destroy sinners. *Castigos* MS A BNM 6559 22.138.

*Q243.7. *Dying man punished for depraved sexual acts* with devil disguised as young woman. *Espéculo* 355.252–54.

Q244. *Punishment for rape: hanging.* Youth falsely accused is put on gallows. Saved by Virgin Mary. *Cantigas* 355.

Q244.2. *Knight who had raped nun captured* when she is mounted miraculously before him on his horse and holds reins until he is taken prisoner. *Castigos* 19.121–22; *Castigos* MS A BNM 6559 (ADMYTE 0 47r–48v).

*Q244.4. *Lustful behavior punished.* Lecherous woman abused and discarded. *a.b.c.* 246: Tubach 1081.

*Q244.5. *Hangman, taken with beauty of murderess,* has sex with her body after he cuts her down. Publicly flogged. *Talavera* 1.24.117.

*Q244.6. *Woman punishes man who had raped her,* severing his head and presenting it to her husband to restore her honor. *Ilustres mujeres* 73.76v–78r (Wife of Orgiaguntes).

Q260. Deceptions punished.

Q260. *Deceptions (treachery) punished.* Hawk breaks promise to nightingale, and is caught by hunter. *Esopete* pp. 62–63.

*Q261.3. *Treachery punished.* Teacher who handed children of besieged city to enemy punished. Grateful citizens surrender. *a.b.c.* 256; *Glosa* 1.2.12.121; cf. Tubach 1082.

*Q261.4. *Emperor severs hand of purported traitor.* Severed hand restored by Virgin Mary. *a.b.c.* 273; Tubach 2419.

Q263. Lying (perjury) punished.

Q263.1. *False accusers of innocent woman* proven to be perjurers. Condemned to death (Susanna and the Elders). *Castigos* 9.70; Tubach 4684.

*Q263.2. *Three false accusers of bishop swear:* if not true first would die of fire; second of erysipelas; third would lose sight. First two punishments occur, and third false accuser cries so much that he loses his sight. *a.b.c.* 235; *Espéculo* 461.359.

*Q263.3.1. *Monk falsely accuses another of theft.* God appears to him in vision and orders him to be punished. *a.b.c.* 359.

*Q263.4.1. *Lender forces lying neighbor to perjure self,* to swear he had not received a loan. Judge punishes lender seriously for sin of destroying another's soul. *Espéculo* 457.357.

*Q263.5. *Heretic conceals on person written declaration of his heresy.* Presents written orthodox statement at same time. Swears to truth of what he had written. Punished later when he miraculously excretes own entrails. *Espéculo* 460.358–59; Tubach 2534.

*Q263.6. *Woman struck by lightning as punishment for perjury.* Had falsely accused saint of rape. *a.b.c.* 158; Tubach 3046.

Q265.1. *Judge who accepted bribes from condemned* punished by king. *Çifar* pp. 107–8.

Q265.3. *Bad judge flayed,* and skin put on the judgement chair. His son, the new judge, taught by fate of father to be good judge. *a.b.c.* 223; Tubach 2859.

Q270. Misdeeds concerning property punished.

Q272.1.1. *Rich man postponed repentance* until dying; pleads with devils to spare him until next day. Plea denied. Is carried off. *a.b.c.* 119, 357.

Q272.2. *Avaricious man has neck broken* when lid of his treasure chest falls on him. *Castigos* MS A BNM 6559 7.99–100 (ADMYTE 0 21r–21v).

Q272.3. *Miser tries to eat his adored money* and chokes to death. *a.b.c.* 39.

Q272.4. *Avaricious woman and her gold in her grave consumed by hell's fires.* *a.b.c.* 40; Tubach 2036.

*Q272.4.1. *Demons in grave throw avaricious man's gold* into throat of dead man. *a.b.c.* 123; Tubach 5039.

*Q272.5. *Executor of will keeps money destined to pay masses for dead archbishop. Damned. *Espéculo* 263.177.

*Q272.6. *Virgin Mary brings avaricious man back* from dead after he has seen hell's torments. He has thirty days to save his soul with prayers. *Milagros* 10.

Q273. Usury punished.

Q273.3. *Man who deserted his usurer father and brother* sees them roasting in hell and blaming each other for their plight. *a.b.c.* 430; Tubach 2006; cf. Tubach 5027.

Q273.4. *Church built by usurer's money made to collapse* by devil. *a.b.c.* 148; cf. Tubach 5031.

*Q273.5. *Usurer and his descendants punished in hell,* ten generations who had benefited arranged on a ladder. *a.b.c.* 385 (not in Paris MS).

*Q273.6. *Saint who accepted alms from usurer* punished in hellfire by burn on his cheek. *Espéculo* 12.9–10.

*Q273.7. *Usurer gave abbot money to pray for him.* God said all but one coin had been earned dishonestly. Accepted only one coin on altar. *a.b.c.* 132.

*Q273.8. *Usurer's soul condemned to eternal torment* despite generosity to monastery. Returns and attacks monks. *a.b.c.* 149.

Q277. Covetousness punished.

*Q277.1. *Covetousness punished.* Fox betrays wolf to shepherd and eats wolf's stores. Shepherd kills fox. *Esopete* p. 63.

Q281. Ingratitude punished.

Q281.1. *Devils torment daughter who abused her mother.* *a.b.c.* 336; *Espéculo* 440.334; Tubach 1442.

Q281.1.2. *Daughter cursed by mother is punished with an illness.* Cured by saint. *a.b.c.* 260; Tubach 975, 1440 c).

*Q281.5. *Ingratitude punished.* Ungrateful serpent freed from captivity; returned to captivity when bites rescuer. *a.b.c.* 312; *Disciplina* 5; Tubach 4254.

Q292. Inhospitality punished.

*Q292.1.1. *Fox punished for serving stork (crane) food in flat dish.* In stork's house given food in tall narrow container. *Esopete* p. 52; Tubach 2170.

Q300. Contentiousness punished.

Q301. *Jealous monks punished.* Dismissed good shepherd who fed poor from flock. Wolves and bears came to eat sheep after dismissal. *a.b.c.* 143; Tubach 4088 (p. 417).

*Q302.0.1. *Envy and covetousness punished.* Twice the reward to other (loss of eye). *Esopete* p. 125; cf. Tubach 3983.

*Q305.1. *King made war against Christians.* Refused to make peace. God helped Christians, and they defeated evil aggressor. Punished him severely. *a.b.c.* 416.

Q312.4. *Fault-finding with God's handling of weather.* Complaining gardener punished. Seeds will not grow. *a.b.c.* 104; Tubach 5233.

Q320. Evil personal habits punished.

Q321.1. *Laziness punished.* Queen insists that idle woman who disdains spinning yarn learn to spin or that she not appear at court. *Castigos* 6.59.

Q327. Discourtesy punished.

Q327. *Nun rebukes prior for the way he addresses her.* He will not choose her for post of prioress of nunnery because of her impatience. *Espéculo* 438.331.

Q330. Overweening punished.

Q331.2.1.5. *Devil rides on long skirt of woman.* Falls off into mud. Other devil laughs at him. *a.b.c.* 407; Tubach 1660.

*Q331.2.1.6. *Woman in a grand procession exposed to ridicule* when her wig is snatched off by a monkey. *a.b.c.* 334; *Espéculo* 431.326; Tubach 2400.

*Q331.2.1.7. *Vain woman prays for green eyes (more beautiful eyes).* Blinded. Prays for restoration of sight. Old eyes are restored. *a.b.c.* 371; *Espéculo* 536.431–32.

*Q331.2.3. *Jezebel's pride punished.* Displays self in window of tower. Tower topples; her flesh eaten by dogs. *Castigos* MS A BNM 6559 6.97 (ADMYTE 0 17r).

*Q331.2.4. *Noble poet writes poor verses.* Demands reward from king because of his lineage. King sends him away unrewarded, telling him his good lineage has worsened in him. *Disciplina* 3; Tubach 3829.

*Q331.2.5. *Man in church boasts of his good deeds* and decries sins of others. Condemned to hell for not confessing his own sins. *Castigos* MS A BNM 6559 86.223.

*Q331.3. *Overweening pride punished.* Boastful rich man and his belongings swallowed up by the earth. *a.b.c.* 287; Tubach 3938.

*Q331.4. *Woman's vanity punished.* Came to mass adorned excessively;

devil in form of spider bit her and could not be removed until abbot brought Host to banish spider. *Espéculo* 429.325–26.

⋆Q331.5. *Vain woman will only bathe in rain water* from the countryside. God punished her with sores that gave off foul odors. *Castigos* MS A BNM 6559 (ADMYTE 0 17r).

⋆Q332. *Vanity of monks punished.* Wearers of silken sashes, silver-trimmed shoes. St. Martin and angel killed them all. *Espéculo* 428.325.

Q340. Meddling punished.

Q341. *Curiosity punished.* Man kills wife for looking at other men through her window. *a.b.c.* 63.

⋆Q341.1. *Inquisitiveness punished.* Monkey sees carpenter astride a beam, splitting wood with a wedge. Tries unsuccessfully to perform task; genitals fall into split and are crushed. Carpenter returns and beats him. *Calila* pp. 125–26; *Exemplario* 11r–11v.

Q380. Deeds punished: miscellaneous.

Q385. *Panther captured in pitfall beaten* by first peasants to find it but released by newcomers. When recovered, panther kills cattle belonging to the peasants who mistreated him. *Esopete* p. 76.

Q386.1. *Devil punishes young woman who loves to dance.* Returns to tell of torment in hell where she must dance forever. *Espéculo* 134.92; Tubach 1429.

Q393. Evil speech punished.

⋆Q393.0.1. *Evil speech punished.* Man spoke ill of bishop. Bit off his own tongue and died. *Espéculo* 176.119.

Q393.1. *Punishment for talking too much.* Talkative nun's dead body cut in half and burned. *a.b.c.* 247; cf. Tubach 4706.

Q393.2. *Gossip punished.* St. Augustine did not tolerate those who spoke ill of others. *Espéculo* 173.117–18.

⋆Q393.3. *Gossipers reproached.* Moribund monk scolds brothers who speak ill of him. *Espéculo* 174.118.

⋆Q393.4. *Flatterer punished* for praising. Beheaded. *Castigos* MS A BNM 6559 35.156 (ADMYTE 0 111r); *Glosa* 1.2.8.100.

⋆Q393.5 *Returned pilgrim* tells others not to make pilgrimage. Punished, falls, and bites own tongue off. *Espéculo* 146.99–100.

Q395. Disrespect punished.

⋆Q396. *Author dreams he is beaten by angry women* for misogyny. *Talavera* 4.3.305; *Grisel* 367–70.

⋆Q397. *Soldiers loot holy person's cell, eat Host, drink sacramental wine, beat him.* Half a league away, one bites own tongue and chokes; others die miserably. *Espéculo* 222.150–51.

Q400–Q599. KINDS OF PUNISHMENTS

Q410. Capital punishment.

⋆Q411.11.3. *Desecrating sanctuary punished.* Consul makes law abolishing sanctuary. Kills enemies captured in church. Later takes sanctuary himself, and emperor executes him. *Espéculo* 211.146.

⋆Q411.16. *Death as punishment for having buried unshriven sinner in church.* Bishop paid by rich sinner, warned by sacristan that he would die in thirty days. *a.b.c.* 353; *Espéculo* 512.405.

*Q411.17. *Treacherous steward who kills Jew under royal protection is executed.* *a.b.c.* 167; Tubach 2799.

Q414. *Burning alive.* Monks, ordered burned alive by king, achieve martyrdom. *Barlaam* p. 31.

*Q414.0.3.2. *Stepmother who lusted after stepson,* rejected, accuses him of rape. Deceit proven. Punished by burning. *Sendebar* p. 155.

Q415.8. *Heretic preaching against God's creation hits fly* that has landed on his head so many times that he falls dead. *Gatos* 6; Tubach 2103.

*Q415.10. *Witch hanged in doorway of man she had poisoned.* Body taken away to be burned. *Talavera* 2.13.198.

Q422. *Punishment: stoning to death.* Evil king stoned by populace. *Çifar* p. 100; *Glosa* 1.2.14.134.

*Q422.1. *Punishment: stoning* as punishment for adultery. *Castigos* MS A BNM 6559 9.103.

Q431. Punishment: banishment.

*Q431.3.1. *Visiting prince who violated royal prohibition against asking why king never laughed is banished from realm.* Sent away in an oarless boat. *Çifar* p. 130; Tubach 4994.

*Q431.20. *Calumniated hero banished.* King's advisers accuse him falsely. *CMC* vv. 11–64; 267.

Q432. Punishment: ejection.

Q432.1. *Owl hatched by hawk* ejected for fouling nest. *Espéculo* 535.422.

Q436. *Unrepentant priest excommunicated.* Dies when begins to say mass. *Espéculo* 268.181; Tubach 3211.

*Q436.1. *Associating with the excommunicated punished.* King stricken dead in house of offending count. *Espéculo* 270.181–82.

Q450. Cruel punishments.

Q451.1. *Hand severed as punishment for treachery.* *a.b.c.* 273.

Q451.4. Tongue cut out as punishment.

*Q451.4.6.1. *Tongue cut out by heretics.* Pious man who sang praise of Virgin Mary punished. *Cantigas* 156.

Q451.4.8.1. *Tongue bitten off* by wife as punishment for adultery. *Talavera* 1.24.119.

*Q451.4.8.2. *Tongue cut (bitten) as punishment.* Man who had told others not to make pilgrimage falls and bites own tongue off. *Espéculo* 146.99–100.

Q451.5. Nose cut off as punishment.

Q451.5.2. *Nose cut off as punishment for theft.* Lawyer stole land from church. Saint appears and tells him to return it. Third time cuts off nose as sign of perjury and theft. *Espéculo* 458.357–58.

Q451.7. Blinding as punishment.

*Q451.7.0.3. *Magic blindness as punishment for perjury.* Monk has said he will go blind if he lies. *a.b.c.* 235.

*Q451.7.0.4. *Eyes fall out magically* as punishment for blasphemy. *a.b.c.* 236; Tubach 1949.

Q451.7.5. *Eyes gouged out as punishment for cruelty* and idolatry. Royal son permitted to rule. *a.b.c.* 22; Tubach 705.

*Q451.7.6. *Blindness punishment used as weapon against enemy.* Covetous and envious. Twice the wish to the enemy. *a.b.c.* 217; *Esopete* p. 125; Tubach 3983.

*Q451.7.7. *Blindness as punishment for adultery. a.b.c.* 224.

*Q451.7.8. *Mother (Empress Irene) orders that her son's eyes be put out. a.b.c.* 295 (not in Paris MS).

*Q451.7.9. *Knight stricken blind* for scoffing at Virgin Mary. *Cantigas* 314.

Q451.10. *Punishment: genitals cut off.* Wife punishes husband for unfaithfulness. *Talavera* 1.24.118.

Q455.1. *Walling up as punishment* for conspiracy to murder seven princelings and their mother. *Ultramar* I.1.66.116.

Q467.1. *Man accused of rape put in sack sealed with pitch* and thrown in river. *a.b.c.* 172.

Q469.7. *Punishment: twisting entrails from body. a.b.c.* 187; Tubach 2534 (excreting).

Q470. Humiliating punishments.

Q492. *Woman must relight magic fires as punishment.* Magician, in repayment for ill-treatment by woman, causes lights of the city to go out. They can only be relighted from the genitals (naked body) of the woman. None can be relighted until all have applied torches. *LBA* cc. 261–68.

*Q493.2. *Devil transforms priest's concubine into mare.* Devil rides her to blacksmith's shop. She identifies self as blacksmith's mother. *Espéculo* 113.73–74.

*Q495.2. *Woman raped and mutilated for lechery.* Impaled vaginally. *a.b.c.* 246.

*Q499.2.3. *Humiliating death questioned.* No sins committed to merit death at hands of asses. *Esopete* pp. 24–25.

Q500. Tedious punishments.

Q501.9. *Man punished for sin; must be perpetual bathhouse attendant.* Saint's prayers free him. *a.b.c.* 372; *Espéculo* 152.106, 159.108–9; Tubach 504.

*Q501.10. *Saintly man punished for single sin.* Must be perpetual bathhouse attendant. Freed because of previous virtuous life. *a.b.c.* 150; Tubach 504.

Q520. Penances.

Q520.2. *Robber does penance.* Will live with next creature he encounters. *Castigos* MS A BNM 6559 82.224.

Q520.4. *King who gave many death sentences accepts penance.* Postpones sentence until thirty days' period of examination has passed. *Glosa* 1.13.68–69; *Castigos* 10.107–8.

Q520.5. *Penance in wilderness as punishment* for two friars who left holy orders to marry. One spent year weeping about sin; second, praising God for having been saved. *a.b.c.* 356; Tubach 3670.

MOTIF INDEX OF

Q522.3. *Penance for desiring to leave monastery to marry:* creeping naked through thorns. *a.b.c.* 251.

*Q522.4.1. *Penance: Man afflicted with leprosy* as punishment makes pilgrimage to Holy Land to die there. *Lucanor* Ex. 44.

Q522.8. *Penitent wears poisonous snake* wrapped around him. Is bitten and dies. *Castigos* MS A BNM 6559 82.224.

Q523.2. *Penance: walking on all fours, naked and grazing like a beast.* *a.b.c.* 387.

*Q523.7.1. *Sinner demands penance of three years:* denied, then one year; denied, then forty days. Told that three days suffice if sincere. *a.b.c.* 296 (not in Paris MS); Tubach 3690.

Q535. Negative penances.

Q535.2. *Penance: lion forgoes meat.* Hunter kills her cubs. Jackal tells her he and other animals have had same experience at her hands. She gives up meat and lives on grass. *Calila* p. 300; *Exemplario* 77r.

*Q535.2.1. *Penance: lion forgoes fruit.* Advised that trees are not bearing enough fruit because of her appetite. Eats grass. *Calila* p. 300.

*Q535.2.2. *Penance for seven days:* covetousness—eat chick peas; pride—vetches; avarice—porridge; lust—spinach; anger—lentils; gluttony—bread and water; envy—beans. *LBA* cc. 1163–69.

Q550. Miraculous punishments.

*Q551.3.2.9. *Punishment: snake transformed into frog-king's mount,* condemned to eat only those frogs given him by king. *Calila* p. 248.

Q551.6.4. *Magic sickness as punishment for theft.* Apostate emperor stole holy vessels and sat on them. Parts of body that had touched vessels when he sat rotted, and he died. *Espéculo* 209ª.145.

*Q551.6.4.1. *Magic punishment for theft.* Priest who stole silver from cross in Virgin Mary's church blinded. His nose grew down to cover his mouth. Could neither eat nor drink. *Cantigas* 318.

Q551.6.5. *Magic sickness as punishment for desecration of holy places (images, etc.).* Military commander urinates on altar; Jew in holy vessels. Excrement pours out of commander's mouth, and he dies; blood pours from Jew's mouth, and he dies. *Espéculo* 210.145–46.

Q551.6.5.1. *Magic manifestation:* blood flows from blasphemer's mouth. *a.b.c.* 55.

Q551.6.5.2. *Magic manifestation:* eyes fall out of sockets of blasphemer. *a.b.c.* 55.

Q551.8.6. *Magic punishment for denying the Virgin Mary:* tongue extends a palm's width and protrudes from mouth; dies. *a.b.c.* 52.

*Q551.8.8. *Magic strangulation for violating holy object.* Chasuble woven for good priest by Virgin Mary strangles bad priest who wears it. *Milagros* 1.

*Q551.8.9. *Magic punishment for arson.* Man who ordered burning of Virgin Mary's church blinded. Cured after he orders its reconstruction. *Cantigas* 316.

*Q551.8.10. *Magic punishment for damaging Virgin Mary's church.* Man kicking door breaks leg, loses senses and speech. Spends rest of life able to utter only her name. *Cantigas* 317.

*Q551.9.2.1. *Magic illness*: Monk says he hopes he will suffer erysipelas if he has perjured himself. *a.b.c.* 235.

*Q551.9.3. *Magic illness*: plague visited on man who attacked saint. *a.b.c.* 100.

*Q551.9.4. *Magic illness*: man who denied Jesus and Mary suffers internal bleeding and dies. *a.b.c.* 55.

*Q551.9.5. *Magic illness*: heretic denied Trinity and was struck dead by three blows from angel. *a.b.c.* 169.

*Q551.9.6. *Magic illness*: man accuses wife unjustly. She prays that God send sign of innocence. Husband miraculously contracts leprosy. *Lucanor* Ex. 44.

*Q551.9.7. *Magic illness*: ghost of St. Gregory strikes mortal blow to head of his successor who had spoken ill of him. *a.b.c.* 100.

*Q551.9.7.1. *Magic illness*: priest falls ill and dies after speaking ill of saint. *a.b.c.* 100.

*Q551.9.8. *Unrepentant sinner's body burned by invisible fires.* Clothing intact, body ravaged by punishing fire. *Espéculo* 120.78–79.

*Q551.9.9. *Punishment from otherworld*: leprosy, erysipelas, and poverty. Executors of usurer's will do not make restitution of his ill-gotten wealth. *Espéculo* 262.176–77.

Q552. Prodigious event as punishment.

Q552.1. *Creditor in pursuit of poor debtor curses God and the Virgin Mary.* Is cleaved in two by lightning. *a.b.c.* 324.

Q552.1.7. *Lightning bolt kills false accuser* of saintly person. *a.b.c.* 158; Tubach 3046.

*Q552.1.7.1. *Mother who lusted after own son*, rejected, accuses him of rape. Struck by lightning and burned to cinders. *a.b.c.* 158, 172; Tubach 2734.

*Q552.1.8.2. *Blasphemer cleaved in two by lightning.* *a.b.c.* 324; Tubach 680.

Q552.4.1. *Voice of sheep comes from thief's belly* when bishop calls for an admission of theft. *a.b.c.* 179; Tubach 4317.

*Q552.18.4. *Bears and wolves miraculously appear* to devour sheep of cruel and unjust monks who have sent away charitable shepherd. *a.b.c.* 143; Tubach 519; see Tubach p. 417 for 4088.

Q554. Mysterious visitation as punishment.

Q554.1. *Punishment.* Devil carries off thief who stole tithes from church. *Espéculo* 170.114–15.

Q554.1.1. *Punishment.* Charlemagne carried off to hell for having given tithes to his knights. *Espéculo* 172.115.

Q558. Mysterious death as punishment.

*Q558.4.1. *Farmer, angered by storm* that destroyed vineyard, curses, raises knife to sky to harm God. Knife falls and cuts his throat. *Espéculo* 80.52.

Q559. Other miraculous punishments.

Q559.5.1 *Birth of child prevented* until woman confesses slander. She had accused saint of fathering her child. *a.b.c.* 89; *Espéculo* 436.330–31; cf. Tubach 648, 1915.

Q559.5.2. *Woman's hand withers as punishment* for breaking oath to God. *a.b.c.* 165.

Q559.11. *Heretic miraculously made to excrete his entrails. Espéculo* 460.358–59; *a.b.c.* 187; Tubach 2534.

*Q559.12. *Man who bared his rear parts to Jesus paralyzed except for tongue* leaving him able to say "Ave Maria." *a.b.c.* 47.

*Q559.13. *Sailor, punished for scoffing at churchgoers,* goes to tavern and body swells to bursting point. Cured when prays to Virgin Mary. *Cantigas* 244.

Q560. Punishments in hell.

*Q560.2.4. *Nun condemned to eternal damnation,* returns to tell sisters that there is no respite in hell. *a.b.c.* 73; cf. Tubach 1188 a) 4.

*Q560.2.5. *Saint would choose to go to hell over committing mortal sin.* Knows he would be released from hell if sinless. *Espéculo* 450.348–49.

*Q560.4. *Sinner condemned to serve eternally as bathhouse attendant* saved by prayers of holy man. *a.b.c.* 372; Tubach 3685.

Q561.3. *Seats heating in hell for sinners.* If they do penance, seat falls away. *Espéculo* 455.353; Tubach 4216.

*Q563.1. *Usurer and his descendants punished in hell,* ten generations who had benefited arranged on a ladder. *a.b.c.* 385 (not in Paris MS).

*Q563.1.2. *Bad Christians in even lower position in hell than Jews.* They had been redeemed and had not valued their redemption. *a.b.c.* 435.

Q566. Punishments by heat in hell.

*Q566.1. *Sinner buried in church. Voice from grave says "I am burning."* Grave opened to find only shroud. *a.b.c.* 400.

*Q566.2. *Angel tells saint that hellfire is hotter than earthly fire.* Tells listeners earthly fire is like a painting; hellfire is real. *Espéculo* 329.231.

*Q566.3. *Fire rises from grave of sinner* showing he was burning in hell. *a.b.c.* 404; Tubach 2037.

*Q566.4. *Man who deserted his usurer father and brother sees them roasting in hell* and blaming each other for their plight. *a.b.c.* 430; Tubach 5027.

*Q566.5. *Lawyers bathe in special hell's fire. a.b.c.* 12.

*Q566.6. *Avaricious woman and her gold in her grave consumed by hell's fires. a.b.c.* 40.

*Q569.6. *Soul wrenched from bodies with pitchforks by devil.* Soul carried off to hell. *a.b.c.* 293; Tubach 4553.

*Q569.7. *Hideous punishment of lecherous cleric.* Cauldron of pitch and sulphur; red-hot metal pans applied to body. *Espéculo* 355.252–54.

Q570. Punishment and remission.

*Q570.2. *Magic foul disease as punishment for persecution of Christians.* Remitted when persecution is ceased. *a.b.c.* 373; Tubach 4362.

Q571. *Magic blindness as punishment remitted.* Woman repents. *a.b.c.* 371.

Q578. *Spirit in hell freed from humiliating punishment* as bathhouse attendant. *a.b.c.* 372; Tubach 2534.

*Q578.1. *Woman unable to give birth until she admits falsehood* of accusing bishop of fathering the baby. Remitted when she confesses. *a.b.c.* 89, 285.

*Q578.2. *Woman's arm withered for breaking vow* not to work on feast day. Repents and repeats her vow. Punishment is remitted. *a.b.c.* 165.

Q580. Punishment fitted to crime.

*Q581.1.1. *Metalworker built a hollow metal bull as instrument of punishment* to curry favor with ruler. Victims put inside and bull heated. Ruler insists that metalworker be first victim. *a.b.c.* 316; Tubach 3134.

Q582.9. *King falls dead when he sees his sons whom he had never punished* killed in battle. *Çifar* p. 83.

*Q583.5. *Punishment for false accusations.* Ghost of evil man appears and mutilates tongue. *Espéculo* 67.46.

Q586. *Son on gallows bites his mother's (father's) nose off:* punishment for lack of discipline in youth. *a.b.c.* 338; *Çifar* pp. 82–83; *Esopete* pp. 112–13; *Castigos* 1.41; *Glosa* 2.2.2.130; *Espéculo* 287.196–98; Tubach 3488.

*Q586.1. *Father who raised dissolute sons punished.* They will die before his eyes, and then he will perish. *Castigos* 1.40.

Q588.1. *Man cruel to his father,* told by his own son that he will be mistreated thus in his old age. *a.b.c.* 337; Tubach 2001.

*Q595.5. *Loss of property as punishment.* Merchant's cargo and vessels lost at sea until he returns ill-gotten gains to church. *Espéculo* 13.10.

*Q595.6. *Loss of property as punishment.* Pet monkey steals merchant's ill-gotten gold coins and tosses them into the sea. *Espéculo* 14.11.

*Q599.2. *Unreasonable threat of punishment* to cook, to baker, and to host's wife to frighten guest. *Esopete* pp. 13–14.

*Q599.2.1. *Gluttony punished.* Three diners at saint's table punished. Floor gives way under them injuring them badly. *Espéculo* 1.4.

R. CAPTIVES AND FUGITIVES

R0–R99. CAPTIVITY

R10. Abduction.

R11.2.1.1. *Soldier recognizes that evil emperor is devil's man.* Devils come and carry off their man. *a.b.c.* 114.

*R11.2.1.2. *A rich man, greedy and avaricious, about to die,* asks for one night's delay. Devils take soul in morning. *a.b.c.* 119, 357; cf. Tubach 1643.

*R11.2.1.3. *Devils carry off daughter* who abused her mother. *a.b.c.* 336; Tubach 1442.

*R11.2.3. *Devils carry off evil judge who had always prayed to Virgin Mary.* Throw him into boiling pit. Virgin rescues him. *Cantigas* 119; cf. Tubach 2852.

R12. Abduction by pirates.

R12.1. *Princess abducted by pirates.* They sell her as slave. *Apolonio* cc. 391–94.

*R12.2.2. *Holy man abducted by Moors.* Ships cannot sail until he is released. *Cantigas* 95.

*R12.5. *Knight's wife abducted in boat by sailors.* *Çifar* p. 27.

R13. Abduction by animal.

R13.1.2. *Lion carries off child.* *Çifar* p. 26.

R13.1.5.1. *Wolf carries off child* beside a stream. *Ultramar* II.2.254–57.370–78.

R39. Abduction: miscellaneous.

*R39.3. *Deacon carried off by enemy* intent on killing him. *a.b.c.* 295.

*R39.4. *Princess abducted by Jupiter* disguised as bull. *Ilustres mujeres* 9.15v–16r (Europa).

*R39.5. *Queen abducted by lover.* Taken away in ship. *Ilustres mujeres* 35.41v–43v (Helen).

R45. Captivity in mound (cave, hollow, hill).

R45.2. *Imprisonment in lion's den.* Lions show reverence for captive (Daniel). *Castigos* 9.69–70.

R70. Behavior of captives.

*R81.2. *Woman suckles imprisoned parent* denied food by jailers. *Ilustres mujeres* 65.69r–70r (unknown young Roman woman); *a.b.c.* 171, 173; *Glosa* 2.2.4.137–38; Tubach 3969.

R100–R199. RESCUES

*R111.4.1. *Young woman betrothed to a prince brought to Alexander (Africanus) for his use.* He sends her back untouched to her betrothed (Tercia Emilia). *Ilustres mujeres* 74.78r–78v; *a.b.c.* 82, 83; *Glosa* 1.2.15.140; Tubach 3971; cf. Tubach 138.

R121. Means of rescue from prison.

R121.6. *Virgin Mary (Santiago) enters prison, breaks devotee's fetters.* She (he) departs without guards seeing him. *Cantigas* 83, 158, 176, 301, 325; *Santiago* 1.45–48, 11.73–74, 20.99–101; Tubach 2768.

*R121.6.3. *Virgin Mary appears to captive Jew, shows him advantages of Christianity.* Freed, he enters monastery. *Cantigas* 85; Tubach 2768.

*R121.6.4. *Virgin Mary appears to Christian captive of Moors*; transports her (him) magically to homeland. *Cantigas* 325, 359.

*R121.6.5. *Rescue from prison by Virgin Mary.* Captive beaten by Moorish captors, rescued magically without captors' knowledge. *Cantigas* 227.

*R121.6.6. *Rescue from prison by Virgin Mary.* Captive tortured by captors. Crosses river without getting wet to reach monastery safely. *Cantigas* 245.

*R121.6.7. *Rescue from prison by Virgin Mary.* Scholar imprisoned for having raped a woman repents and composes a song in praise of Virgin. She frees him so that he will serve her for rest of life. *Cantigas* 291.

*R121.11. *Captive interprets king's dream.* Reward is his freedom and that of all the other captives. *a.b.c.* 61; Tubach 1785.

*R123.1. *Captive prayed for release to Virgin Mary.* Sees doors open, fetters broken, is able to flee Moorish prison. *Cantigas* 83; Tubach 926.

*R123.2. *Prisoners promise to give money to church.* Virgin Mary frees them miraculously. *Cantigas* 106.

*R123.3. *Troubadour imprisoned sings song for Virgin Mary.* Finds himself magically freed. *Cantigas* 363.

R130. Rescue of abandoned or lost persons.

R131.10.2. *Hermit rescues seven abandoned princelings* who had been nurtured by doe in desert. *Ultramar* I.1.56.93–95.

R141. Rescue from well (body of water).

*R141.1. *Virgin Mary rescues royal falconers from drowning.* Had fallen into water. *Cantigas* 243.

*R141.2. *Fox rescued from well.* Persuades wolf to descend into well in one bucket, thereby rescuing fox in other. *Esopete* pp. 144–46; *Disciplina* 23; *Gatos* 14; Tubach 5247; cf. Tubach 2175.

R150. Rescuers.

R152.1. *Wife (wives) rescues husband from prison* by exchanging clothes with him; she remains in prison; he leaves. *Ilustres mujeres* 29.36r–37v (Wives of the Minias); *PCG* 2.718.420–21; *Abreviada* 2.263; *Castigos* MS A BNM 6559 77.209; *Glosa* 2.1.8.42–43; *Jardín* p. 267; Tubach 5328.

*R152.1.1. *Brother rescues sister from brothel.* Exchanges clothes and takes place. *Jardín* p. 258; *Glosa* 2.2.20.214.

*R152.1.2. *Princess frees captive in exchange for promise of marriage.* *PCG* 2.710.413; *Abreviada* 2.255; cf. Tubach 3811.

R153.3.1. *Father and son captured.* One must die, and one must escape. Father chooses to die. *a.b.c.* 339; Tubach 2005.

R153.3.5. *Fathers carry children on head to save them from flood,* even dying. Mothers stepped over and on children trying to escape to safety. *Castigos* 5.55.

*R154.4. *Son-in-law* rescues father-in-law from captivity. *Lucanor* Ex. 25.

R165. *Holy man rescues deacon.* Captors have warned that he will die if deacon flees. Holy man relies on God's protection. *a.b.c.* 295; Tubach 4153.

R165.1. *Rescue of poor young woman.* St. Nicholas tosses a golden apple through poor man's window so that his daughter can marry and not be sold into slavery. *Castigos* 7.62–63.

R165.2. *Hanged youth saved miraculously by saint.* Father returns after three months to find son alive on gallows. Saved by Virgin Mary (Santiago). *a.b.c.* 38; *Santiago* 5.56.61; *Cantigas* 175; Tubach 3796.

*R167.1. *Monk who left monastery rescued* from dragon who intends eating him. Calls for help. Other monks rescue him, and he returns to monastery. *Espéculo* 53.37.

R168. Angels as rescuers.

*R168.1. *Man hanging on edge of cliff* miraculously rescued by angel in form of poor man with whom he had shared food. *Espéculo* 245.164–65.

*R168.2. *Angel enters prison, breaks saint's fetters,* and frees him. *Castigos* 37.174; Tubach 926.

R169. Other rescuers.

*R169.0.1. *Virgin Mary rescues Jewish woman who had been thrown off cliff.* Woman promises conversion and devotion to Virgin. *Cantigas* 107.

R169.6 *Youth saved from death sentence* by father's friend. *Esopete* pp. 137–39; Tubach 2209.

*R169.15.1. *Young woman rescued by pirates.* Her would-be assassin flees. *Apolonio* cc. 384–86.

R170. Rescue: miscellaneous motifs.

*R176.1. *Executioner's arm miraculously frozen in midair.* Condemned holy man saved. *a.b.c.* 295.

*R176.2. *Execution cancelled.* King recognizes long-lost wife and sons. *Çifar* pp. 55–56.

R200–R299. ESCAPES AND PURSUITS

*R243.2. *Deer rescued from hunters by ox.* Owner spies him. Spares him (eats him). *Esopete* p. 67; Tubach 4596.

S. UNNATURAL CRUELTY

S0–S99. CRUEL RELATIVES

S10. Cruel relative.

*S11.3.9. *Father asked to leave child with another for his pleasure* says he would rather leave them all. Draws sword and kills three. *Castigos* MS A BNM 6559 13.118 (ADMYTE 0 52v); *Glosa* 1.3.7.270.

*S11.3.10. *Father asked to leave child with another for his pleasure,* draws sword and dismembers child, leaves the pieces. *Castigos* MS A BNM 6559 13.118 (ADMYTE 0 52v); *Glosa* 1.3.7.270.

*S11.8. *Cruel Jewish father throws son in oven.* Enraged because son went to church and took communion. *a.b.c.* 269; *Milagros* 16; *Cantigas* 4; Tubach 2041.

*S11.9. *Cruel and dissolute father seeks to corrupt son.* Son gives up inheritance and leaves. *Castigos* 1.41–42; Tubach 362.

*S11.10. *Cruel sister.* Kills young brother, throws dismembered parts in path of pursuing father to delay him. *Ilustres mujeres* 16.23r–23v (Medea).

S12. Cruel mother.

S12.2. *Cruel mother kills child* and eats it during siege of her city. *PCG* 1.135; *Castigos* 5.55; *Abreviada* 1.196.

*S12.2.2.2.4. *Cruel mothers step over and on children* to escape flood. *Castigos* 5.55.

*S12.2.4. *Depressed mother kills newborn babies*, offspring of sexual union with godfather. *Cantigas* 201.

*S12.2.5. *Depressed mother plans to kill baby penetrating head with needle*. Virgin Mary intervenes; saves baby; woman enters religious order. *Cantigas* 399.

S12.2.6. *Mother shamed (maddened) by brutal violation by invading army* throws baby into sea. *Ultramar* III.4.155.570.

*S12.3.1. *Cruel mother*. Has lover kill her child to prevent child's revealing their secret. *Talavera* 1.24.117.

*S12.3.2. *Son-in-law killed by order of mother-in-law* who lusted after him. *Cantigas* 255.

S12.4. *Cruel mother*. Empress Irene ordered son's eyes taken out. *a.b.c.* 295 (not in Paris MS).

S12.4.1. *Cruel mother*. Kills children because husband has new love. *Ilustres mujeres* 16.23r–23v (Medea).

S12.8. *All male children* killed by Amazons or given to fathers (Marsepia & Lampedon). *Ilustres mujeres* 11.17r–18r; *Abreviada* 1.467.

*S12.9. *Queen mother kills all heirs to throne* so that she can rule. *Ilustres mujeres* 49.56v–58r (Athaliah).

S20. Cruel children.

*S20.3. *Children do great harm to mother*. She curses them. *a.b.c.* 260.

*S21.6. *Cruel son's victims are his father's servants*. Father is told to yoke young ox to old one to show how cruel son should be disciplined. *Esopete* pp. 64–65.

S21.7. *Cruel son mistreats father*. Told by his own son that he will be mistreated thus in his old age. *a.b.c.* 337; Tubach 2001.

S21.8. *Cruel daughter*. Soul is tormented because she had mistreated mother. *a.b.c.* 336; Tubach 1440.

S22. Parricide.

*S22.4. *Daughter suffocates father and installs lover in house*. *Talavera* 1.24.117.

*S22.5. *Royal son tortures father* and then orders him killed. *a.b.c.* 416.

S60. Cruel spouse.

*S61. *Amazon women kill surviving husbands* so that no woman among them be favored over others. *Ilustres mujeres* 11.17r–18r (Marsepia & Lampedon).

S62. Cruel husband.

*S62.5. *Husbands assault wives*, leave them battered to die in woods. *CMC* vv. 2697–2762; *Abreviada* 3.135.

S70. Other cruel relatives.

S73.3. *King blinds his three brothers* for plotting treason. *PCG* 2.656.376, 2.685.391; cf. Tubach 705.

S74. *Cruel nephew.* Kills uncle for his money. *a.b.c.* 120; Tubach 5020.

S100–S199. REVOLTING MURDERS OR MUTILATIONS
S110. Murders.

*S110.0.1. *Emperor orders death of seven thousand citizens* as punishment for stoning of two officials. *Castigos* MS A BNM 6559 10.107–8; Tubach 1494.

*S110.0.2. *King, told by advisor that he drinks too much,* demonstrates his sobriety by shooting an arrow through heart of advisor's son. *Castigos* MS A BNM 6559 13.118; *Glosa* 1.3.7.270.

*S110.0.3. *Cruel king serves the flesh of his enemy's children* to him. *Castigos* MS A BNM 6559 13.118 (ADMYTE 0 52v); *Glosa* 1.3.7.270–71.

*S110.6. *Queen (Beronice) pursues killer of her sons,* lancing him and running her chariot over his body. *Ilustres mujeres* 72.76r–76v.

*S110.7. *Queen (Clytemnestra) tricks husband with shirt with no opening for head.* Once donned, he is blinded and handed over to assassins. *Ilustres mujeres* 34.40v–41v.

S111. Murder by poison.

*S111.10. *Husband, knowing his wife is inclined to be contrary, leaves her two unguents.* Warns her not to apply poisonous one but to use other one. She disobeys and dies. *Lucanor* Ex. 27; cf. Tubach 5277.

*S111.11. *Husband wants to kill unfaithful wife.* Tells her not to drink poisoned wine (knowing she will disobey). She dies. *Talavera* 2.7.175; cf. Tubach 5277.

*S111.12. *Husband wants to kill wife.* Prepares a chest armed with a crossbow. When opened, arrow will kill opener. Tells her not to open chest, and she does. *Talavera* 2.7.177; cf. Tubach 5277.

S112. *Burning to death.* Man swears he will burn to death if accusation of another's guilt is not true. Burned to death. *a.b.c.* 235.

*S112.8. *Torturer who invented a machine to burn others* is burned to death in his own machine. *a.b.c.* 316; Tubach 3134.

*S113.2.4. *Murder by suffocation.* Daughter suffocates father so that she and lover can live in his house. *Talavera* 1.24.117.

*S113.3. *Murder by drowning.* Husband and wife quarrel over whether she has a knife or a pair of scissors. Murderous husband kicks her into river. She drowns shouting "scissors," using fingers to signal "scissors." She dies. *Talavera* 2.7.178; cf. Tubach 5284, 5285.

*S113.4. *Husband warns wife not to enter empty furnace* (oven) (knowing that she will disobey him). She does so, and it falls in upon her. *a.b.c.* 307; Tubach 5277.

S139. Miscellaneous cruel murders.

*S139.0.1. *Cruel king uses courtier's son as living target.* Shoots arrow at boy to prove marksmanship. *Castigos* MS A BNM 6559 13.118 (ADMYTE 0 52v).

S139.2.2.1. *Heads of slain enemies as trophies. PCG* 742.440.

*S139.7. *Cruel king has courtier's children killed, dismembered, and cooked.* Dish is served to father. *Castigos* MS A BNM 6559 13.118 (ADMYTE 0 52v).

S140. Cruel abandonments and exposures.

*S144.2. *Infants abandoned in wilderness* by compassionate executioner who could not kill them. *Ultramar* I.1.50.92.

*S144.3. *Newborn baby set adrift in chest in sea. Amadís* 1.1.

S146. Abandonment in pit.

*S146.1.1. *Abandonment in well.* Thieves leave cleric in well who cried out to Virgin Mary as he falls; he survives and is rescued by shepherds. *Cantigas* 102.

S160. Mutilations.

S161. Mutilation: cutting off of hands.

S161. *Emperor severs hand of suspected traitor. a.b.c.* 273.

*S161.1.2. *Self-mutilation.* Holy man severs offending hand. *a.b.c.* 273.

S163. Mutilation: cutting (tearing out) tongue.

S163. *Wife bites off deceitful husband's tongue.* Addresses now-mute mate: "With this you will never speak to her again nor deceive another." *Talavera* 1.24.119.

*S163.1. *Punishment for false accusations.* Ghost of evil man appears and mutilates own tongue repeatedly. *Espéculo* 67.46.

*S163.2. *Man (woman) bites off own tongue and spits it in torturer's face* rather than divulge names of co-conspirators. *Ilustres mujeres* 48.55v–56v (Leena); *a.b.c.* 376 (not in Paris MS); cf. Tubach 4911.

*S163.2.1. *Pythagorean virgin spits tongue in face of man who threatens her. Jardín* p. 251; *Glosa* 2.2.21.220.

*S163.3. *Man bites off own tongue and spits it in king's face* rather than let king cut it out. *Castigos* MS A BNM 6559 31.148; *Glosa* 1.2.14.134.

S169. Beheading.

*S169.1. *Prince who had raped kinswoman* is killed and beheaded. *a.b.c.* 62.

*S169.2. *Severed head.* Caesar cried upon seeing Pompey's severed head. *a.b.c.* 66.

*S169.3. *Severed heads of seven sons and their tutor* displayed to father for identification. *Abreviada* 2.287; *PCG* 743.441.

*S169.4. *Victorious queen puts severed head of enemy in wineskin* filled with blood of her soldiers. He will now drink their blood. *Ilustres mujeres* 47.54v–55v (Tamires).

*S169.5. *Wife brings severed head of captor who raped her* to her husband to repair her damaged honor. *Ilustres mujeres* 73.76v–78r (Wife of Orgiaguntes).

S176. Mutilations: sex organs.

S176.1. *Woman cuts off penis of unfaithful lover.* Addresses severed member: "Neither for yourself, nor for me, nor for another woman will you serve." *Talavera* 1.24.118.

S177. *Lecherous duchess physically abused by conqueror.* Used her for one night; handed her over to his soldiers for their use; disposed of, impaled vaginally. *a.b.c.* 246; Tubach 1081.

S200–S299. CRUEL SACRIFICES

S262. Periodic sacrifices to monster (enemy).

S262.2. *One hundred maidens to be sent as tribute to enemy* in exchange for a promise of peace. *PCG* 2.629.329.

S263. Sacrifice to appease spirits (gods).

*S263.2.4. *Man is willing to sacrifice son* (throw him into an oven) to enter monastery. Son saved. *a.b.c.* 109; *Glosa* 1.2.27.201; Tubach 4476.

S300–S399. ABANDONED OR MURDERED CHILDREN

S354. *Abandoned infant (Oedipus) reared at strange king's court. Ilustres mujeres* 23.29v–30r (Jocasta).

T. SEX

T0–T99. LOVE

T24. The symptoms of love.

T24.1. *Love-sickness.* Princess cured of love-sickness by marriage with beloved. *Apolonio* cc. 197–238.

*T24.9. *Love-sickness.* Man gives up his betrothed to friend whose sickness can only be cured by love. *Disciplina* 2; *Çifar* pp. 9–11.

*T24.10. *Love-sickness.* King sends his concubine to ailing prince, his son, to cure him. *Glosa* 2.2.2.129.

T30. Lovers' meeting.

*T32.2. *Lovers' meeting: man in woman's father's (brother's) prison.* They have child. *Abreviada* 2.282; cf. Tubach 3811.

T41. Communication of lovers.

T41.1. *Communication of lovers through hole in wall. Ilustres mujeres* 12.18r–9v (Thisbe).

*T41.3.1. *Mantle used as signal for rendezvous with lover* used by serving-man to deceive her. *Calila* p. 184; *Exemplario* 32v.

T51. Wooing by emissary.

*T51.1.2. *Go-between.* Makes love with client's beloved; disappoints client. *LBA* cc. 113–21.

T53. Matchmakers.

*T53.4.1. *Virgin Mary as matchmaker.* Young couple plighted troth; woman's father married her to rich man instead. Virgin saves her and arranges that she marry her first love. *Cantigas* 135.

T55. Woman as wooer.

*T55.1.2. *Princess gives prince horse and sword* in exchange for promise of marriage in his land. She will convert to Christianity. *Abreviada* 2.145.

*T55.1.3. *Count's daughter helps her father's assassin* in exchange for a promise of marriage. *Abreviada* 2.275; *PCG* 730.427.

T61. Betrothal.

*T61.4.6. *Betrothal arranged by king as "rogador." * Prospective brides handed over by "manero." *CMC* v. 2080.

*T69.6. *Father gives daughter to man who desires her* in exchange for promise to provide for her. *Cantigas* 195.

T80. Tragic love.

T81.8. *Wife swallows hot coals* because husband is unfaithful. *Castigos* MS A BNM 6559 79.211; *Glosa* 2.1.10.51.

T93. Fate of disappointed lover.

*T93.3.1. *Queen Dido immolates self* when consort abandons her. *Abreviada* 1.62.

T100–T199. MARRIAGE

T121. Unequal marriage.

*T121.3.2. *Mysterious empress weds prince* who visits her magic realm. Interdiction: can never return if he should leave her realm. *Çifar* pp. 137–40.

*T121.3.3. *Knight marries queen of underwater realm.* Interdiction: speech with subjects of kingdom forbidden. *Çifar* pp. 67–70.

*T122.4. *King enters queen's bedchamber* only after his men have searched it. *Castigos* MS A BNM 6559 (ADMYTE 0 84v).

T130. Marriage customs.

*T131.1.4. *Woman advises chaste maiden to marry.* Angel rebukes woman. *Castigos* MS A BNM 6559 (ADMYTE 0 74v–75r).

T200–T299. MARRIED LIFE

T210. Faithfulness in marriage.

T211.1.2. *Husband learns from augurs that if he saves self from serpent his wife will die.* Lets self be bitten to save wife. *Castigos* MS A BNM 6559 78.210; *Glosa* 2.1.9.48.

*T211.1.5. *Wife disobeys father's orders to kill new husband.* Imprisoned by father. *Ilustres mujeres* 13.19v–21r (Hypermestra).

T211.2. *Wife immolates self* in husband's funeral pyre. *Castigos* MS A BNM 6559 77.209; *Glosa* 2.1.8.43.

*T211.2.3. *Wife swallows hot coals* because husband is dead. *Ilustres mujeres* 82.84r–85r (Portia); *Jardín* p. 266.

T211.3.1. *Husband falls on sword* when wife dies. *Castigos* MS A BNM 6559 78.210; *Glosa* 2.1.9.48.

*T211.4.3. *Widow ingests husband's ashes.* Builds him a magnificent tomb. *Ilustres mujeres* 55.62r–63v (Artemesia); *Jardín* p. 261.

*T211.4.4. *Wife sees husband's bloodstained clothes; fears he has died.* She dies. *Ilustres mujeres* 81.83v–84r (Julia); *Glosa* 2.1.10.50.

T215. Faithfulness of married couple in misfortune.

T215.4. *Wife puts out one of her eyes in sympathy with her husband.* He has lost an eye in combat and is ashamed to return to her. She shows that it makes no difference in her love. *Lucanor* Ex. 44.

*T215.8.1. *Wife follows husband into exile.* *Castigos* MS A BNM 6559 77.209; *Glosa* 2.1.8.42 (Sulpicia).

*T215.8.2. *Wife hides exiled husband at home* pretending to mourn his absence. *Ilustres mujeres* 83.85r–85v (Curia).

*T215.9. *Faithful wife follows husband into battle* rather than be separated from him. *Ilustres mujeres* 100.101r–102r (Cenobia); *Ilustres mujeres* 78.80v–81v (Hypsicratea); *Ilustres mujeres* 96.97v–98r (Triaria); *Castigos* MS A BNM 6559 79.211; *Glosa* 2.1.10.51–52.

*T215.9.1. *Wife goes to battlefield in defiance of law* to find husband's body and to cremate it. *Ilustres mujeres* 27.34v–35v (Argia).

*T215.10. *During prolonged absence of husband wife fasts.* Eats no meat and subsists on bread and water. *Lucanor* Ex. 44.

*T215.11. *Conqueror refuses to let wives join husbands in captivity.* Women hang themselves. *Castigos* MS A BNM 6559 78.210; *Glosa* 2.1.9.47.

*T215.12. *Wife throws self overboard* to preserve her honor when husband's ship is captured. *Glosa* 2.1.19.93–94.

T221. *Woman's naivete proves her fidelity.* Man is told he has bad breath and rebukes wife for not having told him. She says she thought all men had bad breath. *a.b.c.* 368; Tubach 775.

T222. *Wife hides husband's unfaithfulness* and even shelters his mistress after his death; weds his lover to a man in her household. *Ilustres mujeres* 74.78r–78v (Tercia Emilia); *Castigos* MS A BNM 6559 77.209; 2.1.8.42.

*T223. *Wife unwilling to differ with husband* agrees when he says horses are cows. *Lucanor* Ex. 27.

T230. Faithlessness in marriage.

*T230.3. *Adulteress is like cuckoo.* Puts eggs in others' nests. *Espéculo* 28.19.

*T231.6. *The faithless widow.* For love of a young knight, grieving widow disinters her husband's corpse to conceal knight's neglect of duties. *Esopete* p. 64; Tubach 5262.

*T232.6. *Widow, attracted to handsome beggar,* invites him to dine. She seduces him while he consents declaring his passive acquiescence to exculpate himself. *Esopete* p. 165.

*T238.1. *Adulterous wife vows never to tell husband which of their sons is not his.* *a.b.c.* 174.

T250. Characteristics of wives and husbands.

T251. Ill-tempered wife.

*T251.0.4. *King's favorite wife angered when he praises another.* Hits him with plate of rice. King orders her killed. *Calila* p. 280; *Exemplario* 72r.

T251.2. *Taming the shrew.* By outdoing his wife in disagreeable behavior, husband renders her docile and obedient. Kills dog, cat, and horse when they disobey impossible command to fetch water. *Lucanor* Ex. 35; Tubach 4354.

T251.2.3.2. *Husband tries to frighten wife into obedience.* Kills rooster when it disobeys impossible command to fetch water. She ignores him because she knows he will not hurt her. *Lucanor* Ex. 35; Tubach 4354.

T252. The overbearing wife.

T252.2. *Cock shows browbeaten husband how to rule (serve sexually) his wife.* Can rule many hens; man cannot even handle one woman. *Esopete* p. 167.

T254. The disobedient wife.

T254.1. *Husband knows his wife is inclined to be contrary, leaves her two unguents.* Warns her not to apply poisonous one but to use other one. She disobeys and dies. *Lucanor* Ex. 27; cf. Tubach 5277.

T254.4. *Husband wants to kill wife.* Prepares a chest armed with a crossbow. When opened, arrow will kill opener. Tells her not to open chest and she does. *Talavera* 2.7.177; cf. Tubach 5277.

T254.5. *Husband warns wife not to enter empty furnace* (knowing that she will disobey him). She does so and it falls in upon her. *a.b.c.* 307; Tubach 5277.

T254.6. *Husband warns wife not to drink poisoned wine (knowing she will disobey).* She dies. *Talavera* 2.7.176; cf. Tubach 5277.

T255.1. *Husband and wife quarrel* over whether she has a knife or a pair of scissors. Murderous husband kicks her into river. She drowns shouting "scissors," using fingers to signal "scissors." Husband jests that she will win argument with river and survive. She dies. *Talavera* 2.7.178–79; cf. Tubach 5285.

★T255.1.1. *Husband and wife quarrel over whether bird is a thrush or a throstle.* Enraged, the husband breaks her arm. Their pilgrimage to pray for a child was altered to a pilgrimage for a broken limb. *Talavera* 2.7.179; cf. Tubach 5285.

T257. Jealous wife or husband.

★T257.2.3. *Jealous wife prays to Virgin Mary* to harm her husband's lover. Virgin makes her see that devil made her wish ill to other woman. *Cantigas* 68.

★T257.12. *Jealous husband insists wife prove her innocence.* Virgin Mary protects her when she leaps from a high place and is unharmed. *Cantigas* 341.

T261. The ungrateful wife.

★T261.2. *King indulges wife's every whim.* Creates "snowstorm" of almond blossoms, a "pond with muddy banks" from perfumed water, sugar, and spices. She is ungrateful and complains of his inattention. *Lucanor* Ex. 30.

T280. Other aspects of married life.

T284. *Frightened wife shows marks of affection for husband.* Joins husband in bed for protection. This is so rare that husband is grateful to thief who frightened her. *Calila* p. 238; *Exemplario* 56r.

T299. Other aspects of married life: miscellaneous.

★T299.3. *Young man rendered impotent after placing ring on finger of statue of Venus consults magician.* He is to go to crossroads at certain hour and give letters to mounted woman followed by man (the devil). Devil reads letter and sends for ring on finger of statue to return to young man. *Espéculo* 528.416–17; Tubach 4103; see T376.

T300–T399. CHASTITY AND CELIBACY

T310. Celibacy and continence.

*T310.2. *Virgin Mary grants freedom from lustful behavior* to devoted man. He lives chastely freed from his desires. *Cantigas* 336; Tubach 3098.

*T310.3. *Warrior attains unusual strength* through chastity. *Castigos* 1.38; Tubach 4656.

T311. Woman averse to marriage (sexual intercourse).

*T311.0.2. *Woman's aversion to marriage motivated through promise to Virgin Mary to remain chaste.* Husband inflicts incurable wound with knife. Husband dies in fire; wife is cured by Virgin Mary. *Cantigas* 105; Tubach 3176.

*T311.0.3. *Woman's promise to Virgin Mary to be chaste* causes seducer to renounce his sexual desires. He sends her to convent. *Cantigas* 195; Tubach 5142.

*T311.0.4. *Elderly princess pledged to remain chaste* obliged to wed and produce heir to throne. *Ilustres mujeres* 103.104v–105v (Constancia).

T311.1. *Princess flees* to escape arranged marriage. *Ultramar* I.1.81–82.

*T311.3.1. *Beautiful young woman shuts self in tomb* to save soul of young man who desires her carnally. *Espéculo* 482.380; *Glosa* 2.2.20.215–16; Tubach 4894.

T314.1. *Father kills daughter* lest she become the property of a wicked tyrant. *Ilustres mujeres* 56.63v–65r (Virginia); *Jardín* p. 256; Tubach 3436.

T315. Continence in marriage.

T315.1. *Marital continence by mutual agreement.* Husband and wife to be celibate for two years to do penance for previous sin of husband. *Çifar* pp. 49–50.

T315.2. *Marital continence.* Bridegroom committed to celibacy gives new bride a ring and leaves her. *San Alejo* p. 70.

*T315.4. *Husband and wife enter religious houses.* Husband visits his wife twice; she entices him, and they have two children. He confesses and does penance of seven years. *Espéculo* 390.286–87.

*T315.5. *Husband and wife make vow of future chastity* after God had granted them a child. *San Alejo* p. 99.

T317. The repression of lust.

*T317.1.1. *Repression of lustful thoughts* by visiting places where there was suffering and illness. *a.b.c.* 370.

*T317.1.2. *Repression of lust* by removing one's eyes to avoid temptation. *a.b.c.* 370.

T317.2. *Desert monk who longs for wife he left behind* advised to pray and to do good works. *a.b.c.* 347.

*T317.2.1. *Lustful thoughts* banished by prayer. Young monk must resist to gain God's pardon. *a.b.c.* 326.

T317.4. *Youth counseled to fast and pray in woods to repress lust. a.b.c.* 197; *Espéculo* 4.5; Tubach 1992.

*T317.4.1. *Young man told to work* to avoid sexual temptation. *Espéculo* 90.61–62.

T317.6. *Only abuse and cruel treatment from his fellow monks* can conquer monk's lust. *a.b.c.* 213; Tubach 3097.

*T317.7. *Elderly monk learns that advanced age is no protection against lust. a.b.c.* 176.

*T317.8. *Repression of lust.* Pope severs hand kissed by woman. Restored miraculously by Virgin Mary. *a.b.c.* 391; *Cantigas* 206; cf. Tubach 2419.

*T317.9. *Husband judges wife to be unchaste* because she looks at men from her window. Kills her. *a.b.c.* 63.

T317.10. *Sight of cock and hen provokes lustful thoughts in hermit. a.b.c.* 127; *LBA* cc. 529–43; Tubach 2569.

T320. Escape from undesired lover.

T320.4. *Woman escapes lust of king by shaming him.* Leaves book of laws condemning adultery where he will read it. *Sendebar* Day 1, Tale 1; *Lucanor* Ex. 50.

T320.5. *Beautiful young woman gives up wealth* to escape lecherous emperor. *a.b.c.* 369.

*T326.4. *Chastity preserved.* Noble wife commits suicide rather than submit to emperor's lustful desire. *a.b.c.* 190.

*T326.5. *Chastity preserved.* Noble wife leaps into fire with her two young sons to save self and them from invaders. *Jardín* p. 261.

*T326.6. *Saint, mother, sisters drown* to maintain saint's chastity. *Jardín* p. 257.

T327. Mutilation to repel lover.

T327.1. *Nun sends king her eyes because he had admired them* and coveted her, saying: "You wanted my eyes, take them." *a.b.c.* 370; *Glosa* 2.2.20.215; Tubach 4744 b).

*T327.3.1. *Saint prays for a deformity* to save her from marriage. Loses sight in one eye. *Espéculo* 92.63; *Jardín* p. 259.

*T327.4.1. *Young women smear breasts with foul-smelling rotting chicken flesh to escape rape. a.b.c.* 246.

*T327.8.1. *Woman prays for deliverance from emperor's desires.* Uses knife to disfigure face before meeting with his emissaries. *Espéculo* 483.380–81; *Glosa* 2.2.20.215; *Castigos* MS A BNM 6559 (ADMYTE 0 82r).

T330. Anchorites under temptation.

T331.9. *Celibate man yells "thief" to repel sexually aggressive woman.* When she comes to his bed, he screams. *a.b.c.* 177.

*T331.10. *Bishop saved from temptation.* Evil spirit banished by nonbeliever who made sign of cross. *a.b.c.* 92.

*T331.11. *Holy man refuses to see his mother in this life* so that they will meet in the next. *Espéculo* 391.287; Tubach 3418.

*T331.12. *Holy man, forced to meet his sister after fifty years of separation,* closes his eyes and permits her to see him. *Espéculo* 392.

T332. Man tempted by fiend in woman's shape.

T332. *Monk, suffering from carnal desires, is tempted by devil in shape of woman.* He slapped her, pushed her off his lap, and she disappeared. Foul smell lingered on hands for two years. *a.b.c.* 411.

*T332.2. *Ascetic hermit tempted by woman who appeared at door of his cave.* When he forgets his vows and reaches for her, she disappears and reappears as the devil who laughs at him. *Castigos* 37.177–78; cf. Tubach 912.

T333. Man mutilates self or otherwise removes self from temptation.

T333.2. *Tempted man burns off his finger tips.* An elderly monk was tempted by the presence of a woman in his house. He burned his fingers in a candle's flame to distract himself. *a.b.c.* 253, 254; Tubach 4741.

*T333.2.2. *Man tied to stake in meadow is tempted by lustful woman.* Unable to resist her he bites off his own tongue and spits it at her. *Espéculo* 90^1.62.

T333.3. *Handsome youth, troubled by temptation, used a knife to disfigure his face* so that he would not be admired by women. *a.b.c.* 370; *Glosa* 1.2.15.139; *Castigos* MS A BNM 6559 (ADMYTE 0 82r).

T333.4. *Virgin saves life of pilgrim who, at devil's instigation, had castrated self* to atone for sin of fornication. Offending organ not restored. *Milagros* 8; *Cantigas* 26; *Santiago* 17.86–94; cf. Tubach 3800.

*T333.6. *To escape temptation: man crawls naked through thorns* after almost succumbing to carnal temptation. *a.b.c.* 251; *Espéculo* 90.61–62; *Espéculo* 322^a.225; *Espéculo* 548.439; Tubach 4840.

*T333.7. *Saint applies red-hot iron rod to body.* Pain curbs sexual desires. *Espéculo* 322.224–25; Tubach 3109.

T334.1. *Monk goes into desert* to avoid temptation of women, the source of sin. *a.b.c.* 306; cf. Tubach 5366.

*T334.1.1. *Philosopher retreats to countryside* to avoid temptations of city. *a.b.c.* 370.

*T334.1.2. *Monk unable to endure temptation leaves monastery.* Angel tells him to stay in monastery. His nine years of suffering are his crown and strength. *Espéculo* 542.437.

*T334.1.3. *Elderly monk was tempted in dream.* His pupil directed seven strong thoughts to him that he saw as seven crowns in dream. *Espéculo* 543.437–38.

*T334.1.4. *Abbot, tired of walking, sits down in a cucumber patch.* Preoccupied by his thoughts steals (eats) a cucumber. Says that yielding to temptation of theft is like yielding to carnal temptation. *Espéculo* 544.438.

*T334.1.5. *Saint puts foot in fire.* If this pain is unendurable, how much worse would be eternal pain of hell? *Espéculo* 545.438.

*T334.1.6. *Monk tormented by carnal desire asked for prayers of holy man.*

Prayers do not help him. Holy man sees him surrounded by his desires. Monk must resist. *Espéculo* 546.438–39.

*T334.1.7. *Monk asks why he is unable to free self from temptations.* Told that he has rid himself of temptation but has retained his desires. *Espéculo* 547.439.

*T334.1.8. *Man unable to fight temptation* goes to church and gives self to God. *Espéculo* 548ª.439–40.

*T334.1.9. *Priest must give up fornication.* In exchange, pains are cured by saint's prayers. *Espéculo* 110.72.

T336. Sight or touch of woman as sin.

T336. *Monk on his deathbed refuses to see woman he had loved* before he entered the order (wife before he entered order). He says: "Go away, woman, because even a tiny flame can ignite straw." *a.b.c.* 396; *Espéculo* 393.288.

*T336.2.1. *Holy man will not allow woman, even though she has journeyed from afar to see him.* Later hears that she has a fever and consoles her. *a.b.c.* 305.

*T336.2.2. *Monk will not see his sister in fine clothes* since sight of her is source of sin. Only when she dresses modestly will he see her. *a.b.c.* 299.

*T336.3. *Monk wraps hands in cloths to keep from touching aged mother's body* as he carries her over a stream. Touch of all women is a source of sin. *a.b.c.* 306; *Espéculo* 394.289; Tubach 3419.

T338. Virtuous man seduced by women.

*T338.2. *Celibate prince falls ill* resisting father's pressure to experience sex with a woman. *Barlaam* pp. 277–80.

*T338.4. *Celibate prince's father replaces all his attendants with seductive young women.* *Barlaam* p. 264.

T360. Chastity and celibacy: miscellaneous.

T362.1. *Abbess informed that bishop wished to visit her convent* sent word that she refused to look upon a man. *Castigos* 17.107.

T371. *Youth who had never seen a woman: the Satans.* Sheltered prince shown all forms of human and animal life for first time was told that young women are "devils" who deceive men. Asked what he liked best, chose the "devils." *Barlaam* pp. 261–63.

*T371.2. *Inexperienced young monk (never having seen a woman)* is told that women are goats. Obsessed by what he had seen through window is unable to eat (meat) because he felt so sorry for the poor goat. *a.b.c.* 300.

T376. *Young man mistakenly betrothed to statue.* Puts ring on finger of statue of Virgin Mary. She closes finger over ring; later forbids him the embraces of an earthly wife. *Espéculo* 528.4416–17; *Cantigas* 42; see T299.3.

T376.1. *Canon previously pledged to Virgin Mary marries* because of importunities of family. Leaves his bride on wedding night to continue to serve Virgin. *Milagros* 15; *Cantigas* 132.

*T376.2.2. *Betrothed woman flees to church,* choosing to be God's bride. *a.b.c.* 291.

T400–T499. ILLICIT SEXUAL RELATIONS
T400. Illicit sexual relations.
*T400.0.1. *Princess has baby after secret marriage.* Her brother, the king, imprisons father of baby and sends her to convent. *Abreviada* 2.164.
*T400.0.2. *Daughter, pregnant, thrown off cliff.* Father of baby beheaded. *Glosa* 2.2.21.218–19.
*T400.0.3. *Vestal Virgin has baby.* Punishment: buried alive. *Glosa* 2.2.21.219.
T401.1. *Pregnant abbess secretly delivered of her child* by Virgin Mary. *Milagros* 21; *Espéculo* 362.265–66; *Cantigas* 7.
*T401.2. *Vestal Virgin falsely accused.* Carries water in sieve without spilling any to prove her virginity. *Glosa* 2.2.21.219.
T410. Incest.
T411. Father–daughter incest.
T411.1. *Lecherous father.* Unnatural father wants to marry his daughter. *Esopete* p. 25.
*T411.1.3. *Royal father forces himself on daughter.* Sets unreasonable conditions (riddle) for potential suitors so he will not have to give her up. *Apolonio* cc. 6–14.
T412. Mother–son incest.
T412.1. *Widow guilty of incest with son* forgiven by Virgin Mary. *a.b.c.* 274; *Cantigas* 17.
*T412.5. *Mother treats son as husband.* Found in bed with son, thought to be behaving incestuously. *Lucanor* Ex. 36; *Çifar* p. 55.
*T412.6. *Mother importunes son sexually.* Denied, she falsely accuses him of trying to rape her. *a.b.c.* 172; Tubach 2734.
*T412.7. *Queen justifies incestuous union with her son* by passing law allowing intrafamiliar unions. *Ilustres mujeres* 6r–8r (Semiramis); Tubach 4224.
T415. Brother–sister incest.
*T415.8. *Brother and sister have three children.* She kills them and takes poison. Virgin Mary cures her, and she becomes nun. *Espéculo* 363.286; *Castigos* MS A BNM 6559 82.216.
*T415.9. *Tamar raped by her brother.* *Castigos* MS A BNM 6559 (ADMYTE 0 80v).
T417. Other incest.
*T417.2. *Mother-in-law accused of sexual relations with son-in-law.* *a.b.c.* 272; *Cantigas* 255; Tubach 2737.
*T426. *Noble accused of incest with relative.* Servant to testify that he held candle for master. *a.b.c.* 166.
*T427. *Young woman promised to Virgin Mary has sexual relations with godfather.* Has three children by him. *Cantigas* 201.
*T427.1. *Priest who had sex with goddaughter dies* after seven days. Fire rises from grave consuming it totally. *a.b.c.* 404; Tubach 2037.

T450. Prostitution and concubinage.

*T450.0.1. *Queen, vain about her virtue,* declares she would never surrender her body to a lover for wealth. Challenged with increasingly large rewards, is at last tempted. *Talavera* 2.1.146–47.

*T451.1. *Prostitute shamed by offer of sexual intercourse in public place.* Saint offers to have sex with her before a crowd. She refuses; then how much more shame should she have before God? *Espéculo* 350.250.

*T451.2. *Aging prostitute offers young daughter as substitute* to procurer who will arrange clients for her. *Espéculo* 462.361.

*T451.3. *Whore cheats brothel keeper,* not charging a favorite customer for services. Brothel keeper tried to blow poison through a straw into customer's nose. Customer sneezes, and she inhales poison. *Calila* pp. 138–39.

T452. Bawds, professional go-betweens.

*T452.2. *Procurer sets high price for first use of virgin captive.* Subsequent patrons pay less. *Apolonio* c. 401.

*T452.3. *Go-between tricks woman into believing she will be transformed into a dog* if she does not accede to a man's sexual request. *a.b.c.* 234 (not in Paris MS); *Disciplina* 13; *Sendebar* Day 4, Tale 10; Tubach 661.

*T452.4. *Go-between tricks woman* into believing that sex with a client will solve her marital problem. *Sendebar* Day 5, Tale 13.

*T452.5. *Go-between makes trouble between husband and wife:* the hair from his beard. Tells wife to increase her husband's love by cutting a hair from his beard. Also tells husband that wife will try to cut his throat. *a.b.c.* 370 (not in Paris MS); *Lucanor* Ex. 42; *Esopete* pp. 149–51.

*T452.6. *Would-be-lover employs go-between* repeatedly. *LBA* cc. 77–81, 111–22, 580–891, 1332–1507, 1508–12, 1618–23.

*T459. *Pious maiden convinced by go-between that God does not see what we do at night.* She consents to spend night with go-between's customer. *a.b.c.* 108; Tubach 1436.

*T459.1. *"Prostitute gives great pleasure to men,"* says saint. Prays for whore's soul but also prays for her own ability to please God as the whore pleases men. *Espéculo* 425.324.

T460. Other sexual practices.

T463. Homosexual love (male).

T464. *King uses young man sexually. a.b.c.* 341; Tubach 2598.

T466. Necrophilism: sexual intercourse with dead human body.

T466.1. *Necrophilism: executioner struck by beauty of woman* has intercourse with her after she is hanged. *Talavera* 1.24.117.

T470. Illicit sexual relations: miscellaneous.

T471. Rape and seduction.

*T471.0.2. *Knight who had raped nun is captured* when she miraculously is mounted before him on his horse and holds reins until he is taken prisoner. *Castigos* 19.121–22.

*T471.0.3. *Squire tries to rape woman* who takes refuge in Virgin Mary's church. Trying to kick in door, breaks leg, loses senses, speech, and thereafter can only utter her name. Ends life as a beggar. *Cantigas* 317.

*T471.0.4. *King rapes daughter of courtier.* Father helps enemy to conquer realm to avenge the injury. *PCG* 1.554.307–8; *Castigos* 6.60; *Abreviada* 2.101.

*T471.0.5. *King sends woman's husband to battle in order to be able to seduce her* (See K978. *Uriah letter*). *Sendebar* Day 1, Tale 1; *Lucanor* Ex. 50; *Talavera* 1.12.101–2; Tubach 1453.

*T471.0.6. *Courtier rapes woman; threatens her with revealing secret.* She kills self to guard honor. *Ilustres mujeres* 46.52v–54v (Lucrecia); *Jardín* pp. 257–58; *a.b.c.* 62; Tubach 3095.

*T471.0.7. *Captor rapes enemy's queen.* Ransomed, she orders her soldiers to behead him. She presents head to husband to restore her honor. *Ilustres mujeres* 73.76v–78r (Wife of Orgiaguntes).

*T472.1. *Women of vanquished city given to conquerors.* Two women must perform all duties naked. Out gathering wood, one covers genitals with scrap of cloth. Other one accuses her of lascivious thoughts. Accused, told to look to own thoughts. *Calila* p. 198; *Exemplario* 37r.

*T472.2. *Young woman returns to ask lover to say mass for her.* Their carnal desire was sin. He says mass and enters religious order. *Espéculo* 353.251–52.

*T472.3. *Magic sign shows lover is freed of torment.* Black hair combings secreted by dead lover turn white when she is freed. *Espéculo* 353.251–52.

*T472.4. *Husband and wife sin.* Engage in sexual intercourse on holy eve. Child conceived is possessed by devils. Virgin Mary drives them away. *Cantigas* 115.

*T475.2.2. *Incubus makes sleeping woman think she is having sexual intercourse.* *a.b.c.* 116.

T481. Adultery.

*T481.8. *Woman killed because husband accuses her of lustful behavior.* She looks at other men through window. *a.b.c.* 63.

*T481.9. *The husband locked out,* excessive precautions to assure wife's fidelity. Despite efforts, wife returns home late at night; her husband refuses to admit her. She threatens to throw herself in the well. Husband leaves house to see if she has drowned. She enters the house and bars him from house. *a.b.c.* 303; *Disciplina* 14; *Talavera* 2.1.147 n. 36; Tubach 5246; see K1511.

*T481.10. *The cut-off nose.* Carpenter's wife asks a barber's wife to take her place while she goes to her lover. Carpenter speaks to wife's friend, gets no answer and cuts off her nose. In the morning wife returns and still has nose. Husband made to believe it was restored miraculously. Barber's wife, whose nose has been cut off when she took friend's place, returns home. Her husband made to believe that he has accidentally cut off her nose when he threw razor at her. *Calila* pp. 139–41; *Exemplario* 14v–15r; see K1512.

*T481.11. *The husband in the chicken house (dovecote)*. Husband returns unexpectedly and surprises his wife with her lover. She makes the husband believe he is pursued and hides him in the chicken house. *Esopete* pp. 148–49; see K1514.1.

*T481.12. *The husband's good eye treated* so that lover can leave house unseen (vintner). *a.b.c.* 161; *Disciplina* 9; *Esopete* pp. 147–48; cf. Tubach 1943; see K1516.1.

*T481.13. *The husband temporarily blinded* so that lover can leave unseen. Wife sprays his eyes with mother's milk. He hears noise; she tells him it is the cat. *Talavera* 2.10.188; cf. Tubach 1943; see K1516.9.

*T481.14. *Wife's lover under bed*. Husband returns home. She has husband turn round to brush hair off his clothes. He hears lover leave; she tells him it is the cat. *Talavera* 2.10.188–89; see K1516.1.2.

*T481.15. *Wife's lover under bed*. Husband returns home. Wife tips over candle extinguishing it. Sends husband out for light. *Talavera* 2.10.189; see K1515.3.

*T481.16. *Wife's lover behind curtains*. Husband returns home. Wife shows husband a new kettle she says has holes in it. Holds it in front of his eyes, slaps it loudly. Husband neither sees nor hears lover leave. *Talavera* 2.10.189; see K1516.8.

*T481.17. *Two lovers are pursuer and fugitive*. Wife is visited by two lovers. When the husband arrives, one goes out with drawn sword and the other hides in house. She convinces her husband that she has given refuge to a fugitive. *Sendebar* Day 2, Tale 5; Tubach 4693; see K1517.1.

*T481.18. *Wife entertains lover during husband's absence*. Husband returns, and mother-in-law (guardian) counsels lover to pretend he is fugitive from street ruffians. *Disciplina* 11; *Esopete* pp. 145–46; Tubach 4692; see K1517.2.

*T481.19. *Husband returns while abbot is in house*. Errant wife enlists aid of friar who brings extra habit next day. Abbot escapes wearing friar's habit. *Sendebar* Day 8, Tale 22; see K1517.6.

*T481.20. *Wife outwits husband with extended sheet*. Lover leaves house unseen. *a.b.c.* 162; *Esopete* p. 148; *Disciplina* 10; Tubach 4319; see K1516.

*T481.21. *The enchanted pear tree*. Wife and lover are up in tree. Blind husband hears them and prays to Jupiter for restoration of sight. Prayer is answered. Wife convinces cuckold that her adultery convinced Jupiter to grant his wish. *Esopete* p. 147; Tubach 3265; see K1518.

*T481.22. *Wife, in bed with lover*, knows that husband is hiding under bed. Tells lover how much she loves husband. *Calila* p. 241; *Exemplario* 57r; *Esopete* p. 168; see K1532.1.

*T481.23. *The marked cloth in the wife's room*. A go-between obtains a woman for a client by leaving a marked cloth in woman's house. Husband beats woman; she leaves and is tricked into thinking that sex with the go-between's client will help her solve her problem. Go-between tells husband that she had left the cloth in his house, and husband is deceived. *Sendebar* Day 5, Tale 13.

*T481.24. *Husband unwittingly instrumental in wife's adultery.* Greedy husband supplies his wife to an inexperienced fat prince because he believes him to be impotent. When the prince and the woman evidently enjoy each other, the husband kills himself. *Sendebar* Day 4, Tale 9.

*T481.25. *Husband unwittingly instrumental in wife's adultery.* Believes that wife will spend night with god, Anubis, not with trickster posing as god. *a.b.c.* 385; Tubach 4221.

*T481.26. *Husband unwittingly instrumental in wife's adultery.* Wife's lover (an apothecary) has assistant who substitutes earth for needed medicine. Wife returns with packet; tells husband she was run down by a horse on way and lost money. Used a sieve to find missing money and could not find it. Husband replaces money. *Exemplario* 28v.

*T481.27. *Maidservant is go-between for knight who wants to seduce another's wife.* Convinces wife to don magic slippers she cannot remove sent by suitor. *Cantigas* 64.

*T481.28. *Spanish count's wife runs off with French count.* He follows her to France and kills both offenders. Returns with severed heads. *Abreviada* 2.274–75.

T495. Humiliation or abuse.

*T495.1. *Lover humiliated.* Philosopher (Aristotle) warns against uxoriousness. In revenge, woman tricks philosopher into letting her ride him on all fours. Husband comes and sees them. *Talavera* 1.17.99; Tubach 328.

*T495.2. *Lover humiliated.* Virgil suspended in basket halfway up his lover's tower; not permitted to ascend further. Seen by passersby. *LBA* cc. 262–65; 1.17.100–1.

*T495.3. *Lover humiliated.* Man tricked into escaping from a prison tower to visit his lover. Enemies intercept the descent, catch him in a net, and leave him suspended for all the world to see. *Talavera* 1.17.100–1.

*T495.4. *Lecherous duchess physically abused by conqueror.* Used her for one night; handed her over to his soldiers for their use; disposed of with a stick inserted vaginally until it reaches her upper body. *a.b.c.* 246; Tubach 1081.

*T494.5. *Woman must relight magic fires as punishment.* Magician, in repayment for ill treatment by woman, causes lights of the city to go out. They can only be relighted from the genitals (naked body) of the woman. None can be relighted until all have applied torches. *LBA* cc. 261–68.

T500–T599. CONCEPTION AND BIRTH
T510. Miraculous conceptions.

T526. *Conception because of prayer.* King and favorite wife have son after much prayer. *Sendebar* pp. 66–67; *Cantigas* 171; Tubach 971.

T540. Miraculous birth.

T541. Birth from unusual part of body.

⋆T541.0.1. *Birth from wound in mother's side.* Pregnant woman who goes to aid of slain husband is cut with sword. Baby is born as she dies. *Cantigas* 184.

T547. Birth from virgin.

⋆T547.1. *Birth from virgin.* Divine intervention caused Mary to be impregnated and remain virgin. Angel explained to Joseph that Holy Spirit had engendered Jesus. *Estados* 1.40.

T548. Birth obtained through magic or prayer.

⋆T548.1. *Child born in answer to prayer. Sendebar* p. 67; *Cantigas* 43; *San Alejo* p. 68; *Santiago* 3.50–52; Tubach 971.

T550. Monstrous births.

T551.2 *Child born with two heads,* each one facing the other; two bodies joined at chest (conjoined twins). *Esopete* p. 166.

⋆T551.2.1. *Child born with head on backwards.* Punishment to Jewish father who had denied Virgin and Jesus Christ. *Cantigas* 108.

T554.2.1. *Woman gives birth to animal.* Evil mother-in-law writes to absent son telling him his wife has given birth to seven hounds. *Ultramar* I.1.53.89.

T573. Short pregnancy.

⋆T573.2. *Unusually short pregnancy.* Enchantress gives birth seven days after conceiving child. *Çifar* p. 68.

T574. Prolonged pregnancy.

⋆T574.3. *Woman accuses saint of fathering her child.* Unable to give birth until she confesses. *a.b.c.* 89, 285; cf. Tubach 648, 1915.

T584. Parturition.

⋆T584.0.7. *Jewish woman unable to give birth, prays to Virgin Mary.* Has twins who are baptized. *Cantigas* 89.

T586.1. *Many children at one birth.* Saint's wife, rewarded by God, gives birth to seven children, all of whom are saints themselves. *Castigos* 1.39.

⋆T586.1.2. *Seven children at one birth,* each one wearing a golden chain. *Ultramar* I.1.50.87.

T586.3. *Multiple birth believed to be result of sexual relations with several men.* Magical golden chains around infants' necks proof that their birth is divine. Woman exculpated. *Ultramar* I.1.50.87, I.1.61.106.

T590. Conception and birth: miscellaneous motifs.

T591. Sexual performance.

⋆T591.0.1. *Impotence induced by magic.* Lover is impotent in presence of image of Virgin Mary. Moves to other house to complete sex act. *Cantigas* 312.

⋆T591.0.2. *Impotence induced by magic.* Husband impotent with young wife because he is faithful to Virgin Mary. *Cantigas* 132.

⋆T591.0.3 *Virgin Mary induces impotence* in knight given to lustful behavior. *Cantigas* 137.

*T591.0.4. *Climate (external temperature)* at moment of conception determines sex of baby. *Glosa* 2.1.17.81; *Jardín* 1.9.186–87.

T600–T699. CARE OF CHILDREN
T615. Supernatural growth.
T615.1. *Precocious speech.* Girl at age four appears to be fully grown. Speaks as well as a person of ten or twelve years. *Ultramar* I.1.110.230.
T617. Youth reared in ignorance of world.
*T617.0.1. *Youth raised in ignorance of world.* Must go to spring in woods and fast for 40 days and pray for a wife. Disgusting, odoriferous hag comes to him and tells him she is sin of lust. He returns to celibate life. *a.b.c.* 197.

*T617.3. *Young, inexperienced monk, raised without ever having seen a woman,* is tempted by sight of one. Brother monk tells him she is a goat. He cannot eat meat because of tenderness and pity he feels for goat. *a.b.c.* 300.

*T617.4. *Beautiful young captive woman sent to seduce celibate prince* who had not known women. He tries to convert her to Christianity. She will become Christian if he spends one night in her bed. *Barlaam* pp. 270–72.
T640. Illegitimate children.
*T646.2. *Illegitimate prince counseled to wear special garments* to remind self of both noble and base lineage. *a.b.c.* 189.

*T646.3. *Illegitimate prince,* unaware of fate of parents, reared by royal uncle. *Abreviada* 2.164.

*T647.1. *Crow's egg placed mischievously in stork's nest.* When fledglings recognize that chick is not one of them, they stone mother for adultery. *a.b.c.* 13.

*T647.2. *Illegitimate offspring said to be unable to see magically invisible cloth.* *Lucanor* Ex. 32; cf. Tubach 3577.
T680. Care of children: miscellaneous motifs.
T681.1. *Each likes own children best.* Owl mother sends hare to fetch baby's shoes for a beauty contest. Tells hare to take shoes to the most beautiful among all other contestants. Animals mock her. *Gatos* 7; *Esopete* pp. 122–23; Tubach 4873.

U. THE NATURE OF LIFE

U0–U99. LIFE'S INEQUITIES
U10. Justice and injustice.
U11.2. *He who steals much (Alexander) is called king.* He who steals a little is called pirate. *a.b.c.* 42; *Castigos* MS A BNM 6559 31.147; *Glosa* 1.2.10.110–11; Tubach 113.

*U11.3 *Apparent injustice.* Evil rich man buried with honors; pious hermit devoured by lion. Angel explains that heavenly justice will rectify earthly injustice. *a.b.c.* 105; *Espéculo* 511.404–5; Tubach 223.

*U15.2. *Saint prays for perfection.* Voice tells him he never will achieve the perfection of two saintly women who live in city. *a.b.c.* 216; *Espéculo* 98.66; Tubach 3701.

U21. **Justice depends on the point of view.**

U21.4. *Wolf objects to fox stealing rooster from him,* although he himself is a thief. *LBA* cc. 321–71.

*U21.4.1. *Wolf accuses fox of theft.* Ape judge says that wolf may not have lost anything but that fox had stolen in past. They must watch each other. *Esopete* p. 54.

U25. *Theft to avoid starvation justified.* Youth and sister rob graves to avoid starving to death. *Lucanor* Ex. 47.

U30. **Rights of the strong.**

U31. *Wolf unjustly accuses lamb and eats him.* When all the lamb's defenses are good, the wolf asserts the right of the strong over the weak (usually accused of stirring up water downstream). *Esopete* pp. 32–33; *Espéculo* 72.48; Tubach 5334.

U31.1. *Cat unjustly accuses cock and eats him.* Although all the cock's defenses are good, the cat tells him that she can no longer go hungry and eats him. *Esopete* p. 110.

*U31.1.1. *Dog accuses sheep of taking bread. Esopete* p. 34.

U31.2. *Crow rides on sheep* because sheep cannot prevent it. *Esopete* p. 79.

*U31.3. *Hunter exercises his right of the strong* over the horse when it fails to run down deer. Horse will be saddled forever. *Esopete* pp. 77–78; Tubach 2619.

*U31.4. *Crow (hawk) exercises rights of the strong over dove (nightingale) who cannot defend self.* Dove at crow's request sings to save her brood, but crow kills them because song was not good enough. *Gatos* 41; *Esopete* pp. 62–63; *Espéculo* 71.47–48; Tubach 4388.

*U31.5. *Spider kills fly easily.* Retreats to web when wasp approaches. *Gatos* 52; Tubach 4569.

*U31.6. *Tortoise treads on toad, injuring it. Gatos* 54.

*U31.7. *Pigs exercise rights of strong.* Ants store wheat grains for future use, and pigs come and eat them. *Gatos* 45.

U33. *Cock is killed by its captor* despite his plea of usefulness to man. *Esopete* p. 110.

*U35.3. *Defeated empress turns wealth over to victor. a.b.c.* 295 (not in Paris MS).

*U35.4. *Abbot unjustly strikes monk with footstool,* bruising him badly. Next day, monk asks permission to perform errands. Abbot begs his pardon and monk throws himself to floor so that he can say that he bruised himself when he fell. *a.b.c.* 238.

*U45. *Dog gives up bed to bitch* that is about to whelp. She may keep bed while puppies grow up. Later they help her drive owner off. *Esopete* pp. 35–36; Tubach 660.

U60. Wealth and poverty.

*U61.1. *Saint calls poor masters.* They are honored by God and can help humankind enter heaven. *Espéculo* 448.343.

*U62. *Poor man with a single blanket to cover his feet,* luckier than rich people in hell whose feet are tormented in stocks. *Espéculo* 445.342.

*U62.1. *Abbot, previously rich,* grateful he may now beg in God's name. *Espéculo* 446.342–43.

*U62.2. *Rich man happy to live simply in monastery.* His servant lives luxuriously. Reproached, servant replies that master has what he did not have before, and he too now enjoys what he did not have before. *Espéculo* 502.394.

*U72. *Hermit hides money under pillow.* When robbers enter, he throws it to them so that he will fear robbery no longer. *a.b.c.* 355; *Espéculo* 38.26; Tubach 3364; cf. Tubach 4810.

*U72.1. *Socrates throws great quantity of gold in sea* so that he can drown it before it drowns him. *a.b.c.* 355; *Espéculo* 443.340; *Glosa* 1.1.7.36–37; Tubach 2343, 3366.

*U72.2. *Devil convinces gardener to accumulate sums of money to pay for future medical treatment.* Uses money to cure foot to no avail. Asks God's pardon for having sinned and foot is cured. *a.b.c.* 355; Tubach 2139.

U100–U299. THE NATURE OF LIFE: MISCELLANEOUS MOTIFS

U110. Appearances deceive.

*U111.1.1. *Statue (mask) is beautiful to wolf* but is recognized as lifeless. *Esopete* p. 53.

U114. *Mountain in labor brings forth a mouse (mole).* LBA cc. 98–102; *Esopete* p. 50.

U119.3. *Handsome appearance does not indicate beautiful soul.* Angel holds nose when handsome youth passes by just as he had done when burying a rotting corpse. *a.b.c.* 351; *Espéculo* 351.250–51; Tubach 2559.

U119.4. *An ugly face does not mean an ugly soul.* Rustic refuses to believe ugly man could be the holy man he sought. *a.b.c.* 320; Tubach 5016.

*U119.6. *Bishop with red face* wrongly judged to be drunkard. *a.b.c.* 157.

*U119.7. *Chests adorned with gold and precious stones contain putrefying remains*; chests containing royal treasures covered with pitch. *Barlaam* pp. 56–58; Tubach 967.

U120. Nature will show itself.

*U120.1 *Flea bites man* because it is his nature. *Esopete* p. 113.

*U120.1.1. *Crow, evil by nature,* rides on sheep's back and annoys her. *Esopete* p. 79.

U121. Like parent, like child.

U121.1. *Crab walks sideways.* Mother walks sideways. *Esopete* pp. 119–20; Tubach 1311.

U121.3. *Farmer's son and noble's reared in country.* Son of farmer takes to rustic life; noble's son takes to chivalric pursuits. *Talavera* 1.18.108.

U121.4. *Like father like son.* Alleged son of king proved to be bastard when he displayed habits of his true father. It is his nature to eat raw meat. *a.b.c.* 175; Tubach 500.

*U121.5.1. *Prince whose father was really the court baker* advised to remember both his royal and his humble heritage. *a.b.c.* 189; cf. Tubach 500.

U121.6.1. *Horse behaves like an ass.* Was nurtured with ass's milk. *a.b.c.* 313; Tubach 2611.

*U121.6.2. *Sultan gives bread as a reward* thereby acting like a baker, is not sultan's son, but rather the son of a baker. *a.b.c.* 313; Tubach 500.

*U121.7. *Countess determined that offspring should only be fed on her milk.* They will imbibe her nature with her mother's milk. Causes son who accidentally had been fed by wetnurse to vomit. *Ultramar* I.1.151.300; Tubach 3283.

U122.0.1. *Butterfly visits flowering trees* and returns to dunghill where wife is. Prefers dunghill to all other spots. *Gatos* 30; cf. Tubach 3645.

U122.1. *Beetles treated like oxen are tied to plow* but do not accompany man and oxen to vespers to worship (stop at cowpatch). *Gatos* 33; Tubach 1309.

*U122.2. *Young goat raised in human household.* Owner tries to keep it as a companion animal. She runs off to join other wild goats grazing in fields. His servants bring her back to house and kill other wild goats. *Barlaam* pp. 156–57.

U127. *Fawn (stag) in spite of his strong horns runs from dog. Esopete* p. 63.

*U129.4. *Virgin Mary helps people regain beehives stolen from church.* Thieves abandon them when pursued by justice. *Cantigas* 326.

*U129.5. *Evil and debauchery recognized by physical attributes*: left eye small and squinty, nose inclined to right, wide-set eyebrows, body hair sprouts in threes, watches ground while walking, shifty eyed. *Calila* p. 193.

*U129.6. *Four youths sent out for daily food.* Each one obtains it according to his nature: worker's son cuts wood; noble's son meets woman who supplies food; merchant's son becomes broker; king's son is chosen to reign. *Calila* pp. 323–34; *Exemplario* 83v–86r.

U130. The power of habit.

*U130.2. *Man given to sin of lust* asked by saint to be chaste for three days, then three days more, and three more. Finally man is accustomed to chaste living. *Espéculo* 103.68–69; Tubach 3906.

*U130.3 *Ascetic so accustomed to fasting* and penance found them to be pleasurable. *Espéculo* 105.69–70.

*U130.3.1. *Alexander the Great unable to refrain* from accustomed sins. *Espéculo* 106.70; Tubach 101.

*U130.4. *Heron asks eagle to carry him over the sea.* Eagle refuses because herons have habit of fouling the land wherever they go. *Espéculo* 107.70; Tubach 1828.

U131. Familiarity takes away fear.

*U133.2. *Man used to foul odor of stables* passed a spice shop and fainted because he was unaccustomed to sweet smell. Cured by applications of manure to nostrils. *a.b.c.* 323; *Espéculo* 556.452; Tubach 3645.

U134. *Knight doesn't want to go to heaven* unless there are birds and hunting dogs there. *Gatos* 32.

U135. Longing for accustomed food and living.

*U135.3. *Rustic becomes king and sickens on fancy foods.* Cured by return to accustomed diet. *a.b.c.* 384; cf. Tubach 3652.

U140. One person's food is another's poison.

U144. *Nightingale cannot endure hoopoe's nest* because of manure in nest. Prefers singing and going from tree to tree all night. *Gatos* 42; Tubach 3475.

*U147.1. *At lion's dinner party,* flesh of other animals served. Pig chooses not to attend; prefers eating acorns. *Gatos* 32; Tubach 3774.

*U147.2. *Bees serve honey for dinner to beetles* who eat very little. Beetles invite bees and serve them animal dung. Bees do not eat. *Gatos* 34; Tubach 554.

*U147.3. *At lion's dinner party, a cat is honored guest* so that rats and moles are the fare. Other animals complain and leave. *Gatos* 37; Tubach 3059.

U160. Misfortune with oneself to blame hardest to bear.

U161. *Eagle killed with arrow made with its own feather.* LBA cc. 270–75.

*U161.1. *Last series of rams to die* at butcher's hand rebuke selves for failure to escape when there was time. *Esopete* p. 76.

*U162. *Tree cut down with axe for which it* has furnished a handle. *Esopete* p. 65; Tubach 444.

U180. In vino veritas.

*U182. *Thief in jail will not confess crime.* Given wine and made drunk, he tells truth. *Espéculo* 203.141; Tubach 4789.

*U183. *Man accuses wife of drunkenness.* She accused him publicly of murder. Proven guilty, he was hanged. *Espéculo* 204.141–42; Tubach 5272.

U230. The nature of sin.

U230.0.1. *Monk leaves monastery when he sees devil there tempting brethren.* Returns when in the world he sees scores of devils tempting people. *a.b.c.* 412; Tubach 3324; cf. Tubach 3336.

U231.1. *Monk rebuked other monks for succumbing to temptation.* Later he too succumbs and finally understands power of sin. *a.b.c.* 410.

*U231.2. *Monk is proud he has turned away from sin.* Wise elder tells him to expose himself to sin and to grow strong in resisting it. *a.b.c.* 410.

*U233. *Odor of sin is fouler than that of a rotting corpse.* Handsome sinful youth smells worse than corpse. *a.b.c.* 352; *Espéculo* 351.250–51; Tubach 2559.

*U233.1. *Virgin Mary serves splendid meal that gives off foul odor to sinner who prays to her daily.* Sins make his devoted prayers malodorous. *Espéculo* 352.251.

U235. *Lying is incurable.* Nephew is lustful, gluttonous, and a gambler. Can be corrected, but not for lying. *a.b.c.* 284; Tubach 3102, 4053.

U236.1. *False repentance of a kite.* When sick, kite begs prayers from mother but is reminded that when well had defiled altars and temples. *Esopete* p. 39; Tubach 2933.

U260. Passage of time.

*U261.1. *Time in purgatory more than a thousand times longer than time on earth.* Dead monk explains dying movements of body as torment in purgatory. *Espéculo* 490.386; Tubach 3378.

*U261.2. *Time in purgatory more than a thousand times longer than time on earth.* Man given choice between two days in purgatory or two years of illness. Chooses two days in purgatory but learns that time is longer there. Returns to body and suffers two years of illness. *Espéculo* 491.386–87; Tubach 4001.

V. RELIGION

V0–V99. RELIGIOUS SERVICES

V20. Confession of sins.

V20.1. *Sinners protected by confession.* Devil cannot reveal identity of wife's lover because lover had already confessed and been absolved. *a.b.c.* 354; cf. Tubach 2800, 2804.

*V20.1.3. *Archdeacon cannot confess.* Holy man offers his soul as surety for him. He prays, is able to confess, renounces his worldly possessions, and enters order. *Espéculo* 126.83–84.

V21. *Confession brings forgiveness.* Hermit tempted by devil in human female form confesses and saves self. *Castigos* 37.177–78.

*V21.0.1. *Confession brings forgiveness.* Conspirators suffer torments, confess, and are forgiven. *Milagros* 17.

*V21.1.1. *Good woman unable to confess because of shameful sin (incest).* Prayers of monks free her to confess. *a.b.c.* 133; cf. Tubach 2738.

*V21.1.2. *Two women sinners confess and are forgiven.* Angel declares their pardon. *Espéculo* 124.82–83.

V21.2. *Mother-in-law commits incest with son-in-law.* Murders him out of fear of disclosure. Confesses and Virgin Mary saves her. *a.b.c.* 272; *Cantigas* 255; Tubach 2737.

V21.4. *Prior pardons sinning friar who has confessed.* Hid bread and ate it secretly. *Espéculo* 121.81–82.

V21.5. *Sinner confesses desire* before sinning carnally and is saved by confession. *a.b.c.* 71; Tubach 1161.

V21.6. *Sinner's tear marks on written confession cause bishop to pardon him.* Sins were unusual so were shown to bishop who found that tears had miraculously erased them. *a.b.c.* 72; Tubach 1202, 4421.

*V21.7. *Count unable to enter church without confessing.* Virgin Mary enables him to confess. *Cantigas* 217; cf. Tubach 1062.

*V21.8. *Sinner's list of confessed sins* weighed in moneychanger's balance outweighs all his gold. *Cantigas* 305; cf. Tubach 1501 d).

*V21.9. *Sinner leaves list of sins on Santiago's altar.* Parchment is blank; sins are absolved. *Santiago* 2.48–49.

V22. Condemnation because of death without confession.

*V22.1. *Courtier refuses confession.* Has been shown vision of slim book of his good deeds and great book of his sins. Demons will carry him off to hell. *Espéculo* 127.84–85; Tubach 1501 c).

*V22.2. *Sinner told he has three days to confess before he dies.* Spends one day indulging in carnal sins. Dies before he has time to confess. *Espéculo* 128.85; Tubach 4076.

*V22.3. *Woman reluctant to confess to priests who know her part in her father's death.* Husband tells her to confess to itinerant friars. She does not and kills her three children and herself. *Espéculo* 129.85–86.

*V22.4. *Nun, too ashamed to confess sexual dalliance with knight, died.* Condemned to hell, she appeared to her sisters in convent to warn them. *a.b.c.* 73; Tubach 1188 a) 4.

V23. Miracle to permit confession.

*V23.3. *Knight who built a chapel for Virgin Mary* restored to life to confess a mortal sin. *Espéculo* 208.144; Tubach 2944 c) 1.

*V23.4. *Man, apparently dead, showed signs of life before interment* so that priest could come and hear confession before he died. *a.b.c.* 198.

V24. Miraculous manifestation at confession.

*V24.2. *Confession of adulterous deacon gives him power.* His prayers relieve water shortage. *Espéculo* 123.82.

*V24.3. *Man given silver spoon by devil confesses.* Silver spoon falls to earth from above into his lap. He gives it to confessor. *Espéculo* 130.86; Tubach 4575.

V29. Confession: miscellaneous motifs.

*V29.10. *Queen confesses her adultery.* Confessor miraculously able to help her convince husband of fidelity. Returns lost ring to her. *Espéculo* 125.83.

V30. Sacrament.

V33.1.1. *Doubt about sacramental transformation of Host is dispelled.* Jesus' body and blood appear on altar. *a.b.c.* 433; Tubach 2689.

V34. Miraculous working of the Host.

*V34.5. *Dying man cannot accept Host;* prayers transform it so that he can swallow wafer; he is received by God. *a.b.c.* 154; *Espéculo* 257.173; Tubach 2649; cf. Tubach 2671.

*V34.6. *Corpse rejected by earth.* Host applied and burial is completed. *Espéculo* 42.29; Tubach 1270.

*V34.7. *Host held high by priest* chases demons from church. *Espéculo* 252.171.

*V34.8. *Priest celebrating mass sees Host* in form of the Infant Jesus waving his arms and legs in air. *Espéculo* 253.171–72; Tubach 2689 c).

*V34.9. *Cleric who dropped the Host three days* confesses and does penance. Fallen Host restored self as did wine in chalice. *Espéculo* 454.352–53; cf. Tubach 2654, 2655.

*V34.10. *Host applied to spider bite.* Devil in form of spider bit over-adorned woman. Abbot brings Host to banish it. *Espéculo* 429.325–26.

V35. The stolen sacrament.

V35.1. *Friend brings Host to Jewish friend who promises to convert.* Jew throws it into pig trough where pigs will not disturb it. He repents and is converted. *Espéculo* 260.174; Tubach 2687.

V35.1.1. *Horse kneels before sacrament that priest is taking to a sick man.* Youth misunderstands and tries to make horse rise. *Espéculo* 255.172.

*V35.3. *Thieves leave box that had contained stolen Host.* Pigs kneel before it. Swineherd shows miracle to town and priest restores it to its place. *Espéculo* 256.172–73.

*V35.4. *Woman steals Host to make lover stay with her; hides it in coif.* Head bleeds. *Cantigas* 104.

V39. Sacrament: miscellaneous motifs.

V39.8 *Dying man refuses to take sacrament.* Goes to hell. *a.b.c.* 153.

*V39.10. *Ailing Jew offered Host, attacks it with knife.* Blood flows from Host, curing him. Repents and is converted. *Espéculo* 259.174.

V40. Mass.

V41.1. *Emperor trapped in cave-in in silver mine kept alive a year* by wife's devotion to Virgin Mary and to masses. *Cantigas* 131; Tubach 3892.

V41.2. *Hearing masses causes triumph in tournament.* Knight devoted to Virgin Mary stops on way to tourney to hear mass, never reaches tourney, but attends miraculously in spirit. Others praise his performance. *Espéculo* 232.155, 258.173; Tubach 4925.

*V41.2.1. *Hearing masses causes knight to miss battle.* Virgin Mary (angel) serves miraculously in his stead. *Cantigas* 63; *Castigos* MS A BNM 6559 4.94 (ADMYTE 0 12*v*–13*r*); cf. Tubach 4925.

*V41.2.2. *Stopping to hear mass* causes falsely accused courtier to avoid being burned to death in oven. His accuser burned instead. *Cantigas* 78; cf. Tubach 4925.

*V41.3. *Mass said by priest cures pestilence.* Farmer's family and stock saved. *Espéculo* 246.169.

*V41.4. *Wife had masses said for husband in prison.* Was freed. *Espéculo* 247.169; Tubach 3893.

*V41.4.1. *Prisoner chained cruelly* miraculously released from chains at tierce when mass was said for him. *Espéculo* 249.170; Tubach 926.

*V41.5. *Sailor drowning at sea* saved by mass at moment it was said for him. Magically supplied with bread (wafer). *Espéculo* 251.170–71; Tubach 4148.

*V42.1. *Masses free soul trapped* in block of ice. *a.b.c.* 28; Tubach 2717.

V49. Mass: miscellaneous motifs.

V49.2. *King goes hunting and does not attend mass at appointed hour.* Angel holds mass. King returns and tells priest to celebrate mass. Priest refuses. *a.b.c.* 368 (not in Paris MS); Tubach 3228.

V50. Prayer.

*V51.6. *Nun prays too rapidly.* Virgin Mary teaches her to pray more slowly and more devoutly. *Espéculo* 424.321; Tubach 438.

V52. Miraculous power of prayer.

V52.1. *Prayers save lecher.* He carries Gospel with him and prays to be saved from lechery. Whores reject him because they see his potential salvation. *a.b.c.* 80.

*V52.1.1. *Prayers of holy man do not save monk from temptation.* Monk must also pray. *a.b.c.* 326.

V52.3. *Prayers win battle.* Military leader prays when battle goes badly. Soldiers rally and he prevails. *a.b.c.* 32; Tubach 3875.

*V52.3.1. *Christ's name uttered in battle brings victory.* Enemy defeated by Christians. *Espéculo* 411.306–7.

*V52.3.2. *Prayers to Virgin Mary ensure raiders' success in Moorish territory.* Victorious, they present her with precious cloth. *Cantigas* 374.

*V52.6.1. *Priest swept overboard prays to Santiago* and is tossed back on ship miraculously. Saint appears amid waves. *Santiago* 8.66–68.

V52.10. *Prayers free husband from prison.* Coincident with moments of prayer, he experienced sensations of freedom even while in jail. *a.b.c.* 318; Tubach 3893.

*V52.16. *Prayer cures gluttony.* Monk prays and resists devil who tempts him. *a.b.c.* 111; Tubach 2304.

*V52.17. *Nun teaches young girl to pray to Virgin Mary using knuckles as guide.* Girl dies, and Virgin shows her to grieving nun. Her fingers glow like precious gems. *Espéculo* 377.276–77; Tubach 3915.

*V52.18. *Prayer and work help man free cart from mud.* He had despaired, but then God helped when he made effort. *Espéculo* 408.304; Tubach 3646.

*V52.19. *Even prayers not understood are efficacious.* Simple friar's prayers will protect him from demons even though the words confound him. *Espéculo* 419.318–19.

*V52.19.1. *Prayers best weapon against demons.* *Espéculo* 420.319.

*V52.20. *Prayers to Virgin Mary expedite* reward to illuminator of manuscripts. Royal letter of authorization delayed until Virgin intervenes. *Cantigas* 377.

*V52.21. *Woman prays that Virgin Mary show her her son.* He appears and answers her *Benedictus fructus ventris tuy* with "Well, I am he." *a.b.c.* 280.

*V52.22. *Sinner troubled, enters church,* prays, and leaves protected by an angel. *a.b.c.* 320.

*V52.23. *Priest's prayers relieve suffering* of spirit condemned to serve as bathhouse keeper for eternity. *a.b.c.* 372; Tubach 504.

★V52.24. *Prayers to Virgin Mary cause king to grant land.* Supplicant promises offering to Virgin. *Cantigas* 382.

V57. Purpose of prayer.

★V57.4. *Holy man's prayer brings needed rain.* Friars had prayed for rain but not wholeheartedly. *Espéculo* 423.320; *a.b.c.* 331; cf. Tubach 3885.

★V57.5. *Prayers for child answered.* Childless couple have baby. *Sendebar* p. 67; *Cantigas* 43; *San Alejo* p. 68; Tubach 971.

★V57.6. *Bishop's prayers bring swarm of insects to defeat enemy. a.b.c.* 332; Tubach 2754.

★V57.7. *Prayers miraculously demolish a mountain.* Captives, ordered to move mountain, recall Jesus's words about mustard seed and mountain. *a.b.c.* 170; Tubach 3424.

★V57.8. *Saint's prayers free the emperor Trajan from hell. Espéculo* 160.109, 423ª.321; Tubach 2368.

★V57.9. *Prayers to Virgin Mary cause king to grant land.* Supplicant promises offering to Virgin. *Cantigas* 382.

V60. Funeral rites.

V64.1. *Money placed in coffin* of body cast overboard to ensure burial. *Apolonio* c. 282.

V80. Religious services: miscellaneous.

V82. *Circumcision* to erase original sin and as a mark of difference from others. *Estados* 43.

V85. Religious pilgrimages.

★V85.1. *Man makes pilgrimage to Holy Land* and follows *via crucis.* Prayed to be able to follow Jesus to heaven. Prayer granted. *a.b.c.* 434; Tubach 3797.

★V85.2. *Old woman falls ill on way to Holy Land and dies.* Celestial light descends, and she ascends to heaven. *Espéculo* 143.98–99.

★V85.3. *Sick man, fearful of purgatory, told to make pilgrimage.* Dies and goes directly to heaven. *Espéculo* 144.99.

★V85.4. *Returned pilgrim* tells others not to make pilgrimage. Punished, falls and bites own tongue off. *Espéculo* 146.99–100.

★V85.5. *Empress goes to Jerusalem seeking true cross.* Finds three; tests them; only one cures dying woman. *Abreviada* 1.346.

V86. Sign of the cross.

★V86.1.4. *Sign of cross.* Saint makes spring water safe from serpent with sign of cross. *Espéculo* 136.95–96; Tubach 1347.

★V86.1.5. *Sign of cross.* Saint makes sign of cross and wine glass containing poison breaks and spills contents. *Espéculo* 138.96.

★V86.1.6. *Sign of cross.* Saint makes sign of cross and creates an area free of rain in a storm. *Espéculo* 140.97.

★V86.1.7. *Sign of cross.* Apostate emperor protects self with sign of cross. *Espéculo* 145.99.

★V86.1.8. *Sign of cross* vanquishes evil magic skull. Enchanted skull unable to speak in presence of sign of cross. *Espéculo* 147.100.

★V86.1.9. *Sign of cross.* Magician protects self from devils with sign of cross. *Espéculo* 148.100–1.

*V86.1.10. *Sign of cross.* Youth makes sign of cross to escape assemblage of devils. *Espéculo* 149.101–2.

V86.2. *Martyr with sign of cross and inscription on heart*: "Jesus is my beloved." *Especulo* 29.21.

V100–V199. RELIGIOUS EDIFICES AND OBJECTS

*V101. *Nails that pierced Jesus's hands and feet* given to emperor. Uses them for bit for horse and for helmet. *Abreviada* 1.346.

V110. Religious buildings.
V111. Churches.
V111.2. *Stones for building church miraculously found. Cantigas* 358; Tubach 4638.

*V111.2.1. *Wood for building church* miraculously supplied by Virgin Mary. *Cantigas* 356.

*V111.4. *Church protected by Virgin Mary.* Attack by Moorish soldiers repelled. They are blinded and maimed. *Cantigas* 229.

*V111.5. *Virgin Mary tells pope to build her church* where it snows in August. *Cantigas* 309.

V116. Altars.
*V116.1. *Virgin Mary insists that lamps on altars burn only pure olive oil.* All other oils will not burn. *Cantigas* 304.

V120. Images.
*V121.1. *Impious image carved in marble turns black* near image of Virgin Mary and Son. Prayers restore marble. *Cantigas* 219.

V122.1. *Image of Jesus descends from cross and wounds nun in cheek with nail* when she tries to leave convent to join lover. *Castigos* 19.117–18.

*V122.2. *Image of Virgin Mary prevents father from killing son's slayer.* *Cantigas* 207.

V123. *Image blamed by supplicant for misfortune.* Did not keep safe owner's belongings. *a.b.c.* 436; Tubach 2721.

V125.1. *Woman takes infant from statue of Virgin Mary* because her own son is being hanged. *Cantigas* 76.

V125.2. *Realistic image of Virgin Mary convinces heretic* that a virgin bore a child. *Cantigas* 306.

V126. Image of saint speaks and acts.
*V126.1. *Image of Jesus nods its head* in approval to holy man. *a.b.c.* 94; Tubach 1375.

*V126.2. *Image of Jesus speaks to monk* who is leaving monastery. Will embrace him and save him from the devil. Monk returns to monastery. *Gatos* 43.

*V126.3. *Monk, leaving monastery, salutes image of Virgin Mary.* Devils take his soul after he drowns in river. She saves him. *Espéculo* 369.271–72.

*V126.4. *Image of Virgin Mary and her Son to be washed in clear water.* Child, sick with scrofula, will be cured by drinking this water for five days. *Cantigas* 321.

*V126.5. *Image of Virgin Mary placed in battlements turns away attackers.* *Cantigas* 187, 394.

*V126.6. *King places image of Virgin Mary in church.* Cures many illnesses. *Cantigas* 349.

V127. Image of deity in stone.

V127.1. *Marble stone riven for church construction.* Image of Virgin Mary and child appear in riven stone. *Cantigas* 342.

V128. Motions of various kinds attributed to images.

V128.1.1. *Child offers food to image of Infant Jesus.* Image responds: "Tomorrow you will eat with me in heaven." *Cantigas* 139.

*V128.3. *Woman loses at dice and angrily throws stone at image of Virgin Mary and child.* Image raises arm to protect child. Statue resists restoration by painter. *Cantigas* 136; Tubach 5152.

*V128.3.1. *Woman loses at dice and angrily throws stone at image of Virgin Mary.* Figures of angels intercept stone and save image. *Cantigas* 294.

*V128.4. *Man throws stone at statue of Virgin Mary and Jesus.* She reaches out to keep infant's arm from falling. Blood flows from wounded statue. *Cantigas* 38.

*V128.5. *Sinner's sins to be pardoned* when image of Virgin Mary moves from one side of church to the other. Image moves in response to woman's prayers. *Cantigas* 272.

*V128.6. *Image of Virgin Mary causes cloth in front of her to rise and descend.* *Cantigas* 405.

*V129. *Image of Virgin Mary wears sash characteristic of pregnant woman.* Sash moves miraculously to convince heretic that a virgin could give birth. *Cantigas* 306.

*V129.1. *Bishop moves image of Virgin Mary.* Image repeatedly moves back to original place. *Cantigas* 162.

*V129.2. *Roar of Virgin Mary's image causes earth tremors* to protect monk from prosecution for minting money illegally. *Cantigas* 164.

*V129.3. *Virgin Mary's image kisses hands of king dedicated to her.* Acknowledges his gifts and songs to her. *Cantigas* 295.

*V129.4. *Man, mute for two years, speaks* in presence of splendid image of Virgin Mary. *Cantigas* 324.

V130. Other sacred objects connected with worship.

V132. Holy water.

V132.2.1. *Archbishop sprinkles holy water* and removes mark placed on man's face by the devil. *a.b.c.* 196.

*V132.2.2. *Holy water unable to disperse demons who menace city.* Among citizens of besieged city is a fornicating priest. *Espéculo* 114.74.

V140. Sacred relics.

*V140.5. *Relics of Virgin Mary preserved* miraculously while others were damaged. *Cantigas* 257.

V142. *Devout possessor of false relic* (St. Augustine's finger) miraculously receives authentic one through divine intervention. *a.b.c.* 103; Tubach 2029.

V200–V299. SACRED PERSONS

*V205.2. *Emperor insists on his own divinity.* a.b.c. 360.

V210. Religious founders.

*V211.1.8.4. *Infant Jesus causes date palms to bend and give shade to
his family* in desert. *Castigos* MS A BNM 6559 31.145–46
(ADMYTE 0 92v).

*V211.1.8.5. *Infant Jesus tames dragons (serpents).* Sends them on their
way. *Castigos* MS A BNM 6559 31.145 (ADMYTE 0 91v).

V211.2.1.1. *Christ disguised as leper.* Saint gives him his robes and takes
him to monastery. Rewarded. *Espéculo* 301.209; cf. Tubach 985.

*V211.2.4. *Jesus Christ appears to bishop* to reproach him for praying for
the destruction of sinners. *a.b.c.* 110.

*V211.5.2. *Christ appears in dream to woman* who could not confess.
Tells her to touch his heart through open wound. Now she must
show him hers. She awakens with bloody hand that is cleaned after
confession. *Espéculo* 131.87.

*V211.5.3. *Christ appears to saint attacked by demons.* Saint cured. *Espéculo* 357.258–59.

*V211.5.4. *Christ appears to saint* who erred in rejoicing over sins of an
enemy. *Espéculo* 359.259–60.

*V211.5.5. *Christ appears walking on water* to save ship in stormy seas.
Calms seas and winds. *Castigos* 7.64.

V220. Saints.

V221. Miraculous healing by saints.

V221.2. *Saint restores dumb man's speech.* Esopete p. 3.

V221.6. *Santiago rewards pilgrimage of father.* Sustains falsely accused
son on gallows until innocence is proved. *a.b.c.* 38; *Santiago* 5.56–61;
Tubach 3796.

*V221.13. *Saint frees man's hand magically attached to sickle.* Exacts
promise that man will never again work on saint's day. *a.b.c.* 164;
Cantigas 289, 396.

*V221.14. *Saint's remains cure illness of pilgrims.* Mute regains speech;
blind recover sight; and lepers cured. *San Alejo* p. 81.

V222. Miraculous manifestation acclaims saint.

*V222.1.5. *Unjustly vilified saint denied burial.* Asks that body be placed
outside locked church doors. Magic wind blows doors open so that
he can be buried. *a.b.c.* 33; Tubach 2370.

*V222.6.2. *Bell sounds to call saint for canonical hours.* To escape vainglory, prays to God that only he be able to hear it. *Espéculo* 293.202.

V222.8. *Holy man's cell set afire.* It burns, and he does not. Persecutors
throw him into a baker's oven. Next day he was alive and well
though his clothes had burned. *a.b.c.* 389.

V222.15. *Saint changes maggots in the sores of a nun into precious stones.*
a.b.c. 342; Tubach 2266.

*V222.17. *Christ appears to Saint Francis* and puts the marks of his crucifixion on his body (stigmata). *Espéculo* 443.337.

V223. Saints have miraculous knowledge or powers.

*V223.7. *Saint anticipates arrival of robbers to his garden.* Leaves spades for them and prepares food. They spade his garden instead of robbing him. *a.b.c.* 291.

*V223.8. *Santiago saves ship of Christian pilgrims* from Moorish attack. *Santiago* 7.64–66.

V229. Saints: miscellaneous.

*V229.7.2. *Knight promises a pilgrimage if Santiago helps to defeat Moors.* Promise not kept until he is reminded. *Santiago* 6.69–72.

*V229.7.3. *Knight fleeing battle calls on Santiago for protection* from pursuers. Promises to make pilgrimage. *Santiago* 15.79–81.

V230. Angels.

V230.3. *Angel and mortal (Jacob) struggle. Castigos* MS A BNM 6559 87.223.

V231.5. *Angel appears to woman* to warn her not to force young woman into marriage. *Castigos* MS A BNM 6559 18.132.

V232. Angel as helper.

V232.1.1. *Angel appears and helps young prince* to slay treacherous uncle. *Çifar* pp. 79–80.

*V232.1.2. *Angel as helper.* Teaches through parable that work is prayer. *a.b.c.* 7.

*V232.1.3. *Angels and devils ready to fight for good abbot's soul.* Angels prevail. *a.b.c.* 30; Tubach 1492.

*V232.1.4. *Prophet arranges for army of angels to save king from enemy. a.b.c.* 58.

*V232.3.2. *Angel reveals truth about divine justice to holy man.* Angel had stolen a good man's platter; killed the good man's son; given platter to an evil man. Good man had stolen platter; son had intended to kill father next day; evil man to be damned for possession of stolen property. *a.b.c.* 230; Tubach 2558.

*V232.3.3. *Angel explains why sinful rich man is buried with honors,* and pious monk is devoured ignobly by lion. Evil will suffer in afterlife, good will not. *a.b.c.* 105; *Espéculo* 511.404; Tubach 223.

V232.8. *Angel helps saint escape from prison. Castigos* 37.174.

*V232.11. *Angel assures husband that devil had lied about his wife's fidelity.* Explains she had sent ring to him as token. *San Alejo* p. 107.

*V232.12. *King gives angels disguised as goldsmiths* jewels and gold to create a cross for the altar of his church. *PCG* 2.616.349.

V235. Mortal visited by angel.

V235.3. *Angel bars abbot from his cell* because he has cast out a monk who had sinned. *a.b.c.* 226.

*V235.3.1. *Abbot visited by devil disguised as angel* in vision. Told to change rules in monastery. *a.b.c.* 4; Tubach 19.

*V235.3.2. *Monk sees dark angels over heads of those who were to die. a.b.c.* 203; Tubach 1468.

*V235.4. *Saint shelters freezing, starving beggar.* Beggar is angel sent by Christ. *Espéculo* 303.210; cf. Tubach 3653.

V246. Angel counsels mortal.

*V246.0.3. *Angel appears in vision to king.* He must interrupt journey, sail to Ephesus, and tell his story at Diana's temple. *Apolonio* cc. 577–83.

V249. Angels: miscellaneous motifs.

*V249.3. *Host of angels summoned by Virgin Mary* appear to defend town under attack by Moorish army. *Cantigas* 165, 395.

V250. Virgin Mary.

V251. *Virgin Mary delays death* so as to save sinner's soul. *a.b.c.* 98.

V251.1. *Virgin Mary brings man back from dead after he has seen hell's torments.* He has thirty days to save his soul with prayers. *Milagros* 10; *a.b.c.* 201.

*V251.1.1. *Sacristan had always honored Virgin Mary.* He drowns without time for prayer and repentance. She resuscitates him so that he can die shriven. *Milagros* 2.

*V251.1.2. *St. Peter and Virgin Mary intercede for foolish sinner.* Resuscitate him to save his soul. *Milagros* 7.

*V251.1.3. *Virgin Mary intercedes for sinner.* His soul is permitted to return to body to mend his ways. *Cantigas* 14.

*V251.3. *Virgin Mary helps excommunicated man* to restore self. *Cantigas* 65.

V252.2. *Virgin Mary saves woman responsible for murder of son-in-law* from fire at stake. *a.b.c.* 272.

*V252.2.1. *Virgin Mary saves calumniated wife from fire at stake. Cantigas* 185.

*V252.3. *Virgin Mary saves unjust banker who had sworn falsely* about money in his keeping. *Cantigas* 239.

*V252.3.1. *Virgin Mary saves empress* falsely accused of infidelity. *Cantigas* 5.

*V252.4. *Virgin Mary saves woman devoted to her from three suicide attempts.* She dies and goes to heaven with angels. *Cantigas* 201; Tubach 4672.

*V252.5. *Virgin Mary grants freedom from lustful behavior* to devoted man. He lives chastely freed from his desires. *Cantigas* 336; Tubach 3098.

*V252.6. *Virgin Mary substitutes for woman whose husband has pledged her to the devil.* Devil flees. *Cantigas* 216; *Castigos* MS A BNM 6559 83.216; Tubach 5115.

*V252.7. *Moroccans sally forth against Abu Yusuf with insignia of Virgin Mary* to protect them; they defeat the invader. *Cantigas* 181.

V254. Efficacy of saying "Aves."

V254.1.1. *Virgin Mary supports robber on gallows.* He said "Ave Maria" often. Keeps him alive three days; persuades executioners to cut him down. *a.b.c.* 48, 270; *Cantigas* 13; *Milagros* 6; Tubach 2235.

*V254.1.2. *Nobleman says "Ave" while being dragged behind horse* on way to decapitation. Devotion to Virgin Mary saves him. *a.b.c.* 278.

*V254.1.3. *Virgin Mary saves robber* from hangman's rope and from the knife. He had prayed to her daily. Unable to kill him, they free him.

a.b.c. 270; cf. Tubach 2235.

V254.1.4. Virgin Mary cures leper who had said a thousand "Aves." *Cantigas* 93.

V254.2.1. Virgin Mary saves greedy, evil man from devils who are carrying his soul to hell. He had always said "Ave Maria." *Milagros* 11.

V254.3.1. *Blasphemer paralyzed in all members save tongue.* Power retained to say "Ave." *a.b.c.* 47; Tubach 4904.

V254.3.2. Gambler blasphemes upon losing at dice. Loses power of speech; regains it after praying to Virgin Mary. *Cantigas* 163; cf. Tubach 4904.

V254.7.1. *Criminal who said "Ave" beheaded.* Severed head calls repeatedly "Ave Maria" (or Jesus Christ). *a.b.c.* 46; *Espéculo* 30.21; Tubach 2482.

V254.7.2. Thief, devoted to Virgin Mary, beheaded. Denied confessor, severed head speaks until confessor comes, and he confesses. *Espéculo* 367.270.

V254.7.3. "Ave" appears on leaves of tree planted over grave of person who said the prayer every day. *a.b.c.* 43; cf. Tubach 430.

V254.7.4. Virgin Mary saves life of little boy carried off to sea in the surf. Child, taught by mother to say "Ave," said it as he was carried away. *a.b.c.* 282.

V254.7.5. Virgin Mary teaches nun to say "Ave Maria" to abbreviate prayers. *Cantigas* 71; Tubach 438.

V254.8. *Devil lives in household of robber baron devoted to Virgin Mary.* Awaits day he will not say "Ave" so that he can carry him off. Devil fails. *a.b.c.* 45, 266; *Espéculo* 368.270–71; Tubach 1558.

V254.8.2. Virgin Mary diverts stream from greedy knight's land to monastery land. *Cantigas* 48.

V255. *Virgin Mary has dissolute monk buried in consecrated ground. Milagros* 3.

V255.1. *Virgin Mary causes flower to grow from mouth* of dead devotee so that his grave is discovered. *Milagros* 3; *Cantigas* 24; Tubach 2094.

V255.2. *Virgin Mary gives private mass* to devout woman unable to attend mass in church. *a.b.c.* 265; Tubach 3218.

V255.3. Virgin Mary intercedes for man who has died and gone to hell. Resuscitated, he returns to earth to repent and to do penance. *a.b.c.* 201.

V255.4. Virgin Mary shows greedy cleric the value of humility. She blesses poor old woman who is dying while cleric attends a rich man who is besieged by devils. *Cantigas* 75.

V255.4.1. Monk insists on rich foods and wine in monastery. Virgin Mary offers taste of sacred lectuary to other monks. *Cantigas* 88.

V255.5. Rosebush with five roses grows from mouth of dead nun, reward for five psalms to Virgin Mary. *Cantigas* 56; Tubach 437.

V256. Miraculous healing by Virgin Mary.

V256.1.1. Virgin Mary cures chronic headaches of monk (nun) who always prayed to her. *a.b.c.* 279; Tubach 2488.

*V256.1.2. *Virgin Mary's milk cures dying monk. Cantigas* 54.

*V256.1.2.1. *Virgin Mary's milk cures sinful cleric* given to seizures. Angel intervenes, and image produces milk miraculously. *Cantigas* 404.

*V256.1.3. *Virgin Mary cures shepherd boy.* Boy returns and awakens from dream able to preach even though he was unlettered. *Cantigas* 53.

*V256.1.4. *Virgin Mary cures man who is deaf and mute. Cantigas* 69, 101, 234, 269.

*V256.1.4.1. *Virgin Mary cures blind monk.* In dream is promised he will see after mass. *Cantigas* 92; Tubach 692.

*V256.1.4.2. *Virgin Mary cures girl born blind* in response to mother's prayers. *Cantigas* 247.

*V256.1.4.3. *Virgin Mary restores sight to scoffer.* Knight who scorned wife's prayers punished. Is cured because he prayed to Virgin. *Cantigas* 314.

*V256.1.4.4. *Virgin Mary cures young man's blindness.* Sight regained, he vows to eat nothing but vegetables. *Cantigas* 338.

*V256.1.4.5. *Virgin Mary cures blindness of man who had denied God* and praised devil. *Cantigas* 407.

*V256.1.5. *Virgin Mary cures paralyzed woman. Cantigas* 77, 179, 268.

*V256.1.5.1. *Virgin Mary cures woman whose face is distorted.* Mouth so twisted she could not eat. Prays for nine days and is cured. *Cantigas* 357.

*V256.1.5.2. *Virgin Mary cures woman afflicted with snake in her stomach.* After prayers, snake emerges from her mouth. *Cantigas* 368.

*V256.1.5.3. *Virgin Mary cures man paralyzed* (stroke) by blow to head from falling stone during church construction. *Cantigas* 385.

*V256.1.5.4. *Virgin Mary cures girl whose feet were twisted* and turned to the rear. *Cantigas* 391.

*V256.1.6. *Virgin Mary cures paralyzed man* who promised to make pilgrimage. *Cantigas* 166, 218, 263, 333.

*V256.1.7. *Virgin Mary cures wounds of son* of woman devoted to her. *Cantigas* 114.

*V256.1.7.1. *Virgin Mary pulls out arrow from squire's side.* Cures wound. *Cantigas* 408.

*V256.1.8. *Virgin Mary cures young prince of mortal illness* after queen took him on pilgrimage to pray to Virgin. *Cantigas* 221.

*V256.1.9. *Virgin Mary cures woman's blindness* after vigil. She advises blind man that he pray for sight also. *Cantigas* 278.

*V256.1.10. *Virgin Mary cures twisted mouth and arm* of man punished for disrespect. *Cantigas* 293.

*V256.1.11. *Virgin Mary cures child with grain stalk germinating in stomach.* Stalk miraculously emerges from his left side. *Cantigas* 315.

*V256.1.12. *Virgin Mary cures child (woman) with rabies. Cantigas* 319, 372, 393.

*V256.1.13. *Virgin Mary cures child whose parents promise a pilgrimage* and modest offerings. *Cantigas* 389.

*V256.1.14. *The Virgin Mary's relics cure blind goldsmith* so he can re-place chest that had contained them before fire. *Cantigas* 362.

*V256.1.15. *King's mortal illness cured* by Virgin Mary. *Cantigas* 235.

V256.3. *The Virgin Mary restores severed hand* to Saint John Damascene. *a.b.c.* 273; Tubach 2419.

*V256.3.1. *Holy man severs own hand because a woman had kissed it.* Did not celebrate mass. Virgin restored hand so he could celebrate mass. *a.b.c.* 391; Tubach 2419.

V256.4. *Virgin (Santiago) saves life of pilgrim* who, at devil's instigation, had castrated self to atone for sin of fornication. Offending organ not restored. *Milagros* 8; *Cantigas* 26; *Santiago* 17.86–94.

*V256.4.1. *Virgin Mary restores feet* to man who had severed them be-cause of pain. *Cantigas* 37.

*V256.4.2. *Virgin Mary heals man with kidney stones* (gallstones) so that he can continue to pray to her. *Espéculo* 371.272; *Cantigas* 173; Tu-bach 4632.

*V256.4.3. *Virgin Mary cures leprosy of devoted pilgrim.* In combat with dragon, blood had transmitted disease. *Cantigas* 189.

*V256.4.4. *Virgin Mary cures dropsical woman* who prayed to her. *Canti-gas* 308.

*V256.4.5. *Virgin Mary cures woman whose arm swelled* dangerously. *Cantigas* 346.

*V256.4.6. *Virgin Mary cures king's illness.* Swollen limbs are restored to health. *Cantigas* 368.

V256.5. *Virgin Mary defeats devils who want soul of drowning monk* who practiced lechery but always prayed to her. *a.b.c.* 267; *Cantigas* 111; Tubach 5139.

*V256.5.1. *Sacristan, who always had saluted image of Virgin Mary, was tempted by devil.* On his way he drowns, and he is restored to life be-cause of his devotion. *Milagros* 2; cf. Tubach 5139.

*V256.5.1.1. *Virgin Mary saves life of wife drowned in sack and thrown into sea by husband.* She confronts him in church, and they both go on pilgrimage. *Cantigas* 287.

*V256.6. *Carter lost oxteam in river and contracted St. Anton's and St. Martial's disease.* He put diseased bone in church dedicated to Virgin Mary. She tells him to replace bone and cures him. *a.b.c.* 164; Tu-bach 2139.

V256.6.1. *Virgin Mary cures devotees afflicted with erysipelas.* *Cantigas* 81, 91.

*V257. *Woman prays to Virgin Mary for baby.* Baby is born but is death-ly ill. Virgin cures him. *Cantigas* 21.

*V257.1. *Assassins pray to Virgin Mary.* They are punished with dreadful skin diseases. She cures them. *Cantigas* 19.

*V257.2. *Man with bone stuck in throat prays to Virgin Mary.* As he prays he coughs and expels bone. *Cantigas* 322.

*V257.3. *Virgin Mary cures bandits* who had robbed women who had stopped to eat at a spring. They promise not to rob anymore. *Cantigas* 57.

*V258. *Virgin Mary protects thirty workmen building a church when tower collapses* and falls on them. *Cantigas* 364.

*V258.1. *Virgin Mary saves child after he and his horse fall from high bridge.* Father had called out to her for help. *Cantigas* 337.

V261.1. *Virgin Mary enables unlettered priest to regain his office* because of his faith. Miraculously sews bishop's vestment. *a.b.c.* 264; Tubach 3231.

*V261.1.1.1. *Virgin Mary reproaches bishop* who had denied unlettered priest's right to say mass. (He will die in thirty days.) *Milagros* 9; *Cantigas* 32.

V261.2. *Virgin Mary pardons man who repented* for enlisting devil's help in election to bishopric. *a.b.c.* 261.

*V261.2.1. *Virgin Mary selects simple parish priest to be new bishop* despite his lack of learning. *Milagros* 13; *Cantigas* 87.

*V261.3. *Virgin Mary protects widow accused of incestuous relations* with her son. Woman confesses sin and is absolved. *a.b.c.* 274; Tubach 2734.

*V261.3.1. *Virgin Mary saves woman* who had three sons by her brother. *Castigos* MS A BNM 6559 83.216; cf. Tubach 2728, 2729.

*V261.4. *Knight leaves wife in care of Virgin Mary* when he leaves for battle. *Cantigas* 64.

V262. *Virgin Mary supplies mead (wine)* for unprepared hostess of the king. *Cantigas* 23.

*V262.1. *Virgin Mary sends mountain goats to monastery to be milked by monks.* *Cantigas* 52.

V264. Virgin Mary rescues devotees.

V264. *Virgin Mary rescues drunken cleric* who is attacked by devil disguised as a bull. *Milagros* 20; Tubach 1812.

V264.1. *Virgin Mary brings man pact he signed with devil* and frees him from devil's power. *a.b.c.* 261; *Milagros* 24; *Cantigas* 3; *Espéculo* 361.264–65; *Talavera* 1.13.90; *Castigos* MS A BNM 6559 82.215; Tubach 3572.

*V264.1.1. *Virgin Mary rescues greedy man from devils* who are carrying his soul to hell. He had always said "Ave Maria." *Milagros* 11.

*V264.1.2. *Virgin rescues from falling a painter* whose scaffold has been removed by devil. *a.b.c.* 263; Tubach 3573.

*V264.2. *Virgin Mary rescues pilgrim* whose ship sinks at sea. *Cantigas* 33.

*V264.2.1. *Virgin Mary saves woman whose ship sank.* A sack of flour serves her as raft to reach shore. *Cantigas* 371.

*V264.3. *Virgin Mary exchanges places with wife* of man who had promised to deliver her to devil. Defeats devil. *a.b.c.* 268; *Castigos* MS A BNM 6559 82.216; Tubach 5283.

*V264.3.1. *Virgin Mary takes place of nun* who had left convent to be with lover so that her absence went unnoticed. *Cantigas* 94; Tubach 536.

*V264.2. *Devotee of Virgin stops to pray.* Delay foils ambush. *a.b.c.* 8; Tubach 4925.

*V264.5. *Pregnant woman caught in tides calls on Virgin Mary.* She is rescued and comes ashore holding her baby. *Milagros* 19; *Cantigas* 86; Tubach 4864.

*V264.6. *Virgin Mary saves farmer* wounded mortally by enemies of his master. *Cantigas* 22.

*V264.7. *Virgin Mary protects merchant thrown in sea by robbers.* Despite weight tied to body he surfaces and calls for help. *Cantigas* 193.

*V264.8. *Virgin Mary protects minstrel* waylaid by servants of host sent to rob and kill him. *Cantigas* 194.

V265. *Virgin Mary miraculously prevents nun from leaving convent* to join lover. *a.b.c.* 281; *Cantigas* 58, 59, 285; *Castigos* 19.118–20.

*V265.2. *Monk persuaded to leave monastery and marry.* Virgin Mary convinces him to return to monastery. *a.b.c.* 271.

V268. Miracles performed under protection of Virgin Mary.

*V268.1.1. *Virgin Mary resuscitates boy* killed and buried by Jew because the boy sang "Gaude Maria." *Cantigas* 6.

V268.2. *Virgin Mary restores life to drowned man* who always had saluted her. *Cantigas* 11.

V268.3. *Virgin Mary destroys Moorish army* besieging Constantinople. *a.b.c.* 275; *Cantigas* 28, 264; Tubach 349.

*V268.3.1. *Virgin Mary sends saintly warrior in battle* to kill enemy of Christians. *Cantigas* 15.

*V268.3.3. *Moorish commander spares church because Virgin Mary protects it.* *Cantigas* 169.

*V268.3.4. *Virgin Mary convinces Moorish leader to cede city to Christian rule.* Alcanate becomes Puerto de Sta. María. *Cantigas* 328.

V268.4. *Virgin Mary saves shipwrecked sailor.* *Milagros* 22; Tubach 4334.

*V268.4.1. *Virgin Mary destroys devoted woman's abductors.* Gives her power to sail ship to safe port and to dispose of corpses of enemy. *Çifar* p. 29.

*V268.4.2. *Sailors call upon Virgin Mary* during storm at night. She appears on mast and guides them to port. *Cantigas* 36.

*V268.4.3. *Merchant calls upon Virgin Mary* during storm at sea. Ship's broken mast is restored; storm abates. *Cantigas* 172; Tubach 4649.

*V268.4.3.1. *Cleric calls upon Virgin Mary* during storm. Dove appears, ship is illuminated, and seas become calm. *Cantigas* 313.

*V268.4.4. *Virgin Mary appears to guide lost pilgrims* through mountains. *Cantigas* 49.

*V268.4.5. *Virgin Mary saves storm-tossed ship laden with grain.* Sailors had prayed to her. *Cantigas* 112; Tubach 4649.

*V268.4.5.1. *Virgin Mary calms sea and saves merchant's ship* in storm. Within ten days it arrives safely in port. *Cantigas* 267.

*V268.4.5.2. *Virgin Mary saves sinking ship.* Sailors bail out water, and three fish plug hole in ship bottom. *Cantigas* 339.

*V268.4.6. *Virgin Mary saves mother and baby from shipwreck.* She walks on ocean waves to safety. *Cantigas* 236.

V268.5. Image of Virgin Mary works miracles.

*V268.5.1. *Image of Virgin Mary keeps boy safe from fire* after he is thrown in oven by his father. *a.b.c.* 269; *Milagros* 16; *Cantigas* 4; Tubach 2041.

*V268.5.2. *Moorish invaders defeated* when they try to destroy image of Virgin Mary. *Cantigas* 99.

*V268.6. *Cleric prays to Virgin Mary.* Saves friend from fierce bull running through streets. *Cantigas* 144.

*V268.7. *Woman falling from great height* calls upon Virgin Mary. She lands unhurt. *Cantigas* 191.

*V268.8. *Lightning strikes chapel and burns it to ground.* Seated figure of Virgin Mary and Jesus survives fire untouched. *Milagros* 14.

*V268.8.1. *Monastery chapel* burns, statue of Virgin Mary does not. *Cantigas* 39.

*V268.8.2. *Fire destroys church but does not burn relics* of Virgin Mary. *Cantigas* 35; cf. Tubach 1054.

*V268.8.3. *Virgin Mary saves monastery from boulder.* Course of falling boulder is diverted. *Cantigas* 113.

*V268.9. *Virgin Mary gives youths extraordinary strength.* Able to lift marble slabs for construction of church. *Cantigas* 231.

*V268.10. *Virgin Mary opens closed church doors* late at night for worshiper who had forgotten Sabbath. Opens town gates. *Cantigas* 246.

*V268.11. *Virgin Mary intervenes in fight between sailors* who battle before altar. *Cantigas* 248.

*V268.12. *Thieves steal beehives given to church.* Parishioners call upon Virgin Mary. She sends a man who hunts thieves down. *Cantigas* 326.

V276. Virgin Mary appears to erring person.

V276.1. *Virgin Mary, in unfinished garb, appears to erring cleric* and urges him to resume prayers that will complete her garments. *a.b.c.* 276; Tubach 3913.

*V276.1.1. *Virgin Mary appears to monk fleeing monastery.* She holds unfinished garment he had begun for her. He returns to monastery. *Cantigas* 274.

V276.2. *Virgin Mary appears and pardons young monk* who has been too overworked to pray to her. *a.b.c.* 277; Tubach 5129.

*V276.4. *Virgin Mary causes great wind to open shutters closed against vision of miraculously illuminated church.* Sinning cleric leaves mistress and enters monastery. *Cantigas* 151.

*V276.5. *Virgin Mary defends monk falsely accused of theft.* *Cantigas* 151.

V277. Virgin Mary appears to devotee.

V277.1. *Nun prayed that Virgin Mary would show her her son.* She appears with infant who addresses nun. *a.b.c.* 280.

*V277.2. *Young woman yearned for baby Jesus* from early childhood. Rewarded for devotion, she accepts Host and accompanies Virgin Mary to heaven. *Cantigas* 251.

*V277.3. *Virgin Mary appears to knight given to sin.* Brings him beautiful platter filled with putrid matter to convince him to give up foul ways. *Cantigas* 152.

*V277.4. *Virgin Mary appears to unwilling pilgrim to her shrine.* Insincere woman magically transported to altar. *Cantigas* 153.

V278. *Virgin Mary appears to young girl.* Promises her admission to heaven if she gives up games, dancing, and diversion. Girl dies in thirty days and goes to heaven. *a.b.c.* 85; *Espéculo* 133.91–92; *Castigos* MS A BNM 6559 82.216–17; *Glosa* 2.2.21.220–21; *Cantigas* 79; Tubach 1424.

*V279. *Lovelorn knight prays to Virgin Mary.* He pledges self to her and forgets past love. *Cantigas* 16.

V290. Other sacred persons.

V292.3. *St. Peter appears to martyred pope* who had ordered that he not be buried because of his having sinned. *a.b.c.* 193; Tubach 3851.

V300–V399. RELIGIOUS BELIEFS

V310. Particular dogmas.

V312. *Belief in Virgin Birth.* Divine intervention caused Mary to be impregnated and remain virgin. Angel explained to Joseph that Holy Spirit had engendered Jesus. *Estados* 1.40.

*V312.3. *Monk questions transubstantiation.* Host transformed into bleeding flesh. *a.b.c.* 433; Tubach 2689.

V316. Efficacy of prayer.

*V316.2. *Saint offers prayers to priest in pain in exchange for promise to cease fornicating.* *Espéculo* 110.72.

*V316.3. *Enmity between contemplative and active friars.* Both serve God. *a.b.c.* 329, 425; Tubach 5386.

*V316.3.1. *One of two friars leaves monastery to live like the angels in the desert.* Returns, starving and bitten by flies and wasps, begging to return. Permitted to enter only if he will work. *a.b.c.* 428; *Espéculo* 341.242–43.

V320. Heretics.

*V324. *Heretic king (Arian) orders death of Christian courtier who denied his faith* and became Arian to please king. *a.b.c.* 169.

*V324.1. *Arian bishop, in bath,* visited by angel who kills him. *a.b.c.* 169.

*V327.1. *Heretic is convinced of transubstantiation by actual appearance of the Infant Jesus* on the altar, offering him true body and blood. *a.b.c.* 390.

*V329. *Heretic made to excrete his own entrails.* *a.b.c.* 187; Tubach 2534.

V330. Conversion from one religion to another.

V331.1. *Conversion to Christianity* by miracle of seeing blood flow from crucifix. *a.b.c.* 90, 91; *Glosa* 1.1.13.66–67; Tubach 1373.

V331.1.2. *Conversion to Christianity* through appearance of cross and host of angels in dream (Constantine). Castigos MS A BNM 6559 10.107; *PCG* 1.316.183–86; *Abreviada* 1.339; Tubach 1218.

*V331.1.5. *Unpaid debt (money in stick) scattered on road.* False debtor, lying dead in road. Jewish creditor will not take repayment unless dead man is resuscitated. He will accept baptism if miracle is performed. *a.b.c.* 234; Tubach 3352.

*V331.1.6. *Conversion to Christianity.* Robbery victim and thieves swayed by apparition of St. Nicholas. *a.b.c.* 436.

*V331.1.7. *Conversion to Christianity.* King gives half the realm to son who is a Christian. Subjects in son's kingdom are converted. Finally father is converted as well. *Barlaam* pp. 302–7.

*V331.1.8. *Conversion to Christianity.* Virgin Mary frees Jew from captivity in thieves' lair. Shows him visions of hell and heaven. *Cantigas* 85.

*V331.1.9. *Conversion to Christianity.* Virgin Mary appears to Moorish slave assaulted by devil. Will free him if he converts. *Cantigas* 192, 397.

*V331.1.10. *Conversion through miracle.* Heretic conjures up devil to cure a woman's infertility. Devil is vanquished when priest bearing the Host passes by. Heretic is converted. *a.b.c.* 432.

*V331.1.11. *Conversion to Christianity through miracle.* Generous man's food supply miraculously replenished. He converts after mysterious woman and child (Virgin Mary and child) disappear without trace. *Cantigas* 335.

*V331.1.12. *Jew converted* to Christianity when dead hero's hand is raised against him. *PCG* 2.962.643.

*V331.1.13. *Son of Moorish woman resuscitated by Virgin Mary.* Mother converts to Christianity. *Cantigas* 167.

V331.10. *Conversion to Christianity.* Pagan philosopher converted after disputation with young celibate prince. *Barlaam* p. 298; *Estados* 42.

V331.10.1. *Conversion to Christianity* because of goodness of saintly monk. Pagan priest beats rude monk but admires his teacher. *a.b.c.* 218; Tubach 1237.

*V331.10.2. *Conversion to Christianity* through admiration of happy Christian life in anticipation of heaven. Good king sees happiness of poorest of his subjects. *a.b.c.* 350; *Barlaam* pp. 134–39.

*V331.11. *Conversion to Christianity.* Moorish woman with small son in arms appears on battlements of besieged city. Christians, moved by resemblance to Virgin Mary, spare her. In gratitude she converts and has son baptized. *Cantigas* 205.

V332. *Baptism of pagan.* Is told of Christ and is baptized. *Barlaam* p. 298.

V336. Conversion to Judaism.

V336. *Nebuchadnezzar converted to Judaism.* Convinced by Daniel's miraculous survival in lions' den. *Castigos* 9.69–70.

V340. Miracle manifested to nonbelievers.

V345. *Dove flies out of mouth of monk* who wants the daughter of a pagan. Evidence that he has denied his God. *a.b.c.* 106; Tubach 1760.

*V345.1. *God restores sight of monk*, sightless for forty years, so that he can preach to other monks. When he dies, his soul leaves body in form of a dove. *a.b.c.* 27.

*V348. *Miracle holds fast horses of oppressors.* Horses cannot cross a stream. *a.b.c.* 191; Tubach 2636.

V350. Conflicts between religions.

V351. *Debate to prove which religion is better.* Pagan philosopher acknowledges that simple Christian bishop has convinced him. *a.b.c.* 250.

*V351.1.2. *Debate between Christian and Jewish scholars.* Emperor arranged debate to convert mother. *Abreviada* 1.344.

V352. *Bishop wins debate with pagan philosophers miraculously.* He orders them in Jesus' name not to speak. They lose power of speech. *a.b.c.* 431; Tubach 4560.

*V352.2. *Christian knight in pagan court* accused of disloyalty (political and religious) by envious courtiers. *a.b.c.* 215 (not in Paris MS).

*V353. *Christians defeat foe* who had tried to force them to worship sun. *a.b.c.* 416.

V360. Christian traditions concerning Jews.

*V360.1. *Jew vanquishes devil by making sign of the cross.* Saves saint from sin. Is converted. *a.b.c.* 92.

*V360.2. *King punishes steward who had robbed a Jew.* King had promised safe conduct through a wood. *a.b.c.* 167; Tubach 2799.

*V360.3. *Jew tells Christian his faith tells him he has right to take belongings* of non-Jews. Steals Christian's mule and reminds him of previous warning. *a.b.c.* 202; Tubach 2796.

*V360.4. *False debtor, lying dead in road.* Jewish creditor will not take repayment unless dead man is resuscitated. He will accept baptism if miracle is performed. *a.b.c.* 234; Tubach 2793.

*V360.5. *Bad Christians in even lower position in hell than Jews.* They had been redeemed and had not valued their redemption. *a.b.c.* 435.

V363. *Jewish child thrown into oven* by father for taking communion; revived by Virgin Mary. *a.b.c.* 269; *Milagros* 16; *Cantigas* 4; Tubach 2041.

*V363.1. *Virgin Mary takes synagogue and turns it into church.* *Cantigas* 27.

*V364.1. *Jew stabs statue of Jesus.* Blood flows from wound; he throws it in well. *a.b.c.* 90; Tubach 1373.

*V364.2. *Jew beats statue of St. Nicholas* because it had not protected house from thieves. Saint recovers goods; Jew converts. *a.b.c.* 436; Tubach 3471.

*V364.3. *Ailing Jew offered Host, attacks it with knife.* Blood flows from Host, curing him. Repents, and is converted. *Espéculo* 259.174; Tubach 2689 b).

*V364.4. *Jew steals painted image of Virgin Mary.* Jew dies, and Christian rescues image. *Cantigas* 34.

*V364.5. *Jews crucified wax figure of Jesus Christ.* *Cantigas* 12; *Milagro* 18.

V380. Religious beliefs: miscellaneous.

V385. *Roman council will not include Jesus Christ* in pantheon because he preached poverty and had few followers. *a.b.c.* 349; Tubach 1008.

V400–V499. RELIGIOUS VIRTUES

V400. Charity.

*V401. *King grants all wishes of those who come to him.* They must not leave unhappy. *a.b.c.* 364; Tubach 1459.

V410. Charity rewarded.

V410.1.1. *Poor man who shared the little he had* was rewarded by the Virgin Mary when he died. *Milagros* 5.

*V411.2.1. *Rich man gave fox furs to beggar.* After he died, a religious appeared wearing furs that have kept him warm and safe. *Espéculo* 242.162–63.

V411.3. *Man who had been charitable sinned by saving money against future illness.* Has foot amputated. Restored miraculously when he confesses sin. Previous charity rewarded. *a.b.c.* 355; Tubach 2139.

*V411.3.1. *Saint gives silver plate and contents to poor man.* Hand that gave charity is incorruptible forever. *Espéculo* 237.160.

*V411.5. *Wealth given away by saint restored.* Meets a lad who produces gold magically and gives it to him. *Cantigas* 145.

*V411.5.1. *Merchant gives wealth to God because he will be rewarded hundredfold.* Digs and finds gold worth three hundred silver pounds. *Espéculo* 244.164; Tubach 176.

*V411.5.2. *Saint gives all his money to poor.* Others criticize him. Later sack of money mysteriously left for him. *Espéculo* 402.297.

V411.7. *King gives clothes to leper* and lifts him into his saddle. Leper asks king to blow his nose for him. King does so and finds a huge ruby in his hand. Leper disappears magically. *Castigos* 7.61–62; cf. Tubach 3489.

V411.8. *Jesus appears to St. Martin* when he gives cloak to beggar. *Castigos* 7.62; Tubach 3192.

*V411.10. *Saint gave alms to all comers.* One day Christ came seeking alms. Saint's generosity rewarded. *a.b.c.* 136.

*V411.11. *Angel appears to saint as man who has lost everything in shipwreck*; is given alms. Later comes to him as his guardian angel. *a.b.c.* 137.

V412.1. *Bread taken by St. Nicholas for purpose of feeding poor* is miraculously restored. *Castigos* 7.63.

V412.2. *The more bread (flour) monks give to poor,* the more God places in their bins miraculously. *a.b.c.* 146, 147; *Espéculo* 169.114; Tubach 766.

*V412.3. *Charitable woman's bread dough magically replenished* because prayed to Virgin Mary. *Cantigas* 258.

*V412.4. *Muslim converted to Christianity* when he hears that charity will be returned hundredfold in hereafter. His goods to revert to his children if promise not fulfilled. Grave opened and cadaver held letter certifying that he had received his hundredfold reward. *a.b.c.* 283

(not in Paris MS); Tubach 176 a).

V416.1. *Steward accused of cheating his master* is absolved of guilt. He had given the money to the poor. *a.b.c.* 145; cf. Tubach 4963.

*V417.1. *Young man uses inherited wealth to feed starving populace.* Rebuked, he replies that he had not put it where it could be stolen or destroyed, but rather in a safe place that would benefit kingdom. *a.b.c.* 395; Tubach 4963.

*V418. *Pilgrim carries burden of poor woman who joins party; gives mount to poor ailing pilgrim.* Falls ill; Santiago defeats devils who try to capture his soul. *Santiago* 16.81–85.

V420. Reward of the uncharitable.

*V421.1. *Uncharitable rustic denied food to beggar.* Council of demons in possession of his soul and of his food. *Espéculo* 86.57–58.

*V423. *Bears and wolves miraculously appear to devour sheep of cruel and unjust monks who have sent away charitable shepherd.* *a.b.c.* 143; Tubach 4088, 519 (see Tubach p. 417 for 4088).

*V424. *Usurer leaves wealth to friends and family.* Leaves nothing for his soul. Acknowledges the omission to priest, and then dies. *Espéculo* 659.462–63; cf. Tubach 5050.

*V425. *Alms given with harsh words* shame recipient. Monk told to give charity cheerfully. *Espéculo* 395.291–92; Tubach 168.

V433. Charity of saints.

*V433.1. *Learning that an impoverished man was planning to live off the illicit earnings of his daughters,* St. Nicholas tossed a golden apple through the man's window so that his daughters could marry. *Castigos* 7.62–63.

V440. Other religious virtues.

V441. *Forgiveness.* Holy man forgives slayer of brother when asked in the name of the Holy Cross. *a.b.c.* 94; Tubach 3438.

*V441.2. *Pope convinces father of slain son to forgive killer.* Says he had seen father in devil's power. Will not be free until he can pardon killer. *Espéculo* 506.398.

*V441.3. *Killer of father of knight asks for forgiveness* on Good Friday. It is granted. *Espéculo* 507.398–99.

V450–V499. RELIGIOUS ORDERS

*V452. *Woman who had been betrothed and wed fled to convent.* Granted permission to take habit because she had left her earthly spouse. *a.b.c.* 291.

V460. Clerical virtues and vices.

V461. Clerical virtues.

*V461.0.1. *Bishop* takes captive's place. *a.b.c.* 61; Tubach 4484.

V461.1. *Obedient and industrious nun* (thought to be mad by other nuns) is the worthiest in the convent. *a.b.c.* 406; Tubach 3504.

V461.6. *Monk lives where people speak ill of him* to avoid danger of flattery. *a.b.c.* 49.

*V461.6.1. *Abbot behaves improperly* to avoid worldly praise. Deceit for good ends. *a.b.c.* 5; Tubach 13.

V461.7. *Clerical virtue of absolute faith.* Man captured by robbers is so confident that God will protect him that he is saved. *a.b.c.* 288; Tubach 1961.

V461.8. *Poverty a saintly virtue.* Monk's sin not removed until he gives up his "siete libras de moneda." *a.b.c.* 203; Tubach 4009.

*V461.9. *Saint neglects just once to give alms.* Vows to never neglect duty again. *a.b.c.* 134.

*V461.10. *Harmonious living.* Two elders try to create discord but cannot. *a.b.c.* 249.

*V461.11. *Old monk knows value of keeping* one's own counsel and not talking senselessly. *a.b.c.* 335.

*V461.12. *Preacher, distracted by thoughts of ass tied up outside of church,* gives it away so that he can pray. *a.b.c.* 327; Tubach 381.

*V461.13. *Novice told that a monk's life* is like an ass's constant work. *a.b.c.* 374.

V462. Asceticism.

V462.1. *Ascetic flees man who wants to speak to him.* Silence is to be maintained. *a.b.c.* 387; Tubach 4372.

V462.1.1. *Hermit laughs with joy* because he is alone; all sadness comes from human contact. *a.b.c.* 403; cf. Tubach 2869.

*V462.1.1.1. *Monk counseled to stay in cell* where he will learn all good things. *a.b.c.* 176; cf. Tubach 3327.

*V462.1.1.2. *Aged monk advised not to go to city* for medical help because of danger of fornication. Goes and fathers a child. Returns to monastery to tell his brethren to avoid occasion of sin. Returns to cell. *a.b.c.* 176; Tubach 3323.

*V462.2.4. *Saintly ascetic flees house of rich man* who has never suffered deprivation. Earth opens up and swallows rich man's house and family. *a.b.c.* 287; Tubach 3938.

*V462.2.5. *Monk gives up worldly comforts* in monastery by example of peripatetic ascetic monk. *a.b.c.* 258.

V462.12. *Monk prefers to live with temptation* since he considers it strengthening to have it ever present to test him. *a.b.c.* 410; Tubach 4736.

V465. Clerical vices.

V465.1.1.1. *Hermit gets drunk, rapes woman, kills her, is captured, and executed.* LBA cc. 530–41; cf. Tubach 2569.

*V465.1.1.5. *Fire pours from throat of dead priest* who seduced the young woman he had baptized. *a.b.c.* 404; Tubach 2037.

*V465.1.1.6. *Monk (distracted by thoughts of fornication)* neglects duty to pray. *a.b.c.* 326; Tubach 3906.

V465.1.2. *Nun tempted into sinning with man.* Go-between tells her God cannot see what happens in the dark. *a.b.c.* 108; Tubach 1436.

V469. *Conformity to divine will.* Hermit told that water for garden granted by God; inappropriate seeds do not grow. *a.b.c.* 104; Tubach 5233.

V469.1. *Cleric rejoices in the fiery torments of the sinner* who had converted a Christian to Islam and of the convert. Jesus rebukes him. *a.b.c.* 110; Tubach 3881.

V470. Clerical vows.

V475. Renunciation of clerical vows.

★V475.6. *Christian deacon renounces vows* and is killed by Arian king who reproaches him for disloyalty. *a.b.c.* 169.

★V476. *Pope put incense in receptacle for non-Christian idol.* Repented, but later martyred, body left without burial. *a.b.c.* 193; Tubach 3851.

★V477. *Two hermits leave desert and take wives.* Return and are given penance of a year on bread and water. *a.b.c.* 356; Tubach 3336.

★V477.1. *Monk leaves monastery* because devil is there. Goes to city and sees more devils. Returns to monastery. *a.b.c.* 412; Tubach 3329.

★V478. *Canon previously pledged to Virgin Mary* marries because of importunities of family. Leaves his bride on wedding night to continue to serve Virgin. *Milagros* 15; *San Alejo* p. 70; cf. Tubach 5148.

V500–V599. RELIGIOUS MOTIFS: MISCELLANEOUS

V510. Religious visions.

★V510.3. *Virgin Mary grants vision* to devoted woman. After nine days of prayer, she is rewarded and is carried off to heaven. *Cantigas* 262; Tubach 5123.

★V510.4. *Virgin Mary and chorus of angels* appear to pilgrim. Dies and goes straight to heaven. *Cantigas* 288.

★V510.5. *San Fernando appears in dream vision.* Says that ring placed on finger of his statue be placed on finger of statue of the Virgin Mary. *Cantigas* 292; cf. Tubach 4103.

★V510.6. *Virgin Mary appears in dream three times.* Member of religious order must give king the seal of his order. *Cantigas* 299.

★V510.7. *Virgin Mary appears in dream to doubting monk.* Sees a soul being carried to heaven. *Cantigas* 365; cf. Tubach 4235.

★V510.8. *Virgin Mary appears in dream to sacristan.* He must seek out holy man and permit him to enter the church. *San Alejo* p. 73.

★V510.9. *Angel appears to hero* to predict future triumphs. *CMC* vv. 405–9.

★V510.10. *Saint appears to aging hero.* He will defeat enemy after his death. *PCG* 2.952.633–34.

V511. Visions of the other world.

V511.1. *Vision of heaven, locus amoenus,* golden chairs, glorious people; resplendent city peopled by saints. *Barlaam* pp. 275–76.

★V511.1.3. *Canon hears magical bird song.* Experiences joys of paradise. *Espéculo* 292.202; Tubach 3378.

★V511.1.4. *Hermit's soul will leave body accompanied by David* and heavenly musicians. *a.b.c.* 293.

★V511.1.5. *In vision nun sees remarkable temple with glorious people.* Queen of heaven gives her a candle. *Castigos* MS A BNM 6559 4.95 (ADMYTE 0 13v–14r); cf. Tubach 847.

*V511.2. *Dying man's soul seen in hell* by diabolically possessed woman capable of prophecy. He is there because his piety was insincere. *Lucanor* Ex. 40.

*V511.2.1. *Monk, near death, rescued from eternal hellfire by angel.* Soul returns. *a.b.c.* 200.

*V511.2.1.1. *Monk travels to hell to see those in torment.* Sees a monk whose sin was daily drunkenness. *Espéculo* 196.137.

*V511.2.1.2. *Blacksmith in monastery neglects his religious duties.* Sees place in hell reserved for him. *Espéculo* 230.153–54

*V511.2.2.1. *Man sees torments of hell, sees many acquaintances.* Voice tells him to repent. *Espéculo* 332.23.

V511.2.3. *Woman sees vision of mother suffering in hell* for past sins. Chooses the good life of her father who is in heaven as model. *a.b.c.* 426; Tubach 1450.

*V211.2.3.1. *Priest's soul seen in hell's torment.* *Espéculo* 109.72.

*V511.2.4. *Vision of Nero in hell* bidding a band of lawyers to join him in bathing in hell's fire. *a.b.c.* 12; *Espéculo* 88.61.

*V511.2.6. *Nun condemned to eternal damnation*, returns to tell sisters that there is no respite in hell. *a.b.c.* 73; Tubach 1188 a) 4.

*V511.2.6.1. *Devil punishes young woman who loves to dance.* Returns to tell of hell's torments; she must dance there forever. *Espéculo* 134.92; Tubach 1415.

*V511.2.7. *Man returns from torments of hell* determined to do good works. Reproached because he bathed naked in icy waters, retorted: "Leave off, for I have seen worse." *a.b.c.* 201.

*V511.2.8. *Virgin Mary shows torments of hell to sinners* in dream visions. *Cantigas* 58, 85.

*V511.2.9. *Angels take dying saint to heaven*, but voice says he first must see vileness of devils so that he can confess even small sins he may have forgotten. *Espéculo* 191.131.

V515. Allegorical visions.

V515.4. *Constantine sees vision* of cross in sky after baptism. *PCG* 1.316.183–86; *Abreviada* 1.339; *Glosa* 1.1.13.66–67; *Castigos* MS A BN 6559 (ADMYTE 0 34*r*); Tubach 1218.

W. TRAITS OF CHARACTER

W0–W99. FAVORABLE TRAITS OF CHARACTER
W10. Kindness.
W11. Generosity.

W11.2.1. *Emperor thinks day is wasted* when he has not given any gifts. *a.b.c.* 364; *Castigos* MS A BNM 6559 42.166.97 (ADMYTE 0 55*v*); *Glosa* 1.2.18.161; Tubach 1459.

*W11.2.3. *King gives ragged beggar his own clothes, and carries him to shelter on his horse.* Castigos 7.61–62.

*W11.2.4. *King gives major portion of income to poor.* God increases his wealth as reward. Castigos 14.120.

*W11.2.5. *Holy man shares bread with all who come to beg.* Supply miraculously replenished. *a.b.c.* 146, 147; Tubach 766, 2566.

*W11.3.1. *Steward steals from master to give to poor* where it will be safe. *a.b.c.* 145; Tubach 3363.

*W11.3.2. *Prince gives inheritance to poor* where it will be safe. *a.b.c.* 395; Tubach 4963.

*W11.17. *Christian kind to Jew* who steals his mule. *a.b.c.* 202; Tubach 2796.

*W11.18. *Elderly friar sees another friar stealing from his cell.* Decides to work harder to replace stolen possessions because the other friar must need what he stole. *Espéculo* 346.245.

*W11.19. *Monastery's shepherd feeds poor.* Monks sent him away to keep food for selves. *a.b.c.* 143.

*W11.20. *Learning that an impoverished man was planning to live off the illicit earnings of his daughters,* St. Nicholas tossed a golden apple through the man's window so that his daughters could marry. *Castigos* 7.62–63.

W12. Hospitality.

*W12.3. *Saint gives food and water* to all who come to his home. Christ comes disguised as pauper, receives hospitality, and rewards saint. *a.b.c.* 136; cf. Tubach 987.

*W12.3.1. *Saint gives money and his family silver* to shipwrecked traveler who reveals that he is an angel. Rewards saint. *a.b.c.* 137.

W16. *Self-sacrifice: bishop exchanges places with captive* so that captive can return to his mother. *a.b.c.* 61; Tubach 4484.

W19. Kindness: miscellaneous.

*W19.1. *Kind birds shelter aged parents with wings.* *a.b.c.* 15; Tubach 642.

*W19.2. *Poor man saves his bees by giving all he owns* for their cure from poisoning. *a.b.c.* 15; Tubach 551.

W20. Other favorable traits.

W26.1. *Man passes test of patience,* endures insults at gates of city. *a.b.c.* 214; Tubach 3622.

*W26.2. *Philosopher endures loss of possessions* without anger. *a.b.c.* 220.

*W26.3. *Monk leaves monastery to avoid occasions of anger.* Frustrated filling a jug of water, experiences anger. Returns to monastery. *a.b.c.* 221, 344; Tubach 252.

*W26.4. *Holy man accepts destruction of crops,* his only sustenance, saying that evildoer suffers more than he. *a.b.c.* 343.

*W26.5. *Alexander suffers criticism of dissolute ways patiently.* *a.b.c.* 345; *Glosa* 1.2.14.132–33; *Castigos* MS A BNM 6559 31.147 (ADMYTE 0 94v); Tubach 107.

*W26.5.1. *Alexander frees enemy knight* who had bravely tried to kill him. *Castigos* MS A BNM 6559 31.148 (ADMYTE 0 96*v*); *Glosa* 1.2.14.135; Tubach 114.

*W26.6. *King suffers insults patiently*, and asserts superiority to ambassador who has insulted him. *a.b.c.* 345.

*W26.7. *Julius Caesar permits insults about baldness*. *a.b.c.* 346; *Castigos* MS A BNM 6559 31.147.

*W26.7.1. *Caesar permits man to call him tyrant*. *a.b.c.* 346; *Glosa* 1.2.14.133; *Castigos* MS A BNM 6559 31.147 (ADMYTE 0 94*v*); Tubach 5011.

*W26.7.2. *Scipio answers critic patiently*. Born to be emperor, not warrior. *a.b.c.* 346; *Castigos* MS A BNM 6559 31.147 (ADMYTE 0 96*r*).

*W26.7.3. *Vespasian acknowledges faults patiently*. *a.b.c.* 346; *Castigos* MS A BNM 6559 31.147 (ADMYTE 0 95*v*).

*W26.7.4. *King called dwarf by enemies*, pleased that his own people do not malign him. *Glosa* 1.2.14.135; *Castigos* MS A BNM 6559 31.148 (ADMYTE 0 96*v*).

W26.7.5. *King refuses lavish gifts from vassals*. Rich vassals serve him best. *Castigos* MS A BNM 6559 23.140 (ADMYTE 0 82*v*–83*r*).

*W26.8. *Humble nun endures insults of her sisters* without complaint. She is honored by saint who comes to convent. *a.b.c.* 406; Tubach 3504.

*W26.9. *Cato's teeth knocked out*. Says he is better off without them. *Glosa* 1.2.14.134; *Castigos* MS A BNM 6559 31.148 (ADMYTE 0 96*r*).

W27. Gratitude.

W27.1. *Man weeps with gratitude to God* that he does not resemble a toad. *a.b.c.* 184.

*W27.2. *Mistreated animal spares those who rescued him*. Jackal who escaped from pit attacks only its tormentors. *Esopete* p. 76.

*W27.3. *Caesar grateful for services of old legionary* and lends him legal assistance. *a.b.c.* 319; *Glosa* 1.2.15.141–42.

W31. Obedience.

*W31.1. *Obedience valued more than abstinence in monks*. Value tested on trip. Obedient monk crosses stream and is spared by crocodiles. Abstinent monk thinks he has resuscitated a dead man; abbot tells him it was obedient one's prayers. *Espéculo* 413.312–13.

*W31.2. *Obedience valued over gratitude, charity, asceticism*. In divine judgement, obedient ones are adorned with gold. *Espéculo* 414.313.

W32. Bravery.

W32.1. *King Richard leads army to victory* by leaping his horse overboard to attack enemy (Muslims) on land. His religious devotion in form of brave acts is equal to that of cloistered clerics. *Lucanor* Ex. 3.

W34. Loyalty.

*W34.5. *Courtier refuses physician's proposal* to poison king. Brings traitor to ruler. *a.b.c.* 315; Tubach 3761.

W35. Justice.

*W35.3. *Empress offers judge great honors in exchange for false judgement*.

He replies: "I do not want honors at the price of the truth." *Espéculo* 396.292.

*W35.4. *Cardinal returns bishop's gift* of palfrey given for services at court. Says: "Now I am redeeming my liberty." *Espéculo* 397.292.

*W35.5. *A thief and good man quarrel.* Quarrel settled by saint. When thief is judged guilty of crime, good man pleads for clemency for him. *Espéculo* 100.67.

W46. Compassion.

*W46.1. *Compassion.* Conqueror cries at suffering of conquered. Weeps upon seeing enemy's severed head. *a.b.c.* 66; *Glosa* 1.2.15.143; *Castigos* MS A BNM 6559 12.115 (ADMYTE 0 47r).

*W46.1.1. *Compassion.* Conqueror cries at sight of defeated city. *a.b.c.* 66; *Glosa* 1.2.15.143; *Castigos* MS A BNM 6559 12.115 (ADMYTE 0 47r).

*W46.1.2. *Compassion.* Conqueror does not permit defeated enemy to kneel before him. *Glosa* 1.2.15.144; *Castigos* MS A BNM 6559 12.115 (ADMYTE 0 47r).

*W46.1.3. *Compassion.* Conqueror restores crown of conquered enemy. *Glosa* 1.2.15.143; *Castigos* MS A BNM 6559 (ADMYTE 0 47r).

*W46.2. *Compassion.* Prince forgives man who spat in his face. *a.b.c.* 67.

*W46.2.1. *Compassion.* Emperor forgives traitors, invoking his divine right to rule. *a.b.c.* 68.

*W46.3. *Compassion.* Emperor forgives relative who plotted against him. *a.b.c.* 68.

*W46.4. *Compassion.* Emperor revokes all death sentences. Wild beasts kill people; he does not. *a.b.c.* 397.

*W46.5. *Ailing emperor told to bathe in pool of infants' blood* takes pity on mothers and refuses. God rewards him with cure. *Abreviada* 1.342; *PCG* 316.183–86.

W100–W199. UNFAVORABLE TRAITS OF CHARACTER
W110. Unfavorable traits: personal.
W111. Laziness.

W111.1. *Contest in laziness.* Woman to marry lazier of two suitors. Each cites instances of his laziness. *LBA* cc. 459–67; cf. Tubach 2896, 3005.

W111.1.3. *Man will not move in bed* when water drips in eyes (ear). *LBA* cc. 465; *Esopete* pp. 94–96.

*W111.1.3.1. *Man too lazy to eat* when table is full of food even after fasting for fifteen days. *Esopete* pp. 94–96.

*W111.1.4. *Man so lazy he will not wipe his running nose.* This causes him to lose prospective bride. *LBA* cc. 463.

*W111.1.5. *Man floating in river too lazy to drink to slake thirst.* His voice is damaged. *LBA* cc. 461; *Esopete* pp. 94–96.

*W111.1.7. *Man climbing a ladder* is too lazy to lift foot. Falls and is lamed. *LBA* cc. 460.

*W111.1.8. *Man is so lazy that water that drips in his ear* has caused his brains to leak out. *Esopete* pp. 94–96.

W111.2. The lazy servant.

W111.2.0.1. *Lazy slave* gets others to perform his duties. *Esopete* p. 5.

W111.2.2. *Servant to close door at night.* Leaves it open so that he will not have to open it next morning. *a.b.c.* 195; Tubach 4288.

W111.2.3. *Lazy servant.* "If it is day, give me food; if it is night let me sleep." The master has told servant it is day and time to go to work. *a.b.c.* 195; cf. Tubach 4288.

W111.2.4. *Lazy servant* calls dog in and feels paws to see if it is raining. *a.b.c.* 195; Tubach 4288.

W111.2.5. *Lazy servant,* asked if candles (torches) in house are lit, feels cat to see if she is warm. *a.b.c.* 195; cf. Tubach 4288.

*W111.6. *Lazy animals.* Lazy trout does not escape fisherman as had his two companions. *Calila* p. 149; *Exemplario* 18r.

W121. Cowardice.

W121.2.1. *Ass and other animals attack dying lion.* Humiliated lion, unable to attack them, tears out his own heart. *LBA* cc. 311–16; *Esopete* pp. 37–38; Tubach 3065.

W121.2.3. *Crow sits on sheep's back.* Afraid to sit on dog's. *Esopete* p. 79.

W121.5. *Spider kills fly easily* but retreats to web when wasp approaches. *Gatos* 52.

*W121.9. *Cowardly courtiers hide when lion escapes from cage.* Cid returns it to cage easily. *Abreviada* 3.131; *CMC* vv. 2286–2301.

W125. Gluttony.

*W125.5.1. *Gluttonous wife roasts chicken.* Makes husband give her all the good parts. He is left with roasting spit. Furious, he thrusts her through with the spit. *Especulo* 60.42; Tubach 969.

*W125.6. *Saint eats gluttonously* to please guests. Repents next day. *Espéculo* 298.208.

W126. Disobedience.

*W126.2. *Pharaoh disobeys God's commandments.* He and troops are drowned. *Castigos* MS A BNM 6559 90.226.

W128. Dissatisfaction.

W128.4. *Peacock dissatisfied with his voice.* Wants to sing like nightingale. *Esopete* pp. 75–76; Tubach 3632.

*W128.4.1. *Ass dissatisfied with hard life* and beatings. Even after death, skin is beaten as part of drum. *Esopete* pp. 66–67.

*W128.4.2. *Envious ass, dissatisfied with life of hard work,* desires easy life of pig until he sees him slaughtered for his meat. *Gatos* 35; Tubach 3771.

W128.5. *Monk dissatisfied with what God has granted him* is admonished to accept God's will. *a.b.c.* 103; *Calila* p. 303; *Exemplario* 77v.

*W128.7. *Dying man (usurer) reproaches soul for desire to leave him* despite his great wealth and comfort. *Lucanor* Ex. 4; *Espéculo* 568.462.

W150. Unfavorable traits of character: social.

W151. Greed.

*W151.9.1. *Greedy wolf overeats and drinks* in farmer's larder. Sings and is found and killed. *Esopete* pp. 93–94; Tubach 4092, 5346.

*W151.11. *Greedy horse who overeats* dies of bloat. *LBA* cc. 298–303.

*W151.12. *After solemn funeral mass for wolf,* lion serves a feast to the animal mourners. They hope for another such occasion for a feast. *Gatos* 46.

W152. Stinginess.

*W152.6.1. *Stingy prince deposed.* Never invited guests. *Glosa* 1.2.20.172.

W152.11. *Stingy man takes off shoes to walk on thorns* to save shoes. *a.b.c.* 37; Tubach 4351.

W153. Miserliness.

W153.1. *Dead moneylender's heart found in strong-box.* Saint tells mourners at funeral of moneylender. *Lucanor* Ex. 14; Tubach 2499.

W154. Ingratitude.

W154.2. *Snake ungrateful.* Bites man who saves it. *Disciplina* 5; *a.b.c.* 312.

W154.2.1. *Serpent ungrateful to shepherd* who had carried him to safety. Intends to eat man. Judgement: return to previous hazardous place. *Esopete* pp. 86–87; cf. Tubach 4262.

*W154.2.1.1. *Snake, rescued from winter's cold,* kills rescuer when warm weather arrives. *LBA* cc. 1348–54; *Esopete* p. 36; Tubach 4256.

W154.3. *Crane pulls bone from wolf's throat: wolf refuses promised payment.* "That you were allowed to take your beak from my throat is payment enough." *LBA* cc. 252–56; *Gatos* 2; *Esopete* p. 35; Tubach 5332.

W154.4. *Hunter beats dog that has grown old in his service. LBA* cc. 1357–66; *Esopete* p. 51; Tubach 1701.

W154.5.1. *Fox promises to pay boatman for passage.* Payment is a slap in face with wet tail. *Gatos* 49; Tubach 2020.

W154.8. *Grateful animals, ungrateful man.* Traveler saves monkey, badger, snake, and man (goldsmith) from a pit. Monkey gives him fruit; badger leads him into city to place where he finds jewels. In royal palace, goldsmith accuses traveler of killing king's daughter and of stealing jewels. Serpent saves traveler; bites king's son, and shows traveler the remedy for the venom. *Calila* p. 318–22; *a.b.c.* 207; *Exemplario* 81v–83r; Tubach 256.

W154.19. *Ungrateful Jew steals horse of Christian* who has lent it to him. *a.b.c.* 202; Tubach 2796.

W154.20. *Messenger brings gifts*–one good, one better, two much better. Recipient abuses bearer of king's gifts. Spits in face, throws him into mud, and beats him. *a.b.c.* 206; Tubach 2280.

W154.28. *Magician makes pupil think he has become pope.* Pupil ungrateful. Does not reward magician who returns pupil to previous status. *Lucanor* Ex. 11; Tubach 3137.

*W154.29. *Man laments his ingratitude to God* for having created him in his own image instead of a toad's. *a.b.c.* 184.

W155. Hardness of heart.

W156. *The dog in the manger.* Has no use for manger but refuses to give it up to oxen. *Esopete* p. 93; Tubach 660.

★W156.1. *Fox prefers to bear weight of tail* rather than share part of it with ape. *Esopete* p. 66; Tubach 297.

★W156.2. *Bitch about to give birth* pleads with other to let her use her bed. Later will not give it up. *Esopete* pp. 35–36; Tubach 660.

W158. Inhospitality.

★W158.1. *Fox serves meal to stork in flat dish.* Stork responds with meal served in tall narrow vessel. *Esopete* p. 52; Tubach 2170.

W159. Arrogance.

★W159.1. *Two lepers to cleanse each other's lesions for cure.* First one cured, then refuses to wash the second. *Espéculo* 537.432.

★W159.2. *Saint scrutinizes God's judgements.* Wants to know why some die young; others live long; some are rich; others are poor. God tells him to cease. *Espéculo* 538.432–33.

★W159.3. *Scholar told attempts to understand nature of Trinity are presumptuous* by child who appears to be engaged in fruitless, impossible task of filling a hole with all the water of a river. *Espéculo* 539.433–34; *a.b.c.* 413.

★W159.4. *Dead monk, tortured and ugly, appears to friend* to warn him that pride in disputation and scholarship will be punished. *Espéculo* 540.434.

W167. Stubbornness.

W167.2. *Stubbornness causes loss of chance to go on pilgrimage.* Husband and wife quarrel over whether a bird is thrush or throstle. Infuriated husband breaks wife's leg (donkey's leg). They must return to pray for her welfare. *Talavera* 2.7.179; cf. Tubach 5284, 5285.

★W167.3. *Stubbornness causes wife's drowning.* Husband and wife quarrel over whether he is holding a knife or a pair of scissors. Infuriated husband kicks her into river. She disappears with current, insisting that they are scissors. *Talavera* 2.7.178; cf. Tubach 5284, 5285.

W171. Two-facedness.

W171.1. *Man winks at both buyer and seller.* He tries to appear friendly to both. *Esopete* p. 75.

★W171.1.1. *Bat, because of ambiguous physical traits,* tries to join forces with beasts and with birds. Fails. *Esopete* p. 62; Tubach 501.

★W171.2. *Shepherd betrays wolf* to hunter with wink. *Esopete* p. 75.

W185. Violence of temper.

W185.4. *Monk loses temper* at pitcher and breaks it. *a.b.c.* 221; Tubach 252.

W185.5. *Violence of judge's temper* leads him to condemn man to death unjustly. *a.b.c.* 222.

W185.6. *Insult worse than wound.* The lion to the man: "The wound has healed, but the pain of harsh words still remains." *Castigos* 26.141.

W189. Mischievousness.

*W189.1. *Novice given to antic behavior fears reproach.* Prays to Virgin Mary that pranks be forgotten if she repents. *Cantigas* 303.

W196. Lack of patience.

*W196.1. *Impatience controlled by patience.* Youth counseled to control anger at brother's impatience. *Espéculo* 97.66.

X. HUMOR

X0–X99. HUMOR OF DISCOMFITURE

*X22. *Man whose liver has been temporarily removed* hears passerby ask surgeon to give him the liver to feed his cat. *Lucanor* Ex. 8.

*X35. *Son lies to mother, inventing wild tales* about secret senate debate: men to have two wives; women to have two husbands. She divulges secret to others, and they confront senate. Woman made to look foolish. *a.b.c.* 394; Tubach 5269.

*X36. *Husband tells wife a secret.* He has given birth to a crow. She is unable to keep secret. Is made ridiculous. *Glosa* 2.1.24.119–20.

X52. Ridiculous nakedness or exposure.

X52. *Woman in procession, devils ride on the train* of her skirt. *a.b.c.* 407; Tubach 1660.

X52.1. *Woman in a grand procession* exposed to ridicule when her wig is snatched off by a monkey. *a.b.c.* 334; Tubach 2400.

X54. Humor of self-deprecation.

*X54.1. *Madman in bath* throws pails of hot water at other bathers. Proprietor does same to him. Madman warns other bathers: "Beware. There is another madman in this bathhouse." *Lucanor* Ex. 43.

*X70. *Humor of incongruity.* Woman's timidity inconsistent with her willingness to commit heinous acts. Proverb: "Sister dear, you are frightened by sound of gurgling water but not by sound of the rending of a corpse's neck bones." *Lucanor* Ex. 47.

X200–X599. HUMOR OF SOCIAL CLASSES

X300–X499. Humor dealing with professions.

X310. Jokes on lawyers.

X315. *Dying lawyer says: "I appeal."* Asks for defense. Dies without confession and goes to hell. *Espéculo* 21.15; Tubach 2991.

*X315.2. *Dying lawyer offers self to God.* God says he must be judged. Refuses to be judged by his equals and so dies without communion and confession. *Espéculo* 19.14.

X316. *Lawyers in hell.* Nero has reserved place in hell for lawyers. *a.b.c.* 12; *Espéculo* 88.61.

*X318.1. *Man's lawyer is bribed to lose a lawsuit.* Appears in court saying he has "esquinança" (quinsy) and cannot speak. His client says he does not have "esquinança" but rather "argençia" (money disease). *a.b.c.* 309.

*X319.2. *Widow gives lawyer a cart as fee.* Adversary gives him ox to pull it. She loses and says: "The cart does not go well." He replies that it needs an ox to pull it. *Espéculo* 23.16.

X370. Jokes on scholars.

*X371.1. *Impoverished scholar* gives beggar grammar lesson instead of alms. *a.b.c.* 131.

X372. Jokes on doctors.

*X372.6. *Doctor prescribes same remedy* for a sore eye that he had used to cure his own sore foot. Patient blinded. *a.b.c.* 283; Tubach 3530.

X410. Jokes on clerics.

*X434.3. *Gullible priest believes tricksters* who tell him that deer (bought for sacrifice) is dog. *Calila* p. 236; *Exemplario* 55r; *Esopete* pp. 167–68.

X457. Jokes on monks.

*X457.2. *Abbot advises monk to listen to prisoners.* They ask the right questions: "Where is the judge, and when will he come?" *a.b.c.* 70; cf. Tubach 2867.

*X457.3. *Abbot sends monk for manure.* He returns because a lioness lived where the manure was. Told to rope her, and bring her here. Credulous monk tries, and she resists until he tells her that abbot had sent him. Abbot says: "Just as you are witless, you have captured a witless beast." *a.b.c.* 317; Tubach 3075.

*X457.4. *Inexperienced young monk* (never having seen a woman) is told that women are goats. Obsessed by woman he had seen through window, is unable to eat (meat) because he felt so sorry for the poor goat. *a.b.c.* 300.

X500–X599. Humor concerning other social classes.

X500. Humor concerning royalty.

*X501. *Philosopher spits in king's beard.* It is only place in excessively elegant palace that is suitable. *a.b.c.* 188; Tubach 525.

*X502. *The emperor's new clothes.* Tricksters pretend to make clothes for the emperor. Cloth is visible only to those of legitimate birth. None at court are willing to admit they cannot see it. Finally a slave who has nothing to lose tells emperor he is naked. *Lucanor* Ex. 32; cf. Tubach 3577.

X520. Jokes concerning prostitutes.

*X521. *Only prostitutes* can carry the corpse of a prostitute. *Espéculo* 111.72–73; Tubach 1265.

*X522. *Prostitute shamed by offer of sexual intercourse in public place.* Saint offers to have sex with her before a crowd. She refuses; then how much more shame should she have before God? *Espéculo* 350.250.

*X523. *Queen, vain about her virtue,* declares she would never surrender her body to a lover for wealth. Challenged with increasingly large rewards, is at last tempted. Is in effect potential prostitute. *Talavera* 2.1.146–47.

X590. Jokes on masters and servants.

X591. *Clever servant* asked how much he could eat. Asks if questioner means his food or the food of another. If another, he would eat as much as possible. *a.b.c.* 195.

X592. *Employer says she has eyes in buttocks* to supervise clever slave's actions. He uncovers them while she sleeps. *Esopete* p. 16.

X700–X799. HUMOR CONCERNING SEX
X710. Jokes on husbands.

*X711.1. *The cut-off nose.* Carpenter's wife has another woman, a barber's wife, take her place while she goes to her lover. Husband speaks to her, gets no answer, and cuts off her nose. In the morning, wife returns and still has nose. Husband made to believe it was restored miraculously. *Calila* pp. 139–41.

*X711.2. *Husband hides under wife's bed.* She spends night with lover and tells lover how much she loves husband. In morning, gullible husband commiserates with her over her sleepless night and urges her to stay in bed. *Calila* p. 241; *Exemplario* 57r; *Esopete* p. 168.

*X711.3. *Woman mixes husked with unhusked barley.* Serves it to husband. Only she knows that dog has urinated on husked grain. *Calila* p. 212 n. 116.

*X711.4. *The husband locked out.* He had taken excessive precautions to assure wife's fidelity. Despite efforts, wife returns home late at night; her husband refuses to admit her. She threatens to throw herself in the well. Husband leaves house to see if she has drowned. She enters the house and bars him from house. *a.b.c.* 303; Tubach 5246.

*X711.5. *Parrot (magpie) unable to tell husband of wife's infidelity.* Wife simulates a rainstorm while cage is covered so that parrot gives husband a false report. *Sendebar* Day 1, Tale 2; *Exemplario* 25v–26v; Tubach 632, 3147.

*X711.6. *Husband paints lamb on wife's stomach* to ensure her chastity during his absence. Returns after long absence to find that her lover has repainted it; it is now a full-grown ram. *LBA* cc. 474–87.

*X711.7. *The husband in the chicken house (dovecote).* Husband returns unexpectedly and surprises his wife with her lover. She makes the husband believe he is pursued and hides him in the chicken house. *Esopete* pp. 148–49.

*X711.8. *The husband's (vintner's) good eye treated* so that lover can leave house unseen. *a.b.c.* 161; *Disciplina* 9; *Esopete* pp. 147–48; Tubach 1943.

*X711.9. *Lovers as pursuer and fugitive.* Wife is visited by two lovers. When the husband arrives, one goes out with drawn sword, and the other hides in house. She convinces her husband that she has given refuge to a fugitive. *Sendebar* Day 2, Tale 5; Tubach 4693.

*X711.10. *Wife entertains lover during husband's absence.* Husband returns and mother-in-law (guardian) counsels lover to pretend he is

MOTIF INDEX OF

fugitive from street ruffians. *Disciplina* 11; *Esopete* pp. 145–46; Tubach 4692.

*X711.11. *Wife outwits husband with extended sheet.* Lover leaves house unseen. *a.b.c.* 162; *Esopete* p. 148; *Disciplina* 10; Tubach 4319.

*X711.12. *Husband is made to believe that adulterous wife's pregnancy is gift of God.* *Esopete* p. 149; Tubach 971.

*X711.13. *The enchanted pear tree.* Wife and lover are up in tree. Blind husband hears them and prays to Jupiter for restoration of sight. Prayer is answered. Wife convinces cuckold that her adultery convinced Jupiter to grant his wish. *Esopete* p. 147; Tubach 3265.

*X712. *Greedy husband supplies wife to inexperienced fat prince* because he believes him to be impotent. When the prince and the woman evidently enjoy each other, the husband kills himself. *Sendebar* Day 4, Tale 9.

X740. Jokes on men.

*X741. *Cleric participates passively in sexual acts* with widow. Exculpated because he did nothing actively. *Esopete* p. 165.

*X742. *Clever woman* tells amorous youth to strip off clothes, then shouts for neighbors. Tells him to lie down, puts chunk of bread in mouth, douses him with water, and tells neighbors he had choked. Proves to him he knows nothing of womanly guile. *Sendebar* Day 8, Tale 18.

*X742.1. *Aristotle and Phyllis: philosopher as riding horse for woman.* Philosopher warns against uxoriousness. In revenge, woman tricks philosopher into letting her ride him on all fours. Husband comes and sees. *Talavera* 1.17. 99–100; Tubach 328.

*X743. *Wife frightened upon hearing thief in house,* joins husband in bed for protection. Husband grateful to thief. *Calila* p. 238; *Exemplario* 56r.

X770. Humor of sexual naivete.

*X771. *Naive new bride* compares husband's penis with that of an ass and finds him wanting. *Esopete* pp. 165–66.

*X771.1. *Sheltered princeling,* shown all forms of human and animal life for first time, was told that young women are devils who deceive men. Asked what he liked best, chose the "devils." *Barlaam* pp. 261–63.

*X771.2. *Inexperienced young monk* (never having seen a woman) is told that women are goats. Obsessed by what he had seen through window is unable to eat (meat) because he felt so sorry for the poor goat. *a.b.c.* 300.

*X772. *Absurd ignorance of sex.* Pious young woman convinced by go-between that God does not see what is done at night. Spends night with go-between's customer. *a.b.c.* 108; Tubach 1436.

*X772.1. *Foolish young woman sees copulation between youth and ass.* Told he is giving her sense, asks for same treatment. *Esopete* p. 25.

*X772.2. *Woman's naivete proves her fidelity.* Man is told he has bad breath and rebukes wife for not having told him. She thought all men had bad breath. *a.b.c.* 368.

X800–X899. HUMOR BASED ON DRUNKENNESS

*X801. *Englishman in France in drunken stupor in tavern* as if dead. Taken to confessor, could only say "cup, cup." Priest, unable to understand, left him, and he died. *Espéculo* 201.140.

*X802. *Man in drunken stupor in tavern in foreign land as if dead.* Taken to confessor, cannot speak. A neighbor whispers to him in his tongue: "Neighbor, have some wine." He responds: "Let me drink" and dies. *Espéculo* 202.141; Tubach 1808.

*X803. *Mouse in wine vat.* Promises cat anything if he will save him. Breaks promise, telling cat, "I was drunk when I promised." *Gatos* 56; Tubach 3426.

X900–X1899. HUMOR OF LIES AND EXAGGERATION
X904. The teller reduces the size of his lie.

*X904.2.1. *The great fox: as large as a deer.* Squire tells master he once saw a fox as large as a deer. Master says they will soon be at oracular river that drowns liars. As they near river squire weakens his exaggeration until fox is correct size. *Esopete* pp. 100–1.

X905.3. *Claim of property based on unusual lie.* Goat to be inherited by son who can best exaggerate its size. *Esopete* pp. 94–96.

*X905.3.1. *Claim of property based on unusual lie.* Mill to be inherited by son who tells best lie. *Esopete* pp. 94–96.

Z. MISCELLANEOUS GROUP OF MOTIFS

Z0–Z99. FORMULAS

Z11. *Endless tales.* Hundreds of sheep to be carried across stream, one at a time, etc. The wording of the tale arranged so as to continue indefinitely. *Esopete* p. 144; *Disciplina* 12; *a.b.c.* 156; Tubach 4310.

*Z19.3. *Ages of women.* Speaker attributes qualities to each age from twenty to eighty. *Teodor* p. 118.

*Z19.4. *Beauty of women.* Speaker calculated eighteen qualities in sets of three. *Teodor* p. 118.

Z40. Chains with interdependent members.

Z42. *Stronger and strongest.* Rat-maiden wants most powerful mate of all. Sun covered by clouds; clouds controlled by winds; mountain blocks winds; mountain gnawed by rodents, therefore she must marry a rat. *Calila* p. 244; Tubach 3428.

*Z43.7. *Sequential tale.* Jar of honey suspended over hermit's head. He dreams of selling honey, and through successive transactions becoming tremendously wealthy. In dream he will punish disobedient offspring. Raises stick and shatters jug of honey. *Calila* p. 264; cf. *Lucanor* Ex. 7; Tubach 80.

MOTIF INDEX OF

*Z43.7.1. *Sequential tale.* Jar of honey to be sold. Woman on way to market to sell honey, dreams of future wealth. Inattentive, lets jar drop. *Lucanor* Ex. 7; cf. *Calila* p. 264; Tubach 80.

*Z43.8. *Money will go to its destination.* Man told that money he found belongs to another. Hollows out tree trunk; puts money inside and throws it into sea. Trunk washes up at door of rightful owner. He uses it for firewood; gold begins to melt. His wife finds tree trunk and hides it. First man is beggar now and wife bakes bread with money inside; gives it to him. He sells bread to fishermen who begin to feed it to horses. Wife gives them oats for her bread. Money has returned to owner. *Espéculo* 58.41; Tubach 4954.

*Z43.9. *Squire lost knight's money sack.* Charcoal burner found it. Knight cut squire's foot off. Angel explained: Knight lost money because he had stolen it; charcoal burner found money that had belonged to his father. Squire lost foot for having kicked his mother. *Espéculo* 15.11; Tubach 223.

*Z46.1. *Climax of horrors.* Clever slave, told not to give master bad news, says: pup is dead; (how?) mule frightened it; (how?) mule fell in well and drowned; (why?) master's son fell off roof and frightened mule; mother of child died of grief. (Who is guarding house?) No one; it burned down when daughter's candle tipped over during vigil over mother's cadaver. (How did he escape?) He saw dead daughter and fled. *a.b.c.* 195; Tubach 1705.

*Z46.2. *Climax of horrors.* Drop of honey causes chain of events. Hunter drops honey in a shop; bee lights on honey; storekeeper's cat kills bee; hunter's dog kills cat; storekeeper kills dog; hunter kills storekeeper; villagers and neighbors of storekeeper kill hunter; villagers and neighbors of hunter come, and the two groups kill each other. *Sendebar* Day 3, Tale 7.

Z49.2. Cumulative pursuit.

Z49.2.2. *Sequential pursuit of abductor.* Child carried off by wolf; ape steals it; lions threaten; thieves capture it. Pursuer rescues it from thieves. *Ultramar* II.2.254–57, 370–78.

Z100–Z199. SYMBOLISM

*Z100.01. *Symbolic acts.* Saint sends pupil unclothed to market. He is to bring back meat balanced on his head. Packs of dogs and flocks of birds attack him. They are like the devils who attack ascetics who withdraw from world. *Espéculo* 475.376.

*Z100.02. *Knight's arms represent soul's protection:* tunic is fear of God; chaplet, understanding; shield, faith; lance, strength; sword, justice; legs and feet, humility; hands, chastity. *Castigos* 1.38.

*Z105. *Symbolic dream.* Man in search of eternal happiness rejects: marriage (marital bed inhabited by dangerous beasts); royal power (royal bed inhabited by dangerous beasts); wealth (rich person's bed inhabited by dangerous beasts). Chooses a stair that leads to spiritual happiness. *Gatos* 23.

*Z106. *Father's dream* that sun's rays emanated from pregnant wife's womb. Prophecy of future greatness of unborn child. *a.b.c.* 180; Tubach 647.

Z110. Personifications.

Z111.3.1. *Death allegorically portrayed* as an animal made up of several different animals. *a.b.c.* 296 (not in Paris MS); Tubach 5082 b).

*Z111.7. *Death personified* as human woman or as human man. Appears talking to powerful worldly figures (Dance of death). *Talavera* 4.2.271; *Danza de la muerte.*

*Z121.2. *Truth and Lies personified.* Deceptive crop division: above the ground, below the ground. Truth takes the roots of jointly owned tree, and Lies takes the trunk and branches. *Lucanor* Ex. 26.

*Z121.2.1. *Truth, Wind, and Water debate.* Wind and Water easily found; Truth must be guarded and never lost. Once lost, never regained. *Çifar* p. 136.

*Z121.3. *Evil and Good personified.* Deceptive division of shared wife. Evil takes lower half of wife; Good takes upper half. Child begotten by lower half not permitted to nurse the top half, which belongs to Good. *Lucanor* Ex. 43; Tubach 1921.

Z127.1. *Sin (Lust) personified* as the goddess Venus: as woman because inconstant, naked because shameless, swimming in sea because of pleasure, conch shell because of songs and revelry. *a.b.c.* 429.

Z133.1. *Poverty personified as diseased beggar woman.* Debates with Fortune. *Talavera* 4.2.276–92; *Compendio* pp. 251–73; cf. Tubach 2154.

Z134. *Fortune and Poverty* personified. Fortune a beautiful horsewoman, Poverty a wretched beggar. *Talavera* 276–98; *Compendio* pp. 251–73; cf. Tubach 2154.

Z139.3.1. *Wine personified* with face of young woman, bare breasts, horns on head, riding on serpents (Bacchus). *a.b.c.* 421.

*Z139.9. *Philosophy personified* gives infant hero magical shirt. *Alexandre* cc. 89–103.

Z150. Other symbols.

*Z161.1. *Basket of sand* shows that sins are a burden. *a.b.c.* 1; Tubach 4413.

Z200–Z299. HEROES

Z216. *Supernatural origin of hero*: magic (mysterious) conception. *Alexandre* cc. 19–20, 1063–64.

Z230. Extraordinary exploits of hero.

Z231. *Boy hero kills count in battle.* Captures his sons. *Mocedades* vv. 320–25.

Z300–Z399. UNIQUE EXCEPTIONS
Z310. Unique vulnerability.

*Z311.5. *Witch kills man by means of poison in his armpits. Talavera* 2.12.198.

CORRESPONDENCES BETWEEN MOTIF
NUMBERS AND TUBACH TOPICAL NUMBERS

Imperfect correspondences where circumstantial details differ are marked as cf.

MOTIF NUMBER	TUBACH	MOTIF NUMBER	TUBACH
A163.2	3462	B331.2	1695
A511.1.5.1	124	B363.1.1	3052
A1018.4	3462, cf. 124	B371.1	3052
A1021	3478	B374.1	3057
A1391	570	B381	215, 2771
A2232.1	838	B381.3	cf. 2714
A2232.7	3631	B391.1.4	cf. 4251
A2282.1	cf. 4686	B401.2	2608
A2311.11	501	B411.2	4596
A2325.4	838	B449.4	cf. 2711, 2714
A2326.3.3.1	4589	B449.5	519
A2346.3	547	B525	215
A2441.4.2	1311	B535.0.15	cf. 5350
A2466.3	2176	B535.0.16	cf. 5350
A2492.3	2619	B552.1	125
A2494.12.11	cf. 3014	B581.1	cf. 4251
A2494.13.14	1358	B732	3583
A2497.2	4640	B773.4	5344
A2851	5093	B773.5	642
B39.2	cf. 3556	C12.4.2	1605
B123	4251	C55.3.1	2662
B147.2.2	1366	C94.1.1	1419
B147.3.1.3	293	C94.1.4	cf. 2240
B151.1.1.2.1	375	C94.4.1	1949
B161	4251	C114.4	2734
B242.1.8	3554	C271.1	3283
B259.4	2662	C610.01	5277
B260.1	5357	C770.1	3938
B261.1	501		
B263.3	1358	D117.1.1	3428
B275.1.3.2	5330	D141.1.1	661
B301.1.1	1700	D161.1	1884
B301.8	3057	D315.1	3428

MOTIF NUMBER	TUBACH	MOTIF NUMBER	TUBACH
D361.2	1884	D2011.1	3378
D451.10	5371	D2021.2	677, cf. 4906
D470.2	2266	D2086.1	4697
D812.8	cf. 847	D2136.3.1	3424
D906.1	2370	D2140.1.1	cf. 4649
D906.2	349, 4773	D2143.1.3	3885
D997.1.2	cf. 2497, 2498	D2143.2.1	2091
D1031.1.2	766, 2566	D2152.1	3424
D1053	1103	D2156.5	4279
D1310.4.4	2397	D2161.3.2	2419
D1385.19.1	1118	D2161.5.2.4.1	2419
D1500.1.7.3.5	1373	D2161.5.2.4.5	2419
D1525	123	D2161.5.2.6	2488
D1624.2	1373	D2163.5.4	2754
D1652.1.1	766	D2174	1419
D1654.9.1	1265		
D1712.3	cf. 1785	E121.4	971
D1713.2	4151	E121.5	4082
D1713.3	4151, cf. 4279	E234.0.2	cf. 3817
D1713.4	2239, 4151	E235.4.3.1	5031
D1713.5	4151	E235.7	1498 b)
D1713.6	4151	E243	2424
D1713.8	2091	E301.3	4347
D1766.1.2	1021, 1022	E301.7	1188 a) 1
D1766.1.3	3913	E367.6	1188 a) 4
D1766.1.7.1	3893	E368	1103
D1766.1.8.2	4148	E411	3111
D1766.1.10	519	E411.0.2.2	1188 b) 2
D1766.1.11	519	E411.0.2.3	1924
D1766.1.12	cf. 3885	E411.0.5.1	1254
D1766.1.14	3424	E411.0.6	1270
D1766.1.15	3875	E411.0.9	1137
D1766.7.1.2	4560	E411.0.9.1	2037
D1810.0.3.1	4259	E411.4.1	5031
D1810.0.3.2	3805	E411.12	1464 e)
D1812.5.1.4	1475 a) 3	E412.1	1925
D1816.2.1.1	4102	E412.2	cf. 475
D1817.0.1.7	1018	E412.6	3660
D1817.0.2	697	E412.7	cf. 3213
D1835.7	4656	E415	3667
D1840.1.2	4279	E415.2	3349
D1840.1.2.1	4151	E415.2.1	3349
D1841.1.2	1110	E415.2.2	3349
D1841.3	2038	E415.3.1	3349

MOTIF NUMBER	TUBACH	MOTIF NUMBER	TUBACH
E415.4	cf. 1499	G303.3.5.4	1812
E446.2.1	2276	G303.6.1.8	1660
E481.1.3	1450	G303.9.4.4	1436
E481.1.4	1450	G303.9.4.11	210
E499.5	2424, 3214	G303.10.5	5361
E631.0.2	430	G303.16.1	5283
E631.0.2.1	427	G303.16.1.1	3370
E721.0.1	818	G303.16.1.2	cf. 4948
E722.3.4	4551	G303.16.1.4	214
E722.3.5	4551	G303.16.2.1.2	210
E732.1	1760, 4551	G303.16.2.3.6	1594
E752.1.1.2	3566	G303.16.2.3.7	3276
E752.2	4548	G303.16.2.3.4	3503
E752.2.1	1050	G303.16.5.3	1602
E754.1.9	2717, 4151	G303.16.8.3	3449
E755.2.1.1	4553	G303.16.9	1508
E755.2.7.1	2514	G303.24.1.4.1	1630
E756.1	237	G303.25.3.1	3329
E756.4.2	3572		
E756.4.1	2239	H71.10.8	96
E765.4.3.2	1475 b) 1	H119.3	3420
		H151.4	3796
F565.1	cf. 92	H175.6	2611
F565.1.2.1	cf. 92	H215	4697
F582	3830	H221.2	3109
F591.1	4994	H221.2.3	59
F642.4.1	5391	H251.3.4	3352
F811.2.2.1	430	H473.2	cf. 5278
F912	1326	H473.3.1	cf. 5278
F963.2	349, 4773	H479.3	cf. 5194
F968.1.1	3046	H486.2	1272
F968.1.2	680	H543.1	214
F1066.1	2937	H604	4898, 4916
		H605	275
G72.2.1	1851	H606	4413
G303.1.17	1648	H607.1	2275
G303.3.1.12.2	214	H642.2	214
G303.3.1.12.3	1535	H648.3	214
G303.3.1.12.4	1553	H659.7.3.1	954
G303.3.1.29	cf. 2461	H659.27	3428
G303.3.2.1	1536	H682.1.10	214
G303.3.2.2	19	H696.1.1	cf. 4028
G303.3.2.6	1529	H1111	4310
G303.3.3.1.4	1812	H1376.2.1	5082 b)

MOTIF NUMBER	TUBACH	MOTIF NUMBER	TUBACH
H1511.5	1284, 2759	J148	5383
H1553.3	3622	J152.1	cf. 1673
H1553.4	3619	J152.10	2903
H1553.5	252	J152.17	954
H1553.7	3748	J152.18	cf. 1444
H1554.1	3427	J153.3	3885
H1556.0.4	4485	J155.9	3355, 4969
H1558.1	2216, 2407	J156.5.1	3906
H1558.2	2208	J163.4	cf. 5324
H1558.2.1	2215	J167	2859, cf. 2855
H1565.1	3137	J181.1	484
H1569.4	cf. 5269	J211.2	3281
H1573.2.2	5076	J212.1	2615
H1573.2.4	967	J215.1	2087
H1596.4	cf. 4873	J215.4.1	5386
H1599.1	1663	J215.6	cf. 508
		J217.2	cf. 394, 1747
J15	4251	J217.3	3771
J15.1.1	4251	J221.3	1498
J15.1.1	4251	J225.0.1	2558
J15.1.2	4251	J225.0.1.1	3107
J21.2.1.1	3991	J225.0.4	2558
J21.5	4111	J234	2561
J21.12	cf. 5324	J245.2.1	3843
J21.32	3182	J247.1	1444
J21.53	3323	J341.1	297
J26	4127	J342.2	2917
J26.1	2796	J347.3	362
J28	252	J347.6	4963
J29	3427	J357	381
J31.3	2548	J369.2	3510
J51.1	3069	J410.0.2	2216
J52.2	123	J411.1	3060
J55.1	2855, 2859	J411.3.1	3829
J80.3.2	4413	J445.1	2454
J80.3.3	967	J451.1.1	5228
J80.3.4	275	J451.3.1	2431
J80.4	4994	J452	2999
J80.5	3829	J461.1	570
J83.2	148	J466.2	2829
J88.1	4677	J482.1	3180
J89	4898, 4916	J482.3	955
J94.1	275	J485	1816, 2569,
J121	2001		4130

MOTIF NUMBER	TUBACH	MOTIF NUMBER	TUBACH
J514.1	3608	J1063.1	1311
J571.4.2	3991	J1064.2	4686
J581.3	4787	J1074.1.2	3748
J613.1	4677	J1074.1.3	4627
J621.1	4686	J1114.0.1	4288
J621.1.2	444	J1152.	cf. 632, 3147
J624.3	714	J1153.1	4684
J643.1	2221, cf. 292	J1154.1	cf. 632, 3147
J643.2.1	1755, 3554	J1161.1	3353
J644.1	2169	J1161.4	3352
J651.4	5022	J1162.4	cf. 89
J657.2	625, 1832	J1169.4	3289
J671.1	566	J1171.1	4466
J681.1	3425	J1172.1	874, 4090
J701.2	2909	J1172.3	4254, 4262
J702.2	5383	J1176.2	3524
J711.1.1	2097	J1179.5.1	2081
J711.3	2907	1181.4	4790
J711.5	265	J1181.5	1947
J811.1	3069	J1189.4	1944
J811.2.1	2205	J1215.2	5386
J815.1	304	J1262.5.2	176, 4089
J816.4	954	J1262.5.3	176, 4089
J817.4	1237	J1262.7.1	1229
J869.1	1773, 3606	J1263.1.7	3032
J893.1.2	1950	J1263.4.2	3716
J912.1	4355	J1269.16	539
J912.3.1	5039	J1281	5011
J913.1	3843	J1281.4	2908
J915	2906	J1283.1	cf. 100
J916	13	J1289.10	105
J921	5016	J1289.10.1	cf. 4183
J951.1	386	J1289.21	4181
J951.2	1360	J1289.22	113
J952.6	1692	J1289.24	4694
J953.20	cf. 386	J1289.25	cf. 4911
J954.1	3432, cf. 3829	J1319.2	3426
J955.1	2219	J1341.5	2753
J956	751	J1369.6	2078
J1025.1	1315	J1421	3629
J1032	4596	J1440.1	390
J1041.2	382	J1442.1	1673
J1061.1	3635	J1442.14	4339
J1062.1	1692	J1473.1	1788

MOTIF NUMBER	TUBACH	MOTIF NUMBER	TUBACH
J1546	5269	J2469.6	1605
J1565.1	2170	J2475	2421
J1566.1	525		
J1577	cf. 2169	K171.7	1921
J1592	173	K191	5357
J1607	cf. 4949	K192	2619
J1608.1	3432	K231.3	cf. 4138
J1623.2	cf. 59	K236.5	3469
J1647	4244	K334.1	2177
J1661.1.2.2	500	K344.1.5	2975
J1661.1.5	2611	K354.2	112
J1662	2180	K401.2	2431 b)
J1733	3775	K402.3	717
J1745.1.1	1436	K427.1	2608
J1791.4	1699	K441.3.1	cf. 2851
J1849.5	3075	K444	1789
J1909.1	cf. 2053	K445	cf. 3577
J2071	5326	K476.2	cf. 965
J2072.5.1	838	K477.4	1358
J2119.1.2	3530	K511.1.1	131, 3289
J2131.1.2	698	K513	4229
J2121.1.4	1952	K528.2	4153
J2132.5	3425	K558	4790
J2133.9	701	K558.3	1947
J2135.1.1	570	K561.1.1.1	5228
J2136.5.1	4782	K574	139
J2159.2	2135	K604	322
J2301.4	5361	K651	5247
J2199.4.1	4351	K652	5247
J2301.4.4	cf. 1943	K713.1.2	3425
J2301.4.6	4692	K721.2	3629
J2301.4.7	5246	K730.3	3014
J2301.4.8	cf. 1943	K815.2	4571
J2304	2975	K815.8	1755, 3554
J2312	cf. 3577	K824.2	1529
J2314.1	2570	K871.1	5304
J2339	3432	K943	2570
J2357	1832	K952.1	1326
J2412.1	3530	K959.7	2737
J2413.1	372	K978.1.2	1453
J2413.3	2346	K1011	3530
J2416.1	3843	K1021	2074
J2461.1.9	3075	K1022.1	4092, 5346
J2466.1	4413	K1054	4778

CONCORDANCE

MOTIF NUMBER	TUBACH	MOTIF NUMBER	TUBACH
K1075.1	3432	K2061.1.1	5357
K1081	698	K2061.6	4554
K1085	5361	K2094.1	cf. 1703
K1121.1	2605	K2101.1	134
K1121.2	4554	K2103	2419
K1215	328	K2111.5	2734
K1265	2753	K2111.6	648
K1315.1	4221	K2111.6.1	1915, cf. 3380
K1351	661	K2112.0.2	4684
K1353.2	1081	K2112.0.3	4697
K1397	3095	K2112.2	3020
K1511	5246	K2131.6	3389
K1516	4319	K2155	3796
K1516.1	cf. 1943	K2155.1.2	2431 b)
K1517.1	4693	K2155.1.3	cf. 2431 b)
K1517.1.2	4693	K2213.1	5262
K1518	3265	K2217.1	5020
K1518.1.1	cf. 971	K2242.2	2799
K1536	1803	K2284.0.2	519
K1544.2.1	4221	K2292	134
K1667	3355, 4969	K2294	3790
K1681.1	cf. 3134	K2365.2	317
K1810.2.2	888	K2365.3	112
K1811.4.3	19	K2365.4	5304
K1837.7	1915	K2369.3.1	cf. 1082
K1837.8.2	4224	K2369.6	4109
K1841.3	5283	K2372	3097
K1867.1.1	cf. 2176		
K1955.0.1	4554	L10.3	803
K1955.0.2	2605	L114.1	3005
K1955.0.4	1692	L143.3	cf. 551
K1955.2.2	1833	L146.1	299
K1961.6	5338	L211	967
K1961.7	888	L213	3841
K1962.1	1762	L213.3	1444
K1966.2	89	L302	4388
K2010.3	5357	L315.3	2181
K2031.1	1703	L361.1	3674
K2031.2	4251	L391.1	812
K2031.3	501	L392	3428
K2041.1	3761	L414	4863
K2042	1358	L416.2	4109
K2058.3	1850	L420.0.2	2323
K2061.1	5343	L435.1.1	3389

MOTIF NUMBER	TUBACH	MOTIF NUMBER	TUBACH
L451	3281	N275.5.2	4317
L451.3	5337	N333.1	2103
L452.2	cf. 2615	N340.2	1494
L461	4589	N347.1	2431
L461.1	cf. 4589	N388	698
		N535.1	4950
M2.2	1494	N535.2	2720, 4611
M13	1944	N592	4175, 4702
M14	3101	N635	4892
M101.4	cf. 4138		
M101.4.1	727	P11.7	2907
M122	4224	P12.9	3971
M203.1	2799	P12.9.1	1900
M203.4	139	P13.9.1.1	90
M203.5	131, 3289	P14.25	4994
M205.0.2	2020	P15.1.2	2910
M205.0.3	3426	P232.4	1440 c)
M205.0.4	4388	P233.2.2	4989
M205.1.3	1297	P233.9.1	362
M205.5	cf. 4254	P233.12	2005
M205.7	cf. 4138	P233.13	3796
M205.8	cf. 4138	P233.14	1944
M211	3572	P233.15	3488
M211.1	4540	P233.16	684
M212.2	cf. 2235	P233.17	1272
M217	3566	P233.18	2001
M244.3	322	P234.3	3969
M251.1	1271	P236.2	965
M302.4.3	4703	P315	2208, 2215
M312.0.2.1	293	P317.1.1	1401
M312.0.4	cf. 647	P361	2209
M312.0.4.1	3283	P435.3	375
M341.0.5	1475 b)	P435.4	5031
M341.1	1267	P435.5	cf. 1053
M411.1.3	1440 c)	P435.6	cf. 5027, 5062
M423.1	1440 c)	P435.11	5027
		P435.12	5050
N1.2.1	2239	P435.14	2499
N.1.2.1.1	cf. 2239	P458.1	444
N12	cf. 4354	P465.1	cf. 2991
N111	cf. 2154, 2155, 2156	P465.4	2991
		P482.1.1	3573
N211.1	4102	P511.2	1947
N255.2	387	P511.3	4790

MOTIF NUMBER	TUBACH	MOTIF NUMBER	TUBACH
P525.4	2797	Q244.4	1081
P612	4994	Q261.3	cf. 1082
P691	3462	Q261.4	2419
		Q263.1	4684
Q20.5	2370	Q263.5	2534
Q20.6	1202	Q265.3	2859
Q21.0.1	4963	Q272.4	2036
Q21.1	4089, cf. 176	Q272.4.1	5039
Q39.3	1424	Q273.3	2006
Q44.2	cf. 4963	Q273.4	cf. 5031
Q44.5	4950	Q281.1	1442
Q45.1	2533, cf. 3653	Q281.1.2	975, 1440 c)
Q51.3	2714	Q281.5	4254
Q62.1	5269	Q292.1.1	2170
Q86.1	265	Q302.0.1	cf. 3983
Q111.10	cf. 2720, cf. 4611	Q312.4	5233
		Q331.2.1.5	1660
Q121.2	cf. 1785	Q331.2.1.6	2400
Q141.1	766	Q331.2.4	3829
Q147.1	1271	Q331.3	3938
Q172.0.1.3	3797	Q386.1	1429
Q211.0.5	5020	Q393.1	cf. 4706
Q212.5	4782 b)	Q411.17	2799
Q212.6	2636	Q415.8	2103
Q221.3.2	684	Q431.3.1	4994
Q221.3.3	681, 2240	Q436	3211
Q221.3.4	723	Q451.7.5	705
Q221.3.5	2240	Q451.7.6	3983
Q221.3.6	681, 2240	Q469.7	2534
Q221.3.6.1	2240	Q501.9	504
Q221.3.6.2	5152	Q501.10	504
Q221.3.8	773	Q520.5	3670
Q223.1.1	cf. 4138	Q523.7.1	3690
Q223.1.2	cf. 4138	Q552.1.7	3046
Q223.1.3	4138	Q552.1.7.1	2734
Q223.6.1	cf. 4135	Q552.1.8.2	680
Q223.6.1.1	4135	Q552.4.1	4317
Q223.8	3684	Q552.18.4	519 (see Tubach p. 417)
Q223.8.1	3668		
Q223.9.1	1850	Q559.5.1	cf. 648, 1915
Q225	620	Q559.11	2534
Q225.0.1	cf. 620	Q560.2.4	cf. 1188 a) 4
Q227.4	2636	Q560.4	3685
Q227.5	648	Q561.3.1	4216

MOTIF NUMBER	TUBACH	MOTIF NUMBER	TUBACH
Q566.3	2037	T231.6	5262
Q566.4	5027	T251.2	4354
Q569.6	4553	T251.2.3.2	4354
Q570.2	4362	T254.1	cf. 5277
Q578	2534	T254.4	cf. 5277
Q581.1.1	3134	T254.5	cf. 5277
Q586	3488	T254.6	cf. 5277
Q588.1	2001	T255.1	cf. 5285
		T255.1.1	cf. 5285
R11.2.1.2	cf. 1643	T254.5	5277
R11.2.1.3	1442	T310.2	3098
R11.2.3	cf. 2852	T310.3	4656
R81.2	3969	T311.0.2	3176
R111.4.1	3971, cf. 138	T311.0.3	5142
R121.6	2768	T311.3.1	4894
R121.6.3	cf. 2768	T314.1	3436
R121.11	1785	T317.4	1992
R123.1	926	T317.6	3097
R141.2	5247, cf. 2175	T317.10	2569
R152.1	5328	T317.8	2419
R152.1.2	cf. 3811	T327.1	4744 b)
R153.3.1	2005	T331.11	3418
R165	4153	T332.2	cf. 912
R165.2	3796	T333.2	4741
R168.2	cf. 926	T333.4	cf. 3800
R169.6	2209	T333.6	4840
R243.2	4596	T334.1	5366
		T336.3	3419
S11.8	2041	T412.6	2734
S11.9	362	T412.7	4224
S21.7	2001	T417.2	2737
S73.3	cf. 705	T427.1	2037
S74	5020	T452.3	661
S110.0.1	1494	T459	1436
S111.10	cf. 5277	T464	2598
S111.11	cf. 5277	T471.0.5	cf. 1453
S111.12	cf. 5277	T471.0.6	3095
S112.8	3134	T481.9	5246
S113.4	5277	T481.12	cf. 1943
S163.2	cf. 4911	T481.13	cf. 1943
S177	1081	T481.18	4692
S263.2.4	4476	T481.20	4319
		T481.21	3265
T221	775	T481.25	4221

MOTIF NUMBER	TUBACH	MOTIF NUMBER	TUBACH
T495.1	328	U261.1	3378
T495.4	1081	U261.2	4001
T526	971		
T548.1	971	V20.1	cf. 2800, 2804
T574.3	cf. 648, 1915	V21.1.1	cf. 2738
T681.1	4873	V21.2	273
T647.2	cf. 3577	V21.5	1161
		V21.6	1202 a), 4421
U11.2	113	V21.7	cf. 1062
U11.3	223	V21.8	cf. 1501 d)
U15.2	3701	V22.1	1501 c)
U31	5334	V22.2	4076
U31.3	2619	V22.4	1188 a) 4
U31.4	4388	V23.3	2944 c) 1
U45	660	V24.3	4575
U72	3364	V33.1.1	2689
U72.1	2343, 3366	V34.5	2649, cf. 2671
U72.2	2139	V34.6	1270
U119.3	2559	V34.8	2689 c)
U119.4	5016	V34.9	cf. 2654, 2655
U119.7	967	V35.1	2687
U121.1	1311	V41.1	3892
U121.4	500	V41.2	4925
U121.5.1	cf. 500	V41.2.1	cf. 4925
U121.6.1	2611	V41.2.2	cf. 4925
U121.6.2	500	V41.4	3893
U121.7	3283	V41.4.1	926
U122.0.1	cf. 3645	V41.5	4148
U122.1	1309	V42.1	2717
U130.2	3906	V49.2	3228
U130.3.1	101	V51.6	438
U130.4	1828	V52.3	3875
U133.2	3645	V52.10	3893
U135.3	cf. 3652	V52.16	2304
U144	3475	V52.17	3915
U147.1	3774	V52.18	3646
U147.2	554	V52.23	504
U147.3	3059	V57.4	cf. 3885
U162	444	V57.5	971
U182	4789	V57.6	2754
U230.0.1	3324, cf. 3336	V57.7	3424
U233	2559	V57.8	2368
U235	3102, 4053	V85.1	3797
U236.1	2933	V86.1.4	1347

MOTIF NUMBER	TUBACH	MOTIF NUMBER	TUBACH
V111.2	4638	V268.4	4334
V123	2721	V268.4.3	4649
V126.1	1375	V268.4.5	4649
V128.3	5152	V268.8.2	cf. 1054
V142	2029	V276.1	3913
V211.2.1.1	cf. 985	V276.2	5129
V221.6	3796	V278	1424
V222.1.5	2370	V292.3	3851
V222.15	2266	V312.3	2689
V232.1.3	1492	V316.3	5386
V232.3.2	2558	V329	2534
V232.3.3	223	V331.1	1373
V235.3.1	19	V331.1.2	1218
V235.3.2	1468	V331.1.5	3352
V252.6	5115	V331.10.1	1237
V252.4	4672	V345	1760
V252.5	3098	V348	2636
V254.1.1	2235	V352	4560
V254.1.3	cf. 2235	V360.2	2799
V254.3.1	4904	V360.3	2796
V254.7.1	2482	V360.4	cf. 2793
V254.7.3	cf. 430	V363	2041
V254.7.5	438	V364.1	1373
V254.8	1558	V364.2	3471
V255.1	2094	V364.3	2689 b)
V255.2	3218	V385	1008
V255.5	cf. 437	V401	1459
V256.1.1	2488	V411.3	2139
V256.1.4.1	692	V411.5.1	176
V256.3.1	2419	V411.7	cf. 3489
V256.4.2	4632	V412.2	766
V256.5	5139	V412.4	176 a)
V256.6	2139	V416.1	cf. 4963
V261.1	3231	V417.1	4963
V261.3	2734	V423	4088, 519
V261.3.1	cf. 2728, 2729	V424	cf. 5050
V264	1812	V425	168
V264.1	3572	V441	3438
V264.1.2	3573	V461.0.1	4484
V264.2	4925	V461.1	3504
V264.3	5283	V461.6.1	13
V264.3.1	536	V461.7	1961
V264.5	4864	V461.8	4009
V268.3	349	V461.12	381

MOTIF NUMBER	TUBACH	MOTIF NUMBER	TUBACH
V462.1	4372	W154.2.1.1	4262
V462.1.1.1	cf. 3327	W154.4	1701
V462.1.1.2	3323	W154.5.1	2020
V462.12	4736	W156	660
V465.1.1.1	cf. 2569	W156.1	297
V465.1.1.6	3906	W156.2	660
V465.1.2	1436	W158.1	2170
V469	5233	W167.2	cf. 5284, 5285
V469.1	3881	W167.3	cf. 5284, 5285
V477	3336	W171.1.1	501
V477.1	3329	W185.4	252
V478	cf. 5148		
V510.3	5123	X52	1660
V510.5	cf. 4103	X52.1	2400
V510.7	cf. 4235	X315	2991
V511.1.3	3378	X372.6	3530
V511.2.3	1450	X457.2	cf. 2867
V515.4	1218	X457.3	3075
		X501	525
W11.2.1	1459	X502	cf. 3577
W11.2.5	766, 2566	X711.4	5246
W11.3.1	3363	X711.5	632, 3147
W11.3.2	4963	X711.9	4693
W11.17	2796	X711.11	4319
W12.3	cf. 987	X711.12	971
W11.17	2796	X711.13	3265
W16	4484	X742.1	328
W19.1	642	X772	1436
W19.2	551	X802	1808
W26.1	3622	X803	3426
W26.3	252		
W26.5	107	Z11	4310
W26.5.1	114	Z42	3428
W111.2.2	4288	Z43.7	80
W111.2.3	cf. 4288	Z43.7.1	80
W111.2.4	4288	Z43.8	4954
W111.2.5	cf. 4288	Z43.9	223
W125.5.1	969	Z46.1	1705
W128.4	3632	Z106	647
W128.4.2	cf. 3771	Z111.3.1	5082 b)
W151.9.1	4092, 5346	Z121.3	1921
W152.11	4351	Z134	2154
W154.2.1	cf. 4262	Z161.1	4413

ALPHABETICAL INDEX

Abbess: refuses audience to bishop (man) T362.1

Abbot: behaves badly, avoids praise V461.6.1

covers face to hide worldliness J922

devil convinces to change rules G303.2.2, K1811.4.3, V235.3.1

dresses as beggar, avoids vainglory J916

former rich man, grateful he can beg U62.1

gives knight good deeds, rewarded Q42.8.1

lover, leaves dressed as friar K1517.6, T481.19

not to judge lest he be judged J571.6.1

rich in heaven, with poor saints J1263.1.7

steals cucumber, temptation T334.1.4

stone in mouth, three years, silent J1074.1.3

throws footstool at monk U35.4

Abducted woman: Europa by Jupiter in form of bull R39.4

queen, by lover (Helen) R39.5

Virgin aids, dispose of bodies, sails ship V268.4.1

Abduction: sequential; wolf, ape, lions, thieves Z49.2.2

Abstention, prideful: from meat, mocked J1261.12, J1261.13

Abuse: lustful duchess, by conquering army S177, T495.4

from other monks, conquers monk's lust T317.6

Accuser; false: burned at stake H221.6

condemned to death Q263.1

God appears in dream, punishes Q263.3.1

lightning strikes woman Q263.6

Susanna, elders J1153.1, K2112.02

swear by fire, illness, blindness Q263.2

Advanced age: no protection against lust T317.7

Aged: man counsels travelers J151.6

master solves riddle, saves life J151.1.1

monk, in city, fathers child, returns V462.1.1.2

nursemaid teaches temperance J151.5

sleeping with women, ages men most rapidly H659.28

woman protects another from fraud J155.9

Ages: of women Z19.3

Aging: monk falls to knees, ages D1890.0.1

Air-castle: dream of wealth from honey jar J2061.1

woman drops honey jar J2061.3.1

Alchemist: false, needs money to fetch ingredients K1966.2

Alexander: allows criticism patiently W26.5

debates philosophers J1281.5

descends in submarine D1525

disguised, steals host's flatware K354.2

pirate tells him they are both thieves J1289.22, U11.2

raised with rascal J413.2

recipient of gift protests, gift denied J1283.1

returns captive maiden to betrothed P12.9

Alliance: dog and wolf B267.1

sheep and dogs B267.2

Altar cloth: stolen, underclothes, body twisted Q220.4

Amazons: kill male children or give to fathers S12.8

kill male infants or send them away F565.1

kill surviving husbands S61

women create own kingdom F565.1

Ambush: foiled, man stops to pray N699.3.1, V264.2

Angel: appears to hero, predicts victory V510.9

as beggar to saint's house K1811.0.4

as shipwrecked traveler, saint feeds, clothes W12.3.1

bars abbot, for injustice to monk V235.3

called by Virgin, defend town from Moors V249.3

cures gangrenous foot D2161.5.1.1

dark over heads of those to die V235.3.2

disguise shipwreck man, alms V411.11

disguised as beggar, saint shelters V235.4

disguised as guest, host rewarded Q45.1

dying saint to heaven, first to hell V511.2.9

enters prison, frees prisoner R168.2

explains cut off foot, lost money Z43.9

explains heavenly justice V232.3.2

explains unequal fate, evil, holy V232.3.3

explains unjust acts to hermit J225.0.1

fight devils for abbot's soul V232.1.3

goldsmiths, create cross for altar V232.12

helps prince slay evil uncle V232.1.1

helps saint escape from prison V232.8

kills man who is plotting murder J225.4

mortal struggle V230.3

saves man hanging on cliff edge R168.1

says woman not force other to wed V231.5

sends man to champion his mother H927.3

sets task, man to be defender of weak H927.4

teaches work is prayer V232.1.2

tells man devil lied, saves wife V232.11

Anger: cure for paralysis D2161.5.1, F950.2

monk goes to desert to avoid W26.3

monk experiences, alone in desert W26.3

not to act in, asks another to punish servant J21.2.1.1

to reside in face, not heart J153.6

Animal: allows self to be tied to another J2132.5, K713.1.2, K713.1.2.1

attack dying lion W121.2.1

division of, deceptive: lambs, wool; piglets, wool K171.5

mate only for procreation B299.13

said to be born to woman T554.2.1

saved from pit: grateful and ungrateful W154.8

worship infant Jesus B251.1.1, V211.1.8.5

Anointing: restores dying man D1846.4.2

Ant: carries stored grain out to dry J711.5

dispute beauty with flies J242.6

grateful for rescue from drowning B362

helps dove B481.1

predict infant's future wealth B147.3.1.2

rewarded for industry, has food Q86.1

store grain, pigs eat it U31.7

Ant and fly: ant, safe in winter, fly dead J711.1.1

Ant and grasshopper: ant industrious, grasshopper lazy J711.1

Antelopes: horns entangle in trees A2326.3.3.1

Ape: flees with favorite child, caught L146.1

judges dispute of fox and wolf B274.1

kill bird, told them firefly not fire J1064.1

throws away nut, bitter rind J369.2

Ape-mother: her child to win beauty contest H1596.4

Apostate: protects self, sign of the cross V86.1.7

sat on holy vessels, body parts rot
Q551.6.4

stole church goods, punished Q221.9

Apothecary's aide: dirt not medicine, wife
explains T481.26

Appearance: holy man unprepossessing
J260.0.1

Apple, golden: beseiged city surrenders
K2365.2

    prize in beauty contest, judgement of
Paris H1596.1

    saint tosses in poor man's window
R165.1

Apple tree: who will inherit? K171.10

Apprentice: hungry, calls master insane
J1341.5

    unfed, calls employer insane K1265

Arachne: challenges Athena's skill C54.2

Arian: bishop, angel visits in bath, kills
V324.1

    bishop, blasphemy, heavenly fire
strikes Q221.3.11

    king kills insincere convert V324,
V475.6

Aristotle: returns, no study in hell, only
torment E302

    woman humiliates, saddles, rides
K1215, X742.1

Arm: swollen dangerously, Virgin cures
V256.4.5

Armies: miraculously unable to see each
other F1097

Armpits: poison in, kills man Z311.5

Arms, knight's: tunic, fear of God, shield
faith Z100.02

Arrow: deflected: turn back on archer
D2091.11

    in squire's side, Virgin removes
V256.1.7.1

    intercepted by image of Virgin
D2163.3.1

    removed from face by Virgin
D2161.5.2.7

    shot at heaven, returns bloody F1066

    shows lion how terrible man is J32

    wound of not to be cured: pain
strengthens victim spiritually
J893.4

Ascetic: flees house of prideful man

V462.2.4

flees man who speaks to him V462.1

used to fasting, finds it pleasurable
U130.3

Asking: consort not to ask questions
C411.2

    name of husband forbidden C32.2.1

    not to ask why king never laughs
C411.1

    origin of husband forbidden C32.2.2

Ass: animals flee bray, thinks they fear
J953.20

    back marked with cross A2356.2.7

    carries usurer's body to gallows
B151.1.1.2.1

    ceases to long for death, sees drums
of ass skins J217.2

    envies horse's rich life J212.1

    envies pigs, until sees slaughter
J217.3, W128.4.2

    envious of war horse, sees him woun-
ded L452.2

    heart, eyes cure for disease K961

    hurts where wolf doctor touches it
J1432.1

    lion's skin, unmasked when brays
J951.1

    man mounted on, seen before man
K511.1.1

    masters of progressively worse N255.2

    persuades wolf, kill in privacy
K551.29

    tied up outside church, distracts
preacher, he gives it away
V461.12

    without a heart: fox eats it, denies it
to king lion K402.3

Ave: blasphemer paralyzed, except power
to say V254.3.1

    blasphemer regains speech to say
V254.3.2

    child says, swept away, saved
V254.7.4

    devil awaits day man will not say
V254.8

    leaves on grave, Virgin's devotee
V254.7.3

    leper says one thousand, cured
V254.1.4

prayer, protects robber on gallows V254.1.1

saves greedy evil man from demons V254.2.1

saves man dragged by horses V254.1.2

saves robber from executioners V254.1.3

severed head of criminal says V254.7.1

Virgin teaches nun to say V254.7.5

Babel: tower of A1333, C771.1, F772.1

Bailiffs lead thief to gallows; bystander: great thieves lead thief J1374

Baker: king is illegitimate, is son of J1661.1.2.3

son of, Caesar said to be J1281.3.1

threatened to frighten guest P463.2

uses matter from abscess in bread P463.3

Bald man: hits fly, hurts self J2102.3

Baldness: Caesar permits insults about W26.7

Bandits: rob women, fall ill, Virgin cures them V257.3

Banishing: calumniated hero banished Q431.20

Banker: swears falsely about money, saved V252.3

unjust: deceived by false deposits J155.9, K1667

Banquet: enemy drugged, killed K871.1

Baptism: magic cure D2161.4.9

Barber: hired to cut king's throat, withdraws P446.2

king fears, singes own beard P446.2.1

Bare rear parts: to Jesus, punished by paralysis Q221.3.7, Q559.12

Barley: urine-soaked, wife serves husband X711.3

dog urinates on: woman mixes it K267

Barrenness: relieved by prayer D1925.3

Basket: lover suspended in, on tower T495.2

of sand: abbot's sins J80.3.2

Bat: fur, no feathers A2311.11

joins birds, then quadrupeds W171.1.1

joins birds, then quadrupeds in war B261.1

tries to be bird, then quadruped K2031.3

why flies at night A2491.1

why sleeps by day A2491.1.1

Bathe: woman to use only rain water for, punished Q331.5

Bathhouse attendant: perpetual, punishment for sins Q501.9

in hell freed Q578

Battle: losing, leader prays, soldiers win V52.3

lost due to impiety of emperor P555.0.1

to be won by side whose king dies M362, P711.9

won in Christ's name V52.3.1

Beam, for church: extended magically D1713.1

Bear: and wolves, eat sheep of uncharitable monks Q552.18.4, V423

guards holy man's sheep B449.5

tells traveler not to trust guide J1488

uses tail to fish through ice, loses it K1021

Bear's-food: threat to horses C25

Beard: Jew touches dead hero's beard P672.1.5

not to cut until daughter wed M121.2

pulling, insult P672

vow not to cut until exile over M121.1

Beauty: of women Z19.4

Bedchamber: queen's, searched before king enters T172.4

Beds: dream: marital, royal, wealth, dangerous Z105

man rejects three: marriage, wealth, power J347.5

Beehives: from church, stolen, Virgin sends man to find thieves V268.12

stolen from church, Virgin recovers U129.4

Beekeeper: Host, hive, Virgin, Child appear C55.3.1

puts consecrated Host in hive C55.3

Bees: die after stinging A2232.2, A2346.1
  guard Host in hive B259.4
  king of, no stinger, compassionate A2346.3
  make wax for candles in church B259.4.2
  mortal sting denied A2232.2
  predict baby's future eloquence B147.3.1.2
  serve honey to beetles J1565.2, U147.2
  wish for lethal sting, punished J2072.5.2
Beetles (see also Dungbeetles): serve dung to bees J1565.2, U147.2
  treated like oxen, stop at dunghill U122.1
Beggar: ragged, king gives clothes, ride W11.2.3
Beguine: orders blasphemous painting Q221.3.12
Beheaded: prince who raped kinswoman S169.1
Bell: matins, earliest risers to sound J1179.13
  sound, saint prays he alone hears V222.6.2
  toll when saint's soul departs E533.2
Belling the cat: none willing to bell it J671.1
Belly: debates with other members A1391
Best and worst in world, what is: words H659.37
Best character trait: conscience (shame) H659.7.3.1
Best, what is God's: diversity of human visage H648.3
Betrothal: vassal's daughters, king arranges T61.4.6
Betrothed, married woman: flees to convent, admitted V452
Bird: captured, promises counsels M244.3
  carries dupe aloft, drops K1041
  carries serpent, venom drops in milk N332.3
  caught in net K746
  doubt swallow's warning, hemp-seed J1064.2
  misunderstand trapper's tears J869.1

shelter aged parents with wings W19.1
  song of, power to bewitch B39.2
Birth: delay until false accusation denied Q227.5
  prevented until woman confesses slander Q559.5.1
  of hero: anomalous births of animals F960.1.2
    earth trembles F960.1.2
    hail storms F960.1.2
    sea turbulent F960.1.2
    sun darkens F960.1.2
  multiple: result of sexual acts, several men T586.3
    saint's wife has seven babies, all saints T586.1
    seven at one birth, knight's wife T586.1.2
Bishop: accused, cannot utter "Holy Spirit" H253.1
  bad associates: lawyer lost his soul for him, doctor his life J452
  buries sinner in church, dies Q411.16
  devil helps elect, Virgin pardons V261.2
  invited to eat on fast day taunted, curses inviter who dies J1320.0.1
  judged by king from appearance: king learns from error J56.1.1
  magically silences pagan debaters V352
  prayer of: banishes devil as servant G303.16.2.3.8
  responds with meaningful silence J1074.1.4
  takes captive's place V461.0.1, W16
  to die, prayed from tierce to nones Q21.0.2
  trapped in hill of sand: sustained magically by food D1766.1.8.1
Bitch: pleads for use of bed W156.2
Bitterer than bile, what is: bad children H659.34
Blacksmith: neglects religious duty, sees hell V511.2.1.2
  no blame, if tools damage objects J1891.4

Blasphemer: angrily shoots arrow at sky
F1066

carried off by demons Q221.3.10

curses God's eyes, eyes drop out Q221.3.5

doubts Virgin's slipper, deformed Q221.3.9

gambler loses, curses, dies Q221.3.6.1

knife in ground, emerges bloody F1066.1

punished, blood flows from mouth Q221.3.3

right hand cut off, displayed Q221.3.1

rouses king's anger Q221.1

shows buttocks to Jesus Q221.3.7

struck dead, noxious odor issues Q221.3.6

tongue, elongated Q221.3.8

tongue grows: loses speech D2021.2

Blasphemous portrait, Jesus: artist punished Q222.3

Blind: accidentally hurt each other N388

bishop, detects poison wine D1817.0.2

holy man, knows king is king D1820.1.1

husband thinks wife, lover cure X711.13

told hit pig, hit each other K1081

tricked into hitting each other K1081

woman, told sight is occasion of sin J893.1.2

Blindness: cured by fasting, prayer D2161.5.2.8

cured by Jesus D2161.4.9.1

cured by Jesus's saliva D2161.4.9.1

cured by magic spring D2161.3.1

cured by prayer D2161.4.9.1

cured by saint D2161.4.9.2

cured by Virgin Mary's milk D2161.5.2.3

cured, holy man will see heaven better F952.0.3

penitent, punishment remitted Q571

punishment for adultery Q451.7.7

punishment for perjury Q451.7.0.3

twice the punishment for enemy Q451.7.6

Virgin cures, nonbeliever's V256.1.4.5

Virgin cures girl; mother prays V256.1.4.2

Virgin cures monk's V256.1.4.1

Virgin cures scoffers, wife prays V256.1.4.3

Blood: bathe in infants', emperor refuses Q20.3.2, W46.5

flows from blasphemer's mouth Q551.6.5.1

flows from crucifix, conversion V331.1

flows from wounded image of Virgin V128.4

Boat oarless: comes for man, transports him F841.2.8

transports princess to barren land F841.2.9

Body: aged mother's, source of sexual temptation T336.3

ravaged by invisible fire Q551.9.8

Body and blood of Jesus: appear on altar, doubts dispelled V33.1.1

Body and soul: debate E727.1

Bone: diseased, Virgin restores, cures V256.6

from wolf's throat, crane removes W154.3

stuck in throat, man prays, frees V257.2

Book, dedicated to Virgin Mary: has curative powers D1500.0.2

immersed in water, undamaged F930.1

Book of miracles of St. James: does not burn in fire D1841.3.3

Borrower: bread, not returned, box empty when comes for more J1552.5

pledge Virgin, Christ security P525.4

Boulder: Virgin diverts, saves monastery V268.8.3

Boy: killed by father, Virgin revives E121.3.4

sang Gaude Maria, killed, buried V268.1.1

sends thief into well, steals his goods K345.2

Bravery, knight in battle: equals hermit's devout life J234

Bravest know how to wait: third knight waits for attack J571.6.2

Bread: borrowed, not returned; box empty when comes for more J1552.4

made with abscess fluid N383.2.1

magically supplied to monks D1031.1.2

pre-chewed by fox cures mute D2161.3.6

supply inexhaustible D1652.1.1

thrown at beggar, counts as charity M57

to poor, replenish magically Q44.7, V412.1, V412.2

Bread dough: magically replenished V412.3

Breasts: two, to nurse son, daughter A1313.3.4.2

Bride: compares husband's penis unfavorably with ass's J1744.2, X771

false, detected by mother H51.2, K1911.3.7

modest, wears chemise to bed K2052.1

poor, chosen, virtuous choice L213.3

poor, chosen, wealth revealed L213

Bridegroom: celibate, gives bride ring, leaves T315.2

leaves new bride, serve Virgin T376.1

not going to church but Holy Land K475.4

Brigands: disguised as monks, rob kill K2285.0.1

in monks' garb rob travelers K828.4

Brothel: brother changes clothes with sister in, rescue R152.1.1

whore cheats brothel keeper T451.3

Brother: hostile, unite against common danger P251.3.1

impatience of, youth to curb anger at W196.1

and sister: have three offspring, she kills them T415.8

rob graves, keep from starving U25

Bull: divided, lose fight with lion (wolf) J1022

hollow metal, heated, torture tool Q581.1.1

not to fight goat, must fight lion J371.1

tamed cut off horns, more violent J2107

Burdens, two travelers: one adds to burden, dies J557.2

Burial: denied, wind opens church door V222.1.5

Virgin arranges for dissolute monk V255

Burned alive: stepmother, false accuser, rape Q414.0.3.2

Burning: Image of Virgin Mary resists D1841.3.2

Virgin's church, arsonist blinded Q551.8.9

Butcher: kills sheep, they think he will not P448.1

Butterfly: prefers dunghill over flowers U122.0.1

Buttocks: magic watcher D1317.1

mistress's see, servant bares them X592

shown to figure of Jesus by blasphemer Q221.3.7, Q559.12

watchers of lazy slave J1511.9.1

Cabbages: philosopher's, truth-teller to say he wants them J152.19

Caesar: defends soldier in court J1289.21

grateful to old soldier, legal aid W27.3

permits insults, baldness, lineage J1281.1

responds to insult about stature J1281.3

said to be baker's son J1281.3.1

Cake, magic: chewed by fox restores speech D1507.5

Calendar: Caesar adds leap year A1161

Calumniated: wife, saved from burning at stake V252.2.1

Camel: horns denied to A2232.1, J2072.5.1
offers self as sacrifice K962
why has short ears A2232.1, A2325.4

Candle: if cat warm, they are lit W111.2.5
protects against erysipelas D2161.2.4
received in dream, woman holds on wakening D812.8
tipped over, lover leaves in dark T481.15

Candle, magic: dance on altar D1162.2
kept alight by Virgin Mary D1162.4
will not burn for bishop D1162.3.1
Virgin Mary gives to minstrel D1162.3

Cannibalism: courtiers' children served to him by king G61
siege of Jerusalem G72.2.1
siege of Antioch G72.2.2

Canon: magical bird song, paradise V511.1.3

Captive: animal as, plea for liberty, only joking K561.0.2
bird as, buys freedom with counsels K604
bishop as, confirms king's dream of death M341.0.7
freed, crosses river magically R121.6.6
freed, without captors' knowledge R121.6.5
interprets king's dream, freed R121.11
Jew as, freed from prison, converted R121.6.3
kills renegade priest, profane Host Q222.1.1
persuades captor to talk, release it K561.1
prays for release, Virgin frees R123.1
tells captors, mercy brings peace J817

women as, deprived of clothes K2131.7

Carnality: punished with deluge Q243.0.3

Carnivores: do not eat own species B299.1.2

Cart: four wheels of cart riddle H548.2.8
freed from mud, work, prayer V52.18

Castle: at bottom of lake D1131
underwater, knight lured to F721.5

Castration: self, pilgrim, Virgin (Santiago) cures V256.4

Cat: cock pleads, cat eats him anyway U31.1
disguised as monk, catches mouse K1961.7
feigns death, hangs on wall K2061.9
feigns death, to catch mice K1867.1.1
judges sparrow, hare, eats both K815.4.1
kills mouse, eats cheese J2103.1
not to run off, cut ears, burn fur J156.5.2
only trick, climbs tree to safety J1662
truce, cats and mice, cat eats them K815.13
unite in battle with wolf J1025.2
wears monk's garb, catch mouse K1810.2.2

Cave: two exits, large, small, lion trapped K730.3

Celibate: acquiesces to sexual advances J1261.11
closes eyes, when sister visits T331.12
fears seeing mother T331.11
prince falls ill, sexual pressure T338.2
prince, father surrounds with women T338.4
prince, woman tries to seduce T617.4
yells "thief," repels sexual advance T331.9

Cell: monastic, monks learn goodness there V462.1.1.1

Chains, golden: magic changes when melted D1561.2.5

Champion: judicial combat saves woman H218.0.1

knight regains land for women H218.0.1.1

long-lost son saves mother H218.0.2

Charity: harshly given shames recipient V425

Charlemagne: in hell, gave tithes to knights Q554.1.1

Chastity, test of: wife offered fine gifts by other men H479.3

Chasuble: stained with wine, Virgin Mary returns it to white D454.3.1.2

strangles bad priest D1052.2, Q551.8.8

Chest: choice of, jeweled or tarred L211

golden, hold putrefying matter U119.7

lid, falls, breaks miser's neck Q272.2

no gold found, club to beat oneself P236.2

pitch-covered, hold treasure J80.3.2, U119.7

Chick: crested sign of future greatness B147.3.1.4

crested, baby's future power M312.0.2.3

disregards warning, carried off J1054.1

Chicken house: wife hides husband in K1514.1, X711.7

Child: blasphemed, devils carry off P233.16, Q221.3.2

born in answer to prayer T548.1

born seven days after conception F305.4

born with head on backwards T551.2.1

born with two heads, conjoined T551.2

dead four days, Virgin revives E121.3.2.2

dies on pilgrimage, Santiago revives E121.4

harm mother, she curses them S20.3

is mature in seven days F305.4

killed, dismembered, cooked, served S139.7

mother curses, they suffer affliction P232.4

sheltered, death, aging, sadness J147

Child, horse: fall from bridge, Virgin saves V258.1

Childless: couple, pray, have baby D1925.3, E121.4, V57.5

Children, royal: prepared to work J148, J702.2

Choice of gift: royal wife makes bad choice H511.1.3

Choices: money to Church, family, or poor J235

read holy books, give to others, sell J485.1

sins, covetousness, lust, drunkenness J485

Christ: appears in dream, woman touches heart, hand bloody V211.5.2

appears to bishop, rebukes malice V211.2.4

appears, saves saint from demons V211.5.3

as beggar, saint feeds K1811.0.3, W12.3

disguised as leper, saint shelters V211.2.1.1

puts marks of crucifixion on saint V222.17

rebukes, saint's joy over enemy sin V211.5.4

walks on water, saves sinking ship V211.5.5

Christ's name: nonbelievers rendered silent by D1766.7.1.2

Christian: at pagan court, accused of disloyalty V352.2

becomes Arian, to please king, killed Q232.1.1, V324

does not heed Jew's warning, is his right to take his horse J26.1

resist sun worship, defeat foe V353

throat cut, survives until confess N146.1

Christianity: coming of, prophesied M363.1

conversion to caused by:

   appearance of cross and host of angels in dream V331.1.2

   appearance of Host, heretic V331.1.10

   appearance of St. Nicholas V331.1.6

   appearance of Virgin Mary V331.1.11

   goodness of Christian life V331.10.1, V331.10.2

   Jew, dead hero's hand raised V331.1.12

   Jew, freed from jail by Virgin Mary V331.1.8

   miracle of blood from crucifix V331.1

   Muslim slave, freed from slavery by Virgin Mary V331.1.9

   resuscitation of dead son by Virgin Mary V331.1.13

Church: attacked by Moors, Virgin saves V268.3.3

   build it where snows in August V111.5

   built with usurer's money collapses P435.5

   unable to enter, without confession V21.7

   Virgin's church prevents rape T471.0.4

Churchmen: treacherous, pope warned K2284.0.1

Circumcision: erase original sin, mark difference V82

City: going to, occasion of sin V462.1.1.2

   surrenders, shower of golden apples K2365.2

   under siege likened to ascetic and temptation J81.5

Clemency: for thief, good man pleads for W35.5

Cleric: calls on Virgin, dove calms sea V268.4.3.1

   claims passive part in sex act, not sin X741

   damned for disobedience Q235.2

devil as bull attacks, Virgin saves V264

he will imprison devils in flask K1771.10

in tavern, wrongly arrested N347.1

joyful in suffering of enemy V469.1

leaves mistress, enters monastery V276.4

passive in sexual acts, no guilt K2058.4

prays Virgin, save friend from bull V268.6

resume prayers, finish Virgin's robe V276.1

stubs toe, invokes devil C12.4.3

thieves leave in well, Virgin saves S146.1.1

Virgin teaches humility V255.4

Clever slave: answers biblical and classical riddles H566

Climbing ladder: man too lazy to lift foot, falls W111.1.7

Cloak: droplets burn hand of doubter D1053, E368

Cloth: visible only to legitimate children K445, X502

   marked by go-between, adultery K1543

Clothes: brother changes with sister, rescue R152.1.1

   captive women, deprived of K2131.7

   confer invulnerability D1845.2

   emperor's new, invisible, tricksters K445, X502

   exchange, rich man and poor man K527.3.1

   exchanged with prisoner K521.4.1, R152.1

   hair brushed off, lover leaves, noise is cat T481.14

Cloud: blinds enemy D2091.11

Cock: copulation with hen, hermit aroused by T338.3

   killed by captor, pleads usefulness U33

   pleads usefulness to escape cat K561.1.1

   rules many hens, man fails with

one T252.2
sapphire in dunghill J1061.1
serves sexually fifteen hens, man can only serve one wife J133.7
Coffin: cast overboard with money, burial V64.1
Cohabitation with Jewish woman: punished, king loses battle Q243.0.1
Coin: dropped in water, like tranquil heart J81.6
Coma, abbot in: judged in heaven F11.1
Combings: dead lover, turn white, sign sinless T472.3
Compassionate executioner: hides victim in tomb K512.5
leaves baby in care of shepherd K512.0.3
spares king's wife K512.1.1
Conception: climate determines sex of baby T591.0.4
Condemned man: eyes taken out, choose instrument K558
to select hanging tree K558
Confession: written, contrition erases Q20.6
written, tear marks erase sins in confession V21.5
Conqueror: cries, sees conquered lands W46.1.1
cries, sees enemy's severed head W46.1
does not permit enemy to kneel before him W46.1.2
restores defeated enemy's crown W46.1.3
Conspirators: freed from torment, confess V21.0.1
Constantine: cross in sky, in dream V331.1.2
refuses, bathe, blood infants Q20.3.2, W46.5
vision, cross, after baptism V515.4
Consul: invites captive enemy to consult P12.9.1
Contemplative, active: friars, both prayers valued V316.3
Contest: beauty, golden apple prize, judgement of Paris H1596.1
Cook: threatened to frighten guest P463.2

Corpse: brings bad luck, ship at sea N134.2
disinterred spits gold at robbers E235.7
holds sheep robber fast E235.7
magically too heavy to carry D1654.9.1
prostitutes' carried only by them X521
rolls over, makes room in grave Q147.1
usurer, destroys church E171
Corpse of dead hero: leads troops to victory K97.3
punishes disrespect P672.1.5
Corpse uncorrupted: emit sweet fragrance D2167.0.4
flowers issue from mouth D2167.0.2
saint and wife D2167.0.3
tree bears leaves with "Ave" D2167.0.1
Count: wife runs off, he kills both lovers T481.28
Countertask: hold back rivers to drink sea H951.1
Countess: babies to drink only her milk U121.7
Country mouse: chooses poverty with safety J211.2
Courtier: disguised, pilgrim accompany king K1815.3
hears mass, misses ambush V41.2.2
pretends he will join king in retreat J836
slim book, good deeds, big book sins V22.1
uses tale to teach king J817.5
Courtiers malign king: pardoned because were drunk J811.4
Covetous and envious: twice the wish to the enemy J2074
Cow: snake drinks milk from teats B765.4.2
Crab: mother scolds children for gait J1063.1
mother teaches to walk sideways A2441.4.2

squeezes crane's throat, kills K953.3.5

walks sideways, learned from mother U121.1

Crane: bone from wolf's throat W154.3

carries fish to new lake, eats them J657.3, K815.14

love each other, have laws B773.1.1

serves food to fox in bottle J1565.1

united defeat all enemies J1025.1

Cricket: caught among locusts J451.2.1

Crocodiles: spare obedient monk crossing stream W31.1

Crop division, deceptive: above, below ground K171.1

tree roots, and leaves K171.1

Crop, wheat, divided: trickster covers smaller share K171.0.3

Crops: burned, holy man accepts patiently N252.2

destroyed, holy man accepts W26.4

Cross: arms crossed save victim D1719.6.3

silences magic skull D1719.6.1

Cross, angels: appear, convert emperor V331.1.2

Cross, sign of: bishop's ruddy face cleared D1766.6.4.3

poisoned wine rendered safe D1766.6.4.1

Cross, wood of: David's sling D1719.6.2

Moses's rod D1719.6

Crow: advises eagle to drop shells B321

advises eagle to drop snail, shell breaks J132.1

afraid of dog, sits on sheep W121.2.3

battered, bloody will serve owls K477.4

bird of ill omen B147.2.2.1

care for aged parents B773.5

cure eagle's eyes, onion juice K1955.2.2

drops necklace in snake's hole K401.2.2, K2155.5

drops pebbles in water jug, level rises J101

evil by nature, rides on sheep U120.1.1

imitates partridge's walk J512.6

in peacock's feathers unmasked J951.2

infiltrates enemy camp, spy A2494.13.14, B261.1, K477.4, K2042

pretends to cure eagle, blinds it K1011

rides on sheep, sheep helpless U31.2

seen on left bad omen B147.2.2.1.1

tells eagle to drop snail, crow eats it J758.4

two, good omen B147.2.1.1

Crow (hawk, falcon): song for safety of dove's chicks U31.4

Crow's egg: stork's nest, accused of adultery K2105

stork's nest, stork punished T647.1

Crown: refused, brings excessive cares J347.2, J347.2.1

Crucified: philosopher, can die in air or on earth J1289.27

Crucifix: bleeds when stabbed D1622.4

bleeds when stomped D1500.1.7.3.5

Cup, placed in sack: proof of theft H151.4

Cure: anger cures paralysis D2161.5.1

baptism D2161.4.9

bread chewed by fox restores voice Q94.1

for blindness in magic spring D2161.3.1

magic spring water, blindness Q94.1

marriage cures lovesickness F950.8.1

Cure, marvelous: absent treatment by holy man D2161.2.5

holy man cures at distance F950.7.1

Jesus cures woman at a distance F950.7

Curlew: heron, feed mate fish with stick in it K813.3

leads lover to ambush and death
K813.1

Curse: lifted by prayer, penitence M423.1

Curse on land: man cultivated church
land, cursed M474

Cut-off nose: dupe thinks he cut off wife's
nose K1512

man believes miraculous restoration X711.1

wives of barber, carpenter T481.10

Dancers: cursed to dance until released
C94.1.1, D2174

Daughter: abused mother, soul tormented
P232.3, P232.5, S21.8

helps kill father, promise to marry
T55.1.3

mother curses, saint cures
Q281.1.2

saves father from attacker P234.5

saves father from death sentence
P234.6

suckles imprisoned parent P234.3

suffocates father, installs lover S22.4

ungrateful, devils torment Q281.1

Daughter-in-law: deserted, stays with husband's family P266

Daughters: treacherous, afflicted with illness K2214.1

Daw: imitates eagle, fails J512.16

Deacon: abducted by enemies R39.1

renounces vows, Arian king kills
V475.6

Deacon, confession of: power to relieve
drought V24.2

Dead: give responses to prayer for dead
E499.7

grateful for good priest's prayers
E481.1.4

rise grateful for holy water, prayer
E499

Dead abbot and monks: punish cellarer
for alms not given E425.2.3

Dead apostate's hand: swells, points to
heaven in defeat E369

Dead brother: returns to do penance
E325

returns, saved by pilgrimage
E326.1

Dead canon: asks canons to pray for him
E411.12

Dead cleric: returns, insincere prayers of
no use E301.7

returns, masses not paid for
E415.3.1

returns, scholar saved, bishop not
E301.2

Dead knight: friend to make amends for
his sin E411.11

Dead man: penance completed by friend
E412.2

returns, chains are his debts
E415.3.1

returns, stolen goods, be returned
E415.3.1

Dead monk: brothers must give goods to
poor E415.2.2

returns grateful for masses E301.6

returns to ask brothers for prayers
E301.2

returns to restore shoes to owner
E301.3

returns to warn against pride
E301.5

returns, tells friend of salvation
E301.1

returns, tells how Virgin saved him
E366

returns, twisted, demons torment
him E366

Dead mother: returns, covered with fiery
snakes E323.9

returns, grateful for son's prayers
E323

returns, tells hell's pain, heaven's
joy E323.4

Dead nun: abbess, nuns complete her
penance E412.2

Dead pilgrim: returns, warns that their
lord to die E301.8

Dead prior: returns to tell of torment
E243

Dead pupil: returns, tells master studies
are futile E368

Dead scholar: in hell for vainglory, greed,
lust E412.8

Dead sister: returns grateful for saint's
prayers E325

Dead son: commended to Virgin, revived E121.3.5.1

Dead thief: returns to do penance thirty days E411.0.2.1

Dead usurer: restless in grave in church E411.4

returns from grave, attacks monks E411.4.1

Dead woman: returns, asks lover for masses E312

returns, condemned to comb forever E301.10

returns, confesses character flaw E365

returns, grateful for prayers E361.4

returns, offended mother in past E365.0.1

Deaf, mute: Virgin cures V256.1.4

Death: bishop's foretold M341.1

by burning if testimony is false S112

dragging by asses, humiliation Q499.2.3

God tells deacon bishop to die M341.1.1.1

human figure leads worldly dance Z111.7

monk names those to die M341.0.4

seen as composite beast Z11.3.1

sentences, king revokes all W46.4

Death predicted: abbot and pupil die at same time E765.4.3.2

Death, respite from beating: beat ass when dead, skin is drum W128.4.1

Debate: belly and other members A1391, J461.1

body and soul E727.1

cat, cock, usefulness K561.1.1

Christian, Jewish scholars V351.1.2

hear masses, hear sermons J466.3

simple bishop, pagan philosopher V351

Debate, which saint is greater: saints, in dream, urge peace J466.2

Debt not owed, better to pay: than to suffer dishonor J221.3

Deer: freed from net by friends B545.1

unite, safe from hunters J1025.4

Demands: excessive to prevent marriage

H301

Demon: carry off robber's soul E121.3.6

dwell in pagan idols G303.16.8.2

flee at hearing Jesus's name G303.16.8.1

leave at Virgin's command G303.16.8.3

monk, knight's wife run off, Virgin saves G303.16.1.1

tricked into losing power D630.1.1.1

Deny: Trinity, punished, three mortal blows from angel Q551.9.5

Virgin, punished, internal bleeding Q551.9.4

Depraved sexual acts: dying man punished Q243.7

Desecration, image of Christ: mob storms rabbi's house Q222.2

Destiny: better than work, intelligence, charm N142

Devil: appears to dying man G303.6.2.8;

as angel: abbot to revise rules G303.3.2.2

monk to fast nine days G303.3.2.6

tells abbot change rule V235.3.1

visits abbot, strife K1811.4.3

as: bull to drunken cleric G303.3.3.1.4

as: Christ, imposture detected G303.3.2.1

as hermit's childhood love G303.3.1.12.3

as incubus exorcised G303.16.5.4

as Jew, wants cleric to renege G303.3.1.15

as monkey, will steal money G303.3.3.2.7

as old woman, monk to leave G303.3.1.12.4

as pagan god G303.9.4.12

as spider, bites woman G303.3.2.11

as victualler, tempts monks G303.9.4.11

bishop to renege for new post G303.9.4.8.1

carry off: abusive daughter R11.2.1.3

    evil emperor R11.2.1.1

    evil judge R11.2.3

cast out of calumniator E728.1.2

cause injuries at mock battle D2163.3.1.1

dead son, endangers mother G303.3.1.16

defeated by bishop riddler G303.16.1.4

defeated by sinner's confession G303.16.9

deny delay to miser, carry him off R11.2.1.2

disguised as gentleman G303.3.1.3

disguised as raffish traveler G303.3.1.3.1

distressed woman, shelter G303.1.12.3.1

dying man, pleads for time G303.6.2.8.1

grateful, churchmen send sinners J1263.1.6

haunts house, exorcised G303.15.3

in brothel, fights monk reformer G303.3.1.31

induces bishop and nun to sin G303.9.4.4

laughs when other falls in mud G303.6.1.8

magician promises wealth G303.3.1.26

magician, Moors taught him G303.3.1.26

makes offer for man's soul G303.3.1.3.1

man must be his vassal G303.9.4.8.2

neighbors who come to dine G303.1.17

pact with, returned to signer, saved M211, V264.1

paralytic's prayer vanquishes G303.16.5.5

pilgrim attacks asceticism G303.3.1.28

pilgrim, charity over asceticism G303.3.1.28

pulls scaffold away from painter P482.1.1

putrid odor of G303.4.8.1

rides on woman's long skirt, falls off, other devils laugh Q331.2.1.5

seductive woman with bishop G303.3.1.3.1

sends old woman, for discord G303.10.5

sends snake to tempt humans G303.10.20

take cleric's hoarded fortune G303.16.1.2

tells monk fast nine days, almost dies K824.2

tempts youth to deny Christ G303.9.4.8.11

tricks hermit into killing father K943

unable to name wife's lover who confessed V20.1

unable to record names of all who misbehave in church G303.24.1.4.1

unbearably hideous G303.3.0.1

with herd of boars attacks G303.3.1.29

Devil as false priest: accuses woman of incest G303.3.1.30

Devil begs for apple: cannot utter "charity," flees G303.16.19.21

Devil changes form: bull, hairy savage, lion G303.3.5.4

    hairy, huge teeth, fiery nostrils G303.3.0.2

    lion, bear, basilisk, griffin G303.3.5.5

Devil defeated: by simple friar's prayers G303.16.2.3.6

    cannot go where monk prays G303.16.2.3.7

    chased away by holy man G303.16.15.2

    cheated of promised soul K218.4

    confession protects against G303.16.9

    vanquished by sign of cross G303.16.3.4.1

vanquished when Host passes
G303.16.5.3

Devil disputes saint: saint wins for humility G303.16.11.5

Devil gets woman's ring: uses it to accuse her G303.9.4.3.1

Devil has monk's soul: monk's penance, soul returns G303.16.15.1

Devil in church: frustrated by length of list G303.24.1.4.1

thrown out by holy man G303.24.1.10

writes names of misbehavers G303.24.1.3

writes names of sleepers G303.24.1.7

Devil reigns in parts of monastery: cannot enter chapter G303.25.3.3

Devils attack fleeing monks: Virgin protects them G303.16.8.4

Devils attack witch's grave: capture her soul G303.25.20

Devils in monastery: do mischief among monks G303.25.3.4

prefer it because sinners resist G303.25.3.1

Dice game: won by saint D1713.4

Die, broken: saves gambler's soul N1.2.1

Virgin helps gambler win N.1.2.1.1

Disease: remitted when persecution ceases Q570.2

Disguise: in clothes of other sex K521.4.1

lover as priest to escape husband K521.6

to enter enemy's castle K2357

wolf changes voice to fool kids K1832

Disputation: pride in, punished in hell W159.4

Distance: earth to heaven, devil knows H682.1.10

Doctor (*see also* Physician): hot onion cures foot, cures eye P466

poisons princess, to drink poison too K824

same remedy, sore eye, sore foot X372.6

Doe: raises abandoned babies B535.0.16

Dog: accuses sheep of theft of bread K1290

begs at table, indifferent elsewhere K2094.1

chooses safety over thief's reward J211.3

eats kill first, crow eats remains A2545.3.1

friendly at home, fierce on street K2031.1

gives bitch bed, she drives him away U45

keeps master's body afloat B299.13

proud of its clog J953.1

saves child, killed in error B331.2

says sheep stole bread U31.1.1

takes food to imprisoned master B301.1.1.1

tricked by wolves K815.3

Dog, sent out, called in: paws wet, rains, paws dry not W111.2.4

Dog, testament of: given Christian burial J1607

Donkey: given to poor, distracts priest J352.2

Doors: church, sinner may not pass through C611.1.2

church, Virgin opens for worshiper V268.10

shatter, pilgrims may enter D1557.1

Doubting monk: sees Virgin in dream V510.7

Dove: elect hawk as their king J643.2.1, K815.8

flies out of dying monk's mouth V345.1

flies out of sinful monk's mouth V345

grateful for rescue from drowning B362

have king B242.2.2

lead man to treasure B558.1

not to throw chicks to fox K601.3

not to throw fledglings to fox, fox to climb to get them J21.54

trained to eat grain, prophet's ear K1962.1

Dove's family killed: builds nest in same place J16

Dovecote: husband hides in, wife with lover T481.11

Downfall of emperor: persecutes Christians, will die M342.1.3

Downfall of king: dream interpreted falsely M342.1.1

philosopher knows M342.1

Dragon: guards hermit's food B11.6.5

holds victim down with tail B11.10.4

rescued, breaks promise, returned M205.5

Dragon's blood: causes leprosy B11.2.13.1

venomous B11.2.13.1

Dream: angel advises in D1814.2.1

angel predicts future victories M312.10

baby girl, found royal line M312.0.4.1

baby, drink only mother's milk M312.0.4.1

bishop's death fulfilled M370.2

captive interprets D1812.3.3.0.4

deacon sees bishop's death D1812.3.3.12

enemies will attack duke M342.1.2

false interpretation D1712.4.1.1

father sees infant's future D1812.3.3.8.1

hermit's, knight to be king M314.5

Jesus appears D1813.5

king judged in J157.4

king will be assassinated M342.3

king's, interpreted by bishop D1712.3

knight's, conquer territory M314.6

lineage to free Holy Land M312.0.4.2

pope's death fulfilled M370.3

pregnant woman, son's greatness M312.0.4

pregnant woman's D1812.3.3.8

re-interpreted J1528.1

son will avenge Christ's death M312.0.4.3

son will kill father M312.0.4.4

sun's rays from wife's womb Z106

Virgin shows hell's torments V511.2.8

warns of danger D1813.1.3.1

women beat author for misogyny Q396

Dream beasts attack: interpreted, enemy will come H617.1

Dream bread: rustic tricks townsmen K444

Dream of birds of prey: must hunt usurers D1814.2.2

Dream vision: hero will defeat enemy when dead V510.10

Dream, holy city encircled by entrails: interpret: lineage will be honored H617.2

Dreamer: offered price for sheep, wants more J1473.1

Drop of honey: causes chain of events Z43.7.1

Dropsy: woman devotee's, Virgin cures V256.4.4

Drover: leaves wounded bull to die K2255.3

Drowned: man, prayed to Virgin, revives him V268.2

man, Virgin resuscitates V256.5.1

wife, sack in sea, Virgin saves V256.5.1.1

Drowned child: on pilgrimage, Virgin revives E121.3.5

Drowned girl child: Virgin revives during funeral E121.3.1

Drowning: husband, kicks wife into river S113.3

image of Virgin Mary resists D1841.4.6

man, without confession, revived V251.1.1

monk, Virgin saves soul of V256.5

Drowning man: saved by Santiago's name D1766.7.1.2

Drowning woman: prays to Virgin, is saved D1841.4.7

Drum: makes noise in wind, is empty J262.1

Drunk: unable to speak to confessor, dies X802

Drunkard sees double: sees four children, kills wife J1623.1

Drunkard's wife to undergo ordeal: he must hand wife red-hot iron J1623.2

Drunken taunt: punished, man dies J1320.0.1

Drunkenness: leads hermit to covetousness, lust J485

sin of monk in hell V511.2.1.1

Duchess: abused, impaled vaginally S177

handed over to common soldiers T495.4

Duke: sacrifices self to win battle P711.9

Dungbeetle (*see also Beetle*): defeats eagle L315.7

destroy eagle's eggs A2431.3.9

Dwarf: Caesar called, replies he needs stilts J1281.3

king called, by enemies, not by own people W26.7.4

Dying man: prays for good end, not cure J893.5

refuses Host, goes to hell V39.8

Dying monk: knows who will die M341.0.5

Eagle: arrow from own feathers kills U161

brings fish to saint B469.11

do not nest, dungbeetle season A2431.3.9

drops official's ring in slave's lap N352.1.1

drops tortoise and kills it J657.2

flies close to sun, is consumed B32.2

king of birds B242.1.1

lays eggs, Zeus's lap, beetles shake L315.7

leads rescuer to treasure B361

not carry heron over sea; they foul U130.4

threatens falcon who caught heron L315.9

Earth: rejects body, Host applied, accepts V34.6

Earthen pot: river can destroy J1476.1

Eel: opens clams with pebble B749

Elders: try, fail, create discord, monastery V461.10

Election: king of birds B236.1.1

Emetic: detects theft of food J1144.1

Emissary: killed in place of intended victim N341

Emperor: answers, born to rule, not fight J1281.3.2, W26.7.3

aspire be gods, live like sinners L420.0.2

daily gifts to courtiers, subjects W11.2.1

descends to sea floor, glass barrel P15.1.3

elected, to choose stone for tomb J914.5

forgave enemies, ruled in peace Q20.3

gives son to woman, son died P233.2.2

in boiling oil in hell for murders Q211.0.3

insists on own divinity V205.2

never laughs, punishes questioners C951, F591.1

offspring to be trained to rule J148

orders death of 7,000 citizens S110.0.1

pardons defeated foe P15.1.3

refuses cure, bathe in infant blood Q20.3.2

rewarded, treasure under floor Q44.5

shows faith in physician friend P317.1.1

trapped in mine, wife's prayers sustain V41.1

Emperor's new clothes: invisible, tricksters K445, X502

Employer: falsely called insane K1265

says her buttocks have eyes to check on work D1317.1, J1511.9.1, X592

Empress: defeated, turns over wealth U35.3

falsely accused of infidelity, saved V252.3.1

Jerusalem, seeks true cross V85.5

orders son's eyes put out P231.4.1

Enchanted pear tree: blind husband, lovers in tree, cured K1518

Enemy: carries off deacon, will kill him
R39.1

lured by banquet, ambushed
K2365.4

make peace in order to rule jointly
J218.2

of Christians defeated, son killed
L416.3

overcome, banquet, doctored wine
K871.1

persuaded by show of wealth
K2365.3

Enemy brothers: unite, fight common enemy J624.3

English, short-lived: drink excessively
J1320.0.1

Englishman: in France drunk, cannot
speak X801

Enmity: carnivores and herbivores
A2494.7.4

falcon and kite A2494.13.13.1

falcon and nightingale
A2494.13.13

lion and leopard A2494.12.2

mongoose and snake A2494.12.2

monkey and lion A2494.7.1

owls and crows A2494.13.14,
B261.1. K477.4, K2042

Entrails: twisted from body, to punish
heresy Q469.7

Entry into enemy's camp: pretending mistreatment in own K477.4

Erysipelas: devotees', Virgin cures
V256.6.1

magic candle protects against
D2161.24

punishment for desecrating church
Q222.5

usurer's heirs subject to P435.9

Escape: invader convinced he would suffer K574

substitute sand for treasure
K525.11

Evil and Good: share wife, upper and
lower parts K1635, Z121.3

Evil rich man: bury with honors, lion eats
hermit U11.3

Evil spirit: expelled from bishop's enemy
E728.1

Evil thoughts, inability to hinder: bare
chest, wind, inability to hinder
J80.3.1

Excommunicated person: association with,
punished by death Q436.1

bones restless in grave E411.12

grave filled with foul boiling water
E411.0.2.3

helped to restore self V251.3

Excreta: why humans look at A1599.4.1

Execution: cancelled R176.1

escaped by false confession J1189.5

three knights K512.5

Executioner: arm frozen in mid-air
D2072.0.1, R176.1

has sex with hanged woman
T466.1

spares wife and princelings
K512.0.1.1

spares woman K512.0.1.2

unable to kill innocent woman
H215

Executor of will: does not pay masses for
dead Q272.5

Executors, usurer's will: no restitution, afflicted with illness Q551.9.9

Expenses, royal: exceed income J342.2

Eye to the one-eyed person: remove remaining eye to match J1512.2

Eyes: fall out, punishes blasphemy
Q451.7.0.4, Q551.6.5.2

gouged out as punishment
Q451.7.5

mother orders son's eyes put out
Q451.7.8

removal of, cure for headache
K1011.1

remove to repress lust T317.12

sent to king who admired them
T327

wife removes one to match husband's loss T215

Eyes torn out: magically replaced
D2161.3.1.1

Face: woman disfigures, saves self from
king T327.8.1

youth disfigures, to avoid temptation T333.3

Fairy gift: cloak protects from fear and
  sloth F312.1

  tunic protects against evil-doing
  F312.1

Falcon: attacks threatening eagle, wins
  L315.9

  dies, wax figure, Virgin revives
  E169

  eats chicks, hunters catch L302

  leaves hunter's hand, strangles
  B331.1.2

Falcon lost: found miraculously
  D1816.2.2

Fall: great height, Virgin saves woman
  V268.7

Farmer: enemies wound, Virgin saves
  V264.6

  raises knife to God, falls, kills
  Q558.4.1

Fast, failure to: devils, flames torment sinner Q223.9.1.1

  dragon carries off sinner Q223.9.1

Fasting: excessive, kills devotee of Virgin
  J557.2

  represses lust T317.4

Fasts fifteen days: too lazy to eat, table of
  food W111.1.3.1

Father: chooses husband for daughter
  J482.2.2

  dies instead of son P233.12

  dismembers child, over depravity
  S11.3.10

  dying overhears children's greed
  P236.8

  kills three children, over depravity
  S11.3.9

  kills daughter, save from tyrant
  T314.1

  lets son play in river, both drown
  P233.16.1

  seeks to corrupt son, son leaves
  S11.9

  sees bad sons die, he dies Q586.1

  tests son's loyalty H1569.04

  throws infant across stream P234.4

  tries to marry daughter T411.1

  weds daughter to man who provides T69.6

Father and son captured: one must die,

father dies R153.3

Father of slain son: forgives killer, asked
  by pope V441.2

Father, Jewish: kills son who sang "Gaude
  Maria" E121.3.4

  Jewish, puts son in oven S11.8

Father's advice: find treasure, dig soil in
  vineyard J154

  in form of sententiae J1540.2

  weed small patch every day J154.2

Faults: emperor acknowledges patiently
  W26.7.3

Favorite: accused of disloyalty by courtiers
  K2141.1

  to accompany king in retirement
  J1634

Feast day: leatherworker, sews, needle in
  throat Q223.1.3

  man uses sickle on D1206.1.1

  woman works, right arm afflicted
  Q223.1.2

February: number of days, Caesar determines A1161

Feet: self-severed, Virgin restores V256.4.1

  twisted, turn to rear, Virgin cures
  V256.1.5.4

Fields: set afire, owners burned to death
  K812.2

Fight: between sailors, Virgin intervenes
  V268.11

File: thought to be food J1772.15

Fingers: knuckles guide to prayers V52.7

Fire: chapel, statue Virgin, unharmed
  V268.8.1

  church, image Virgin, Child, safe
  V268.8

  church, Virgin's relics unharmed
  V268.8.2

  kindled magically D2158.1

  priest's throat, raped goddaughter
  V465.1.1.5

  Virgin's veil extinguishes D2158.2

Firefly: thought to be fire J1761.3

Firewood, magic: bleeds when cut D1298

Fish: caught magically D2156.12

  keep little one in net J321.2

  swallows hook, is caught K746.1

Fish for royal guests: Virgin Mary supplies
  magically D1032.1.1

Fisherman: fails to make fish dance to flute J1909.1

goods to shipwrecked sailor, reward Q45.0.1

Five: magic number, five joys D1273.1.2.1

magic number, five wounds D1273.1.2.2

Five-fold death: prince cannot avoid M341.2.4

Flatterer: punished, beheaded Q393.4

reply to, "This arrow wound proves I am mortal" J1281.8

Flea: bites, it is its nature J1179.5.1, K551.30, U120.1

thinks it controls camel J953.10.1.1

Flesh of child: eaten by starving mother G72.2.1

Flesh of children: king serves to father G61

Flies and stinging insects: afflict enemy D2163.5.4

Flies have eyes: only blind humans have soul's eyes J893.1

Flies, sated preferred: over hungry ones J215.1

Flight to heaven: eagles pull vehicle, punished L421

Floating in river: man too lazy to drink W111.1.5

Flood: as punishment, Neptune, Athens A1018.4

escape in boat (ark) A1021

Neptune punishes Athens A163.2

world without kings punished A1018.5

Flood dried: bishop's prayers protect city D2151.9

Flood waters: church saved from by prayer D2143.1.3.1

Flower grows from mouth of dead: Virgin causes, grave discovered V255.1

Flute, extra hole in: valued more than mosque J372

Fly: bite, create filth, make noise A2522.8

dispute beauty with ants J242.6

excommunicated D1443.2

on heretic's head J2102.3.1, N333.1

threatens to bite mule, mule scorns J953.19

Flying tower: touches neither earth nor sky F772.2.6

Food: Christ's wounds sweeten D1039.3

generous man's supply replenished V331.1.11

humble, chosen over rich fare J245.2.1

supplied magically D2105.2.1

Fool: passes as wise, remains silent N685

Foot severed: restored by Virgin Mary D2161.5.2.4.2, D2161.5.2.4.8

Fornicating priest: disables power of holy water V132.2.2

Fortuna: personified as goddess N111

personified as beautiful equestrian Z134

Fox: bears tail's weight, will not share it W156.1

betrays wolf to eat his stores J1521.1.1, Q277.1

blames thornbush for injury J656.1

burns tree with eagle's nest L315.3

feigns illness, enters roost K828.2

grapes, out of reach, they are sour J871

great fox, squire lies, changes tale in fear X904.2.1

laps blood shed by goats, is killed J655.3

lures wolf into well K810.1.2

meal to stork, flat dish W158.1

plays dead to trap prey A2466.3

punished for inhospitality Q292.1.1

rescued from well, wolf trapped R141.2

serves crane food in flat dish J1565.1

sheds coat but not heart J1281.3.3

tail not to be shared with ape J341.1

tails tied together, set afire, destroy enemy K2351.1

tells lion, wolf skin is remedy K810.1

tracks going in lion's den, none exit J644.1

tricks: bear, fish with tale in ice K1021

bird, head under wing K815.20

cock to receive kiss of peace K721.2

wolf into nearing ass's hoof K1075.1

wears sheepskin, enters fold K828.1

Fox plays dead: does not permit removal of heart J351.2

Fox, and wolf: well, fox ascends, wolf descends K651

Fox, cock: gnaws trunk, cock descends tree K815.21

Friar: critic, idolatry, bad luck rest of life Q220.3

hid bread, ate secretly, confesses V21.4

prayers, without understanding V52.19

promises rain to flock if they pray D2143.1.3.1

replaces goods stolen by other friar W11.18

to desert, returns starving, bitten V316.3.1

Friar leaves monastery to control anger: alone, he is angered filling jug J28

Friar scorns garden work: waits hungrily in cell J215.4.1

Friends: offer to die for each other P315

Friendship: mouse and dove A2493.36

test of H1558.1, H1558.1.1, H1558.2, H1558.2.1, H1558.11

Frog: demand a live king from Jupiter J643.1

fear increase of sun's power J613.1

inflates self, bursts J955.1

physician, unable to cure self J1062.1

tries to be physician J952.6, K1955.0.4

Fugitive: husband believes lover is X711.10

Future: foretold by queen D1712.4

Gallows: robber on, supported by Virgin V254.1.1

youth, supported by Santiago V221.6

Gambler: blasphemes, tongue grows N9.2

calls profanely on God's eyes C94.4.1

curses Virgin Mary C94.1.4

cuts out own tongue, Virgin Mary restores it D2161.3.6.1

lost, threw stone at Virgin Q221.3.6.2

Gardener: punished, criticized God's weather Q312.4

Garland of roses: magically protects knight D2163.3.1.1

Garment for Virgin Mary: woven by prayer D1766.1.3

Gem: bird says she has precious gem in body J21.12

merchant hires artisan to polish gemstone J1522.3

Genesis: story prophesied by pagan M364.7.2.1

Genitals: cut off by wife for adultery Q451.10

woman's, magically re-light fires D2158.1, Q492, T494.5

Ghost: attack bishop, defend good priest E243

kills evil person who mocked it E235.1

returns, lover say mass, carnal sins T472.2

Ghost, pope: kills evil successor Q551.9.7

Giant: small hero defeats (Goliath) L311

Gift: cardinal refuses, maintains liberty W35.4

good, better, much better W154.20

magical, fairy gives hero, exchange for love F302.3

recipient protests unworthiness, gift denied J1283.1

Girl: age four, fully grown, articulate T591.0.3

bleeding from eyes, Virgin revives E121.3.8

Virgin promise heaven, no dancing V278

Give and you shall be given: punning J1262.3.1

Glass: breaks, spills poison, sign of cross V86.1.5

Glass, magic: from shrine cures sufferer D1171.6.5

Gloves and ring received in dream: sent for as proof D812.16

Gluttons: floor gives way, they fall Q599.2.1

Gluttony: monk prays, resists temptation V52.16

    monk's, Virgin reproaches V255.4.1

Go-between: creates discord, husband, wife T452.5

    makes love with client's love T51.1.2

    marked cloth, client, wife husband T481.23

    says puppy is woman who refused lover T452.3

    tells maiden sex act at night unseen T459

    tells nun God cannot see in dark V465.1.2

    tells wife, wear lover's slippers K1584.1

    tells woman sex will solve problems T452.4

    tells woman, don magic slippers T481.27

    tricks maiden into sex with client J1745.1.1

    used repeatedly by failed lover T452.6

Goat: claims holiness, hair for hair shirt A2311.10

    kept as pet, runs off B575.2.1

    raised in house, runs to wild goats U122.2

    thinks able to fight wolf L461.1

    Virgin sends to monastery for milk V262.1

Goat, largest description of: all rope cannot hold it; eagles see K171.11

Goats shed blood in fight: fox laps up blood, killed by goats J624.1

Goblet: planted in luggage, accuse theft K2155

God: abducts princess, rapes her R39.2

bad, good beasts created by J1262.6

disguised as pilgrim sees theft of pig D1817.0.1.7

voice heard A139.6.1

Goddaughter: has sex with godfather, three children T427

Gold: found, hidden, burned, in fish, return Z43.8

    thrown in sea, before it drowns owner U72.1

Gold statue: reward to one who finds treasure Q111.10

Golden eggs: kill hen, get them all at once J2129.3

Good counsels bought: different prices J163.4

Good deed: boasts of, man damned Q331.2.5

    reward for, lions spare life Q151.11

Goose: crow tries to teach to fly J1849.6

    golden egg D876

Grain: trickster covers partner's share K1712.1

Grain to poor, promised: God to extinguish fire, promise broken M242.4

Grateful: man, he does not resemble toad W27.1

Grave: cursed woman's, severed arm thrust out E411.0.6.1

    dead child's, hidden in stable E410.3

    flowering plant, leaves "ave" E631.0.2

    opens, sinner's body thrust out E411.0.2.3

    priestly sex abuser's, burns E411.0.9.1

    rich man's, demons drag to unblessed ground E411.0.2

    room in promised, body turns, makes room M251.1

    sinner's, malodorous E721.0.2

    sinner's speaks, says "I am burning" E411.0.6.1

Grave, golden: sages see, power no longer matters L413

Greeks and Romans: disputation by signs H607.1

Griffins: pull chariot through air B552.1

Guest: drinks foul water, at dinner vomits P324.2.1

    eat meat during Lent to please host P324.5

    leaves plate empty, bones on other guest's J1511.21

Hag: appears to fasting youth, is lust T617.0.1

Hailstorm: Virgin Mary protects vineyard D2143.4.2

Hair: burned to prevent witchcraft D2176.5

    fleeing man's, caught on tree limb K747

    not to cut until daughter wed M121.2

    queen not to bind until victory M122

Hair burning: banishes evil ghost E425.2.3

Hair combings: turn white D1310.4.4

Half-friend, father has: son has hundreds J410.0.2

Hand: self-severed, Virgin restores V256.3.1

    severed for treachery Q451.1

    severed, replaced magically D2161.3.2

    severed, restored by Virgin Mary D2161.5.2.4.1, D2161.5.2.4.5

    severed, saint's restored V256.3

    withers, punishes broken oath Q559.5.2

Hands and eyes: restored by Virgin Mary D2161.5.2.4.3

Handsome: youth malodorous like rotting corpse U119.3

Hangman: sex with body of hanged woman Q244.5

Hare: frogs are more timid than they J881.1

    race with wolf K264.3

    shows lion its reflection, lion afraid K1715.1

    tells elephants moon is angry K1716

Hawk: breaks promise, caught by hunters Q260

eats nightingale chicks, caught J651.1.1, M205.4

    magically catches all prey B172.5.1

Head: pagan's, soul is in hell E411

    severed, as trophies S139.2.2.1

    severed, enemy's in wineskin S169.4

    severed, Pompey's, Caesar weeps S169.2

    severed, rapist's, to husband S169.5

    severed, repeats "Ave Maria" V254.7.1

    severed, seven sons, shown to father M2.5, S169.3

    severed, speaks until confessed V254.7.2

Headache: cured by Virgin Mary D2161.5.2.6

    Virgin cures nun's V256.1.1

Healer: poisons king, seizes throne P16.1.6

Heart: bears image of Virgin Mary D997.1.2

    martyr's, bears sign of cross V86.2

    moneylender's in strong box W153.1

Heaven: daughter visits father E481.1.4

    golden chairs, glorious people V511.1

Heaven, journey to: man, able to speak foreign tongues F11.3

Heir: inheritance to poor V417.1

Hell: daughter sees mother suffer E481.1.3

    monk travels to F88

Hellfire: consumes avaricious woman, grave Q566.6

    hotter than earthly fire Q566.2

    lawyers special fire Q566.5

    rises from grave of man in hell Q566.3

Hemorrhage stopped: test of truth H252.7

Hen: scratches ground, so woman will seek men J99.4

Herbivores: eat only what they need B299.12

Herbs: power to resuscitate sought D978, E105

Heretic: excretes entrails Q225.1, Q415.8, Q559.11, V329
hits fly, kills self J2102.3.1, N333.1
power of Host converts V331.1.10
two declarations, swears to truth of both Q263.5
Hermit: asks God, wealth to benefactor M201.0.1.2
curses men who killed his bear M411.8.2
dream of, knight will become king M314.5
drunk, rapes, kills, executed V465.1.1.1
feigns madness to return to cave K523.1.1
finds coins in mouse's hole N534.7.2
laughs alone, sad in company V462.1.1
leave monastery, take wives, return penitent V477
prayers bring bear companion D1766.1.10
rescues seven abandoned princelings R131.10.2
secret sinner, blasphemous art K2064.1
tempted by woman, confesses, saved V21
throws money to thieves, no more fear U72
to choose one sin, covetousness, lust, drunkenness J485
woman at door of cave, disappears T332.2
Hero: boy, kills count, battle, captures sons Z231
conceived miraculously Z216
engendered magically A511.1.5.1
leads lion to cage by collar D2156.13
welcomed to otherworld by women F174.2
Hero-king's corpse: leads troops to victory P12.5.0.1
Heron leads mongoose to snake: mongoose kills snake and heron K1632.1

Hole, fill with sea water with spoon: like explaining Trinity J80.5
Holy man: counsels emperor, no vengeance against offenders J152.15
cures hyena cubs, mother grateful Q51.3
denies woman traveler audience T336.2.1
dreads judgement in heaven J191.3
helps others build cells J373
in brothel to save whores, accused N347.2
is surety for deacon R165
faith, more convincing than heretic's words J31.3
kind words convert pagan L350.2
moves close to water, angel rebukes him, moves J215.5
never laughs, laughs when devil is discomfited F591.3
piety rewarded, elected bishop Q39.2
preaches after God restores sight Q20.4
safe from persecutor's fire V222.8
shares bread with all comers W11.2.5
soul, sinner's surety, able to confess V20.1.3
Holy water: removes demon's mark, man's face V132.2.1
Honey: droplet, causes sequential tragic events N381, Z46.2
on lips of baby, future orator M312.0.2
Honey jar: hermit (woman) dream, future wealth, jar drops Z43.7
Honors: judge refuses at price of honesty W35.3
Horn, magic: saved from fire D1222
Horse: agrees to be saddled K192
dying, wax figure, Virgin revives E169.1
fed milk of ass, acts like ass J1661.1.5
finds lodgings for pious pilgrim Q28.1
gait proves him son of ass H175.6

grab's thief's arm, foiled theft B401.2

kneels before Host, will not rise V35.1.1

magic, swift, neither eats nor drinks B184.1.1.4

oppressor's, cannot cross stream V348

overeats, dies of bloat W151.11

permits self to be saddled A2492.3

thieves's horses unable cross river Q212.6

unite against lion J1025.3

walks like ass, son of ass U121.6.1

Hose of saint: protects woman D1385.19.1

Host: ailing Jew attacks, blood cures him V39.10

appears to priest as baby Jesus V34.8

cleric drops, it restores self V34.9

cures spider bite V34.10

held high chases demons V34.7

honored by king, kneels in mud D1841.1.2

Jew puts in pig trough, pigs respect it V35.1

keeps dead person's goods K2294

stolen, hidden in coif, head bleeds V35.4

stolen, pigs kneel before container V35.3

surrenders wife to guest P325

transformed, dying man can swallow V34.5

Host's wife: threatened to frighten guest P463.2

Hostess: Virgin supplies wine for royal meal V262

Humble man becomes king: cannot eat rich food J913.1

Hundredfold: merchant digs up three hundred coins J1262.5.3.1

Muslim leaves money to God, return V412.4

return of alms J1262.5.2, J1262.5.3

steals coin for beggar, owes one hundred J1263.5.4

wealth to God, returned V411.5.1

Hunter: beats old dog, no longer useful W154.4

falls into she-devil's power G405

horse lost liberty, failed to catch stag U31.3

Husband: absent, believes wife's child divine gift K1518.1.1, X711.12

accuses wife: falsely, punished with leprosy K2112.0.1

of drunkenness, she accuses husband of murder, he is hanged U183

she survives execution K2112.0.3

assaults wife, abandons in woods S62.5

barley, wife serves urine-soaked barley to X711.3

believes: cat has made noise, not wife's lover K1516.3, T481.14

had cut off wife's nose K1512, T481.10, X711.1

lover is fugitive from street bullies K1517.1, T481.17, X711.9

wife is unfaithful, devil has her ring G303.9, V232.11

wife is unfaithful, leper in her bed K2112.2

wife to mate with god K1544.2.1, T481.25

blind, wife, lover in pear tree K1518

blinded: breast milk in eye K1516.9, T481.13

candle has blown out K1516.3, T481.15

extended sheet K1516, T481.20, X711.11

eye treated (vintner) K1516.1, T481.12, X711.8

hair washed K1516.7

kettle obscures view K1516.8, T481.16

breaks wife's leg W167.2

chest, armed crossbow, warns wife S111.12, T254.4

chicken house, hides in K1514.1,

T481.11, X711.7

corpse of, widow substitutes for
hanged man, K2213.1, T231.6

drowns wife: after trivial argument
S113.3, T255.1, W167.3
sack thrown in sea V256.5.1.1

drugged, tonsured, in monastery
K1536

excessively jealous, locked out
K1511, T481.9, X711.4

falls on sword, wife is dead
T211.3.1

forbids wife to ask his name, or origin C32.2.1

genitals, angry wife cuts off
Q451.10

gifts to wife to test loyalty H479.3

gives wife to devil for promised
riches Q111.9

gives wife to impotent prince
J2199.5, K1544.2, T481.24,
X712

hollow threat, fails T251.2.3.2

kills gluttonous wife, wants share of
chicken W125.5.1

kills wife, devil warns she is dangerous G303.10.5, J2301.4,
K2155.4

lets serpent bite him, saves wife
T211.1.2

loves other woman, Virgin Mary,
wife stabs self E63.3

outdoes wife in disagreeability
T251.2

oven, warns wife not to enter
C610.0.1, H473.2, T254.5

paints lamb, wife's stomach, chastity index H439.1.1, J1531.4,
X711.6

parrot, to report on wife's fidelity
J1154.1, X711.5

poisoned unguent, warns wife
S111.10, H474.4.1, T254.1

poisoned wine, warns wife
S111.11, T254.6

precautions fail, wife meets lover
T481.9

presumed impotent prince, wife
enjoy T384

proves wife's obedience, she agrees
to all H474.1, N12, T223

punished for doubting wife, leprosy
K2112.0.1, Q551.9.6

sacrifices life to save wife T211.1.2

sends wife to apothecary (lover)
K1544.2.1

sends wife to lie with god
K1544.2.1

sent to battle to die (Uriah)
K978.1.2, T471.0.5

to deliver wife to devil for wealth
Q111.9

told of pursuit, hides in dovecote
K1514.1

tongue, bitten off by wife S163

under bed, wife and lover in bed
J2301.4.3, K1532.1, T481.22,
X711.2

Husband, wife: agree to be celibate
T315.1

enter religious orders, lapse T315.4

good eye covered, lover leaves
house K1516.1

old wife plucks black hair, young
grey J2112.1

penis compared to that of ass
J1744.2, X771

sin, sex on holy eve T472.4

vow chastity after baby is born
T315.5

wife, given magic slippers by lover,
Virgin Mary helps her remove
them D1065.21, K1584.1,
T481.27

Hydrus: enters crocodile, kills from within
F912, K952.1

Hyena: brings food to hermit B437.2
hermit cures cubs B381.3

Identity: saint not to reveal identity to
father C436

Illegitimate: offspring, unable see magic
cloth T647.2

prince, illegitimate, not forget lineage T646.2

prince, unaware of fate of parents
T646.3

Illness: brings human closer to God J893.8

mortal, king's, Virgin cures V256.1.15

sign of divine attention J893.6, J893.7

Image: bishop moves, it moves back V129.1

blamed for misfortune V123

infant Jesus, child offers food V128.1.1

infant Jesus, taken, woman son died V125.1

Jesus, nods head, approval V126.1

Jesus, wounds nun leaving convent V122.1

Image of Virgin Mary: angels protect image of Virgin V128.3.1

appears to be in labor D1622.4

causes cloth to rise and fall V128.6

causes mute man to speak V129.4

convinces heretic of virgin birth V125.2

keeps boy safe in oven V268.5.1

keeps man from killing V122.2

king puts in church, cures V126.6

kisses king's hands V129.3

moves, response to prayers to pardon sins V128.5

raises arm, protects baby V128.3

roars, quake, protects monk D2152.6, V129.2

saves painter D1639.2

speaks to monk, not to leave order V126.2

thrown in sea, fish die Q222.2.3

turns away attackers V126.5

washed, water cures scrofula V126.4

wears sash that moves V129

Image, impious: turns black near image of Virgin V121.1

Impaled: vaginally, woman punished for lust Q495.2

Impotence: devotion to Virgin causes T591.0.2

in presence of image of Virgin T591.0.1

Virgin cures lascivious knight T591.0.3

Impotent: husband thinks wife's companion is X712

Imprisonment: lion's den, lions show respect R45.2

Incest: brother, sister T415.9

king, daughter T411.1.3

mother, spurned, cries rape C114.4

nobleman's servant holds candle C114.3

punished in this life and next Q242

widow forgiven by Virgin Mary C114.1.1

Incest with son-in-law, murder: confesses, Virgin saves her V21.2

Incest, brother-sister: woman bitten by spider Q242.5

Incest, father-daughter: both struck by lightning Q242.2

Incest, woman commits: cannot confess, prayers free her V21.1.1

Income: king, major portion to poor W11.2.4

Incubus: holy man's token banishes F471.2.0.2

woman asleep thinks having sex T475.2.2

Incurable illness, most, what is: shameless daughter H659.35

Industrious nun: thought mad, worthiest of all V461.1

Infant: abandoned, raised at royal court S354

executioner abandons seven in wilderness S144.2

Infant Jesus: causes palms bend, give shade D171.9, V211.1.8.4

chases dragons (serpents) away D1713.10, V211.8.5

magic spring at foot of palm tree F933.1.2

Ingratitude: human, in God's image not toad's W154.29

Injured person: learns to embrace offender J80.4.1

Injuries: emperor must pardon injuries J811.5

Injustice: explained by angel J225.0.4

Jupiter: bee offends asking lethal sting
C51.4.1.1

Kettle: held, look for holes, lover goes
T481.16

Kicking door of Virgin's church: leg
breaks, loses sense, speech
Q551.8.10

Kid: obedient, denies entrance to wolf
J142.3

Kidney stones (gall stones): Virgin heals
V256.4.2

Kind: Christian, to Jew who stole his
mule W11.17

King: abdicates to live ascetic life P16.1.6
abdicates, son cruel, king returns
P16.1.5
advised to kill family and court
N340.2.1
angry, shoots courtier's son
S110.0.2
asserts superiority to insulters
J1281.2
avoids giving money to friend
J1283.2
bestiality punished, live like beast
L410.1.2
blinds three treasonous brothers
S73.3
blows leper's nose, ruby left in
cloth Q42.10, V411.7
cannot protect self from fly J913.2
cannot take wealth with him J912.3
captured, laughs at captor L416.1
cares for subjects like physician
L350.1.1
chosen by people, eats at iron table
P11.8
converts, happy life of poor
V331.10.2
demands great privileges P13.9.1.1
disobeys law, enters court armed,
kills self P19.4.2
does not permit executions P14.24
evil, destroyed by divine power
P16.1.3.1
feigns illness, lures traitors K911.6
forbids tides to rise, fails L414

forgives critics who were drunk
P12.16
goes among subjects secretly
P14.19
grants all wishes, none leave sad
P19.3.1, V401
hears subjects call him fool P14.19
humble lineage, flattery not permitted J915
humbled, all will be dust L410.1
hunts, misses mass held by angel
V49.2
ignores plea, kills subject's three
sons M2.2
in bathhouse, angel takes place
L411
in haste kills thousands N340.2
invited to public execution, trapped
K811.3
man forced to become P11.02
murdered innocents, punished
Q211.0.4
never laughs, punishes inquiries
C411.1, P14.25, Q431.3.1
offers drink to saint, saint to aide
J914.2
propounds riddles, clever minister
solves H561.5
proves sobriety, arrow in child's
heart M2.3
punished for war against Christians
Q305.1
says power is hollow, temporary
P12.15
sends woman captive back unharmed P12.9
sends woman's husband to battle
K978.1.2, T471.0.5
serves enemy flesh of sons J1281.7
serves flesh of enemy's child
S110.0.3
serves flesh of subject's sons to him
M2.3
singes beard, saves self from barber
J634.1
son of baker, bread rewards
J1661.1.2.3
spares life of stranger P14.26
spends nights studying J1012

stoned by hostile crowd K811.3

uses young men sexually T464

vows to convert for saint's cure M177.1.1

worshiped, when wounded repents L410.1.1

King David: dances before Ark J914.1

King descends to bottom of sea: learns from fish J52.2

King for a year: provides food on island exile J711.3, P11.7

King improves kingdom: leaves it to sons J701.2

King leaves bathhouse: wears rags, unrecognized J1072.3

King vows to be contrary: asked to destroy city, saves it J1289.10

King, bird injure each other: bird refuses reconciliation J15.1

King, election of: one whose arrow kills four birds H171.0.1

who will first see sun at daybreak H561.11

King, wife: pray for son, she gives birth T526

King's own son: to lose two eyes, king gives one M13, P233.14

Kingdom: subjects, Christian prince, convert V331.1.7

Kingdom and hand of princess: reward for virtuous life Q112.0.5

Kissing: empress's hands forbidden C604

Kite: ailing, prayers denied, fouled altars U236.1

carries so many partridges, drops all J514.1

Knife, scissors: quarrel leads to wife's death S113.3, T255.1, W167.3

Knight: asks captor, death over disloyalty Q72.1.1

beats blasphemer J1164

breaks tabu, set adrift in oarless boat C951

cuts horseshoe with sword J1289.24

flees battle, calls on Santiago V229.7.3

follows *via crucis*, soul follows E754.2

gave sword to duke not strength J1289.24

hears mass, angel in battle for him V41.2.1

hears mass, wins tourney in absentia V41.2

illiterate, read only "Ave Maria" E631.0.2, J142.3

lame, will stand and fight J1494.1

leaves wife in Virgin's care V261.4

not go to heaven, if no birds, dogs U134

promises pilgrimage, defeat Moors V229.7.2

queen weds, no speech, subjects T121.3.3

rapes nun, flight halted magically T471.0.2

Knuckles: nun teaches use of, guide to prayer V52.17

Ladder: hell, bad Christian lower than Jew Q563.1.2

in hell, usurers at bottom Q273.5, Q563.1

Lamb: flees dogs, hides among wolves K1111.4

painted on wife, is ram after years H439.1.1, J1531.4

prefers foster-mother, goat J391.1

Lamb chooses death in temple: to being eaten by wolf J216.2

Lameness: asset in battle, knight will not flee J1494.1

Lamp: altar, burn only olive oil V116.1

device to supply oil for through the night J1012

Land: grant, prayers obtain V57.9

granted, prayers to Virgin, facilitate V52.24

Language of animals: Aesop given magic knowledge B217.9, D1815.2

Lapse of time: cleric spends three hundred years, returns F377.1.1

in paradise, three years equals three days F377.1

Lawsuit: ape is judge B274.1

between dog and sheep B270.4

between wolf and fox B270.3

fox, wolf suspects, cannot sue J1179.1.1

stag, sheep, in presence of wolf P521.2

wolf, fox; ape judge P521.1

Lawsuit over property: plaintiff sleeps during trial J1162.5

Lawyer: bathe in special hell fire P465.6

bribed, lose (esquinança / argençia) P465.3, X318.1

cart as fee, loses, needed ox to pull X319.2

dying: asks for appeal P465.4

offers self to God, not peers P465.1

refuses to be judged by peers X315.2

says, "I appeal" X315

fee, cart; opposition ox to pull it P465.2

special place in hell X316

stole church lands, nose cut off P465.5

two fees, same case, higher wins K441.3.1

Laziness: queen makes idle women spin Q321.1

water drips in ear, brains out K171.12

Leader: prays, soldiers rally, win battle V52.3

Leaf: falls, mistaken for sky falling J1810.0.1

Leatherworker: works feast day, needle in throat M205.8

Lecher: carries Gospel, whores reject him V52.1

Leeches, sated: preferred over hungry ones J215.1.3

Leg: broken saves man from ambush N178.1

Lender forces borrower to lie: punished for damage to soul Q263.4.1

Lentil, one lost: monkey lets fall others to find one J344.1

soup prepared with only one J2469.1

Leopard: fruit of adulterous union, cause of mutual enmity A2494.12.11

guide holy family through desert B562.1.3

traps lion in cave K730.3

why leopard is aggressive A2562

Leper: king to blow nose; ruby in cloth V411.7

Lepers, cleansing lesions: first cured, refuses to help other W159.1

Leprosy: pilgrim's, Virgin cures V256.4.3

punishment, penance pilgrimage Q522.4.1

Leprosy to accuser: calumniated wife's innocence Q551.9.6

Letter: altered, care for wife, kill wife K2117.1

certify dead had hundredfold reward V412.4

forged, accuse man of treason K2156.1

reward delayed, Virgin intervenes V52.20

substituted letter accuses falsely K2117

Letter in hand of dead convert: removed only by bishop D1654.11.2

Letter in hand of dead saint: removed only by pope D1654.11

Letter, forgery: evidence of treason, Virgin saves accused K2103

Liar: rewarded by ape-king J815.1

Liar, greatest: water drips in ear, brain out K171.12

Life: spared, loyalty valued over liberty Q151.8.1

Lightning: cleaves blasphemer in two F968.1.2, Q552.1.8.2

cleaves creditor who cursed God Q552.1

impossible to avoid, emperor struck N174.1

kills mother, accused son, rape Q552.1.7.1

kills saint's false accuser F968.1.1, Q552.1.7

Lightning, emperor fearful of: out hunting struck by lightning J656.2

Lion: allows self to be roped by monks J1849.5

brings food to rescuer B361

carries off child R13.1.2

dinner party of meat served, pig leaves, eats acorns U147.1

escapes cage, courtiers flee W121.9

follows man who rescued him/her B301.8

grateful for: removal of thorn from paw B381

rescue B301.8

rescue from snake B374.1

grateful to mouse for release B363.1.1

injured by man refuses reconciliation B336

king of beasts B240.4

led peacefully to cage by hero D2156.13

male lion kills adulterous mate A2497.2

offers to cure horse, kicked K1955.0.2

saves child, nurtures it B535.0.15

spares: Androcles B525

Daniel B525.2

mouse B363.1.1

saintly woman B525.1

tells sons to fear man J22.1

Lion and ass: ass laughs, lion ignores J411.1

Lion and statue (sculpted by human): depicts human supremacy J1454

Lion disregards warning: seeks out man, is caught and beaten J17.2

Lion kills wolf for taking greater share: fox learns to take little J51.1, J811.1

Lion king: avenges mistreatment of vassals P50.0.2

Lion raised by man: cannot forgive insults J15.2

Lion, dinner party of: cats guests, served rats, moles U147.3

Lion, man: agree not to touch, man uses club K810.1.1

Lion's breath: kills those who say it smells J811.2.1

List of sins: left on altar, later is blank V21.9

outweighs moneychanger's gold V21.8

Liver: removed, passerby requests it to feed cat X22

Loan repayment: arrives miraculously by sea P525.4

Loaves and fishes: multiplied by Jesus D2106.1.5

Locked out: husband, wife tricks X711.4

Logic: parentage of horse, runs like ass F645.3

Logic applied: perceives worm in warm stone F642.4.1

Lost falcon: Virgin Mary helps find it D1816.2.2

Lost ring: found in fish belly D1816.2.1.1

returned by Virgin Mary D1816.2.5

Lost sheep: returned by Virgin Mary D1816.2.3

Lot's wife: pillar of salt Q221.5.1

Lots: queen casts to see future N126.3

Love-sickness: cured by marriage F950.8.1, T24.1, T24.9

father sends own concubine to son to cure him T24.10

friend gives betrothed, cures friend T24.9

princess, cured by marriage T24.1

Lovelorn: knight, Virgin helps forget loss V279

Lover: caught in net, humiliated, suspended mid-tower K1211.1.2

disguised as pursuer and fugitive K1517.1

enters bedchamber in basket K1343.1

fugitive from street ruffians K1517.1.2, T481.18

hidden, wife sends husband for kindling K1521.4.1

in basket, humiliated, suspended mid-tower K1211

meet, man is prisoner T32.2

quarrels about escape route J581.2

speak through hole in wall T41.1

treacherous, leaves Dido K2232.1

Lucretia seduced: threatened with loss of honor K1397

Lust: man, freed from lustful behavior V252.5

personified as Venus Z127.1

repressed by fasting T317.4

repressed, crawls through thorns T333.6

stimulated by actions of cock and hen T317.10

Lust, gluttony, gambling: curable, lying is not U235

Lustful: man, chaste for brief periods U130.2

Lustful thoughts: monk must pray T317.2.1

repressed by seeing suffering T317.1.1

repressed, removing eyes T317.1.2

Lying: incurable, other sins are not U235

Madman: in rich man's garb, unrecognized J1072.4

questions good sense of hunters J156.5

warns against other madman in bath X54.1

Madness: caused by grief F1041.8.2

cure for, stand in water J1434

cured by Virgin Mary F959.6.3, F1041.8.2

Maggots in nun's wound: transformed into jewels D470.2, V222.15

Magician: defeated by scripture D1745.1.1

protects self, demons, sign of cross V86.1.9

shows pupil reality D2031.5

Maiden: told sex at night not seen by God J1745.1.1

Maidens: one hundred, tribute to enemy S262.2

Maidservant: go-between, tells woman to don magic slippers sent by knight K1584.1

Man: burden of precious stones, drowns J651.2

created in God's image A1212.1

granted freedom from desires T310.2

in coffin, Virgin revives E63.4

in peril, comforts self with honey J861.1

maligns bishop, bites off tongue Q393.0.1

never known unhappiness, punished L424

perched on branch, ignores danger, eats honey, falls J651.3

returns from heaven knows who will die, pestilence M341.0.6

returns from hell, bathes in icy water V511.2.7

thought to be devil by lion J1781.4

tied to stake, tempted, bite tongue T333.2.2

transformation to woman D12.01

treacherous, winks at both buyer, seller W171.1

unworthy, looks heavenward, rewarded Q61

wants three wives, marries one, debilitated by love J21.32

Manger: dog in, no need, not give it up W156

Mantle: signal, lovers' rendezvous T41.3.1

Marriage of cleric: cure for illness, Virgin reproaches F950.4.1

woman counsels maiden to wed, rebuked T131.1.4

Mask: mistaken for face J1793, U111.1.1

Mass: protects from snake venom D1515.2.2

Master: servant saves life, solves riddle for servant J151.1.1

Master, when angry: withholds punishment J571.4.2

Mastiff: magically brings down all prey B182.1.3.2

Matchmaker: Virgin helps woman to wed her love T53.4.1

Mayor: takes church lands, falls ill Q222.4.1

Measure land with hide of ox: cut into long thin strips H1584.3

Measuring the dregs: fraud detected by J1176.2

Meat: ascetic vows not to eat meat C221.0.1

belonging to lion, put in jackal's room K2155.1.3

eating on Sabbath forbidden C221.0.2

men eat meat on Sabbath, lose battle C221.0.2

poor saint serves during Lent C235.1

Medicine, bitter for weaning: like bitter punishment for carnality J81.7

Merchant: denies pay to artisan, play music J1522.3

gold to God, dig, find hundredfold V411.5.1

requests music, refuses payment K231.2.2

storm, Virgin restores broken mast V268.4.3

thieves throw in sea, Virgin saves V264.7

worries over goods on ship at sea C777.1

Messenger: face, marked by devil J1263.1.7

to arrange death, first to arrive, burned to death K1612

Military leader: discards arms and prays D2163.5.3

Milk: baby forbidden to have wetnurse C271.1, M312.0.4.1

Virgin Mary's cures dying monk V256.1.2

Virgin Mary's cures seizures V256.1.2.1

saint's mother, nursed own children P231.3

Mill, who will inherit: greatest liar K171.12

Miller, son, ass: not to heed opinions of others J1041.2

Minerva: naming of Athens, dispute A163.2

Minister: advise taxes, debased coinage K2248.0.1

banished, recalled to court P111

falsely accused, cleverness saves K2101

falsely accused, Virgin Mary saves K2101.2

spares royal wife, pardoned P111.1

Minstrel: waylaid, Virgin saves V264.8

Miscreant: hidden in hollow tree, smoked out J1172.3.3

Miser: in grave, demons throw gold in throat Q272.4.1

lid of chest falls, breaks neck Q272.2

teased into giving bread to poor N67.1

tries to eat gold, chokes to death Q272.3

Virgin grants thirty days to repent Q272.6

woman, gold, hell fire consumes Q272.4

Monastery swallowed by earth: reappears magically after year F941.2.2.1

Money: devil advises saving for future U72.2

given to poor, safe from thieves J347.6, W11.3.1

returns to owner, series of events N212.2

saving for future care, sin U72.2

tied to hare, for rapid repayment J1881.2.2

Money in the stick: literal repayment of debt J1161.4, K236.5

Moneylender: dead, heart found in money chest P435.14

deceived, chests filled with sand K1667.2, P435.15

Mongoose: tricks heron, eats snake, and heron A2494.12.2, K401.1.1

Monk: abstinence from meat, prideful L491

accuses other, attend own faults K2131.6

adorned with silk, silver, punished Q332

ascetic teaches, give up world V462.2.5

attention to possessions rebuked L491.1

avoids sin, told to experience it first U231.2

beast kills, entry in heaven Q172.0.4

burned alive, achieve martyrdom Q414

burns finger tips, repress lust
T333.2

busy, no prayers, Virgin pardons
V276.2

chooses contemplative life J495

chooses work over contemplation
J215.4

cures hyena cubs' blindness, rewarded B381.3

deathbed, had eaten when fasting
K2058.3

desert, longs for wife T317.2

devil, in woman's shape, tempted
by T332

devil, victualler tempts, prays, saves
self G303.16.2.1.1

devils menace, call on Virgin to
save them G303.16.1.3

disobeys, lifts plate, releases mouse
H1554.1, J29

dissatisfied, must accept God's will
W128.5

drives demons out of attacker
D2176.3.4

dying, fears seeing woman he loved
T336

dying, scolds brothers for gossip
Q393.3

enemies quarrel, thief to steal cow,
devil his soul J581.2

erysipelas if commits perjury
Q551.9.2.1

flees devil, devil in city too V477.1

flees, Virgin appears, to finish robe
V276.1.1

follows bird of paradise, returns
after two hundred years
D2011.1

goes to desert, avoid temptation
T334.1

hides book in other's bed
K2155.1.2

inexperienced, told woman is goat,
cannot eat goat J1745.5,
T371.2, T617.3, X457.4

knows who will die, including self
M341.0.4

learn from prisoners, ask where
judge is, when come X457.2

life like an ass's, constant work
V461.13

lives where criticized, avoids flattery
V461.6

lives with temptation, strengthens
V462.12

loses temper at pitcher, breaks it
W185.4

no cooked food, pride rebuked
L491.2

old, knows to keep own counsel
V461.11

pains of people, not prayed for
Q220.2

penance: await soul in cave, soul
returns E752.2.1

punished, wolves, bears eat sheep
Q414

rebuked for fault-finding L435.1.1

reforms whores, accused falsely
K2176

refuses wine, singularity rebuked
L492

repents, devil denied his soul
E754.1.10

replaces gold with ashes, flees
K476.1.3

rescued from dragon, returns
R167.1

rescued from hell, soul returns
V511.2.1

salutes Virgin's image, safe from
devil V126.3

scolds others for sin, sins himself
U231.1

see his sister, she must dress modestly T336.2.2

sees devil, goes out, sees more
U230.0.1

sent for manure, returns with lion
J1849.5, J2461.9, X457.3

share bread with poor, magically
replenish Q141.1

sight restored to preach to others
V345.1

silence justified with scripture
J1074.1.5

survives burning cell D1841.3

tempted, holy man prays, monk

must pray too V52.1.1

thoughts of fornication distract V465.1.1.6

to leave monastery, Virgin saves V265.2

told not to go to city, fornicates, fathers child J21.53

treacherous, kills friend's bear K2284.0.2

unwilling to speak, admonished L494

vows silence, can see departing souls of dying E721.11

wants pagan woman, sign of sin V345

wants to leave monastery T334.1.2

Monkey: flesh of, cure for illness B335.2

have king B241.2.2

heart, cure for disease K544, K961.1

imitates carpenter, crushes genitals Q341.1

steals merchant's stolen coins Q595.6

Monkey-king: punishes traveler who tells truth, eyes torn out D2161.3.1.1

Monogamy: storks and lions practice A2497.2

Monster: half-human, half-fish B80.2

Months: February, days determined by Caesar A1161

naming of, Rome A1162

Monument: sign of king's mortality J912.2

Moon: looks like cheese in well, wolf J1791.3, K810.1.2

Moonbeam: thief to climb down to exit house K1054

Moorish: army destroyed by Virgin who saves city, destroys V268.3

child, Virgin Mary revives, Mother converts E121.3.2

pirates, forced to return to port, Virgin caused storm D2141.0.9

slave, Virgin Mary appears, frees from devil V331.1.9

woman, son of, Virgin revives, converts V331.1.13

woman, son, battlements, spared, grateful converts V331.11

Moors: abduct holy man, ships cannot sail R12.2.2

attack church, blinded, maimed V111.4

Moribund refuses sacrament: offered by inferiors J1261.4.1

Mosquitoes, horse flies: sting Pharaoh L392.1

Mother: breaks vow, child dies, Virgin saves M205.6

curses children who mistreated her M411.1.3, P232.4

invader's persuades him to be merciful J816.6

kills children, husband has lover S12.4.1

kills newborns, father is godfather S12.2.4

kills, eats child during siege S12.2

king's, urges clemency J816.5

lover kills child, guard secret S12.3.1

plans to kill newborn, Virgin saves S12.2.5

pledges son as security for loan P524.3

rebuffed by son, accuses rape K2111.5, T412.6

rescue selves, step on, over children, in flood S12.2.2.4

son's eyes put out S12.4

throws child into sea S12.6

treats son as husband T412.5

Virgin saves baby, walk on sea, safety V268.4.6

Mother's milk: spray in husband's eye, lover goes T481.13

Mother-in-law: accused of incest with son-in-law T417.2

kills son-in-law, rejected advances S12.3.2

orders son-in-law's murder K959.7

puts slave in daughter-in-law's bed K2218

says daughter-in-law gave birth to seven hounds K2115

Mountain: falls, seals off captives
D2152.1.2

God causes to fall on enemy
D2152.1.1

in labor, gives birth to mouse
U114

leveled by prayer D2152.1

moved by prayer V57.7

Mountain woman: grotesque long breasts
F460.1.2

Mouse: gnaws net: frees doves A2493.36,
B437.2.1

frees lion B437.2

to free animal B545.2;

pleads inebriety, breaks promise,
J1319.2, M205.0.3, X803

stronger, sun, wind, clouds, mountain L392

torments bull L315.2

Mule: ashamed of low-born father, ass
J80.5, J954.1

half-flayed, Virgin revives E171

identity written on hoof, kicks fox
J1608.1

Murder: in church, punishment, erysipelas Q222.5

man, accused of, Virgin saves
K2116.5.1

Muslim, leaves money to Christian God
V412.4

Mute: sees demons carry off souls
D1821.7

Muteness cured by need to warn of danger F954.5

Nails: metal, from crucifixion, given to
emperor V101

Naive wife: thinks all men have bad
breath X772.2

Naive young woman: compares husband's
penis with ass's J1744.2, X771

sodomy, youth, ass, gives sense
X772.1

thinks sex at night, not seen by
God X772

Naked captive: covers self, sign of lasciv-
iousness T472.1

Nakedness: shame for A1383.1

Nebuchadnezzar: Daniel, lions, converted
to Judaism V336

impiety, wander naked, eat grass
Q220.6

Necklace: returned by Virgin Mary
D1816.2.2

Neglect to attend church: man sees his
place in hell Q225.5

Neighbor: saves sheep from wolf, eats it
J1374

Nephew: murders uncle, caught, killed
Q211.0.5, S74

treacherous, kills uncle for money
K2217.1

Neptune: naming of Athens, dispute
A163.2

Nero: vision of in hell with lawyers
V511.2.4

Net: lover suspended in T495.3

Newborn: adrift in chest S144.3

deathly ill, Virgin cures V257

Nightingale: not endure hoopoe's nest
filth U144

why sing at night A2491.6, U144

Niobe: challenges goddess's fecundity
C54.1

No bad news: pup dead, events mount in
horror Z46.1

Noble: and son both enter monastery
J1289.10.1

forces son to return to lay life
J1289.10.1

gives up fine garments in monastery J922.1

Noble wife: kills self, escapes emperor's
desires T326.4

leaps into fire with sons, escapes
invaders T326.5

Non-believer: sign of cross, saves bishop
T331.10

Nose: bitten off by son on gallows Q586

cut off, mark of perjury, theft
P465.5

cut off, punishment for theft
Q451.5.2

cut off, barber's wife K1512,
T421.10. X711.1

poison, straw, inserted in K1613.1,
T451.3

thief's grows, seals off mouth
Q551.6.4

Not the same purse as was lost: greedy owner foiled J1172.1

Novice: prays, freed from antics W189.1

Nun: ashamed of sexuality, cannot confess V22.4

eats unblessed lettuce, G303.16.2.3.4

endures insults of sisters W26.8

leaves convent, Virgin takes place V264.3.1

prays rapidly, Virgin helps slow down V51.6

prays Virgin show son, she does V277.1

punished for impatience Q327

raped by knight, magically reins his horse Q244.2, T471.0.2

returns from hell to warn sisters Q560.2.4

returns, says no respite in hell V511.2.6

sends eyes to king who wants them T327.1

talkative, corpse halved, half burns Q221.3.4, Q393.1

Virgin stops her leaving convent V265

vision, heavenly temple V511.1.5

Obedience: of wife, wager N12

valued over all other qualities W31.2

Obedience, test of: man warns against poison unguent H473.3.1

not to enter oven H473.2

wife agrees with absurdities H474.1

Odor, foul: of stable, rustic prefers over spices U133.2

foul, sinner's food U233.1

sin, fouler than rotting corpse U233

Office-seeker: denied post, for use of perfume J1281.6

Ointment: revives drowned woman E101

Omen: bird drops serpent egg in lap D1812.5.2.12

bird lands on head D1812.5.0.2

crested chick good omen D1812.5.2.13

crows birds of ill omen B147.2.2.1

crows seen on left bad omen B147.2.2.1.1

eclipse evil D1812.5.1.4

two crows good omen B147.2.1.1

Omens sneezing (flatulence): wolf leaves food for better D1812.5.0.1

One devil suffices for usurer's dwelling: many needed for monastery G303.25.3.1

Ordeal: boiling oil, saint not hurt H221.3

jumping from height, innocent wife unharmed H412.7.3

red-hot iron, saint walks on H221.2

repeated, woman burned cold iron H221.2.3

woman confesses, can handle redhot iron H221.2.3

Otherworld: journey to, oarless boat F129.4

queen, second sight (past only) F185

Oven: collapses, husband warns wife S113.4

woman forbidden to enter C610.01, H473.2

Overboard: husband killed, wife throws self T215.12

priest prays, swept back on ship V52.6.1

Overhearing: king tells revilers to move along J1281.4

Overhears, husband: wife tells lover she loves husband K1532.1, T481.22, X711.2

Owl: hatched by hawk, ejected Q432.1

king of birds B242.1.8

song portends death B39.2

mother, calls chicks most beautiful T681.1

war between owls and crows A2494.13.14, B261.1, K477.4, K2042

Ox: hides fugitive stag B411.2, R243.2

yoking of, origin A1441.2

young and old yoked together
J441.1

Ox-hide measure: deceptive land purchase
K185.1

Pact with devil: for worldly success
M217.1

owns body and soul, disappears
M211.1

to get desired woman M217

Virgin regains, saves signer M211,
V264.1

Pagan: beats rude monk, admires saint
J817.4

philosopher, converts after debate
V331.10

priest converts, saint's goodness
V331.10.1

told of Christianity, baptized V332

Pain cured: prayer and celibacy
D1766.1.4

Painter: devil takes scaffold, Virgin saves
V264.1.2

Painting on wife's stomach: chastity index
H439.1.1, J2301.4.12, X711.6

Palace: elegant, king's beard only place,
spit X501

entry to forbidden C603

rosewater lagoons, spice sugar
F771.2.4.1

Panther: avenges injuries done him/her
B299.1.2, Q385

sweet smell attracts other animals
B732

Paradise lost: forbidden fruit A1331.1

one sin A1331

Paralysis: blow to head, Virgin cures
V256.1.5.3

Virgin cures woman's V256.1.5

Paralyzed: man vows pilgrimage, Virgin
cures V256.1.6

Parents: must chastise children when
young P230.4

Parrot: tricked into giving false report
J1154.1, X711.5

Parrots, cannot speak foreign tongue:
learn accusation in foreign· tongue
J1152

Partridges: doubt that teary hunter to kill
them J1064.3

Passage: payment for, slap of fox's tail
M205.0.2, W154.5.1

Paternity: son and father eat raw meat
U121.4

Paternity, test of: son to shoot arrows at
corpse H486.2

Patience: man endures insults, gates of
city W26.1

Payment: choices: forty marks, take
blows, eat forty onions J210.3

for passage, fox hits boatman with
tail M205.0.2, W154.5.1

Peace fable: fox lures cock from tree
J1421

Peace of mind: work and prayer J94.1

Peacock: ashamed of ugly feet A2232.7

envies nightingale's voice W128.4

Peacock and crane: dispute usefulness
J242.5

Pear tree: lovers in, cure blind husband
T481.21

Peasant: ashamed of being thrown by ass
J411.4

betrays fox, winking K2315

Pebbles in water jug: crow drops, water
level rises J101

Penance: embrace next creature seen, is
serpent who kills him, man
goes to heaven Q172.4

for each of seven mortal sins
Q535.2.2

given three days, sinner fails
Q223.8

grave, sinner kill, mild sinner repent L361.1

king, agrees to postpone death sentences Q520.4

lion forgoes meat Q535.2

man dies before he has chance
Q223.8.2

true, effective, time period unimportant J557.1.1

Penis: naive bride compares husband's
with ass's J1744.2, X771

unfaithful lover's, cut off S176

Pennant, magic: ensures victory
D1400.1.16

Perfection: saints not equal to two saintly women U15.2

Persecutor: of Christians, struck down Q225.4.1

Pestilence: cured by mass V41.3

Pharaoh: disobeys God, drowned in Red Sea Q220.5, W126.2

Philosopher: advises courtier, deceive king J152.8

answers riddle for king J152.17

confines self and pupil six months J152.11

deep in study, killed by marauders J235.1

does not believe friend maligned him P317.1

king to act contrary to advice of, advises destroy city J1289.10, M203.4

lives in earthenware vessel J152.1

reads gloomy epitaph, becomes hermit J30.01

re-interprets royal dream J152.16

retreats to countryside T334.1.1

simple man tells, wisdom preceded learning J1217.2

spits in king's beard J1566.1

studies, forgets to lift food to mouth J235.2

superior to king, guided by reason J152.14

tells father to marry daughter to good man J152.18

tells knights that robbing is wrong J152.9

urinates while walking, keeps feet cool, escapes odor J152.7

woman ridicules, rides him like horse X742.1

woman tricks, rides him on all fours K1215

writes royal epitaph J152.13

Philosophers see disparity: between golden tomb and reality J30.02

Philosophy: personified gives infant magical shirt F312.1, Z139.9

Phoenix: renews youth B32.1

Physical attributes: reveal evil nature U129.5

Physician: falsely accused, vindicated K2101.1

offers to poison king K2041.1, K2292

sham: crow, to cure eagle's eyes, blinds him K1955.2.2

frog tries to be, sham recognized K1955.0.4

has universal cure, needs camels, money to find it K1955.10

lion asks to cure horse K1955.0.2

poisons princess, king poisons him K1613.6

warns tyrant, only he can cure J1289.25

wolf pretends to help sow give birth K1955.0.1

wolf will treat sick ass K1955.0.3

Physiognomist's nature: contradicts his features H1551

Pig: friends with sheep, carried off J411.5.1

shriek on way to slaughter J1662

waits under fig tree, ape throws figs J514.4

Pig's feet: too many in pot J1539.2.1

Pigeon: wrongly kills mate for stealing wheat N346

Pilgrim: aids all, falls ill, Santiago saves him V418

castrates self, atone for fornication E121.3.1, T333.4

fears purgatory, goes to heaven Q28.3, V85.3

follows *via crucis*, prays to die Q172.0.5, V85.1

helped by Santiago in fight Q28.4

insincere, Virgin transports to altar V277.4

lightning strikes, Virgin revives E63.5

lost in mountains, Virgin guides V268.4.4

sees Virgin, angels, dies, to heaven V510.4

Virgin rescues in sinking ship V264.2

warns against pilgrimages, punished V85.4

woman, falls ill, climbs celestial light Q28.2

Pilgrimage: knight in Jerusalem, to heaven E754.2, Q172.0.5

woman dies, goes directly to heaven Q28.2

Pine and thorn bush: dispute usefulness J242.5

Pious man: heretics cut out tongue Q451.4.6.1

in alley of whores J453

Pirate: does what emperor does J1289.22, U11.2

Pirates: abduct princess R12.1

rescue young woman, attack R169.15.1

Virgin Mary causes storm, forced to return to port D2141.0.9

Pitch: sulphur, red-hot metal, applied to sinners in hell Q569.7

Pitcher, magic: Virgin Mary's tears fill it D1171.7.2

Pitchforks: devils wrench souls with Q569.6

Plague: visited on saint's attacker Q551.9.3

Plants: mature in miraculously short time F815.1

Plants, wild: grow better, God tends them J1033

Platter: putrid matter, Virgin brings to sinner V277.3

Plotter: against emperor, forgiven W46.3

Poet: humble birth, rose born among thorns Q85.1

noble, demands reward, king rebukes Q331.2.4

noble, disdains base-born poets J411.3.1

rewarded, acknowledged base parentage J80.5

Virgin Mary gives perfect line D1811.3

Poison: armpits, poison in kills man Z311.5

damsel, exudes poison, kills men F582

false physician poisons princess, king makes him drink it too K1613.6

senators warn enemy against, prefer victory in battle K2369.7.1

Poison blown into victim's nose: sneezes, poison kills poisoner K1613.1, T451.3

Poor: feet cold, rich, feet in stocks in hell U62

power to help humankind U61.1

Poor man: saves bees, rich man poisoned L143.3, W19.2

sees another worse off than he J883.1

share his goods, dies, Virgin rewards V410.1.1

shares food with disguised angel R168.1

Pope: humbles self, bathes in river J914.3

incense for pagan idol, denied burial V476

not to enter church C601.1

severs hand kissed by woman T317.8

Porters: steal treasure J2092

Possession: demonic, freed by saint's humility G303.16.15

philosopher loses without anger W26.2

Potiphar's wife: empress demands sex, refused K2111

Pots, earthen and brazen: earthen fears association J425.1

Poverty: diseased beggar woman Z133.1

Prayer: best weapons against demons V52.19.1

bishop's dry up flood, save city D2151.9

brings rain D1766.1.12

defeats devil D1766.1.9

holy man's causes evildoers to die D1766.1.11

in church, enlightens literally D1766.1.13

moves mountain D1766.1.14

obedient monk's, over abstinent monk's W31.1

prisoners freed by saint D1766.1.7

produces food for workmen D1766.1.8

saint offers, priest to stop fornicating V316.2

saint's brings sinner back from dead D1713.2

to Virgin to show her son D1766.1.2

warrior's, defeats enemy D1766.1.14

woman's see Jesus, fulfilled V52.21

work, man makes rope and prays H605

Preacher: reproaches king who misses sermon J1647.1

Precentor: curses false flatterer J1369.6

refuses to accept praise J916.1

Pregnancy: illicit, husband believes God's gift X711.12

illicit, woman thrown from cliff, father of baby beheaded T400.0.2

unusually short, seven days T573.2

Pregnant woman, tides catch: Virgin saves, emerges with newborn V264.5

Prescription: symbolic, given to king H605.1

Price: horse, falcon, doubled each day K227

Pride, overweening: proud man swallowed by earth C621

Priest: asked to preach short sermon J1647

falls ill, after maligning saint Q551.9.7.1

gives up fornication, pain leaves T334.1.9

ignorant, sent to Church by devil J1263.1.5

man, interment delayed, revived by E121.5

neglects hearing confession Q233.4

prayer save bathhouse keeper, hell V52.23

sex with goddaughter, dies seven days T427.1

trick woman, sex with pseudo god K1315.1

unlettered, Virgin helps regain post V261.1

unlettered, Virgin Mary protects V261.1.1.1

unrepentant, dies as he begins mass Q436

vision of soul in hell V211.2.3.1

Priest's concubine: transformed into mare Q493.2

Prince: court baker's son, remember origins P463.4, U121.5.1

does not eat meat, queen's lover not eat meat J1661.1.2.2

forgives man, spat in his face W46.2

gives wealth to poor where safe Q21.0.1

ignorant of sex, wife supplied to T481.24

illegitimate, to wear garments to recall lineage J152.12

in quest of knowledge of death H1376.1

promises Virgin candles to find lost hawk M201.0.3

queen weds, may not return if he leaves T121.3.2

told women are devils J1745.4, T371, X771.1

treacherous, sells justice K2246

violates prohibition, banished Q431.3.1

wild horse bows to H71.10.8

Princess: elderly forced to wed T311.0.4

flees arranged marriage T311.1

has baby, secretly wed, imprisoned T400.0.1

prince horse, sword, promise wed T55.1.2

sickens, dies, Virgin revives E121.3.1.3

will marry successful riddler H540.3

Prisoner: chained cruelly, mass said, freed V41.4.1

masses, paid by wife, free him V41.4, V52.10

promise money to church, freed R123.2

released at time of mass D1766.1.7.2

senses wife's prayers D1766.1.7.1

Privy in churchyard: odor is offensive C93.3.1

Procurer: sets high price on virgins
T452.2

Prodigal son: favored over faithful son
N172

returns P233.8

Promise: broken, youth cursed M205.2

calf for rescue at sea, broken
M205.1.3

calf to Virgin, broken, calf runs to
Virgin's church M242.6

help dying companion, broken
M256.2

hostage returns to captor M202.2

king's to protect Jew M203.1

king's, not to do as sage requests
M203.4

literal, hunter not to touch lion,
clubs it K2310.1

moribund to return to tell, suffers
in purgatory M253.1

pilgrim, bring back Virgin's image
M202.0.2

pilgrimage broken, son dies
M101.4.3

to join order if cured, broken
M101.4.2

Property: inherited, by unusual lie
X905.3, X905.3.1

Prophecies: unfulfilled M372, M372.2,
M372.3

Prophet: calls angels to save kingdom
V232.1.4

dove eats grain from ear K1962.1

predicts victory J673.2

tells wife palsy is divine message
K1962.2

takes servant's wife, says angel sent
her K1962.1

Proposal: poison king, courtier rejects
W34.5

Prostitute: aging, offers daughter as substitute T451.2

cheats brothel owner T451.3

only ones permitted to carry prostitute's corpse X521

pleasure to men, soul to please
God T459.1

queen sets high price for her body
X523

shamed by offer of sex in public

T451.1, X522

Pupil: fox, unsuccessful hunter, tried to be
master before pupil J2413.5.1

naked, meat on head, dogs, birds
attack J80.3.6, Z43.7.1

not to retaliate when hurt J153.7

ungrateful to magician W154.28

Puppy: woman to be transformed into
D141.1.1.

Purgatory: time is thousandfold U261.1

two days in, or two years of illness
J210.2, U261.2

Purse: not the one lost J1172.1

Pursuer, fugitive: husband thinks lovers
are X711.9

Queen: abducted by lover R39.3

bedchamber searched before king
enters T172.4

blinds husband, assassins kill him
S110.7

brings her rapist's head to king
T471.0.7

confessor helps her clear name
V29.10

counsels kindness with enemy
L350.1

disguised as son, heir to throne
K1837.8.2

immolates self, lover abandons her
T93.3.1

insists that idle woman spin cloth
P29.4

kills all heirs to throne S12.9

lances sons' killer, runs him over
S110.6

passes law, legalizes incest T412.7

raped, brings rapist's head to king
T471.0.7

succumbs to offer for sexual act
T450.0.1

Quest: find herbs to resuscitate dead
H1185.2

see face of Death, horrible composite beast H1376.2.1

Raft: sack flour, Virgin rescues woman
V264.2.1

Raiders: pray to Virgin, win in Moorish
land V52.3.2

Rain: area, free of in storm, sign of cross
V86.1.6
comes if people repent sins
D2143.1.3.1
holy man's prayers, bring V57.4
prayer for, presumptuous J153.4
prayers of holy man bring
D2143.1.3
Ram: do not flee butcher, killed U161.1
small, mock large ram fleeing
danger J952.7
wears mastiff skin, detected J951.6,
K1810.2.1
Rape: punished by beheading S169.1
punished by hanging, Virgin saves
youth Q244
sister raped by brother T415.9
Rapist: writes song for Virgin, freed
R121.6.7
Rat and frog: tie paws together, kite kills
both J681.1
Rat, cat: cat freed, rat leaves time to es-
cape J426.1
Rat-maiden: transformed D117.1, D315.1
Ravens: quarrel, prince learns governance
from J83.1
Recognition: daughter by lamentation
H11.1.5.1
husband by life story H11.1.5.2
mother in humble, not fine, clothes
H119.3
saint by life story H11.1
Red-faced: bishop mistaken for drunkard
U119.6
Reed: bend before wind, oak uprooted
J832
pricks dog when it urinates L391.1
Reflection: dog thinks it other dog, drops
meat in mouth J1791.4
Rejuvenation: monk prays to Virgin
D1882.1.1
Rekindling: magic fire from genitals of
woman Q492, T494.5
Relic: cure goldsmith sight, fix reliquary
V256.1.14
false, divine intervention makes real
K1684.1, V142
of Virgin Mary, preserved miracu-
lously V140.5

of Virgin Mary, protects ship
D1381.20
Religious teachings: like braying of asses,
asses violate scoffer's funeral
Q225
like greyhound's baying, scoffer
attacked Q225.0.1
Remains: saint's cures mutes, lepers, blind
V221.14
saint's, cures blind, mute, halt
V144.3
Remedy: eye pain, take them out
J2119.1.2
overheard from animal meeting
B513
Reminder of foolishness in past: bad
judge's skin used on stool J55.1,
J167
Repress lust: fast and pray in woods
T317.4
Reptile: wise, refuses reconciliation B123
Rich man: angrily throws bread at poor
Q172.2.1.1
buried with gold, corpse spits it
J912.3.1
dying, asks for delay, devils take
soul E752.2.1
dying, wealth to poor, pardoned
Q172.2
earth swallows, house and goods
Q331.3
finds money on way to church
N181.1
fox fur to beggar, later cleric wears
V411.2.1
gives up more than poor man
J1269.16
lives poorly, servant richly U62.2
postpones penance, devils come
Q272.1.1
seeks eternal life in monastery
P152
trial in heaven, bread on scale
Q172.2.1
worries over investments J347.4
Rich sinner buried with honors: pious
monk eaten by lion J225.0.1.1
Riddle: ages man most rapidly: sleep with
many women H659.28

anchor H548.2.6
based on chance event H561.11
bathhouse and bather H548.2.5
bitterer than bile: bad children H659.34
boats and water H548.2.3
calendar H548.2.1
conscience (shame), best character trait H659.7.3.1
distance from earth to heaven: devil knows H682.1.10
distant stallions impregnate mares H572
empyrean: highest H642.2
enigmatic answer to H561.5.1
fish in river H548.2.2
four wheels of cart H548.2.8
heavens, what is higher than: empyrean H682.1.11
human heart: faster and more burning than fire H659.32
impossible, princess unwed T411.1.3
incurable illness, most: shameless daughter H659.35
mirror H548.2.7
obligations: heaviest burden H659.29
posed to rival monarch H548.2
reed grass and paper H548.2.3
responder's origin, place of birth H594.4
saint defeats devil, answers H543.1
sharpest: tongue of men and women H659.29
strongest of sun, wind, mountain, rat: rat H659.27
strongest of wine, women, truth: truth H631.5.1
sun at daybreak: first to see it looks west H561.11
sweeter than honey: parental love H659.33
thoughts: faster than arrow H659.31
truth: easiest lost, hardest to recover H659.19
visage, human, diversity of: God's best work H648.3

water in sea, measure: stop all rivers H696.1.1
where first see sun at daybreak H561.11
words: best and worst in world, H659.37
Riddle contest: customer, entertainer in brothel H548.6
Riddle test: failure brings death H540.3
Riddling: clever slave beats rivals H548.3
Ring: half, identification token H94.5
lost, found in fish D1816.2.1, N211.1
official's, dropped in slave's lap N535.3
on image of Virgin's finger, man who placed it there, impotent T299.3
seen as token of infidelity H84.5
wife's, sign of infidelity H94.0.1
Ringdoves: rise up in net, fly away together J1024
River: carries worldly debris D915.8
drowns liars who pass over it D915.8, F715.7.1
feeds moat, diverted, city won K2369.6
magically carries off debris D915.7
Roasting: in hell, usurers Q566.3
Robber: penance, live with next creature he sees Q520.2
saved by devotion to Virgin Q171
soul carried off by demons E121.3.6
soul carried off, Virgin revives E121.3.6
Robbers: capture man, sure God protects him V461.7
Rogue: in tree trunk, judge sets afire K451.3
Romans: disputation by signs with Greeks H607.1
learn from enemy, kindness better than cruelty J26
not include Jesus, preached poverty V385
Rope: twisting as work like prayer J80.3.4
Rosebush, five roses: grows from mouth of dead nun V255.5
Ruler: forgets nothing, save injuries J811.5

ALPHABETICAL INDEX

forgives offenses, returns love Q20.3

learns mercy, tale of bees dying after sting J57

Running nose: man too lazy to wipe, loses bride W111.1.4

Rustic: as king, fine food sickens U135.3

denies beggar food, demons take him V421.1

Sabbath: origin, feast dedicated to Venus (Mary) A1441.2

violated, sinner disabled Q223.6.1.1

woman sews on, loses use of hands Q223.6

Sack of wheat: sinner pulls, holy man pulls against J80.3.5

Sack sealed with pitch: man thrown in river, punish rape Q467.1

Sacristan: Virgin says, dream, to seek holy man V510.8

Sailor drowning: saved by mass said for him D1766.1.8, V41.5

Sailors: abduct knight's wife R12.5

Virgin guides, storm at night V268.4.2

Virgin saves, bail out water, fish plug holes V268.4.5.2

Saint: accepts usurer's alms, hellfire marks P435.7

accused of fathering child T574.3

alms to all, Christ comes as beggar V411.10

causes throne to burn D1713.7

changes maggots into gems V222.15

chooses hell over mortal sin Q560.2.5

did not tolerate gossip Q393.2

disguised as pilgrim, dies, father's house K1815.1.1

disinherits sisters, God will provide J1577

dying, tells monks, love each other J153.5

dying, to see hell first to confess sins J172.1

eats gluttonously to please guests P324.4, W125.6

enters jail, breaks fetters, frees captive R121.6

falsely accused of fathering baby K2111.6

fear of God like fire, wastes body J352.2

flees rich man's house V462.2.4

frees hand stuck to sickle V221.13

gives good deeds to sinner, saved D1840.1.4, Q21.2

gives up hair shirt, avoid singularity L492

gold to poor, magic sack of money V411.5.2

has second sight D1713.6

helps young woman to marry, avoid slavery R165.1

holds back flood water D1713.7

keeps pilgrim's son alive on gallows R165.2

leaves cryptic message, later explained J154.1

leaves spades, food for robbers V223.7

makes sign of cross, frees area of rain or snow D1841.4.4

moribund, gives monks rules J153.8

moribund, never exercised own will L493.1

neglects to give alms, will not again V461.9

perceives cheat: knows boy has hidden basket D1810.0.2

knows where pilgrims hid clothes D1810.0.3.2

prays for deformity, loses eye T327.3.1

puts foot in fire T334.1.5

questions God's judgment, cease W159.2

red-hot iron to body, repress lust T333.7

restore mute's speech, for kindness V221.2

revive foolish sinner, save soul V251.1.2

revives son of pleading mother
E121.5.2

saves man pledged to Satan
D1714.2

saves poor family's daughters from
prostitution V433.1, W11.20

sees face of death D1713.5

sends witch away D1745.3

shares fish with helpful eagle
B469.11

silver plate to poor, hand blessed
V411.3.1

sustains man on gallows P233.13

Saint's day: violated, king punished
Q223.6.2

Saliva: of Jesus, cures blind man
D1500.1.7.2

Salt: pillar of, Lot's wife C961.1

Salvation: ensured by one generous act
M58

San Fernando: ring on statue, to go on
Virgin's finger V510.5

Sanctuary: abolisher seeks sanctuary, fails
Q411.11.3

violated, violator punished
C901.4.2

Sand: basket of, like sins H606, Z161.1

Sandalwood buyer: burns a bit to show it
is worthless J2084

Sandalwood merchant: profits from scarcity N411.5

Sandpipers: eggs caught by tide, bird king
intervenes K1784.3

Santiago: carries pilgrim's body to shrine
M256.2

God's warrior knight J153.9

rewards pilgrim, sustains on
gallows V221.6

saves pilgrim's ship, Moorish attack
V223.8

Satan (see also Devil): fall from heaven
A106.2.2

tempts Eve with apple A106.2.3

Satiric legacy: father tricks greedy children
P236.2

Satisfied subjects, small territory: chosen
over large, rebellious J245.3

Satyr: fears man, blows to cool, to warm
J1820.1

half-human, half-goat B24

Scholar: gives grammar lesson instead of
alms J1592, X371.1

in hell E412.8

Scholars in tavern: arrested with criminals
J451.3.1

Scipio Africanus: gained name from campaign J1289.23

Scissors, knife: husband, wife quarrel
S113.3, T255.1, W167.3

Scoffer: attacked by greyhounds Q225.0.1

at Virgin blinded Q451.7.9

body swells to bursting Q559.13

grave violated Q225

Scoffing woman: transported through air
to shrine F1021.5

Scorpions: held safely by saint D1713.3

Scourge marks: prove events of dream
H242.2

Scribe: abbot calls, returns, work done in
gold Q69.1

illuminates book, enters heaven
Q172.0.3

Sea: Virgin calms, saves ship V268.4.5.1

Seats: heating in hell for sinners Q561.3

Secret: of animals (dwarfs) overheard
from hiding place N451.1

overheard, used in court N455.2.1

wife unable to keep, husband says
gave birth to crow H1569.4,
X36

Seducer: shamed by woman's child
J122.1

Sentence, death: postponed until thirty-
day period Q520.4

Sentence, eye put out: permitted select
tool, unable to find J1181.5,
P511.2

Sentence, hanging: permitted select tree,
unable to find J1181.4, P511.3

Sentence, obligatory loss of both eyes:
judge gives one eye, son loses one
eye J1189.4

Sentry asleep: tells evil king devils will
come for him J1489

Serpent (see also Snake): advice of, brings
wealth to human B581.1

bites prince, gives friend remedy
W154.8

causes farmer to prosper B161
deceiver in paradise B176.1.1
enters crocodile, destroys from within F912
guards monastery garden B256.13
house spirit brings prosperity F480.2
injures human, refuses reconciliation J15, J15.1.1
saves accused man from death B522.1
ungrateful for rescue, returned J1172.3, Q281.5, W154.2.1
warns against advice from victims, not heeded J21.13.1
Servant: abused by knight, saint saves him L416.5
called "devil," devil appears C12.4.2
dies in place of master P361
how much could eat, more if another's J1114.0.2, X591
witness to noble's incest T426
Servant to close door at night: leaves open, will be open in morning W111.2.2
Servant to master: feed if day, let sleep if night W111.2.3
Service to God: knight fights infidels, ascetic prays J234
Serving-man: disguised, sex with master's love K1317.1
Severed head: proof of slaying in battle H105.8
Sex with dead woman: punished, public flogging Q244.5
Sexual intercourse forbidden: before church attendance C110.2
in public place C116.1
on consecration day C116.1
on feast day C119.1.2.2
Sexual temptation: youth to work and pray T317.4.1
Sham physician: extorts riches from emperor K1955.10
too near horse's hoof, kicked K1121.1
She-wolf: repents stealing holy man's bread B773.4

Shearer: says wolf ate sheep, detected K2061.1.2
Sheep: breaks promise to deer, wolf present L396
carried across stream, endless tale Z11
persuade wolf to sing K561.2
shelter others from sun B701
Sheep, wolves: peace between them, send away guard dogs for peace K191
Sheep's voice: from belly of thief N275.5.2, Q552.4.1
Sheet: extended, blinds husband J2301.4.5, K1516, T481.20, X711.11
Shepherd: alms, sent away, wolves eat sheep Q44.1
betrays wolf to hunter W171.2
cried "wolf" too often P463.4
feeds poor, monks send him away W11.19
Virgin, in dream, teaches to preach V256.1.3
winks, betrays hidden wolf J1442.15
Ship: held back magically D2072.0.3
sinks, Virgin helps, fish plug holes V268.4.5.2
Shipwrecked: sailor, Virgin rescues V268.4
Shirt: no opening for head, blinds victim S110.7
Shirt, magic: protects in battle D1381.5
Shoes: save, walk barefoot on thorns W152.11
Shrine: dead child revived at E121.3.2.3
Shroud: of king displayed, sign of mortality J912.1
Sick man denied cure: rust is to iron, sickness is to human J893.3
sickness cleanses soul J893.2
Sickle, magic: stuck to man's hand D1206.1.1
Sight, magic: stars over heads of good or bad persons D1825.3.2
Sign of cross: banishes evil spirits of dead E425.2.3
Silence: gives man power to see spirits J1074.3

philosopher in desert serene C400.02

sign of wisdom C400.01

Simple person: advises ascetic to regain strength J156.5.1

Sin: monk's, removed, gives up money V461.8

save money against future illness V411.3

Sinner: confesses carnal desire, saved V21.5

demands long penance Q523.7.1

enters church, dark, leaves light V52.21

eternal bathhouse keeper in hell Q560.4

in hell, Virgin revives, do penance V255.3

magically unable to enter church Q233.1

three days to confess, sins more, dies V22.2

Sister: dismembers brother, delays pursuit S11.10

ˌkills brother to gain throne P253

Skin: disease, assassins', Virgin cures V257.1

Skirt of Virgin Mary: repels besiegers of city D1381.5.1

Skull: evil magic, muted, by sign of cross V86.1.8

Skull, magic: tells political secrets D992.4

Slaughter: babies, unborn to avoid danger M375.2.1

Slave: cleverly confounds master J1114.0.1

gets others to perform his duties W111.2.0.1

Slayer of brother: holy man forgives V441

Slipper: magic, removed by Virgin Mary D1065.2.1

Virgin's applied to deformity, cure Q221.3.8

Snails: travel little, carry own house A2543

Snake (see also Serpent): bites man who saves it W154.2

enemy mongoose A2494.12.2

frog king's mount J352.2, Q211.4.3, Q551.3.2.9

grateful for shelter B391.1.4

helps farmer prosper, harms him K2031.2

offspring, kills human's child B391.1.4, J15.1.2

rescued in cold, bites in spring W154. 2.1.1

woman's stomach, Virgin cures V256.1.5.2

wrapped around waist, penance Q522.8

Socrates: asked king not to block his sunshine J152.1

Soldier: loots monastic cell, bites tongue, dies Q397

Solomonic judgement: divided child J1171.1

Son: abuses father's servants S21.6

chooses exile over life at court J347.3

cruel to father, own son will repeat J121, P233.18, Q588.1, S21.7

denied horse, accuses mother K2110.2

farmer's son rustic, noble's son courtly U121.3

hanged, uncorrected in youth P233.15.1

imprisons, tortures, kills evil father P233.9.2

last surviving, dead three days, Virgin revives E121.3.3

least truthful to inherit L114.1

leaves dukedom, licentious father P233.9.1

mocks drunken, naked father P233.9.3

mother's champion in combat H151.4

newly betrothed, dies, Virgin revives E121.3.2.1

never punished, die in battle, father dies Q582.9

of king chosen to reign U129.6

of merchant becomes broker U129.6

of noble finds woman to feed him U129.6

of worker cuts wood U129.6

on gallows, bites mother's (father's) nose P233.15

sacrifice, in oven, enter monastery S263.2.4

tortures, kills royal father S22.5

Virgin revives, mother converts V331.1.15

Son-in-law: frees captive father-in-law K640.1, R154.4

Soul: after death, good fly, bad fall to earth D1825.3.3.1

angels, music transport good E755.2.1.1

asked to stay in body J321.4

carried off by devil E752.2

departing, seen by men at sea E722.3.4

dissatisfied, wants to leave body W128.7

dove leaves mouth of dying person E732.1

dream is extra-corporeal trip E721.0.2

gambler's, saint wins in dice game E756.4.1

good abbot's, angels and devils fight for E756.1

hermit, with David, musicians V511.1.4

insincere man seen in hell E755.2.7.2

invisible as it departs E722.2.1.2

invisible in living and in dead J1262.10

judged in heaven, returns, tells E721.0.2

just rewarded, unjust tormented E751

moribund's, in hell, insincere V511.2

nun's, returns, preaches repentance E366

priest's seen in hell's torment E755.2.1.1

promised to devil E752.1.1.2

returns: at moment of death E586.0.1

time on earth wasted E301.9

to body on blade bridge E721.0.2

to body, to sin no more V251.1.3

seen as black or white spirit E722.1.1

ascending by travelers at sea E586.1

by brother, moment of death E722.3.4

sinner's, pitchforks wrench from body E755.2.1.1

speaks as it departs E722.2.13

taken by Jesus E722.2.14

trapped in ice freed by masses E754.1.9, V42.1

views four fires, returns to body marked E631.0.2

visible only to one person E415.3.1

youth's, saint regains from devil E756.4.2

Sow and reap badly: better than not at all J99.3

Speaking: consort not to speak to subjects C411.2

forbidden during seven days C401.2

Speech: recovered, eat, bread pre-chewed by fox D2161.3.6

recovered magically D2025.6, D2025.7

Spell: magic, knight's horses die after ten days D2089.3.2

Spider: afraid of wasp, kills fly U31.5, W121.5

bite, cured by Virgin Mary D2161.5.2.5

bites over-adorned woman Q331.4

invites wasp, rest on "white curtain" K815.2

swallowed, leaves body through arm D2161.5.2.5.1

Spiritual food: not nourishing as earthly food J1215.2

Spoon, silver: devil gives to man V24.3

Spring: bursts forth in front of altar F933.1.4

flows at command of infant Jesus A941.7.4, F933.1.2

gods create in desert D927.1

magic, curative powers D1505.5.4

safe from serpents, sign of cross V86.1.4

transforms man into woman D927.6

Squire: tries to rape, disastrous injuries T471.0.3

St. John Damascene, hand of severed D2161.5.2.4.1, Q261.4, V256.3

St. John Patriarch: humbly uses clay vessels J914.4

St. Martin: gives cloak to beggar V411.8

St. Nicholas: appears, victim, thieves, convert V331.1.6

bread to poor, replenished V412.1

tosses golden apple in house V433.1

St. Peter: tells pope he merits Christian burial V292.3

Staff, iron, symbolic sin: carried, dropped, end of pilgrimage H606.1

Stag: has horns, but runs from dogs U127

hides, found by master J1032

intimidates sheep, wolf present J1510.1

proud of horns, tangled in tree L461

Stairway set with razors: does not kill man H1531.2

Stallions: neighing, impregnate distant mares B741.2

Star: prince not see fire, sunlight M302.4.4

prophesy, crisis at age twenty M302.4.2

reflection, duck thinks it fish J1791.8

say prince to be silent seven days M302.4.3

Star, celestial sign: birth of hero E741.1.1.2

Statue: fool kicks it, money inside J1853.1.1

Stealing contest: friends compete K305.2.1

Stepmother: accuses prince of rape K2150

Steward: gave master's money to poor Q44.2, V416.1

kills Jew under royal protection

K2242.2, Q411.17

mismanages estate K2242.3

steals king's money, watchers too K2242.1

Stick, money in: breaks, thief betrayed H251.3.4

Still-born child: Virgin Mary revives E121.3

Stinginess: prince deposed W152.6.1

Stolen goods: hidden in dupe's house K401.2

Stolen meat: hidden in fasting man's house K401.2.3.1

Stone: for church, found magically V111.2

magic powers of D1300.4.1

riven, Virgin, Child appear within V127.1

warmth of, worm inside F642.4.1, J1661.1.6

with image of Virgin Mary, power to enlighten D1071.2

Stonecutter: finds treasure in wall N511.1.6.1, P462.1

Stoned: king tricked into talking to crowd K811.3

Stonemason: saved from falling by Virgin D2149.4.3

Stoning to death: evil king stoned by populace Q422

punishment for adultery Q422.1

Stork: among cranes, killed J451.2

male, kills adulterous mate A2497.2, Q241.4

male, punish offspring of adultery Q241.4

meal to fox in tall thin vessel W158.1

Storm: stilled magically D2140.1.1

Storm at sea: impedes pirate's escape D2141.0.9

Santiago calms D2149.4.5

Storm-tossed ship: Virgin saves V268.4.5

Stream: Virgin diverts to monastery land V254.8.2

Strength: in hair (Samson) D1831

lost, after conjugal activity J21.32

secret of, revealed K975

unusual, Virgin gives to workmen V268.9

Strength, magic: in lion skin and magic club D1831.4

moral rectitude D1831.7

Strong man: mighty slayer F628

Stubborn husband, wife: quarrel, husband breaks wife's leg W167.2

quarrel, husband pushes wife in river W167.3

Submarine: Alexander descends in D1525

Substitution: deacon for captive K528.2

Suffocation: daughter, father S113.2.4

Suicide: three attempts, woman saved V252.4

Suitors: lazier of two, woman to marry W111.1

Sultan: behaves like baker's son, gives bread as reward H175.6, P463.1, U121.6.2

Sun weds, creates more suns, dry world: thieves wed, create thieves J88.1

Sunlight: hunters block, philosopher protests J1442.1

Supernatural beings: bestow gifts at birth of hero F312.1

Susanna: accused falsely by elders J1153.1

exonerated by clever deduction K2112.0.2

Swallow: divine messenger B291.1.11

warns other birds about hemp seeds J621.1

why nest near humans A2282.1

Swallows and crows: dispute beauty J242.6

Swallows' loud chirp, sporadic: chosen over low constant sparrows J215.1.4

Swallows, sparrows: choose between J282

Swan: draws knight's boat through water B558.1

golden neck chains transform them to men D361.2

leads knight in magical boat B469.12

man transformed into D161.1

signals departure time to knight B752.1.1

Swine: men transformed into D136

trample ant hills B16.1.4.3

Swollen limbs: king's, Virgin heals V256.4.6

Sword: death to foe when drawn D1402.7

into plowshares J642.2

is lost, has lost many lives J1600.1

lovers, pursuer, fugitive T481.17

magic, given to infant D1344.11

Sword blows: image of Virgin Mary resists D1840.1.4

Synagogue: Virgin turns into church V363.1

Tablets, golden: unearthed, warn against avarice N592

Target: living, child's body S139.0.1

Task: buy best possible food, slave buys tongues H1185.2

carry sheep across stream H1111

drink seas dry H1142.3

fill magic pitcher, Virgin helps H984.1.1

gather multicolored fleas, sort males, females H1129.10.1

impossible, find man without cares H931.3

replace one-eyed man's eye, remove eye to match H919.4

retrieve royal heron, Virgin protects courtier H1154.7.4

symbolic, dip sea out with spoon H1143.1

Teacher: delivers city's children to enemy K2369.3.1, Q261.3

gives pupil rhetorical rules P344

puts wisdom on wall, pupil confined P344.1

Tears: of hunter, birds mistake for pity J1821.2

of Virgin, fill magic picture D1171.7.2, H984.1.1

penitents fill barrel F1051.1

wash away thumb mark on palm F1051.1.1

Teeth: knocked out, ruler says better off W26.9

mother dog's benign, rabid dog's dangerous J88.2

Temples: teach, with figures, inscriptions J168.1

Test: ability to reign, youngest son prevails H1569.2

anger, royalty suffers criticism without H1553.2

curiosity, mouse between plates, not to lift plate H1554.1

evil, devils, winner makes saint touch woman H1596.4

fear, threat of killing innocents H1406.1

friendship: whole friend H1558.2, H1558.2.1

half-friend H1558.1

least loved of three is best H1558.1.1

take publicly, slap from friend H1558.11

generosity, saint gives special food to visitor H1573.2.2

gratitude: magician's pupil fails H1565.1

three gifts, three recipients H1565

loyalty, vassals drink foul exudations H1556.0.3

parental love, fathers save children, mothers not H491.2

paternity, shoot father's corpse P233.17

patience: monk endures blows of abbot H1553.3

monk fails, loses temper at cup H1553.5

pupil endures philosopher's insults H1553.7

visitors suffer insults at city's gate H1553.3;

valor, knight who waits until attacked H1561.2.4

wisdom, choose among three chests H1573.2.2;

wit: prince poses riddles to youth H548.4

sages pose riddles to slave woman H548.5

worry-free nature, peasant unmoved by threats H1569.3

sexual identity, choice of playthings H1578.1.4.3

Theft: false accusation, Virgin saves monk V276.5

Theft of meal for fritters: knife pierces thief's mouth, prays Q212.8

Thief: arm bruised Judgement Day E411.0.2.1

attacked by poor victim K335.1.0.3

excommunicated, returns funds J1141.14

frightened, leaves sheet behind K335.1.0.2

mistakes lion for horse, rides it J1756.2

oath of innocence, steals again M102

of holy man's horse, detained magically at river Q227.4

of sheep, belly bleats in church N275.5.2, Q552.4.1

on gallows, devil supports, then lets him hang M212.2

paralyzed, blind, returns loot, cured Q212.7

prevented from leaving church by Virgin Mary D2072.0.3

sent into well by boy K345.2

trapped by horse K427.1

trapped in hermit's cell Q222.5.4.1

tricked into stealing from self K439.3

tricked, climb down moonbeam K1054

tries to bribe watchdog K2062

trusted by cleric steals K346

wife hears, joins husband in bed X743

Thorn: creep naked through, penance for wanting to leave order Q522.3

removed from lion's paw B381

Thread magically supplied: sews altar cloths D811.3

Threat: to child to throw it to wolves C25.2

to horses to throw them to bear C25

to ox to throw to wolf C25.2.1

Thrush or throstle: husband, wife quarrel W167.2

quarrel, wife's leg broken T255.1.1

Tiger learns from experience: fears man J17

Tithes: Charlemagne gives to his knights, punished Q554.1.1

unpaid, pestilence, poor crops P532.1

Tongue: bitten off: by betrayed wife Q451.4.8.1

by wife S163

spat at king S163.3

spat in face of inquisitor S163.2

bitten, man discouraged pilgrims Q451.4.8.2

cut out, restored magically D2161.3.6.1

extends, denying Virgin Q551.8.6

heretics cut pious man's tongue Q451.4.6.1

man bites, throws it at king J1289.25

mutilated for false accusation Q583.5, S163.1

pilgrim bites, told others not to go Q393.5

spiced, bitter served at dinner H604

tempted man bites, spits at woman T333.2.2

Tongue severed: restored by Virgin Mary D2161.5.2.4.4

Tongues seasoned, well or poorly: kind or unkind speech J89

Toolmaker: makes tools, God makes creatures J1262.6

Torments of hell: man sees, hears warning voice V511.2.1.2

Tortoise: treads on toad, injuring it U31.6

Torturer: invents machine to burn others S112.8

Tower: confinement in, avoid prophecy M372

Town mouse and country mouse: liberty preferred to ease L451

Traitor: emperor severs hand, Virgin restores Q261.4, S161

forgiven, ruler invokes divine right W46.2.1

Trajan: freed from hell, saint's prayers V57.8

Transformation: human to swine D136

maggots to precious gems D470.2, V222.15

maiden to rat D117.1.1

man to swan D161

man to woman D12.01

rat to maiden D315.1

swan to man D361.2

water, river to copper D470.1

woman to puppy D141, K1351

wood to stone D451.10

Transubstantiation: Jesus appears to heretic, convinces V327.1

monk doubts, Host, bleeding flesh V312.3

wine to blood, Host to body V133.1.1

Treasure: buried in roots of tree N511.1.9.1

buried in vineyard, sons to dig soil P233.19

doves lead man to treasure B562.1.3, N511.1.9.1

eagle leads rescuer to treasure B361, N545.1.1

found in broken statue N514.3

found in ruined wall N511.1.6.1

magic, gives mouse access to food D1561.2.2

soul leaves body, finds N538.1

statue's extended finger points to N535.2

stone cross marks on palace floor N535.1

Virgin, dream vision tells king N531.6

Treasure-seeking sons: to dig up soil in vineyard H588.7

Treaty: sheep and wolves B260.1

Tree: axe from own wood cuts it down U162

fruit of one tree forbidden C621

king of J956

not to supply wood for axes P458.1

on grave, leaves bear "ave" F811.2.2.1

supply wood for axe handle J621.1.2

Tree, apple, division, deceptive: roots, branches K171.10

Trickster: fool owner, goat is worthless K344.1.5

    insults another, says only joking K1771.10

    tell gullible cleric his deer is dog X434.3

    wife believes is god, spends night T481.24

Triple tax: poet collects coins at city gates N635

Trophies: severed heads as S139.2.2.1

Troubadour: sings for Virgin, freed magically R123.3

Troubles, personal: king chooses over political ones J369.0.1

Trout: pretends to be dead K522.4.1

    too lazy to escape fishermen W111.6

Trout, in danger: two evade, third lazy one is caught J321.5

Trout, lazy: disregards danger J16.1

Trumpet: announces death sentence P612

Truth and Lies: share tree, branches, roots Z121.2

Truth, Wind and Water: Wind, Water easily found, Truth not Z121.2.1

Truthful man: reveals secret cures to king Q94.1

Twice the reward to other: envious, covetous, loss of eye Q302.0.1

Two (three) joint depositors: all must be present to redeem J1161.1

Two-headed: baby born F511.0.2.1

Tyrant: Caesar permits man to call him J1281.3, W26.7.1

Tyrant preferred: over uncertain future ruler J215.2.1

Ugly: holy man, rustic doubts holiness U119.4

    holy man, embraces those who call him ugly J921

Unbaptized person: needs baptism to stay in paradise E412.2

Uncle: treacherous, tries to usurp power K2217

Unconfessed person: restless in grave, returns E411.0.2.2

Under wife's bed: husband believes wife's love for him X711.2

Understand Trinity: intellectual arrogance W159.3

Uriah letter: man carries orders for own murder K978

Urinate, in holy vessels, blood from mouth Q551.6.5

    on altar, excrement pours from mouth Q551.6.5

    sage, as he walks, J152.7

Usurer: alms to abbot, only one coin is honest P435.8, Q273.7

    cheated, chests filled with sand J1510.2, P435.15

    father and son seen in hell P435.11, Q273.3

    forebears, descendants in hell P435.6

    gives alms to saint, saint marked Q273.6

    heart found in strong box P435.14

    in hell, lineage arranged on ladder Q273.5

    leaves nothing for soul, confess, dies V424

    leaves wealth, family not to church P435.12

    legacy brings illness, poverty P435.9

    one devil enough in usurer's house, many needed in monastery G303.25.3.2

    pays to build church, collapses Q273.4

    rebukes soul for wanting to leave P435.13

    soul condemned, despite alms P435.10

    soul in torment, despite charity Q273.8

Usurer, corpse of: ass carries to gallows, not church B151.1.1.2.1, P435.3

    rises up, destroys church E235.4.3.1, P435.4

ALPHABETICAL INDEX

Vegetables, division, deceptive: turnip, root; cabbages, leaves K171.5.1

Vendor, accused of theft: ring found in fish belly K2103.1

Vessels, lost at sea: until merchant church goods Q595.5

Vestal virgin: buried alive if pregnant T400.0.3

falsely accused, proves virginity T401.2

Victim: avoids death, stops to pray K1612

Vintner: eye wound, wife treats, lover goes K1516.1, T481.12, X711.8

Vipers: controlled by saint D2156.5

Virgin birth: belief in V312

Virgin Mary: appears three times in dream vision V510.6

beam not to fall in church D2149.4.5

brings man back from dead V251.1

casts out demons D2176.3.4.1, D2176.3.5.1

causes storm at sea D2141.0.9

causes winds to free ships D2142.0.2

convinces Moors to cede city V268.3.4

delays death, sinner to do penance V251

drives devil out, robber baron castle V254.8

explains Host to doubting monk J164.1

frees Christian, transports home R121.6.4

gives birth, Holy Spirit engenders T547.1

halts volcanic eruption D2148.3

in place of woman pledged to devil K1841.3

rescues royal falconer from drowning R141.1

restores speech of child D2176.3.6

saves: falling man D2149.4.3

Jewish woman falling, cliff R169.0.1

men trapped in sand hill D2149.4.4

says private mass, ailing devotee V255.2

tells monk he must love her J164.2

Visitation: carries off thief of church tithes Q554.1

Visitor: takes beautiful courtier for king P15.1.2

Voice: from grave, "I am burning" Q566.1

God's, counsels humility J164

Volcanic eruption: Virgin Mary halts D2148.3

Vow: keep feast day, broken, hand wither M101.4

not to comply with request, destroy city, will not M203.4

not to eat meat, bone stuck throat M101.4.1

not to leave convent, nuns stand firm in face of fire M183.5

sacrifice first creature seen, man riding ass, ass beheaded J1169.4, M203.5

Vulcan: gives infant hero sword and shield F312.1

Vulture: invites birds to feast, eats them J1577, K815.4.1

why drop bones from height A2441.5

Wager: drink seas dry J1161.9, N67.1

Walk on all fours: graze like beast, penance Q523.2

Walk on water: magical power D2125.1

Wall, sheltering: falls on man pursued by mishaps N253

Walling up: for conspiracy to murder princes Q455.1

Walls: inscribed with condensed education J168

thrown down magically D2093

War: between birds and quadrupeds B261.1

between crows and owls A2494.13.14, B261.1, K477.4, K2042

Warrior: abstain from meat, victors C221.02

choose death in battle over death in retirement J216.5

promises Virgin one thousand masses for military success M201.0.4

rises from sick bed to battle P711.7

saint, Virgin sends to battle V268.3.1

strength through chastity T310.3

Watchdog: refuses thief's bribe B325.1

Water: divide D1551

for garden, sent by God V469

Water drips in ear: washes out brains K171.12, W111.1.8

Water drips in eye: man too lazy to move, loses eye W111.1.3

Water in river: transformed into copper D470.1

Water in spring: made safe by sign of cross D788.1

Water spirit: gives silver axe to woodman F420.5.1.7.4, P458.2

Waves: hares mistake sound for danger J1812.2

Wax figure: dying horse, Virgin revives E169.1

falcon in church, Virgin revives E169

Wealth: given away, magically returned V411.5

refused, fear of covetousness J347.1

Weasel: caught with mice, killed J451.1.1

dusts self with flour to fool mice J951.4

plea, keeps house free of mice K561.1.1.1

royal pet, killed, Virgin revives E169.2

tries to bite file J552.3

Weather: controlled by prayer D2140.1

Weeping bitch: woman, transformed into puppy K1351

Wheat grains: lips of baby, future wealth M312.0.2.1

Widow: attracted to handsome beggar T232.6

disinters husband, to help lover T231.6

falsely accuses saint of rape K2111.6.1

incest with son, Virgin forgives T412.1, V261.3

ingests husband's ashes T211.4.3

of Ephesus, husband's corpse, for hanged man K2213.1

prevents husband's interment E121.5

proves dead husband innocent H1511.5

refuses second marriage J482.1

Wife: abandoned, kills self P214.2

agrees with husband, horses, cows T223

breast milk blinds husband K1516.9

calumniated, survives burning at stake H221.6

counsels: against killing courtiers J571.5.1

delay J155.4

king, return good for evil J155.4.1

disobeys warning: applies poison unguent T254.1

drinks poison T254.6

enters oven T254.5

opens armed chest T254.4

division of, deceptive, above, below waist K171.7

eats chicken, husband left with spit, stabs wife W125.5.1

eats hot coals: husband unfaithful T81.8

husband reported dead T211.2.3

extends sheet in front of husband K1516, K1516.1.4

extinguishes candle, lover leaves K1516.3

fasts during husband's absence T215.10

fears thief, joins husband in bed T284

follows husband into battle T215.9

follows husband into exile T215.8.1

forbidden to join men, hang selves T215.11

frees husband from prison R152.1

has drugged husband made monk K1536

hides husband at home, mourns T215.8.2

holds pot before husband's eyes K1516.8

husband: indulges whims T261.2
   kills for looking at men Q341
   under bed, tells lover she loves husband K1532.1
   husband's bloody clothes, dies T211.4.4

immolates self in husband's pyre T211.2

jealous, hits king, he kills her T251.0.4

lover under bed, husband turns, coat brushed K1516.1.2

mistaken for another, killed Q211.3

old, plucks husband's black hairs J2112.1

ordeal by leaping off cliff T257.12

pledged to devil, Virgin takes place G303.16.1, V264.3

prays to harm husband's lover T257.2.3

puts out eye, to match husband T215.4

retrieves husband's body T215.9.1

shelters husband's mistress T222

spares husband's life T211.1.5

stabs self, Virgin revives E63.3

takes husband's place in prison R152.1

thinks all men, bad breath T221

thought unchaste, looks at men T317.9

washes husband's hair, lover leaves K1516.7

will not tell which son not husband's T238.1

young, plucks husband's grey hairs J2112.1

Wig: monkey snatches, woman mocked Q331.2.1.6, X52.1

Wild pigs: killed for eating sheep B275.1.3.2

Wild tales, invented: woman repeats them, is mocked X35

Wilderness: penance in, friars who left order Q520.5

Wind: blows arrows back against enemy D906.2, F963.2
   frees warships trapped in narrows D2142.0.2
   magic, transports saint's boat D1524.9.1
   opens church door, pope enters D906.1, Q20.5, Q147.2
   Virgin causes, open shutters church V276.4
   woman able to cause winds D2142.1

Window: look at men through, adulterous woman T481.8

Wine: four characteristics of A2851
   Virgin Mary supplies D1040.1
   woman, bare breasts, horns, seen as Z139.3.1

Wisdom: before learning, says simple man J1217.2
   "Consider the end": barber heeds warning hired to cut king's throat, confesses J21.1
   "Do not act when angry": man sees man in wife's bed, his son J21.2
   "Do not believe what is beyond belief": bird tells man it has gem in body J21.13
   "Do not leave the highway": short cut proves long J21.5
   "I know where my shoe pinches": says man who left wife J1442.1.4
   "Never give up what you have in your hand": man releases bird, for better J21.12.1
   "Never try to reach the unattainable": man cannot attain height of birds J21.14
   "Not to try to acquire what cannot be acquired": man tries to recapture bird J21.12.2
   "Rue not a thing that is past": man lets bird go, tries to recapture it J21.12

taught by parable: good shepherd J80.0.1, J80.0.7

    invited guests, not attend, idolaters J80.0.4

    prodigal son J80.0.6

    seed sown on good and sterile soil J80.0.2

    seven wise and foolish virgins J80.0.5

    ship in storm at sea J80.0.3.1

    unjust steward J80.0.8

    yoking calf and oxen J80.0.9

Wise man: unable to describe God J152.10

Wishes: third used to remedy foolish two J2071

Witch: hung in victim's doorway, burned Q415.10

Withdrawal: from world earthly death J1217.3, J1217.4

Wolf: as shepherd, detected K2061.1

    betrayed by fox J1521.1.1

    disguised as monk, detected K1961.6

    entices goat, high place, detected K2061.4

    funeral feast, animals hope more W151.12

    judges race before eating rams K579.5.1

    killed for eating sheep B275.1.3.2

    leaves food, hopes for better J344.3

    makes friends with lion, killed J411.5

    offers to help pregnant sow K1955.0.1

    overeats in larder, cannot leave K1022.1, W151.9.1

    permits captive ass to lead it K713.1.2.1

    proposes dismiss guard dogs K2061.1.1

    says lamb dirties water downstream U31

    scorns salt meat, hopes for better J2066.4

    skin is cure for lion king's disease K961.1.1

    sow kicks into stream K1121.2

    steals, complains of fox thefts U21.4

    to be midwife to sow, detected K2061.6

    to cure ass, fraud detected K1955.0.3

    treaty with sheep, dogs to go away K2010.3

    tries to eat bowstring, shoots self J514.1

    uses mother goat's voice to fool kids K1832

    waits for children to be thrown away J2066.5

Wolf and dog: liberty preferred over ease L451.3

Wolf, fox: guard against each other's theft U21.4.1

Wolf-food: threat to ox C25.2.1

Woman: accedes to rape, kills self T471.0.6

    accused falsely, execution magically impeded K2114.1

    accuses bishop falsely, unable to give birth Q227.5

    ages of Z19.3

    beauty of Z19.4

    betrothed, flees, will be God's bride T376.2.2

    captive, prince returns to betrothed (family) R111.4.1

    chastity discourages seducer T311.0.3

    chosen to sleep with enemy, kills K872

    condemned to dance forever in hell Q386.1

    confess sins, angel pardons them V21.1.2

    created from man's rib A1275.1

    created to procreate A1212.1

    damned for one adulterous act Q241.3

    deceived, thinks invader will spare her K1353.2

    delays sexual act, must bathe first K551.4

    disfigures face, saves self from king T327.8.1

disguised as man is abbot K1837.7

dupes married couple, kill each other K1085

falsely accused, wise man saves K2110.2

genitals, to magically kindle fire D2158.1

gives only cow, hundredfold reward Q21.1

gives up wealth, escapes king T320.5

hide in tomb, save youth's chastity T311.3.1

husband pledges to devil, saved V252.6

ignorant, believes sex act, injection of sense J1745.3

inconsistent, timid, but able to rob corpses X70

in disguise becomes pope K1961.2.1

Jewish, unable to give birth, twins, baptized T584.0.7

killed, Virgin revives, confesses E121.3.7

lechery punished Q244.4

lose vote to appease Neptune P691

lose voting privilege Athens A1018.4

of conquered city, kill children, selves M161.7

prays for green eyes, blinded, wants sight Q331.2.1.7

pregnant, dreams: child's greatness M312.0.4, M312.0.4.1, M312.0.4.2, M312.0.4.3

child will kill his father M312.0.4.4

promises chastity, ruins marriage T311.0.2

puts leper in bed, only roses found K2112.2

raped by captor, severs his head, carries to husband Q244.6

restrains amorous king J816.4

returns, dances eternally in hell V511.2.6.1

saved from burning at stake V252.2

sees mother hell, father heaven V511.2.3

sews holy day, stricken, Virgin cures M205.7

shames lustful king T320.4

shipwrecked, ointment revives E101

smear foulness on breasts, not raped T327.4.1

three sons, brother, Virgin pardons V261.3.1

told false secret J1546

told to hold razor near man's throat K2155.4

tricks amorous youth K1227.4.2

unable to confess, kills self, children V22.3

vision of blessed, prays, heaven V510.3

wrongly called drunk N340.3

yearns, baby Jesus, joins him heaven V277.2

Wood: for building church, Virgin supplies V111.2.1

transformed into stone D451.10

Words: hurt more than wound, says lion W185.6

Work on feast day: sickle adheres to farmer's hand Q223.1.1

woman breaks promise, works on feast day K231.3

Workmen: saved, church tower collapses V258

Would-be philosopher: endures insults, proves self J1074.1.2

Wound: in mother's side, baby born T541.0.1

new battle's, soldiers to forget old ones J215.6

of Christ, food touched to, improves D1039.3

Virgin cures, mother prays, son's V256.1.7

Wraith: appears to announce death E723.6

Years not counted: real life began with service to God J181.1

Young woman: rewarded for not dancing
Q39.3

Youngest: daughter will marry elderly
warrior L54.2

son only genuine one, tested
P233.17

son, best fitted to reign L13.2

son, wisest L10.3

Youth: calls king fool, proves case J1162.4

choose, wife, mother, grandmother
chaste J482.3

disfigures face, avoid temptation
T333.3

escapes devils, sign of cross
V86.1.10

father's friend saves from death
R169.6

in love with ugly old woman
J445.1

invents false report to keep secret
Q62.1

ridiculed by older woman X742

takes poison instead of benefactor
F959.6.3

to abandon religion, be Christian
M351

told woman is goat, loves goats
X771.2

told women are devils, likes devils
T371, X771.1

tricked by woman, appears ridiculous K1227.4.2.25